LEARNING CULTURE THROUGH SPORTS

LEARNING CULTURE THROUGH SPORTS

Perspectives on Society and Organized Sports

Second Edition

Edited by
Sandra Spickard Prettyman
and
Brian Lampman

ROWMAN & LITTLEFIELD PUBLISHERS, INC.
Lanham • Boulder • New York • Toronto • Plymouth, UK

Published by Rowman & Littlefield Publishers, Inc.
A wholly owned subsidiary of The Rowman & Littlefield Publishing Group, Inc.
4501 Forbes Boulevard, Suite 200, Lanham, Maryland 20706
http://www.rowmanlittlefield.com

Estover Road, Plymouth PL6 7PY, United Kingdom

British Library Cataloguing in Publication Information Available

Library of Congress Cataloging-in-Publication Data

Learning culture through sports : perspectives on society and organized sports / edited by Sandra Spickard Prettyman and Brian Lampman. — 2nd ed.
    p. cm.
Includes bibliographical references and index.
ISBN 978-1-4422-0630-4 (cloth : alk. paper) — ISBN 978-1-4422-0631-1 (pbk. : alk. paper) — ISBN 978-1-4422-0632-8 (electronic)
    1. Sports—Social aspects—United States. I. Prettyman, Sandra Spickard, 1957– II. Lampman, Brian, 1973–
    GV706.5.L43 2011
    306.4'83—dc22
                                    2010022155

∞ ™ The paper used in this publication meets the minimum requirements of American National Standard for Information Sciences—Permanence of Paper for Printed Library Materials, ANSI/NISO Z39.48-1992.

Printed in the United States of America

Contents

Acknowledgments

THIS BOOK IS THE RESULT OF OUR WORK in sport, which does not always take place on the field or in the locker room. Instead, much of our work with sport takes place in our homes, in our classrooms, and in our conversations with others. We take up this work in all of these venues because we are deeply committed to creating positive change in sport, and we believe this can only happen by engaging others in the larger conversation about the role of sport in society. Our families, students, and conversations with friends and family have influenced our thinking about sport and contributed in significant ways to the development of this book. In addition, authors, activists, and athletes—from the past and the present—have inspired and influenced us to pursue this project. All of these people have had an impact on our ideas and beliefs about sport and our relationship to it, and their deep commitment to social justice, in sport and in society, continues to remind us of the importance of this work. We thank all of those folks who have listened to our ideas for this book, who have questioned those ideas, and who have pushed us to expand our thinking. We thank our children whose experiences, both positive and negative, and whose enthusiasm for life continue to teach us and nourish us. Finally, we thank all of those who contribute in positive ways to sport—they are the ones who will change the game and help sport achieve its fullest potential.

Introduction

Studying Sport—What Can We Learn and Why Do We Care?

Sandra Spickard Prettyman

S INCE THE FIRST EDITION OF *Learning Culture through Sport* was released, a lot has happened in the world of sport, both good and bad. It is certainly easy enough to point to the scandals that have erupted in recent years: the Duke University men's lacrosse team rape scandal; steroid and drug use from the Tour de France to Major League Baseball; the Northwestern University women's soccer team hazing incident. However, it is also true that in other ways, positive growth has happened. More athletes feel they can come "out of the closet" to the public and their peers, and more research is being done in this area; sport organizations and franchises are taking the use of steroids and drugs seriously and implementing testing processes and strong penalties; and the number of young women playing sports continues to increase, as does the number of their fans. What is clear is that sport remains a contested territory, and our very definition of what constitutes sport and who is an athlete is unclear. What is also clear is that sport is a billion-dollar industry that has infiltrated almost every area of our lives. It is in our clothing, in our media, in our textbooks and schools, in our music, and in our language.

However, sport is rarely examined critically, despite the fact that it is an integral part of our society, and an important force in our lives. Each year, over 30 million young people participate in youth sport activities and programs. While sport participation wanes as young people take on adult responsibilities, you can still find adults on soccer fields, tennis courts, football fields, and basketball courts across the country every day. Many others participate by watching sporting events, either in person or on television, on a regular basis. Others, both young and old, reject or resist organized sport programs, and a growing number of people are turning to alternative forms of sport for activity and entertainment.

Given all of this, it is fair to say that sport has an impact on all of our lives. Whether we play a sport or not, our lives are influenced by it, in part because it is a cultural force that permeates our world. Our culture places a tremendous value on the behaviors and attributes associated with sports and athletes, which is in part why sport matters in our lives. A commonly held assumption is that sport teaches young people important lessons about teamwork, about discipline, and about respect (for their bodies, for others, for winning). Thus, the assumption is that participating in sport is important for communicating desired behaviors, values, and skills. However, these are only assumptions, and in order to assess their voracity, it is important to examine them from different perspectives. Have they always been true (a historical perspective)? Are they true for some groups of people in some situations (a sociological perspective)? How do individuals respond to sport and these assumptions (a psychological perspective)? This edition again utilizes these perspectives as a foundation for this book. We believe it is important to carefully consider the role and influence of sport in our lives, how sport is conducted and for what purposes, and the consequences and outcomes of sport in our lives. Our goal in this book is to examine these issues from multiple perspectives, in order to better understand how sport influences our lives and our culture, both positively and negatively.

A (Feminist) Mother's and Researcher's Perspective

I have a hard time believing it, but my daughter recently graduated from college. In high school, she did not become an athlete until the end of her sophomore year, and I still find it hard to believe that for three years she was a college athlete, running cross country and track. As a high school student, she was much more interested and involved in the arts, and because our culture often dichotomizes these two worlds (athletics and the arts), it was difficult to imagine her becoming an athlete. But she did become an athlete, and I believe her identity today is shaped in part by her sense of self as an athlete, as well as by her sense of self as a student. However, many of her college and high school experiences surrounding sport were negative, and certainly gendered, which contributed to her particular understandings about sport and her role in it. These experiences ultimately caused her to leave college athletics, which she found sad but necessary. However, these experiences also helped her better understand the importance of sport and athletic participation. She is now an avid sport fan, still runs regularly, and hopes in the future to work in some capacity with a middle school or high school running program.

Her experiences, and those of my other children, caused me to question our understanding of sport as an institution. While my daughter might argue that many negative experiences in sport are due to individual influences, I believe we must examine those individual experiences within the larger context of the institution if we want to truly create change. Brian and I began the challenge of putting together this book based on a belief that sport has tremendous potential for good, but that this potential is not always realized, in part due to the way sport is currently defined, designed, and implemented. As a scholar, I am interested in understanding how sport shapes our lives in all kinds of ways, and the potential it has for positive and negative influences, opportunities, and outcomes, sometimes inadvertently. As a mother, I began working on this book as a mechanism to better understand and improve the sport experiences of young people. It is with these goals and interests in mind that we decided to pursue a second edition of the text.

A Critical Sociological Perspective

As with the first edition of this book, the authors in this edition take a particular perspective toward the study of sport. This is not a book about the benefits of sport or a book about the demographics of sport. Rather, it is a book about what sport means in people's lives and how these meanings are constructed culturally and socially by our experiences with and in sport, whether directly or indirectly. This book examines sport in relationship to the meanings it holds for individuals, for groups of people, for organizations, and for society. Today, both in education and in business, the focus is on developing our ability to think critically—the ability to synthesize, apply, and evaluate information. The authors in this volume recognize that sport and our society are intimately connected, and that sport is connected in complicated ways to our individual lives. In order to best understand these connections, we need to utilize different perspectives, some of which may represent thinking very different than our own. The goal is to understand the relationship between the individual and the social, between the patterns, practices, and events in the broader social world and in our own lives. The ability to develop this "sociological imagination" relies upon three different, but connected, approaches: the historical, the comparative, and the critical.

It would be difficult to escape the historical nature of sport—it came from somewhere, was created in particular ways for particular purposes. Understanding this history is important if we want to understand the current context and effects of sport in our world, and ultimately create changes in it. In addition, it is clear that sport means different things to different people in different contexts. Thus, a comparative approach becomes important because it allows us to examine sport from perspectives other than our own. Finally, adopting a critical approach to sport means that we critique the way sport is constructed and enacted. This does not imply an anti-sport perspective, only that we ask questions about and examine taken-for-granted assumptions about the way the sport operates in our lives and in our world. This critical approach provides a space in which we can explore contradictions and complexities in sport and in society, thus moving us toward thinking and acting critically to create change where necessary.

When we examine sport with and through these different perspectives, we are able to see the ways in which sport is linked to the historical, political, social, and economic forces in our world. We recognize that this is certainly not how most people think about sport, especially as they are engaging with and in it. However, we hope such an examination can help readers to be more reflective about sport in their world. This reflection can help move us forward in our own thinking, causing us to (re)consider our views and beliefs about sport, evaluate them in relationship to new ideas presented, and decide whether or not to hold onto, discard, or change them based on these new understandings. Without such analysis, it is difficult for us to recognize how our own ideas about sport are influenced by social, economic, political, and historical influences. The goal is to be able to examine a variety of different viewpoints, including our own, through a critical lens.

We recognize that it is often difficult to engage in such a critical analysis. We have grown up in a world in which our understandings about sport become part of the cultural landscape, and rarely are we asked to critically examine that land-scape. We just look at it every day and assume it is the way it is and should be like that. Rarely do we question how and why sport operates the way it does. One re-sult is that when presented with a critical perspective, we become uncomfortable, or angry, or upset. This is the *cognitive dissonance* that often occurs when our thinking is challenged by new ideas that are not in harmony with what and how we currently think. As teachers, coaches, authors, parents, and/or the many dif-ferent positions that the authors in this text represent, we believe that cognitive dissonance provides the power for change—both individually and collectively.

Thinking Critically versus Being Critical

Questioning what is taken for granted is never easy, especially when it is some-thing as revered as sport. However, such a critical analysis can help us move be-yond the status quo toward better practice. This book examines the role and in-fluence of sport in society, taking a critical approach that asks readers to consider the relationship between sport and the larger society of which it is a part, as well as the relationship between the individual and sport as an institution. The goal is to provide a space for the development of a social consciousness about sport—to move readers beyond simplistic slogans and taken-for-granted assumptions to a more critical understanding of sport. This type of analysis is often assumed to be negative. On the contrary, the authors in this book believe wholeheartedly in the potential of sport, but not always in its current practice. It is only with such critical analysis that we can recognize the problems and the possibilities of sport. Such critique has the potential to be a more powerful form of support (and change) than unthinking acceptance of current practices.

The critical analyses presented in this book are not a criticism of sport itself, nor of those who participate in it. Rather, they are a means by which to uncover and acknowledge the ways in which historical, social, economic, and educational practices construct sport in ways that often foster discrimination, injustice, and abuse. Thus, the critical perspectives presented here represent a way to demonstrate our commitment to sport while at the same time working for change. Often, we want easy and fast solutions to problems when presented with such a critical analysis: "If things are so bad, then what's your plan to change them?" However, this book is not about presenting solutions, but about beginning a dialogue about sport in our world. We believe it is the responsibility of all those associated with and concerned about the institution of sport to work for change. The authors in this book care deeply about sport in our world, which is why they are willing to engage in such a public discussion of it. They also have particular perspectives about sport and its role in society, perspectives that recognize both the problems and the possibilities of sport in our world. These authors write about sport as accurately, intelligently, and critically as they can, recognizing its strengths and its weaknesses. We hope the diversity of ideas and perspectives represented in this book moves readers toward engaged debate about the ideas and perspectives represented. We believe such debate about sport (and about our world) is necessary in order to create change, both individually and institutionally.

This volume once again presents cutting-edge research and writing about a variety of issues facing the world of sport today. Whether we consider ourselves sport fans or not, whether we are (or were) athletes or not, it is clear that sport influences all of our lives. It is everywhere around us, in film and television and advertising, on our clothing and apparel, in our language and communication patterns. Even our decision to actively ignore it sends a message about sport. Recognizing its importance in our world and in our lives brings us closer to understanding the relationship between sport and society, and thus how to create change, possibly in both realms. Sport is not just a game; it is a serious piece of our culture that needs to be examined critically from multiple perspectives.

Overview of the Book

This edition, like the first, is broken into parts that each deal with particular issues in sport. First, the part on "Youth and Sport" has chapters that examine how sport influences young people in both positive and negative ways, and about the purposes it supposedly serves. Two parts of the book deal with sport and identity: "Gender, Sexuality, and Sport," and "Race, Ethnicity, and Sport." Authors in both parts address issues that all of us face as we negotiate the world of sport, and specifically focus on the discrimination and bias that is assumed, accepted, and enacted through sport. "Sport, Media, and Big Business" examines sport as entertainment, information, and commerce, with chapters that examine sport and economics, as well as sport and media representation. The final part, "International Perspectives on Sport and Participation," represents work by authors from around the globe who deal with global issues facing sport today. We believe this edition presents new and exciting avenues for exploring sport in our world, allowing us to recognize its tremendous influence, both positive and negative, in our lives and in our world. We hope this recognition will help us to *change the game* in positive ways.

1

Sport Specialization and Its Effects

Jay Coakley

PEOPLE OFTEN SET PRIORITIES FOR what they wish to learn and do, especially when they have multiple opportunities and choices. In other words, they *specialize* in learning and doing some things rather than others. For example, when college students choose sociology as their major field of study, they take courses enabling them to become specialists in the study of social relationships, interaction, and the organization of groups and societies. When a student accepts a scholarship to play soccer for a college team, he or she chooses to specialize in soccer rather than other sports.

We can't do and be experts in everything. Therefore, specialization is a normal and even necessary way of keeping our focus and sanity as we negotiate our lives in complex social worlds. But specialization can have negative effects when it prevents us from experiencing things that contribute to normal development and maturation.

When it comes to the psycho-social development of children and adolescents, it's important to understand the dynamics and possible consequences of specialization in youth sports. Through the mid-1970s, most people believed that *all-around athletes were the best athletes.* For example, young men who played and "lettered" in three or more varsity sports in high school were given special status in their schools and communities. It is important to note that in this case it is about young men because prior to the late-1970s girls had very few opportunities to play sports because schools provided very few if any teams for girls. The students who played only one sport were seen as athletically inferior to their multi-sport peers. But this perspective began to change in the 1970s as people discovered that the highly talented, medal-winning Olympic athletes from the communist nations of the Soviet Union and East Germany had specialized in their sports from a young age.

By the beginning of the 1990s, most young people in the United States specialized in formally organized sports controlled by adults and they spent less and less time playing informal games that they created and controlled. At the same time, young people were encouraged to specialize in a single sport through the year so they could develop elite skills and move to higher levels of competition where the rewards were greater. These two types of specialization, (a) playing only in adult-controlled, formally organized sports and (b) playing in only one sport for most or all of the year, have dramatically changed youth sport experiences over the past two generations.

What do we know about these two forms of specialization? Do they have positive or negative consequences for young people? Should we encourage them, or should we think about "de-specializing" youth sports for the sake of young people and their overall development? These are the questions discussed in this chapter.

Youth Sport Experiences Then and Now

When I was growing up in the 1950s, I spent at least ten hours playing in "pickup games" and informal, player-controlled sports for every hour I spent playing games or practicing in an organized sport. Few of my sport experiences were ever seen or evaluated by parents, coaches, or referees. They were my experiences and it was up to me to give them meaning, because neither parents nor coaches were there to interpret my experiences for me. I decided if I had fun, played well, succeeded or failed. My judgments were influenced by my peers with whom I played, but there were no spectators. Further, there were no official statistics, scores, records, game films, or coaches' ratings to influence how I judged and then integrated these experiences into my life.

Because I was interested in many sports I played five different sports in high school, and then played other competitive sports during summers. Only in college did I specialize because I had a full scholarship to play basketball and my coaches prohibited us from playing other sports that might lead to injuries or disrupt our basketball training. However, I played softball and golf every summer and played in a number of summer basketball leagues (in the 1960s this was not against National Collegiate Athletic Association rules).

Two generations later, Maddie, my 10-year-old granddaughter was chosen to be on a "select" soccer team organized by a non-profit club. The team is scheduled to play two seasons, one in the fall and another in the spring. About half of her games are out of town and involve three to seven hours of round-trip driving. Her team also plays in three to four major tournaments that require significant out-of-town travel, and all team members are encouraged to play in one or more summer and "between season" soccer camps administered and coached by people associated with the soccer club. This specialization is required if Maddie wishes to play soccer at a level that offers her challenging competition and a chance to be with friends she's made in past soccer seasons. When I was 10 years old or when Maddie's parents were 10, we were never asked to specialize in this way, and we would have found it to be disruptive of our lives and our participation in the diverse sports we wanted to play.

Playing on the select club team requires major time commitments and expenses. Therefore, Maddie will drop karate, another sport she loves, and she won't have time to play basketball in a league that she's enjoyed the last two years. Her interests in gymnastics, swimming, and ice- and inline-skating will be put on hold for the most part, as she plays on the soccer club "select" team and follows team rules.

Maddie has played in organized sports since she was 4 years old, but she's played few informal sports and "pickup games" with friends. Parents today feel uncomfortable allowing their kids the freedom to roam around the neighborhood and play informal games in whatever open spaces they might find. And parents fear that their kids might get into trouble if they are not supervised by an adult. Therefore, for every hour Maddie has spent playing informal sports, she's spent at least ten hours practicing or playing games on organized teams under the watchful eyes of adult coaches and parents.

Maddie and I typify our respective generations. Informal games were the major part of my sport experiences, whereas Maddie's sport experiences have occurred almost exclusively on organized teams controlled by adults. I didn't specialize in a sport until I was a 19-year-old college student, and Maddie is specializing in soccer as a 10-year-old fifth-grader.

Does this mean that "playing sports" involved different learning experiences for me than for Maddie and her peers? If there are differences, can we say that one set of experiences is better than the other? The answers to these questions are important because so much individual and family time today is being used to enable young people to play a single organized sport that requires nearly year-round participation. I explore these questions in the rest of this chapter.

Experiences in Informal versus Organized Sports

The experiences of children in adult-controlled, organized sports differ from those that young people have when they play informal games and sports that they create and control. Research indicates that each of these experiences involves opportunities to learn important but different things, and neither set of experiences is without problems. However, people tend to overrate the importance of organized sports in the lives of young people, whereas they underrate the importance of informal games and sports (Schultz, 1999).

Informal sports are *action-centered,* whereas organized sports are *rule-centered.* Organizing and maintaining informal sports involves creativity and interpersonal skills. Games involve decision making and conflict resolution in response to unanticipated situations and problems. Unless the participants understand and accept the rules they create, the games will end in disagreements. This means that the players must learn to cooperate with peers and follow the rules on which their game is based. Such experiences provide important learning opportunities for young people as they mature and enter adolescence and adulthood.

Research shows that playing informal games and sports involves cooperation, planning, creativity, decision making, organizing, negotiating, problem solving, and the ability to distinguish self-interest from the common good of the group playing a game. After spending eight years studying the everyday lives of children and adolescents in an upper-middle-class community, sociologists Patricia and Peter Adler (1998) concluded that young people learn valuable lessons when they create and control their own games and sports. But the Adlers were not able to measure the types and extent of learning that may have occurred during these games, nor were they able to say whether the learning that occurred in these games carried over to other settings and relationships.

Playing organized sports involves different experiences than those observed by the Adlers and others who have studied play and informal games and sports (Coakley, 1983; Schultz, 1999). Young people in organized sports must manage relationships with adult authority figures, learn the rules and strategies used in their sports, and abide by the schedule of practices and games that they are given. Playing organized sports acquaints young people with the operation of formal organizational structures, rule-governed teamwork, and adult models of work and achievement (Adler & Adler, 1998). But we don't know if their experiences teach them how to effectively manage relationships in formal structures, or if they teach them to passively accept formal structures without question.

As we discuss these issues, it's important to recognize that some sport experiences occur in contexts that are partly informal and partly organized by adults. For example, adults may provide subtle guidance to young people as they play informal games and sports, and young people may have opprtunities to be creative and make decisions in organized sports controlled by adults. These "hybrid" sport experiences can be valuable contexts for learning. The adults involved in hybrid games say that it takes tact and patience to put up with children's mistakes and oversights, but they also say that it is a joy to see the creativity and compassion shown by many children as they play these games.

Because organized sports are so prevalent today and informal sports are rare, many experts in child development have tried to remind people of the benefits of play and informal games in the lives of children (Bloom, 1985; Chudacoff, 2007;

Elkind, 2007, 2008; Laumann, 2006; Sternheimer, 2006). For example, a recent report of the American Academy of Pediatrics (Ginsburg, 2007) emphasizes that without experiences in self-initiated games, young people miss opportunities to learn critical skills needed to be successful in the world today. Creativity, innovation, sharing, conflict resolution, decision-making, group skills, and self-advocacy, the report highlights, are learned in free, unstructured and self-structured play and games rather than in organized, adult-controlled sports. Similarly, leadership skills based on calculated risk taking and thinking outside the box are more likely to be learned in unstructured and self-structured activities than in formally organized activities controlled by adults.

Former international soccer star Brandi Chastain suggests that sport experiences for children today are "overly organized" and that young people need to play informal games and sports if we want them to learn "to be independent, creative, and self-motivated" (2004, p. 125). She also notes that young people are more likely to develop a long-lasting love of physical activity and sports when they "dictate the place, the time, the rules, and the structure—or lack of it" in their sports. Chastain's point is that it is difficult to feel a sense of ownership and an intimate connection with a sport if you've always played it according to the wishes of an adult with a whistle.

Recent research shows that young people who regularly participate in diverse informal games and sports between the ages of 6 and 12 have lower dropout rates than those who specialize from a young age (Baker & Robertson-Wilson, 2003; Côté & Hay, 2002; Côté & Fraser-Thomas, 2007; Fraser-Thomas & Côté, 2006; Fraser-Thomas, Côté, & Deakin, 2005; Kirk, 2005; Weirsma, 2000). Additionally, athletes who have not played informal games are more likely than others to retire early after reaching an elite level (Barynina & Vaitsekhovskii, 1992).

Pressure to Specialize in Organized Sports

Despite what we know about the value of play and informal games and sports, there are social factors that push children toward specializing in organized sports at the same time that they impede the revival of informal sports. These factors influence both children and their parents. They include the media, cutural changes in the definition of a good parent, the privatization of youth sports, and misinformation about the benefits of specialization.

Television introduces children to organized sports at a very young age. They quickly learn that these sports are highly valued by those around them, including parents and family members, and that playing organized sports brings positive feedback in the form of status and social acceptance. Further, once they play an organized sport, they see how their parents alter the family to accommodate their sport involvement. This makes them the center of attention, especially the attention of their fathers and, for many children, this feels so good that they give high priority to playing organized sports.

For parents, specializing in organized sports fits their desire to find for their children supervised activities after school and on weekends. This, parents believe, keeps their children out of trouble, and provides a constructive activity that they believe teaches children valuable lessons about achievement, teamwork, commitment, and competition at the same time that it serves as a basis for them to claim moral worth as parents (Coakley, 2006). These factors are very important in families where both parents work, worry about child-care issues, and seek to meet the expectations that people have for parents today. This is crucial in neo-liberal societies where parents are held totally accountable for the actions and whereabouts of their children twenty-four hours a day, seven days a week. In this cultural context, organized, adult-controlled activities become a necessity for parents trying to meet this standard, which has never before existed in a society. Organized sports come to be highly valued in comparison with other activities, because they are culturally valued, highly visible, and structured in ways that make achievement quantifiable and understandable to everyone (Coakley, 2006). To claim you are a good parent because your child plays informal games will not work in a neo-liberal culture where individual choices and self-control are the basis for establishing moral worth.

Specializing in a Single Sport at an Early Age

Early specialization and decreased involvement in diverse physical activities is becoming increasingly common in youth sports (Côté & Hay, 2002; De Knop, Engström, Skirstad & Weiss, 1996; Ewing & Seefeldt, 1996; Hill, 1988; Hill & Hansen, 1988; Hill & Simons, 1989). Most adults, including parents, realize that specialization does not provide all that their children need in terms of overall physical, psychological, and social development, especially when a child is younger than 14 years old. But concerned parents also know that youth sports today are often organized in ways that demand early specialization if children are to succeed and progress to higher levels of competition. Specialization has even become a prerequisite for playing on certain high school teams and elite club teams where players come out of a preparatory pipeline that gives them the "sport resumés" that are favored by high school and college coaches.

Many parents today are confused about what to do. They know that early specialization involves excessive costs for them and their children, but they believe that playing organized sports is good for their children. Additionally, they know that their moral worth as parents will be evaluated in terms of how they manage their children, and keeping children in organized sports is seen by nearly everyone as a responsible child management strategy.

When a child specializes in a "select, club team sport," parents must make commitments and devote personal and family resources to their children's sport participation to a degree that is unprecedented in human history. The money and time required to sponsor early sport specialization is so great that it often undermines alternative family activities and opportunities for siblings to play sports other than the one played by an older brother or sister.

When specialization occurs, many parents find that they become part of a "sport and team culture" in which the sport-related needs of their child must come first in their lives. If they don't set priorities in this way, other parents and coaches question their moral worth as mothers and fathers. For this reason, parents of children in highly specialized youth sport programs often make sure that other people know about the money they spend on their child's sport participation, how many miles they drive, how many mornings they wake up before dawn to drive a child to before-school practices, how many weekends they spend driving to and watching games, how many vacations they've organized around tournaments, and how many days they leave work early to accommodate the sport-related needs of their children. These sacrifices become parents' "moral worth merit badges," and parents display them for everyone to see.

Many parents don't realize that the current emphasis on early specialization in youth sports is due in great part to the privatization and professionalization of youth sports. When sport clubs, both non-profit and commercial, hire staff and coaches, there needs to be a way of ensuring that payrolls, facility costs, and other expenses can be paid twelve months a year. The only way this can be done is to convince parents that year-round participation is in the best interests of their children, and that dues must be paid every month of the year. But this approach is grounded in the logic of economic profit, and it has nothing to do with the best interests of children.

Children who specialize in a single sport at an early age often develop impressive skills sooner than other children and are more likely to be age-group standouts among pre-teens in a particular sport. However, there is little evidence that specialization is the best or the only way to produce highly skilled athletes. In other words, specialization may not pay off as many parents hope and as advertised by many sport clubs (Côté & Fraser-Thomas, 2007; Côté, Lidor, & Hackfort, 2009).

Research shows that early specialization in youth sports is more likely than diversified sport participation to be associated with higher rates of overuse and overtraining injuries (American Academy of Pediatrics, 2000; Gorman, 2005; Pennington, 2005), an overly focused self-concept, weak and highly variable self-esteem (Coakley, 1992; Côté, 2004), burnout and early retirement from sport (Barynina & Vaitsekhovskii, 1992; Bompa, 2000; Boyd & Yin, 1996; Coakley, 1992; Wall & Côté, 2004), and restricted psycho-social experiences that can interfere with normal maturation and development (Côté, 2004; Côté & Hay,

2002; Wright & Côté, 2003). Long-term specialization through childhood and adolescence may also put young people into a developmental rut that makes it difficult to see and experience the world from vantage points unrelated to their sport. When this occurs, young people will face developmental and maturational challenges as they reach early adulthood. Therefore, even when young people achieve athletic success after specializing in a sport from an early age, we cannot assume that their experiences will lead to positive developmental outcomes or even good physical health (Côté & Fraser-Thomas, 2007; Côté, Lidor, & Hackfort, 2009).

Steve Swanson, who has coached Stanford, Dartmouth, and the University of Virginia to conference championships and has coached U.S. national teams at the U-16 (under 16 years old), U-17, U-18, and U-19 levels, notes that elite soccer players today often suffer serious self-esteem problems, despite their skills. He explains that the long-term, year-round specialization that is now the norm in soccer puts young people in a situation where their sense of self and self-esteem is tied exclusively to their performance and identity as a soccer player. This means that every mistake, every loss, and every time that perfection is not reached spins these athletes into emotional turmoil and creates doubt about their competence in soccer and their self-worth as a person. Consequently, many of these elite athletes experience dramatic emotional swings corresponding to their latest performance on the field. As elite athletes, they've learned that success in the past means little when compared to what you do today. This puts them on a perpetual self-esteem roller coaster at the same time that outsiders look at them and assume that they are supremely self-confident on and off the field. Swanson says that this changes what he must do to be effective as a coach. In addition to being a teacher of tactics and techniques, he must also be a "clinician" who reassures highly skilled athletes that they are worthy people.

An expanding series of studies by Jean Côté and his colleagues provide support for the idea that early diversification, rather than early specialization, is the most effective way to develop elite athletes (Baker & Côté, 2006a, 2006b; Baker, Côté & Abernethy, 2003; Côté, 1999; Côté, Baker & Abernethy, 2003, 2007; Soberlak & Côté, 2003). It appears that when children play a variety of sports before they are 12 years old and then gradually become more specialized during early adolescence, they are more likely to be motivated and committed to their sport than those who have specialized from a young age. It's not clear why this is so, but it may be that when young people gradually come to choose a sport in which to specialize, they feel a greater sense of "ownership" of their sport career. If this choice comes during mid-adolescence when the young person can make an informed decision about the sport that he or she wants to take seriously, participation is more likely to occur on terms set by the athlete rather than parents and coaches. When young people specialize in a sport from an early age, they may never feel a similar sense of ownership, because they've never had the opportunity to make an informed choice about the sport they play. Consequently, they see their participation occurring on everyone else's terms rather than their own, and this can lead to burnout and early retirement, even when they are at the top of their game.

From the perspective of sport development, early specialization has additional problems. First, it cuts out young people who are "late bloomers" when it comes to skills in a particular sport. In fact, once young people become part of the specialized, highly select club team structure in a community, they may have a very difficult time becoming re-involved after skipping a year or two of participation. Newcomers have even more difficulties because they are unknown and outside the pipeline through which players in a particular sport go as they move to higher levels of competition.

Second, early specialization often leads to high rates of burnout among "early bloomers" who are selected to play on the select teams that have demanding practice and season schedules. By the time these children are 11 or 12 years old, they feel that they've been in their sport ever since they can remember, which may be literally true, and they are now bored or stressed out by the sport because it gives them little freedom of choice.

Third, early specialization often puts those who stay in the sport through mid-adolescence into a developmental rut and presents them with the challenge of digging themselves out if they wish to move successfully into adulthood. This occurs when young people focus so exclusively on their sport that they have little time to expand their interests, identities, and experiences beyond the confines of their sport. This compromises the normal development that occurs during adolescence.

Overall, a youth sport system that emphasizes early specialization is organized to *cut out* late bloomers, *burn out* early bloomers, and force successful athletes to *dig out* of developmental ruts. Furthermore, long-term specialization often turns young athletes into "one-trick ponies" who excel in one sport, or even one position in a sport, but have a difficult time when they are asked to do something that does not involve the highly specialized skills they've spent their lifetime learning. This suggests an obvious conclusion: If we're interested in the overall development and health of young people as well as the development of athletic talent in general, it would be best to emphasize playing a variety of sports, both formal and informal, rather than specializing in one formally organized, adult-controlled sport, and to delay year-round participation in a single sport until mid-adolescence, when young people can make an informed decision about what they'd like to do for the next decade or two of their lives. The message that parents and young people need to hear today is that de-specialization is the way to go—until young people have enough experience, maturity, and knowledge to choose a sport in which they'd like to specialize.

References

Adler, P. A. & Adler, P. (1998). *Peer power: Preadolescent culture and identity.* New Brunswick, NJ: Rutgers University Press.

American Academy of Pediatrics (Committee on Sports Medicine and Fitness). (2000). Intensive training and sports specialization in young athletes. *Pediatrics* 106 (1), 154–157.

Baker, J., & Côté, J. (2006a). Shifting training requirements during athlete development: The relationship among deliberate practice, deliberate play and other sport involvement in the acquisition of sport expertise. In D. Hackfort and G. Tenenbaum (Eds.), *Essential processes for attaining peak performance* (93–110). Germany: Meyer and Meyer.

Baker, J. & Côté, J. (2006b). Shifting training requirements during athlete development: Deliberate practice, deliberate play and other sport involvement in the acquisition of sport expertise. In D. Hackfort & G. Tenenbaum (Eds.), *Essential processes for attaining peak performance* (pp. 92–109). Oxford: Meyer & Meyer Sport.

Baker, J., Côté, J. & Abernethy, B. (2003). Sport-specific practice and the development of expert decision-making in team ball sports. *Journal of Applied Sport Psychology* 15, 12–25.

Baker, J. & Robertson-Wilson, J. (2003). On the risks of early specialization in sport. *Physical and Health Education Journal* 69(1), 4–8.

Barynina, I. I. & Vaitsekhovskii, S. M. (1992). The aftermath of early sports specialization for highly qualified swimmers. *Fitness and Sport Review International* 27(4), 132–133.

Bloom, B. S. (1985). *Developing talent in young people.* New York: Ballantine Books.

Bompa, T. O. (2000). *Total training for young champions.* Champaign, IL: Human Kinetics.

Boyd, M. P. & Yin, Z. (1996). Coginitive-affective sources of sport enjoyment in adolescent sport participants. *Adolescence* 31, 383–395.

Chastain, B. (2004). *It's not about the bra.* New York: Harper Resource.

Chudacoff, H. (2007). *Children at play: An American history.* New York: New York University Press.

Coakley, J. (1983). Play, games and sports: Developmental implications for young people. In J. C. Harris & R. J. Park, (Eds.) *Play, games and sports in cultural contexts* (pp. 431–450). Champaign, IL: Human Kinetics.

Coakley, J. (1992). Burnout among adolescent athletes: A personal failure or social problem? *Sociology of Sport Journal* 9(3), 271–285.

Coakley, J. (2006). The good father: Parental expectations and youth sports. *Leisure Studies* 25(2), 153–164.

Côté, J. (1999). The influence of the family in the development of talent in sport. *The Sport Psychologist* 13, 395–417.

Côté, J. (2004). Education through sport participation: A developmental perspective. European Launch of the European Year of Education through Sport (EYES), Dublin, Ireland.

Côté, J., Baker, J. & Abernethy, B. (2003). From play to practice: A developmental framework for the acquisition of expertise in team sport. In J. Starkes & K. A. Ericsson (Eds.), *Expert performance in sports: Advances in research on sport expertise* (pp. 89–113). Champaign, IL: Human Kinetics.

Côté, J., Baker, J. & Abernethy, B. (2007). Practice and play in the development of sport expertise. In G. Tenenbaum & R. Eklund (Eds.), *Handbook of sport psychology* (pp. 184–202; 3rd edition). Hoboken, NJ: Wiley.

Côté, J. & Fraser-Thomas, J. L. (2007). Youth involvement in sport. In P. R. E. Crocker (Ed.), *Introduction to sport psychology: A Canadian perspective* (pp. 266–294). Toronto: Pearson Prentice Hall.

Côté, J. & Hay, J. (2002). Children's involvement in sport: A developmental perspective. In J. M. Silva & D. E. Stevens (Eds.), *Psychological foundations of sport* (pp. 484–502). Boston: Allyn & Bacon.

Côté, J., Lidor, R. & Hackfort, D. (2009). ISSP Position Stand: To sample or to specialize? Seven postulates about youth sport activities that lead to continued participation and elite performance. *International Journal of Sport and Exercise Psychology* 7(1), 7–17.

De Knop, P., Engström, L., Berit Skirstad, B. & Weiss, M., Eds. (1996). *Worldwide trends in youth sport.* Champaign, IL: Human Kinetics.

Elkind, D. (2007). *Hurried child: Growing up too fast too soon.* Cambridge, MA: Da Capo Lifelong Books.

Elkind, D. (2008). *The power of play: Learning what comes naturally.* Cabridge, MA: Da Capo Lifelong Books.

Ewing, M. E. & Seefeldt, V. (1996). Patterns of participation and attrition in American agency-sponsored youth sports. In F. L. Smoll & R. E. Smith (Eds.), *Children in sports: A biopsychosocial perspective* (pp. 31–45). Indianapolis: Brown & Benchmark.

Fraser-Thomas, J. & Côté, J. (2006). Youth sports: Implementing findings and moving forward with research. *Athletic insight: The online journal of sport psychology.*

Fraser-Thomas, J. L., Côté, J. & Deakin, J. (2005). Youth sport programs: An avenue to foster positive youth development. *Physical Education and Sport Pedagogy* 10(1), 19–40.

Ginsburg, K. R. (2007). The importance of play in promoting healthy child development and maintaining strong parent-child bonds. *Pediatrics* 119(1), 182–191. Retrieved from http://www.aap.org/pressroom/playFINAL.pdf.

Gorman, C. (2005). Why more kids are getting hurt. *Time* 165 (June 6): 58.

Hill, G. (1988). Celebrate diversity (not specialization) in school sports. *Executive Educator* 10, 24.

Hill, G. M. & Hansen, G. F. (1988). Specialization in high school sports—the pros and cons. *Journal of Physical Education, Recreation and Dance* 59(5), 76–79.

Hill, G. M. & Simons, J. (1989). A study on sport specialization in high school athletes. *Journal of Sport and Social Issues* 13(1), 1–13.

Kirk, D. (2005). Physical education, youth sport and lifelong participation: The importance of early learning experiences. *European Physical Education Review* 11, 239–255.

Laumann, S. (2006). *Child's play: Rediscovering the joy of play in our families and our communities.* Toronto: Random House Canada.

Lyman, S. L., Andrews, J., Fleisig, G. S. & Osinski, E. D. (1998). Youth pitching injuries. *Sports Medicine Update* 13(2), 4–9.

Pennington, B. (2005). Doctors see a big rise in injuries for young athletes. *The New York Times,* Section A (February 22): 1.

Schultz, B. (1999). The disappearance of child-directed activities. *Journal of Physical Education, Recreation and Dance* 70(5), 9–10.

Soberlak, P. & Côté, J. (2003). The developmental activities of elite ice hockey players. *Journal of Applied Sport Psychology* 15, 41–49.

Sternheimer, K. (2006). *Kids these days: Facts and fictions about today's youth.* Lanham, MD: Rowman & Littlefield Publishers, Inc.

Wall, M. & Côté, J. (2004). The influence of early sport participation on future sport investment or dropout. Paper presented at the meeting of the Association of the Advancement of Applied Sport Psychology, Minneapolis, MN.

Weirsma, L. D. (2000). Risks and benefits of youth sport specialization. *Pediatric Exercise Science* 12, 13–22.

Wright, A. & Côté, J. (2003). A retrospective analysis of leadership development through sport. *The Sport Psychologist* 17, 268–291.

2

The Power of a Coach

Sport and Life's Lasting Lessons

Brian Lampman

Dreams for a Daughter

One BY ONE, FRIENDS AND FAMILY entered the church to remember and honor the man whose infectious smile, cunning wit, selflessness, and passion for helping others made him such a beloved figure. Victims of his panache for the "zinger" aimed at one's golf prowess (or lack thereof) or the extra pound or two put on at the holidays or just the bad hair day that never escaped his attention shared their stories as a badge of honor. The message in his clever banter never escaped them: He cared about me, too. A shining light had been extinguished by the cruelty of amyotrophic lateral sclerosis, more commonly known as ALS or Lou Gehrig's disease, and the magnitude and unfairness of the loss was difficult for all to comprehend. Yet, the day would serve as a celebration of life lived to its fullest: a well-orchestrated eulogy that brought one special story after another of family, love, integrity, and kindness. His body had been broken, but his spirit resonated with all in attendance and his life lessons would live on in the hearts and minds of all who honored him that day.

My heart beat faster as I watched his daughter gracefully stride to the podium. I still remembered her as a young girl, a member of the women's freshman soccer team that I had coached years ago at her high school. It was my first coaching job, and I had approached it with a mix of excitement and trepidation. Would they like me? Would I instill a passion and appreciation for the game that had made such a difference in my own life?

Before me today stood the same girl who had matured into a brilliant young woman. She was an Ivy League graduate and former Division I athlete with dreams of becoming a doctor. She still possessed all of the same qualities that, years ago, I had found made her so unique: a passion for learning, a commitment to family and team, a love of life, and her father's ability to bring out the best in those with whom she came in contact. Gazing out confidently at the packed church, she started to speak and I choked back tears before the words came out of her mouth.

To this day, I am unable to recall the subtle nuances and eloquence of her words, but I vividly remember the loving tapestry of family stories that captured the spirit of her father, the love he had for her, and the dreams he had for her future. She recounted the close bond they shared, strengthened by their mutual passion for sport. She offered a myriad of examples of his commitment to whatever sport she played and his efforts to master all of the complexities that sport had to offer. He had varying degrees of success, which resulted in moments that brought them to tears of laughter—he was certainly not the MVP of demonstration, but his status as MVP of fatherhood was unmatched.

She spoke of the countless high school games that he attended, despite a dizzying schedule as an attorney at one of the finest law firms in the state, in addition to the countless hours serving numerous charitable organizations in the area. She glowed with pride describing the sports banquets he attended and the questions he often asked her: "Are you having fun?" he asked. "Are you being a great teammate?" As she spoke, it was evident that their conversations were never just about sport—he was always teaching, nurturing, encouraging, and offering pearls of wisdom to assist her as she navigated her own life and participated in the games that bonded them.

Those who came to pay their respects to her father knew of the state championship she helped earn as a member of the field hockey team in high school. They knew she went on to Harvard and became a member of their prestigious field hockey team. What they did not know about were her struggles as a member of the highly competitive team at arguably one of the finest academic institutions in the country. But throughout these struggles, her father continued to be her guiding light as she expressed her fears, her dreams, her triumphs, and her failures to him as she had done so many times while growing up. Her father listened thoughtfully as he had done countless times in the past. He chose his words carefully and offered his insight and encouragement to his daughter, now hundreds of miles away. In his daughter's most difficult time, he offered these words: "Sports are a tool to learn life's great lessons." This was the mantra by which her father chose to live his life. Now, she passed his wisdom on to all who came to honor her father. I left feeling that I had been moved, once again, by this special man. I also left with a renewed sense of the transformative power of sport and the lasting opportunities it offered for life's great lessons.

This chapter will explore my own efforts as a secondary educator, a varsity high school coach, and a father to harness the many life lessons that sport offers for my own children and the athletes I coach, and the profound opportunity a parent and coach has to impart these lasting lessons. I will use examples from my own teaching and coaching to examine the power of sport to teach these lessons. The names of players and others mentioned in this chapter have been changed, and conversations and events are conveyed as accurately as possible, given my memory of them. The goal is to highlight the power of sport and the opportunities coaches, parents, and the public have to use sport to create powerful teachable moments and thus contribute to positive social change.

New Uniforms and New Books: Redefining Masculinity

"Coach, what's the book this year?" a bleach-blond junior inquired. I was delighted beyond belief with the question. A couple of years into my varsity men's coaching tenure, I had decided my players would read a book of my choice each season. The book would serve as a teaching tool for athletes accustomed to receiving uniforms and soccer balls the first day of practice, not books. My vision for my players was an understanding and appreciation for not only the X's and O's of soccer, but the X's and O's of life.

Sports are a tool to learn life's great lessons.

"Coach, what is it?" he asked impatiently. "A book about a football coach," I responded. "A football coach?" he asked incredulously. "This is no ordinary coach," I said, careful to impress upon him the book's importance with my words. His tone suggested I would have to overcome some of my players' stereotypical beliefs about football coaches as archaic relics of the past consumed only with football and winning, with little understanding or appreciation of other sports. "OK, but it better be as good as last year's book!" he replied. "I assure you that you will enjoy it and learn from it," I promised.

Fortunately, I was able to keep that promise. My chosen book, *Season of Life* by Jeffrey Marx (2003), was a gem of a book, one that I knew would resonate with my young male athletes. My players were quickly hooked by the story of Joe Ehrmann, the former NFL star who turned to coaching high school football. In the process, he was able to transform his players' lives and shift the paradigm of their concepts of masculinity, fatherhood, and relationships. Coach Ehrmann stressed the importance of character, integrity, and teamwork from his players and focused on his number one job as their coach: to love them.

What might have been an unusual sight prior to the soccer season now became an accepted practice ritual: players reading their books prior to practice or even during time set aside at some practices. Discussions with my players about Coach Ehrmann's teaching pedagogy and unorthodox methods convinced me my players were taking notice. I always viewed sport as far more than just fun and games; in this case, my players were actively using their own participation in a high school sport to read about how they could challenge dominant constructions of masculinity, and possibly change the culture of what it meant to be a man at their school.

Sadly, young men are conditioned to believe that being a "real man" means being in control, hiding feelings of emotion, engaging in hyper-masculine posturing, and achieving sexual conquests with women (Katz, 2006). The pervasive media culture often saturates boys with very narrow conceptions of masculinity, creating dire consequences for their healthy physical, social, and emotional development. Participation in sport often exacerbates these limited constructions of masculinity with its emphasis on winning through the use of power, dominance, intimidation, and even violence on and off the field (Coakley, 2001). I truly believe that sport provides numerous teachable moments for deconstructing some of the fallacies associated with contemporary images of masculinity. We, as coaches, are in a unique and important position to debunk some of the most toxic images of what it means to be a man. The book *Season of Life* would serve as the impetus for discussions of masculinity. I believed this was important since masculinity is not a fixed projection but a fluid construction that my players were in a position to understand and alter (Katz, 2006). I wanted my players to recognize the importance of understanding deficiencies in the manner masculinity is often framed for them and the ways in which its construction is heavily influenced by their involvement in high school athletics. Ultimately, I wanted to empower players to acquire a greater level of self-awareness about being a man and become agents of positive change in their school and community.

"How does Coach Ehrmann frame false masculinity?" I asked the team. They stared back at me. I was not going to let them touch a soccer ball until we thoroughly dissected Coach Ehrmann's ideas about masculinity. "What is false masculinity?" I asked them, curious to gauge their understanding of Coach Ehrmann's definition of false masculinity and the triumvirate pieces that define what it means to be a man.

A flick of a cleat released a shower of small rubber pellets from the beautiful new turf field as one player cleared his throat and began to speak. "False masculinity is what Coach Ehrmann feels is wrong about masculinity. We're conditioned to think we should act a certain way because we're men; Coach Ehrmann wants us to think about it in different ways," one of my players responded with confidence. I beamed with pride; the player had captured the essence of Coach Ehrmann's ideas. "That's a great answer," I said, still glowing. Perhaps the lessons, about masculinity and soccer, were starting to have the desired impact and raise a new level of consciousness among my players about what it meant to be a man.

We had a big game the next day against our cross-town rival, but I sensed my players understood the importance of this moment as our conversation triggered discussions about their development as young men and relationships with other men and women. I pulled out my weathered copy of *Season of Life*, the pages folded and torn from months of reflection, and began:

> Masculinity, first and foremost, ought to be defined in terms of relationships. It ought to be taught in terms of the capacity to love and to be loved. If you look over your life at the end of it . . . life wouldn't be measured in terms of success based on what you've acquired or achieved or what you own. The only thing that's really going to matter is the relationships that you had. It's gonna come down to this: What kind of father were you? What kind of husband were you? What kind of coach or teammate were you? What kind of son were you? What kind of brother were you? What kind of friend were you? Success comes in terms of relationships. (Marx, 2003, p. 36)

I paused and looked around the huddle of young men. Some made eye contact, some shifted, and others appeared engaged in reflection. What was clear, however, was that they were carefully digesting each new idea about their role as young men in the soccer program. They gained a greater appreciation of the importance of their own relationships and understood a greater sense of purpose about their participation in sport at their school. The quote further helped to debunk stereotypes of males as incapable of showing emotion and unwilling to cultivate meaningful relationships with others. It was truly a powerful teachable moment we shared together on that day.

As the season progressed, we reflected back to the book on numerous occasions. Coach Ehrmann's words, eloquent themselves and so skillfully crafted by Jeffrey Marx, served as powerful starting points for discussions of life's great lessons. The season ended with a gut-wrenching loss in the district final, but with a young lineup and a victory over the sixth-ranked team in the 2006 district semifinals, the team knew they had achieved more than anyone expected. I sensed not only their commitment to one another, but a genuine love and a sense of brotherhood nurtured with every practice, game, and team activity. The team had become a family, a circle of brothers united in their passion and love of sport. I wondered, however, once the season ended and they went their separate ways, what would the lasting lessons be? What lessons did they take away from the season about being a great student, a great community member, a great teammate, and our shifting paradigm of what it meant to be a man? Furthermore, would they remember what they learned about false masculinity from reading *Season of Life*? My answer would come at next season's summer soccer camp.

Be a Man

"Coach, I need to talk to you," said Joe, one of our tri-captains for the upcoming season. He had a grave expression on his face. "Of course, what's wrong?" I responded. "You need to know what one of the summer coaches said to us at camp," Joe said. My heart sank as I considered the most egregious thing a coach could have said to provoke Joe's reaction. "Ben had difficulty controlling the ball in a morning drill and the camp coach said something that I don't think he should have. He said, 'What, are you a fag or something? You can't do this?'"

I paused for a moment and immediately thought of Coach Ehrmann and *Season of Life*. I thought about the soccer posters that our varsity team had created, which hung in every school in our district with a picture of the team. One said, "Real men don't discriminate," and the other said, "Real men respect women." My players were invested in creating an inclusive school community that practiced tolerance and respect for all people. I knew they had the confidence to stand up to their peers, but what about an adult? And, this was not just any adult but a coach from a high-profile Division I college whom they were all desperate to impress.

"What happened after he said that?" I inquired, hoping my players would be leaders not bystanders, and challenge the overtly homophobic statements by the coach. "Nothing," Joe said. "There was an uncomfortable silence on the field," he continued. "No one said anything to the coach and nobody laughed. After a moment, we just all started playing again. The coach was very quiet for the remainder of the morning session," he exclaimed, a sense of satisfaction etched on his face that he and the team had resisted the efforts of the coach to denigrate homosexuals.

Later, my captain revealed to me what he had said to the coach in private. "We don't do that here," Joe had said to the coach after all players had been excused for lunch after the morning session. His words, so simple, yet so brave and eloquent, captured every hope and dream I had for my players as young men. The captains (and upperclassmen) had the power to create a climate in the locker room and on the field that, in turn, had the potential to impact the school climate as a whole. Too many coaches look the other way when their athletes engage in sexist and homophobic banter; sadly, some coaches model this to their athletes themselves. All too often, coaches excuse this type of language as innocent high school machismo—the type of "boys will be boys" mentality that has, historically, been allowed to fester in athletic programs across the country. The normalization of homophobia in sport often rears itself through the overt objectification of women (locker room bravado) and the use of the term "fag"—both methods of distancing oneself from homosexuality (Prettyman, 2006). When coaches take a stand against this type of boorish behavior from their male athletes, the possibility exists to affect the entire team and potentially even the school climate in the most extraordinary of ways. When the team captains and older members of a team create an environment where this type of behavior will not be tolerated, sub-varsity programs and players are more likely to follow suit.

I wish I had known about this incident when it occurred. In truth, I found out about it some time after the fact, and heard about my soft-spoken captain's comments to the coach even further down the line. As parents, teachers, and coaches, we want the best for our kids, but we will not always be there to protect them or urge them to do the right thing. We hope that our influence equips them with the backpack of knowledge and experience that allows them to make thoughtful and calculated responses to the most difficult of situations life has to offer. On that day, my captain, Joe, exceeded my expectations.

When I first created a sports sociology course while teaching in middle school, I always posed this question to my students: Have you ever had a coach who used racist, homophobic, or sexist language towards the team? The results were always the same—the majority of the female players had coaches who, at times, used swear words as a tool to motivate, but seldom, if ever, used homophobic, racist, or sexist language. What was so stunning was what the young males had to say about the language coaches had used with them. This language was laced with homophobic and sexist references, spoken in crass and vulgar tones. While the results of my queries were purely anecdotal, they certainly provided insight into the ways in which boys and girls are socialized through sport. They also further motivated me to be a coach who harnesses sport as a vehicle for positive social change.

The noted cultural theorist Jackson Katz (2006) explores the subculture of male high school student-athletes and the problems and possibilities of sport. He comments:

> Men and boys in the male-dominated school sports culture often have disproportionate impact on what sorts of masculine styles and sexualities in that school are accepted or marginalized, celebrated or bullied. But while many critiques of the relationship between sports culture and gender violence understandably stress its complicity in covering up, if not actively promoting, men's violence against women, the male sports culture can also be a source of creative anti-sexist strategies. (p. 247)

Katz's description of the significance of sport in the lives of young men offers a critical glimpse into their socialization through sport and the need to rigorously confront abusive social norms in male culture. Narrow constructions of what it means to be a man not only damage young men's self-image but their ability to form positive relationships with other men, as well as lasting relationships with women. By deconstructing masculinity in sport, coaches have a unique opportunity to challenge stereotypical and confining definitions of manhood that are still prevalent on the playing field and in the locker room. But in order to do this coaches not only have to seize teachable moments, but also proactively take the initative to raise difficult topics with young men—such as sexual violence, relationship abuse, and bullying.

Sports are a tool for life's great lessons.

Defining Moments in My Education as a Coach and Father

I walked through the aisle of the supermarket with my oldest son as I had done hundreds of times before. My summer vacation was in full swing and I appreciated how teaching provided me with treasured time with my children; today we were picking up some items for dinner. I was normally one of the few fathers in the supermarket during the day, and I often reflected on how lucky I was to have so much quality time with my sons.

As I reached for the final item to put in my cart, I saw a former student's parent out of the corner of my eye. I had always had a great relationship with her son and valued the way he carried himself as a student, an athlete, and a young man. I knew his parents were very supportive and nurturing and great stewards of his development—the kind of parents all teachers and coaches dream of working with. I smiled as she started to approach me—but I was met with a concerned look. I tried to imagine what could be so upsetting to her; I was unprepared for her words.

"A sub-varsity coach from another athletic program called your soccer team pussies," she said. She shook her head in disbelief. "Bill came home and said the coach had called the soccer team a bunch of pussies last year while addressing his team. Bill was very upset. I knew I needed to tell you; Bill just couldn't bring himself to do it."

I felt like my body was a balloon and all the air had been let out of it. I fumbled for the right words, and managed to mumble a "thank you" to her and that I would contact her after I looked into it further. I felt sick to my stomach as I left the supermarket—I had worked so hard to model a form of positive masculinity to my student-athletes, and this was how it was being characterized? It is difficult to measure the lasting effect of these words, uttered by a colleague in front of a group of impressionable young men. Needless to say, it would be another battle to fight for the hearts and minds of players whose coach, presumably to bolster his own team and perhaps his own self-confidence, had degraded ninety young men in another program.

After taking my concerns to the athletic director and head coach of that particular sport—both of whom were very supportive of my efforts—I approached the coach who had made the comment. I immediately sensed he knew what I intended to speak with him about. I asked him about the comment and he looked me dead in the eye and denied ever making the remark. I knew this was an outright lie (from other sources beyond the one parent) and I probed further; he continued to deny ever making the comment. I tried one more tactic—I implored him to understand how that type of language tears at the fabric of our athletic community and reinforces dangerous—and outdated—notions of masculinity among athletes. And then I did something that I wish I hadn't done—I urged him to consider how tough and aggressive a sport soccer actually is, and what mental and physical toughness it requires. In the process of confronting this coach about the sexist nature of his language, I had retreated to time-honored definitions of masculinity: power, control, physical size, physical prowess, and aggressiveness (Katz, 2006). It was truly a watershed moment for me as I recognized my own bias and the difficulty we all have in moving beyond current conceptualizations of masculinity and sport. While on this day I did not see the intended progress with the coach, I did not hear of any further incidents and, hopefully, it was a learning experience for both of us.

Sports are a tool to learn life's great lessons.

Penguins and Fatherhood

It was a beautiful September day in the fall of 2008, the kind without a cloud in the sky and the pleasant hint of autumn looming on the Michigan horizon. But I was worried about approaching my athletes with a concern. "I need to ask you guys an important question," I said, unsure how they would respond to my request. "I need to leave practice early each Wednesday. I have the opportunity to coach my son's soccer team and this is very important to me." I felt that I had said enough to garner their understanding and acceptance, but I decided to disclose a bit more.

I explained further: "Guys, my own dad was a world-class athlete. He ran at Penn State, nearly breaking the four-minute mile and narrowly missing a spot on the 1968 United States Olympic team. He went on to become a successful Masters age group runner and even competed in local triathlons. But," I paused, "I just wish my father had taken the time to coach me in a sport. As a young athlete I rarely got the chance to strengthen our bond through our mutual passion for athletics."

Through pee-wee soccer, Little League baseball and varsity high school soccer, cross country, track, and basketball, he had never once coached me. There had always been the informal tips administered by my father when we ran together: "Stop pronating and swing your arms!" he had barked like a drill sergeant. "Get your head up and drive up the hill." Sometimes, he would comment on one of my soccer games, a sport he never played. The fact that he lacked any participatory background or proper coaching in the sport did not escape my brother or sister, and was something we all found rather humorous. My father's success on the track had convinced him that he understood the intricacies of soccer—and there was no convincing him otherwise.

He often gave me tips after games he attended: "Be more aggressive off the ball! . . . Use your left and right foot! . . . Shoot when you're in front of the goal!" But what I yearned for was his voice in the huddle. I wanted to look into his eyes as he explained the proper technique for a pick-and-roll or how to hit a fly ball or catch a hard grounder. But it never happened. As was often the case when I was growing up, my father, an avid hunter, spent a good portion of the fall in northern Michigan. Hunting fulfilled my father's need to be outdoors and enjoy the beauty of the countryside that undoubtedly brought him back to his own childhood; in the process, he missed out a great deal on ours. Hunting, coupled with a full slate of after-work endeavors, which on any given day might include running, swimming, and biking, left him little time with his kids. At best I was left with a sense of longing for what could have been with our relationship; I also vowed that, if given the opportunity, I would never miss out on the experience of coaching my own children and the indelible bond that would create between us.

Sports are a tool to learn life's great lessons.

When I reflect upon this interaction with my team and my request to leave early on Wednesdays to coach my son, I think I surprised them with the personal nature of my story. But I trusted them, and they trusted me. They all knew my level of commitment to the soccer program; I wanted them to know as well my level of commitment as a father. I realized that helping my players understand my involvement with my own children would teach them something positive about fatherhood. I never loved my players more than when one of my captains said out loud, "Coach, you need to be there; we'll be fine."

And so it began, my new job as assistant coach of my son's first-grade team, the Penguins. Each Wednesday, I raced from varsity practice to first-grade practice. My coaching lexicon quickly shifted from "track the runner through and close space in the defensive third" to "give yourselves room; you can't all chase the ball like bumblebees!" I traded my expensive black Under Armour warm-up gear from my high school for a lime green recreation-department-issued coach shirt. My son grinned when he saw our shirts matched as we walked hand in hand to his first game. I beamed with pride as we rounded the cracked concrete of the school, brightly decorated with colored chalk from siblings at earlier games. I reminisced back to my formative years and thought of all my magical memories of my own childhood park: The uneven slopes of the schoolyard and hot asphalt of the basketball court had provided endless hours of freedom, and glorious camaraderie with friends. I thought of my first coach, Mr. Carlson, and the passion he instilled in me for the game of soccer at that park; how perfect the imperfect field with the uneven goal crossbars and faded yellow sidelines seemed to me thirty years later.

The memories flooded my mind as we approached the field. After a short warm-up where soccer balls seemed to fly in every direction except towards their intended target, the referee called all players to the center of the field for game instructions. The Penguins and the Coyotes fidgeted as the referee offered final instructions. Following a quick discussion on proper throw-in technique (all but ignored by every player during the game) he released the teams to their respective coaches and they took the field. My son's charge as a defensive player was to keep the opposing team from scoring; he would, however, have other objectives once the whistle sounded.

Once the game began, it appeared from the sidelines that Kale had never before seen such a blue sky or such an explosion of yellow dandelions. They must have been calling out for his immediate and undivided attention. The ball, and the swarm of players chasing the ball, did not offer the slightest distraction for him as he surveyed his surroundings. "Kale, watch the ball," I implored. But it did not matter; he was content to be on the field, literally watching the grass grow. I watched with amusement as he picked up a handful of grass and tossed it into the air. When he finally touched the ball for the first time—a chance carom off his right shin guard when the hive of players got too close—his interest in the game seemed to come alive. From that point on, he became part of the pack of Penguins and Coyotes giving chase to the black-and-white checkered ball. While running down the sideline close to our bench, he stopped and looked at me. With his glasses precariously perched on his nose and his long, curly hair blowing in the wind, he uttered words that I will never forget: "Dad, can I hug you?" he said. The hive of other players pushed down toward the opposing goal as my son walked over and gave me a hug and a kiss and awkwardly ran off to rejoin his teammates. I could still feel his touch as I watched him pursue the ball. I owe a debt of gratitude to sport for this special moment with my son; my dreams of fatherhood were fulfilled on the soccer field that day.

Sports are a tool to learn life's great lessons.

It Takes a Village to Raise a Good Sport

The video that I played for my sports sociology class discussed some insurance agencies that now offered life insurance for referees. I shook my head at the mounting evidence that our sports landscape had sunk to this all-time low. Each student in my class seemed to validate my worst fears as they shared stories of parents or players "losing it" with a referee, an opposing player, or even a coach during various sporting events. No sport seemed immune from these examples of poor sportsmanship—from basketball to football to cheerleading, there always seemed to be a negative story to be told. Sport experts from the National Alliance of Youth Sports to local recreation and education programs have taken extensive steps to make sport as meaningful as possible for the athletes who participate, and the families and friends who cheer them on. However, in too many instances, the healthy physical and social development of young people has been compromised by misguided parents and coaches. In many instances, parents and coaches can develop a win-at-all-costs mentality that harms the development of the athlete.

I recall an incident that occurred at my son's second soccer game where the opposing coach lost perspective about his son's involvement in organized sport. After a goal by my son's team, wild gesticulations by this coach suggested his profound displeasure with the call. "Ref, that was not a goal! What are you thinking!" he shouted. Most of the first-graders nervously looked at one another; some seemed visibly scared. "Ref, come over and explain the call!" the man screamed. The referee, who could not have been more than fourteen, slowly walked over to the opposing coach. His shoulders were slumped over and his head was down; it was evident that he expected the worst. I watched with a mixture of sadness and anger as the opposing coach dissected the play with the young referee and expressed his displeasure with the call. After what seemed like an eternity, the referee walked back to the middle of the field for the kickoff; he quickly wiped a tear from his eye.

Play resumed, but the opposing coach was not going to let go of this difference of opinion with the referee. He continued to stalk the sideline barking out comments directed at the referee. A moment later, the whistle sounded. Again, the young referee made the walk over to the opposing coach; this time, his body language was full of conviction for what he knew he must do. A short conversation ensued and the coach threw his hands up in disgust; the referee had bravely returned the game to the kids. The coach collected his coaching bag, made one last inaudible comment to the referee, and walked away from the field for the duration of the game. I can remember feeling embarrassment for the opposing coach's son and his team—it must have been difficult for them to watch this spectacle. Sadly, what the coach failed to recognize were the consequences his behavior held for his young team. By treating the first-grade game and its outcome as if it were the World Cup (soccer's most competitive global tournament), he robbed his players of the reason kids participate in sport: fun. His actions modeled poor sportsmanship to his players and normalized his intimidating behavior toward the referee as part of the game and this was a first-grade competition! A coach has such powerful opportunites to create meaningful experiences for his or her athletes. In this instance, the coach did teach his young charges a powerful lesson about life and sport, but it was not through his positive example.

Sports are a tool to learn life's great lessons.

I tried to keep the image of the coach in my head during my high school games as a reminder of the importance of my own conduct. No one (except maybe that opposing youth coach) would mistake the intensity level of a youth game for that of a high school varsity game. But while the competitive nature of the two might differ, each level creates many opportunities for lessons of fair play and appropriate conduct by athletes. This past fall season, my team had a great deal to celebrate after securing their third trip in the last six years to the Division I State Final Four. Along the way, we defeated the number one team in the state and finished with a high state ranking and our first national ranking. But I would not consider this season a success if I did not see my players make strides academically. I would not consider the season a success if my players did not practice the highest levels of sportsmanship at all times. I would not consider the season a success if my players did not use their platform as athletes to create positive social change in their school and community.

Finally, I believe that sport participation must also be a partnership between coaches and parents to best support our athletes. Both parties must recognize the importance of their mutual efforts to ensure a quality experience on and off the field, one that honors and respects the game. While parents and coaches will always differ on playing time and strategy, the healthy support and development of the athlete must be the overarching concern. A coach's decisions will not always sit well with players and parents, but hopefully most coaches will make these decisions with the good of the team in mind. Players and parents must also always have the opportunity to speak honestly and openly with their coach. And coaches and parents must understand the influence they have over their athletes and the type of sportsmanship they exhibit. Together, this partnership can make a tremendous difference in each child's experience.

Dreams for My Sons

On the final competition of my son's soccer season, my father made it to the game. A stunning myriad of fall colors surrounded the field; it was fall, and my dad was with his son and grandson. As all three of us stood on the sidelines, sport bound three generations of a family together. The moment was one of sheer brilliance—my son was thrilled to have his grandfather there, matched only by my own excitement for having my father there, too. The outcome of the game hardly mattered; the fact that we were together made it a defining memory for all of us.

I hope my sons will always participate in sport and that their involvement will provide them with their own special memories. I hope their involvement will bring them euphoric triumphs that teach them the value of hard work and the deep sense of satisfaction that comes with achieving one's goals. I hope they will learn from the sting of losing, and that individual and team setbacks will teach them the importance of perseverance and equip them with the tools to handle the inevitable rejection that life has to offer. I hope they will carry themselves with honor and integrity during practice and competition, and treat their participation as a gift that not all children and young adults have available to them. I hope they will forge strong, lifelong friendships through sport that will enrich their lives. I hope they will be able to share sport with their future children and strengthen their bonds through meaningful participation. I hope they will see the leadership role they can play at their school because of their involvement with sport. And I hope, perhaps that one day they, too, will choose to coach and create the "ripple effect" with their positive involvement in the lives of others.

Sports are a tool to learn life's great lessons.

References

Coakley, J. (2001). *Sport in society: Issues and controversies.* New York: McGraw-Hill.

Katz, J. (2006). *The macho paradox: Why some men hurt women and how all men can help.* Naperville, IL: Sourcebooks, Inc.

Lapchick, R. (2005). *100 heroes: People in sports who make this a better world.* Orlando, FL: NCAS Publishing.

Marx, J. (2003). *Season of life: A football star, a boy and a journey to manhood.* New York: Simon & Schuster.

Prettyman, S. S. (Eds). (2006). If you beat him, you own him, he's your bitch: Coaches, language, and power. In Prettyman, S. S. & Lampman, B. (Eds.). *Learning culture through sports: Exploring the role of sports in society.* Lanham, MD: Rowman & Littlefield.

3

Achieving Equal Opportunity in Youth Sports

Roles for the "Power of the Permit" and the "Child Impact Statement"

Douglas E. Abrams

EXPERIENCE IN SPORTS, WROTE James A. Michener, "enlarge[s] the human adventure" (1976, p. 451). For most Americans, this experience begins at a tender age. An estimated 30 to 35 million boys and girls—about half the nation's children—play each year in at least one organized youth sports program conducted by a private association or club, or by a public parks and recreation department (Bigelow, Moroney & Hall, 2001; Demorest, Bernhardt, Best & Landry, 2005; Federal Interagency Forum, 2009). Some of these children play on "select," or "travel," teams, which enroll children who are judged to be the most talented in a particular age group, usually to compete against teams from other communities. Other children play in "house leagues," which enroll youngsters without tryouts, usually for local intramural competition. At one level or the other, nearly all children have some experience with organized sports before they turn 18 years old (Stryer, Tofler & Lapchick, 1998, p. 697), and no other activity outside the home and schools holds greater potential for influencing the next generation.

Many communities, however, squander much of this potential by perpetuating youth sports systems that begin weeding out children as young as 7 years old and lead most children to quit playing altogether by their early teen years. A "youth sports system" refers to the totality of private and public sports programs available to boys and girls in a community and its environs. In too many communities, the youth sports system overemphasizes select teams that cut elementary school students before they can explore their sport or develop their talents; the system then lavishes practice and game time on select teams while pleading a shortage of available facilities to justify constricted house leagues or avoidable waiting lists that shut out many children altogether. To determine whether a youth sports system truly serves all young athletes, we need to ask only one question: "What opportunities does the community provide its least talented players?" Decision makers in many towns and cities could not answer honestly with a straight face.

Systemic reform is long overdue. In poll after poll, Americans express firm belief that playing sports enhances children's physical fitness while teaching citizenship, commitment, teamwork, and other lifelong character lessons (Abrams, 2002, p. 258; Tharp, 1996). At the same time, Americans tolerate inequitable community sports systems guaranteed to produce bumper crops of young athletic dropouts year after year (Engh, 1999, pp. 128–129; Wolff, 2003, p. 21). Sports can do nothing for a child who has quit playing. We might prefer that more boys and girls achieve self-esteem through academic excellence or community service, but the reality is that our sports-steeped culture induces children of all ages and abilities to seek much of their self-esteem on the playing field. For better or worse, lessons learned in sports complement lessons learned at home or in the classroom.

Former Boston Celtic Bob Bigelow pinpoints the true mission of youth sports in our nation, whose public policy strives to "leave no child behind" (No Child Left Behind Act of 2001). Now a leading national advocate for reform of organized youth sports, Bigelow says: "Youth sports systems that are created for the greatest good of the greatest number of children will be the right choices for all children—from the child who appears to have the greatest athletic potential at a young age, to the child who may not show that potential until later, to the child who never shows any athletic talent" (Bigelow, Moroney & Hall, 2001, p. 37). This chapter advances a blueprint for creating a community youth sports system that strives to ensure a meaningful place for all children who wish to play.

Equal Opportunity in Youth Sports

Systemic reform begins with acknowledgment that both select teams and house leagues enrich the community. I played ice hockey at both levels when I was growing up in the late 1960s, and each of my teams made me a better person and athlete. As a coach of select and house league hockey teams ever since, I have seen play at both levels promote positive youth development.

I would not want either level to eclipse the other because equal opportunity in youth sports means enabling each player, to the extent possible, to compete against players of similar ability. Players with five years' experience, for example, would be better off not competing against beginners, and beginners would be better off not competing against seasoned veterans. Experienced players may become bored, beginners may become intimidated or embarrassed before quitting, and wide disparities of talent invite injury, particularly in contact or collision sports.

But equal opportunity also means viewing the community youth sports system as a pyramid. The strongest part of a pyramid is at the middle and base, not the top. Select teams assume an important role because the relatively few players at the top, particularly older pre-teens and teenagers, deserve the chance to compete at their own general ability level once they have shown commitment and mastered the basics. For most of these players, select teams and high school varsity teams provide the last chances to pursue excellence in organized sports because the collegiate and professional ranks will be out of reach.

Most young athletes, however, are not select-level players. In communities with an abundance of players, the select ranks cannot realistically include more than about 20 percent of the boys and girls who compete in a particular sport. A community fails its children unless the youth sports system offers meaningful participation to the remaining 80 percent of interested youngsters lower on the pyramid, including the least experienced youngsters at or near the base (Abrams, 2002, p. 283).

A community's failure hits many children particularly hard. Until the rapid growth of suburbia following World War II, "youth sports" usually meant pickup games arranged by children themselves on the nation's sandlots and playgrounds, without participation by parents or other adults (Berryman, 1988, 1996; Coakley, 2006; Reiss, 1989; Wiggins, 1996). The "adultification" of youth sports gathered momentum by the 1960s, and today nearly all sports for children are conducted by adults, who create, incorporate, administer, outfit, coach, and officiate programs and leagues (Eitzen & Sage, 2003). Many children today graduate from high school without ever having played a pickup game. The virtual adult monopoly means that most boys and girls seeking athletic competition have little choice but to depend on whatever the community youth sports system offers.

The "Power of the Permit" and the "Child Impact Statement"

Each private sports program is only one spoke in the wheel, and no one program can easily reform the community's youth sports system, even if the program's board members happen to be amenable to change. Systemic reform depends on two public officials—the school superintendent and the parks and recreation director, whose agencies together manage nearly all local youth sports venues. Most private youth sports programs do not own their own fields, gymnasiums, or other facilities; the school district or the parks department grants these programs permits to use public facilities. These permits often come at favorable rates or even free, on the rationale that the private program performs a public service by conducting a wholesome youth activity.

Many school districts and parks departments act as little more than real estate agents (Seefeldt, 1996), assigning scarce field and gymnasium time to private programs that under-serve children at the middle and base of the youth sports pyramid (Bigelow, Svare, Irving, Fisher & Abrams, 2006, pp. 21–24). The real estate agent approach may seem like the path of least resistance because school districts are not charged with conducting sports programs unrelated to interscholastic athletics, and understaffed parks departments may not feel equipped to conduct sports programs. But when these authorities shut their eyes to what happens after they grant permits for public facilities, the meaningful access of most children to sports depends on the goodwill of private programs that remain essentially unaccountable to public scrutiny (Coakley, 2001). Most private sports programs are conducted by parents and coaches who know they will participate for only a few years while their own children play, and these "short termers" may or may not value a youth sports system that serves all children.

To help ensure equitable community youth sports systems, school districts and parks and recreation departments need to craft equity when they exercise the "power of the permit" (Bigelow, Svare, Irving, Fisher & Abrams, 2006, p. 23). This is the power, firmly established in the law, to determine whether and under what regulations a private individual or entity may use a public facility. Government agencies have long held discretionary authority to grant or deny permits regulating private use of public property that charters, statutes, or ordinances commit to agency management (McQuillin, 1999; Russo, 2004).

Working together in the exercise of their power of the permit, the school district and parks department should require a "child impact statement" annually from each private sports program that applies to use a field, gymnasium, or other public facility. The statement is akin to an environmental impact statement, the disclosure document required before federal agencies decide whether to grant permits for actions by private entities that would significantly affect the quality of the environment.

The child impact statement would significantly affect the quality of a child's environment by disclosing the number of boys and girls the applicant program enrolled last season, and the percentages of time in public facilities the program allotted to select teams and house leagues. Most important, the statement would disclose the program's commitment for allocating public facilities among select teams and house leagues this season. Fulfilling the commitment would be a condition for renewing the permit next season.

With child impact statements in hand, school and parks officials together can draft a community-wide master plan, based on facility availability and the number of children likely to enroll in all local sports programs that have applied to use public property. Without micro-managing the day-to-day operations of private sports programs, the officials can maintain public access by allocating available facilities in a way that provides meaningful opportunities for each boy and girl who wishes to play.

House leagues require particular vigilance because they can be the first to suffer in unregulated community youth sports systems. To encourage broad participation by children seeking to play, the master plan must ensure house leagues sufficient use of public facilities during convenient hours. In many communities these days, priority may work the other way, with first choice going to select teams, or to programs that favor select teams and constrict their house leagues (Meyer, 2005). Open-enrollment house leagues are left to settle for whatever facilities and inconvenient time slots remain, which may amount to very little in communities where real estate development has turned playing fields into residential or commercial tracts. House leaguers deserve sufficient time for practice sessions because schedules top-heavy with games deny youngsters fair opportunity to develop their skills and perhaps move on to select teams. Youth sports specialists understand that without patient instruction during practice sessions, players simply fine-tune their mistakes in games because athletes have trouble processing instruction in the heat of competition. USA Hockey, for example, recommends that from the youngest age levels until age 18, house league and select teams alike schedule at least two practices for each game (USA Hockey, 2009).

The community's master plan should tolerate house league waiting lists only as last resorts, and should insist that private programs maintain unavoidable waiting lists on a first-come, first-served basis. No waiting list should be tolerated where careful scheduling, such as modest reductions in practice and game time for select teams, would create room for new house teams rather than leave some children with nothing.

At the same time, allocating select teams a modestly greater amount of facility use than house leagues may actually enable a community's youth sports system to enhance access for families at all income levels. House leagues may offer attractive alternatives to the four- and five-figure costs, extensive travel, and heavy practice and game schedules characteristic of many select teams. Even some families that can afford higher costs balk at these accommodations that select team membership may impose on family life (de Lench, 2006, pp. 98–115; Smith, 2004). House leagues may continue enrolling these families that might otherwise drop out, but lower costs and less burdensome schedules may also mean modestly less facility use throughout the season, particularly where the school district or parks department charges private programs a user fee. The key here is "modestly" because house leagues provide little or no opportunity for children who get only minimal game schedules and practice time, for wait-listed children, or for children shut out altogether by the voracious appetites of select teams.

Eyebrows were raised in a Minneapolis suburb a few years ago, for example, when about two hundred 9- and 10-year-olds signed up for the local youth basketball program, through a private organization that held permits to use all the available gymnasiums operated by the public schools and the parks department (P. Bearmon, interview, June 8, 2006). About 30 of these youngsters made select teams, and the remaining 170 or so were placed in the house leagues. During the season, each select team received about 130 hours of court time (two or three practices each week, plus three or four games every weekend), but each house league team received only about twelve hours of court time.

Dr. Paul Bearmon felt that the suburb's youth sports system was out of kilter when less than 20 percent of its 9- and 10-year-old basketball players would get more than 1,000 percent more court time than the remaining 80 percent of players. And when school and parks department officials said they were powerless to correct the imbalance because the youth basketball program was a private organization, Bearmon and like-minded parents founded "Keep'em All Playing," a citizens' alliance that seeks greater accountability from the schools and parks department. The alliance advances the core principle that public authorities should indeed correct imbalances in public use amounting to more than 1,000 percent (P. Bearmon, interview, June 8, 2006). The principle is well-grounded in law because, as discussed earlier, authority to regulate private use of public facilities rests with the appropriate public agency and not with the private users.

Reform and Resistance

Calls for equitable allocation of public youth sports facilities may spark fireworks because people with privilege do not normally yield their favored positions without a fight. Select teams have enjoyed favored positions in many communities ever since these teams began proliferating in the past generation or so, and bruising turf battles can become particularly nasty when parents stoked by emotionalism argue as surrogates for their children (Bigelow, Moroney & Hall, 2001, pp. 217–247). Defenders of the status quo may tar advocates of equity as troublemakers, malcontents, whiners, or the like. Name-calling can make for good press, but can also upset parents who find themselves in the public spotlight for the first time. Parents may also choose silence if they sense that by publicly advocating equity, they invite retribution that would jeopardize their own children's future prospects for select team membership.

When communities debate equitable use, the arguments of select team parents normally reduce themselves to four. First, the parents may say that reserving the lion's share of public facilities for select teams is equitable because fair preseason tryouts separated select players from house leaguers. Second, these parents typically say that assigning select teams substantially greater access than house leagues to public facilities is equitable because select teams play at a higher level, and thus need more practice and game slots to keep pace with the stronger competition. Third, these parents argue that their sons and daughters have earned extra time in public facilities by working extra hard to achieve top athletic skills; the community, the argument goes, should "reward" and not "penalize" their children's success. Finally, these parents remind authorities that they are willing to pay for extra use of public facilities necessary to accommodate their children's select teams (Bigelow, interview, June 24, 2007). I examine these four arguments below, highlighting the problems with each.

Tryouts. A few years ago, in the Minneapolis suburb discussed previously, the youth basketball program's Board of Directors defended its skewed allocation of court time as equitable because select and house teams for the elementary school students were created following tryouts that the board said were conducted fairly by impartial evaluators.

As a threshold matter, athletic tryouts for elementary school students are inherently unfair because evaluators seek to measure the physical skills of pre-pubescent children. These measures are little more than predictions, and frequently inaccurate ones at that (Cary, Dotinga & Comarow, 2004; Ginsburg, Durant & Baltzell, 2006, pp. 49, 58; Magill & Anderson, 1996). Time has a way of humbling 9-year-old superstars when other youngsters catch up, as many do by their early teen years unless adults have already stigmatized them with premature evaluations that no coach is capable of making, and that no coach should be entitled to make. Evaluating other people's children is serious business.

Personally, I have seen very few youth sports tryouts truly conducted fairly from top to bottom at any age level. The first few roster selections may seem relatively apparent because some youngsters appear to stand out. The last few slots, however, leave coaches plenty of room to favor some players, such as their own children's friends, or players whose parents volunteer as assistant coaches, can pay the stiffer select team fees, or hold personal or professional standing in the community.

But even if tryouts could somehow evaluate each child, coaches and league administrators confuse individual fairness with systemic fairness when they invoke tryouts to justify grossly inequitable assignment of fields and other public facilities. The suburban Minneapolis youth basketball program, which assigned about 80 percent of elementary school players a minuscule fraction of practice and game time, remained inequitable regardless of how tryouts were conducted; the system helped ensure that most children would never have reasonable opportunity to develop their skills, and that many other children would feel so frustrated and embarrassed by an adult-imposed caste system that they would join the ranks of the 70 percent or so of athletes who quit playing by their early teen years (Wolff, 2003, p. 21). When elementary school students seek to play sports with their friends, the role of adults is to hold the doors wide open, without retreating behind the cloak of gerrymandered tryouts.

Keeping pace. A private select team's perception of its own level of play is no warrant for denying equity to house leaguers. Equitable access to public youth sports facilities provides parents not a gratuitous handout, but a return on their taxes, which build and maintain the facilities. A community can provide access only to the athletic facilities it has, which may be less access than some parents would like. If a select team parent wants an unreasonable "slice of the public pie" at the expense of other taxpayers' children, the parent always has the option of joining with like-minded adults to build and maintain their own private athletic facilities, as some private youth sports programs have done.

Reward and penalty. Nearly forty years as a youth hockey coach convince me that no correlation necessarily exists between a young player's skill level and work ethic. House leaguers can work and compete every bit as hard as their select team counterparts. I have watched many devoted players work their hardest, make necessary personal sacrifices, and yet not reach the select level for lack of natural skills. I have also watched many innately gifted players approach the top without a solid work ethic, and indeed sometimes with laziness that would embarrass a truly serious athlete.

Nowadays money may further erode any correlation between a youngster's skill and work ethic. Some families may find themselves unable to afford a few thousand dollars yearly for the pro-style uniforms, private tutoring, interstate gas mileage, weekly hotel bills, and other expenses that increasingly accompany select team participation. As the "youth sports arms race" continues to produce longer seasons and greater costs, membership on a select team may depend as much on the family's ability to pay as on the youngster's prowess on the field.

Willingness to pay. No self-respecting public school educator would provide extra history or chemistry instruction only to students in the top 20 percent of the class, or only to students whose parents could afford the stiffest fees. No parks department would allow a patron, regardless of wealth or sense of self-importance, to rent a park's entire picnic grounds during the most convenient hours all season and leave other members of the public with little or nothing. Sports instruction is essential to childhood education, and leisure time at any age is essential to public health and well-being (Eccles & Gootman, 2002; U.S. Department of Health and Human Services, 1992, 1996, 2000). School districts and parks departments should allocate public youth athletic facilities as they allocate their classrooms and picnic grounds—by acting as trustees of scarce yet productive public resources, and not as auctioneers dispensing these resources to the highest bidders.

Conclusion

Parents bear primary responsibility for raising their children, and neither the community nor its public officials can duplicate parental influence. The community youth sports system plays an integral role in children's lives, however, not only because the virtual adult monopoly over organized sports leaves most children without other athletic opportunities, but also because no family alone can provide teams, leagues, or competitions for their children.

Wholesome athletic participation enriches all boys and girls who wish to play, and not just the ones selected by adults as the "best." Heywood Hale Broun often said that "sports do not build character. They reveal it" (Michener, 1976, p. 16). To people working with children, Broun's axiom meant that youth sports programs were not expected to take bad kids and somehow make them good. Nor were these programs necessarily expected to keep good kids from going bad. The conventional wisdom was that most youngsters who played organized sports were already on the right track; athletic competition merely revealed their predisposition to solid citizenship.

Today, however, the impact of youth sports on solid citizenship is more direct. Too many communities remain uneasy about high rates of teen alcohol and illicit drug use, yet tolerate youth sports systems destined to exclude most children by their early teen years, when participation in sports programs conducted by adults with positive values can help counter these unsavory temptations (Eccles & Gootman, 2002; Micheli, 1990; Thompson, 2003). Private sports programs in these communities may offer teens only select teams, sending everyone but the most talented home empty-handed. Varsity and junior varsity teams may enroll only the top 20 percent or so of high school athletes, while cutting everyone else or allowing them to hang around in practice sessions without a realistic chance of ever seeing game action. "Double dipping" may permit the same athletes to play both select and high school competition in the same season.

In communities that systematically exclude most interested teens from sports, no one should be surprised when many excluded youths travel the wrong path. Teens sense a need to belong, and many teens unable to belong to a sports team drift toward other peer groups, including ones prone to causing trouble (Eccles & Gootman, 2002). Unable to "turn on" to sports, some teens may turn on to something else, including drugs or alcohol (Ginsburg, Durant & Baltzell, 2006, p. 48; Micheli, 1990, p. 235). The downward trajectory is unfortunate and avoidable, yet predictable. Until communities stop taking children's sports away from children, we will all be the losers.

We can do better. Systemic youth sports reform depends on a community's resolve to straighten out its priorities and take affirmative steps to ensure equal opportunity for children who wish to play. This resolve, in turn, depends on public commitment to redefine the meaning of "winning" in youth sports (Thompson, 2003, pp. 17–60). When school districts and parks departments use the power of the permit and child impact statements to allocate scarce public sports facilities among wholesome private programs in the best interests of all children who wish to play, the youngsters win because the challenges, successes, and disappointments of athletic competition help them grow. Parents win because sport provides their children lifelong memories of victory and defeat shared with family and friends. The community wins because values learned on the field help build solid citizens, many of whom remain in the community to raise families years later. America wins because these values help shape the next generation—long after the scores of distant games have faded from memory.

References

Abrams, D.E. (2002). The challenge facing parents and coaches in youth sports: Assuring children fun and equal opportunity. *Villanova Sports & Entertainment Law Journal,* 8, 253–292.

Berryman, J.W. (1988). The rise of highly organized sports for preadolescent boys. In F.L. Smoll, R.A. Magill, & M.J. Ash (Eds.), *Children in sport* (pp. 3–6). Champaign, IL: Human Kinetics Press.

Berryman, J.W. (1996). The rise of boys sports in the United States, 1900 to 1970. In F.L. Smoll & R.E. Smith (Eds.), *Children and youth in sport: A biopsychosocial perspective* (pp. 4–14). Madison, WI: Brown & Benchmark.

Bigelow, B., Moroney, T. & Hall, L. (2001). *Just let the kids play.* Deerfield Beach, FL: Health Communications.

Bigelow, B., Svare, B., Irving, R., Fisher, S. & Abrams, D. (2006). An open letter to communities: What community leaders can do to improve youth sports. In S.S. Prettyman & B. Lampman (Eds.), *Learning culture through sports: Exploring the role of sports in society* (pp. 15–25). Lanham, MD: Rowman & Littlefield Education.

Cary, P., Dotinga, R. & Comarow, A. (2004, June 7). Fixing kids' sports. *U.S. News & World Report,* 44.

Coakley, J. (2001). *Sport in society: Issues and controversies.* Boston: McGraw-Hill Higher Education.

Coakley, J. (2006). Organized sports for young people: A 20th-century invention. In S.S. Prettyman & B. Lampman (Eds.), *Learning culture through sports: Exploring the role of sports in society* (pp. 3–14). Lanham, MD: Rowman & Littlefield Education.

de Lench, B. (2006). *Home team advantage: The critical role of mothers in youth sports.* New York: HarperCollins.

Demorest, R.A., Bernhardt, D.T., Best, T. & Landry, G.L. (2005). Pediatric residency education: Is sports medicine getting its fair share? *Pediatrics,* 115, 28–33.

Eccles, J. & Gootman, J.A. (Eds.) (2002). *Community programs to promote youth development.* Washington, DC: National Academy Press (National Research Council and Institute of Medicine).

Eitzen, D.S. & Sage, G.H. (2003). *Sociology of North American sport.* New York: McGraw-Hill Higher Education (7th ed.).

Engh, F. (1999). *Why Johnny hates sports: Why organized youth sports are failing our children and what we can do about it.* Garden City Park, NY: Avery.

Federal Interagency Forum on Child and Family Statistics (2009). *America's children in brief: Key national indicators of well-being.* Retrieved April 6, 2010, from http://www.childstats.gov/pdf/ac2009/ac_09.pdf.

Ginsburg, R.D., Durant, S. & Baltzell, A. (2006). *Whose game is it, anyway?* Boston: Houghton Mifflin.

Magill, R.A. & Anderson, D. (1996). Critical periods as optimal readiness for learning sports skills. In F.L. Smoll & R.E. Smith (Eds.), *Children and youth in sports: A biopsychosocial perspective* (pp. 57–72). Madison, WI: Brown & Benchmark.

McPherson, B. (2002). The child in competitive sport: Influence of the social milieu. In R.A. Magill, M. Ash, & F.L. Smoll (Eds.), *Children in sport* (pp. 247–278). Champaign, IL: Human Kinetics Press.

McQuillin, E. (1999). *The law of municipal corporations.* Vol 10. Minneapolis, MN: West Group (3d ed.).

Meyer, P. (2005, July, 24). Cities make the pitch to catch growing youth sports market. *The Dallas Morning News*, 1A.

Micheli, L.J. (1990). *Sportswise: An essential guide for young athletes, parents and coaches.* Boston, MA: Houghton Mifflin.

Michener, J.A. (1976). *Sports in America.* New York: Random House.

No Child Left Behind Act of 2001, Pub. L. No. 107–110, 115 Stat. 1425 (codified in scattered sections of 20 United States Code).

Reiss, S. (1989). *City games: The evolution of American urban society and the rise of sports.* Urbana: University of Illinois Press.

Russo, C.J. (2004). *The law of public education.* New York: Foundation Press.

Schock, B. (1987). *Parents kids and sports.* Chicago, IL: Moody Press.

Seefeldt, V. (1996). The future of youth sports in America. In F.L. Smoll & R.E. Smith (Eds.). *Children and youth in sports: A biopsychosocial perspective* (pp. 423–435). Madison, WI: Brown & Benchmark.

Smith, M.L. (2004, December 5). A timeout on youth sports: As athletics blocks out other priorities, more families are saying "enough." *The Minneapolis Star Tribune*, 16A.

Stryer, B.K., Tofler, I.R. & Lapchick, R.E. (1998). A developmental overview of child and youth sports in society. *Child & Adolescent Psychiatric Clinics of North America*, 7(4), 697–724, vii.

Tharp, M. (1996, January 15). Sports crazy! *U.S. News & World Report*, 30.

Thompson, J. (1995). *Positive coaching: Building character and self-esteem through sports.* Palo Alto, CA: Warde.

Thompson, J. (2003). *The double-goal coach: Positive coaching tools for honoring the game and developing winners in sports and life.* New York: Quill/HarperCollins.

USA Hockey. (2009). *2009–11 Official Rules of Hockey*, xiii. Retrieved April 6, 2010, from http://www.usahockey.com/uploadedFiles/USAHockey/Menu_Officials/Menu_RulesEquipment/USAH%20Rulebook%200911_WEB.pdf.

U.S. Department of Health and Human Services. (1992). *Healthy children 2000: National health promotion and disease prevention objectives related to mothers, infants, children, adolescents and youth.* Washington, DC: U.S. Government Printing Office.

U.S. Department of Health and Human Services. (1996). *Physical activity and health: A report of the Surgeon General.* Atlanta, GA: Centers for Disease Control and Prevention, National Center for Chronic Disease Prevention and Health Promotion.

U.S. Department of Health and Human Services. (2000). *Healthy people 2010: Understanding and improving health. Leading health indicators: Physical activity.* Washington, DC: U.S. Government Printing Office.

Watson, D.G.A. (1988). Evaluating sports skills. In J.C. Hellstedt, D.S. Rooks, & D.G.A. Watson (Eds.), *On the sidelines: Decisions, skills, and training in youth sports* (pp. 21–60). Amherst, MA: HRD Press.

Wiggins, D. (1996). A history of highly competitive sport for American children. In F.L. Smoll & R.E. Smith (Eds.), *Children and youth in sports: A biopsychosocial perspective* (pp. 4–14). Madison, WI: Brown & Benchmark.

Wolff, R. (2003). *The sports parenting edge.* Philadelphia: Running Press.

4

Jocks Rule—Girls Drool

Middle School Definitions of a Jock

Sandra Spickard Prettyman

ONE DAY I NEEDED TO VISIT MY local middle school, and was struck by how similar the scene was to my own time in school. The hallways were filled with laughter and chatter and movement, with the energy of adolescence. I watched one boy saunter down the length of the hallway, slowly and confidently making his way from his locker to a classroom down the hall. His pace was slow and easy, and he swayed back and forth as he walked; it seemed as if he owned the hallway, and several other boys moved out of his way as he passed them. Several students spoke to him as he passed and he nodded, flashing a smile at several girls who stuck their heads out of one classroom to yell something at him. As he approached me, I noticed he moved to the right, closer to a boy who was still at his locker. As he passed, he whacked him with his notebook and said: "Faggot." The boy, who was much smaller and had several books in his hands, did not look up, but replied: "Stupid." The other looked back laughing, and raising his hand in the air he said: "At least I can throw a football." His arm arced through the air as if indeed he was throwing a football, and he entered the classroom, giving his teacher a high-five as he passed. This scene seemed all too familiar, resonating both with my own schooling experiences and with the social categories prevalent in the literature (Eckert, 1989; Foley, 1990; Mac an Ghaill, 1994; Willis, 1977). There was the popular and confident "jock" and the much-maligned "nerd," engaged in a scene that seems all too familiar for many of us. Foley (1990) describes a similar "ritual" of picking on and "terrorizing" effeminate males as a means of creating and enacting a "culturally defined boundary between effeminate and masculine behavior" (p. 32) that signals the power and prestige of the jocks, both as individuals and as a group.

Peer groups exert a tremendous force on and in the lives of students. Eckert (1989) argues that the peer groups and social categories created by youth are a powerful force by which students understand themselves and their relationship to others and to the school. In her early work on student social networks, she details how these networks represented the "competition among adolescents for control over the definition, norms, and values of their life-stage cohort" (p. 5). Eckert argues that these social networks also mirror and help to reproduce the social class structure students come in with, serving as "training for correspond-ing adult roles" (p. 23). In addition, they are built upon and help to reproduce a gender order dominated by hegemonic forms of masculinity—a form of masculinity that typically is constructed around sexism and homophobia, and uses these as tools to dominate and "other" different forms and expressions of masculinity (Connell, 1987). Kimmel (1994) argues that hegemonic masculinity works to "maintain the power that some men have over other men and that men have over women" (p. 125).

This chapter presents findings about how middle school students define and interpret the peer group networks and relationships they live in and with, focusing specifically on how students understand, define, and live out the role of jock in school culture. In addition, it demonstrates how this peer group is constructed around and utilizes hegemonic masculinity to maintain power and control. It must be noted that while I have characterized these groups, using names that come from the students' own words, there are limitations in using such a typology. It often masks the complex forms and meanings inherent in the relationships between groups and the individuals that constitute them. However, as Eckert (1989) and Connell (1987, 1989) have noted, these groups exist in relationship to each other, and delineating a social structure provides a means by which to speak about types of relationships, not types of individuals. Given the scenario depicted above, I was interested in exploring how students define and perceive the category of jock, and the role it played in not only creating and sustaining peer group relationships, but also in creating and maintaining a posi-tion of privilege and power.

Context and Methods

Pristine Middle School (PMS) is situated in a small but growing middle- to upper-middle-class bedroom community in a Great Lake state. This chapter presents findings from a yearlong study conducted at PMS that included daily participant observation in classrooms, hallways, the lunch room, the cafeteria, the library, and other school spaces, as well as at sporting events, concerts, and other extra-curricular activities. All names used here are pseudonyms, and all quotes from participants represent verbatim speech transcribed from digital audio files, except for those excerpts denoted in < >, which represent near verbatim speech captured during a field observation and written in jotted notes. Data analysis utilized both deductive and inductive approaches to develop a coding schema, as well as in the subsequent identification of themes that cut across the data.

In order to discover social categories and networks at PMS, including the groups students identified and the hierarchy that existed among and within them, I employed a two-stage interview process. At the end of a semi-structured interview, I asked students to list all of the groups they thought were present at PMS, circle the groups to which they belonged, and identify the groups with which they associated and spent the most time. Asking students to indicate the groups they associated with and the time spent with each group gave me an idea of the social networks at PMS. For example, one student, Amanda, listed more than fourteen different groups or "kinds of kids" (1-20:1) at PMS, and indicated that she affiliated with ten of them, although most of her time was spent with two, "smart girls" and "band kids" (1-20:1). Another student, Landon, could only name five different groups of kids, and said he affiliated with only one of those groups (1-6:1). These students clearly had different understandings of the existing social network at PMS and its importance in their lives.

I then conducted second-stage interviews where I gave students cards with the most commonly used terms for social groups written on them and asked them to sort the cards in whatever way made sense to them. Next, I asked students to explain why they had sorted the groups in this way. Lastly, I asked students to rank the groups based on popularity, and to lay them out in whatever way made sense to them. From this data, I was able to construct a scatter chart of peer group popularity and relate it to how students categorized the groups. This process, combined with extensive participant observation and additional student interviews, provided a detailed and rich description of the world these middle school students inhabited, and allowed me to place the peer group networks they identified in context.

Gendered Categories—Gendered World

Toward the end of each sorting and ranking interview, I asked students if they thought any of the groups were made up of mostly boys or mostly girls. Their answers to this question demonstrate interesting gender dynamics at work. The data from these interviews reveal that the categories students create, inhabit, and use are often gendered. One student noted that "it's just like life" (Amanda—1-20:2), recognizing that the broader social world they inhabit is gendered, just as their adolescent world is. Seemingly generic categories such as alternatives, computer geeks, and jocks were most often denoted as male groups.

Girls seemed to need separate designations and hence specific gendered group names were used, such as "pretty girls" and "smart girls." "Cheerleader" was another term always designated as a girls-only group. The only terms used for both males and females, according to the responses for this question, were "athletes," "band kids," and "preps."

While band kids seemed to be a generic category, "orchestra kids" was more often than not referred to as a girls-only category, even though many boys were in orchestra. When I asked some students about this, they responded that orchestra was seen as "a girl thing, more feminine, ya know" (Amanda—1-20:2), or "well it's just like more, I don't know gay-like for a guy, even though I know guys do it" (Brent—1-7:2). Referring to orchestra kids as a girls-only group represented a legitimate means by which to express and reconfirm the public and private positions of hegemonic masculinity within a gender order that values heterosexuality and power. In addition, "athletes," like "band kids," referred to both girls and boys, while "jock" was a designation used only for boys. Students responded that this was because "not all athletes are jocks" (Ken—1-3:2). Who gets to be a jock, how they come to be a jock, and what the implications of being a jock are represent questions I take up in the ensuing analysis. The ways in which the category of jock is defined and enacted, and its relationship to hegemonic masculinity, are explored in the following sections.

Examining Jockdom

Negotiating the everyday relationships within a peer group network is a complicated and often contradictory experience that demands students "perform" different forms of masculinity and femininity (Butler, 1990). The adoption and performance of hegemonic masculinity is predicated upon dominance, which is achieved through the demonstration of particular cultural norms. While hegemonic masculinity is constructed differently in different places and spaces, it always relies on socially and culturally sanctioned roles and behaviors (Connell, 1987). At PMS, like in many schools across the U.S., hegemonic masculinity is demonstrated through adherence to cultural norms of heterosexuality, control, physical prowess, competition, and homophobia—that while enacted individually, are constituted through group norms and behaviors. Similar to the jocks in both the Eckert (1989) and Foley (1990) studies, jocks at PMS were able to regulate and enforce the expression of masculinities and femininities within the school at large. Robinson (2005) notes that hegemonic masculinity "is generally rewarded with power and popularity for young men in schools and the broader community" (p. 22), and jocks at PMS used this power and popularity to maintain their social and cultural dominance. Below, I detail how jocks are described, defined, and embodied by students at PMS.

Becoming a Jock: Social Class and Status

When I asked students how one gets to be a jock, the answer was clear: play a sport. However, while the answer was clear, it was not simple. Not all athletes were jocks, and not all jocks were athletes. So how did one become a jock?

Brian: Jocks are guys who play sports.

SSP: So all guys who play sports are jocks?

Brian: OK, well no, but lots are.

SSP: So how does an athlete become a jock?

Brian: Like I guess, I don't know, like maybe it's the kind of sport you play, like harder sports like football or hockey, or basketball, maybe it's easier, or like most of those players are jocks. But not all even, it's also kind of what you look like, like I hate to say it, but yeah, like what you look like.

SSP: So, is what you look like more important than playing a sport?

Brian: Well no, not to be a jock, but maybe to be popular, but like there are some like guys who aren't really athletes, but they like sports a lot, and they're good-looking, ya know, and so they're jocks too. They like hang out with us and stuff, and so they're jocks too like. (1-4:3)

As Brian's interview above illustrates, becoming a jock was a far more complicated process than just playing a sport. It was about what you play and how you play (hard), whom you associate with (other jocks), and what you look like (traditional "good" looks).

All of the boys I interviewed articulated the complexity of becoming a jock, noting that while jocks were associated with athletics or athletes, it was not that simple. Kent, a tall self-identified jock, noted, "It's like who you grew up hanging out with maybe. Like where you live, who you're used to like hanging out with" (Kent—1-2:2). Brent, another self-identified jock, who played football, basketball, and baseball and called himself "a pretty good-looking guy" (Brent—1-7:1), expressed the same idea, saying: "Jocks, well, like, well they're guys who play sports, or like guys who like sports too. It's more like if you're popular too, like who you hang with" (Brent—1-7:2). In order to become/be a jock, one needed to have already developed a relationship with other students likely to be jocks, by growing up with them, living near them, or hanging out with them (which is not likely if you did not grow up with and live near them). In this respect, social class was represented in jock status.

Brent noted this link between social class and being a jock most explicitly in response to a question about how students were able to become jocks: "Lots of us play club sports, like hockey and stuff, and it all costs like a lot of money, so I would say it's like about money sometimes" (Brent—1-7:1). Students who were not self-identified jocks also noted the relationship between social class and being a jock. Donald, who saw himself as a "cheever" (an academic achiever), noted, "Jocks are sport freaks; they're guys who are into that you know. But like also they're like the guys who think they're cool, think they're better than everybody. Like they have money and stuff and think they're cool" (Donald—1-11:1). To a large extent, being a jock meant coming from a family with money. It was clear that it had to do with more than just athletic participation, and included where a student lived, the way he dressed, and the access he had to friends and activities.

The Jock Dress Code

In general, jocks were well-dressed, sporting designer labels or clothes from high-end clothing stores. They tended to dress in either dark or neutral colors, with a lot of navy and gray being worn; rarely did I see any of them in bright colors, or in anything that would set them apart or focus attention on them. They gravitated to khakis and jeans, T-shirts and striped rugby-type shirts. There was little variation in the way they dressed, as I noted early on in my field notes.

> I'm sitting in history class right now, but as I roam the hallways or sit in classes or hang out in the cafeteria, I'm struck by how similar many of these students dress. There are certainly some kids who dress differently (some "Goth-like" dress for example), but the boys especially seem to dress all the same (*PN: so much for individuality!*). All the boys who I know to be jocks, for example, are all dressed about the same—jeans or maybe khakis, with T-shirts or rugby-type shirts. While it seems pretty casual, their clothes often come from high-end stores (as evidenced by visible labels or writing on them). (*AN: I wonder if there is a relationship between clothing and being a jock? Certainly other kids wear expensive clothes, but is this one way social class gets played out and represented in school?*). (FN27:pp. 3–5)

A boy who was not part of the jock group noted this same tendency in an interview.

> Oh yeah, like those jocks, they're weird; you'd like think they had a dress code thing or something going, like they always dress the same. It's like sooooo boring, all blue and gray and designer stuff and all, a way to show off, but not maybe show off or like stand out. Like I know they think the way I dress is weird, but at least like I have my own style. (Landon—1-6:2)

It seems that just as jocks came from the same neighborhoods, played the same sports, and hung out with the same kids, they also tended to wear the same clothes. These markers expressed and reconfirmed group membership and identification, and policed the boundaries of who was "in" and who was not. They served to create a sense of identity and solidified the social class relations present in the school, and in our society.

When I asked several students who self-identified as jocks about the idea of a jock "dress code" they laughed and said that was ridiculous. But after reflection, several of them recognized that perhaps it might be true.

> Well, like with the dress code thing, I guess it could be kinda true, like we do all wear kind of the same colors and same like kinds of clothes, but not the SAME (very emphatic) clothes, because that would be like not cool. But we do like dress similar. (Kent—1-2:3)

> A dress code, no, like no, we like wear whatever we want. But, well, I guess, like if you want to fit in you don't wear just like anything, but so there is some like structure maybe to what you think about wearing, like I'm not gonna wear Hawaiian shirts or anything. That would like be flashy or like in your face. I don't need to stand out like that; I think like we get noticed for who we are, for our efforts and other stuff, not our clothes, and maybe some other kids need to wear flashy stuff like that to get noticed. (Brent—1-7:3)

Dress seemed to unite these students, and be a visual reminder of who they were in the school. Eckert (1989) argues, "Many jocks' enhanced economic status is indeed reflected in their ability to follow the fashions and in their emphasis on 'designer' clothing . . ." (p. 63). Certainly the fact that many of the jocks at PMS wore expensive clothing depicted a particular form of status, implicating social class in the construction of jock status.

Jock status was related to where you live (the ritzier parts of town), to how you dress (designer clothes), and to what you do (club sports that cost a lot of money and take a lot of time). These contingencies made the group relatively closed to students from families who had less money, and exposed the relative homogeneousness of the group. The ability to become a jock was influenced by the intersection of multiple sites of identity that allowed some boys access, while it denied others. The ability to control others, or in this case to control access to being a jock, allowed jocks to maintain a position of superiority in the peer group network at PMS and helped construct their hegemonic position.

Jocks Rule—Girls Drool: Sexism and Homophobia in the World of Jocks

While it was not simple to define a jock, one thing did seem clear—to be a jock meant being a guy. When Brian stated earlier in the chapter, "Jocks are guys who play sports," his use of the male noun was not random. When boys and girls, jocks and non-jocks, spoke about jocks, they always spoke about them as male. This emerged early on in the research, during the sorting and ranking interview, when I asked students if any of the groups were exclusively made up of girls or boys. Students easily recognized the gendered nature of the group, and how girls did not fit into it.

> . . . jocks are really guys, well except for Josie maybe. Because being a jock is like being like a certain kind of, like a type of person, not just any athlete. (Brian—1-4:2)

> Jocks are yeah guys who are athletes, like into sports, but girls, like they can play sports, but they're not really jocks you know, not like most of 'em, like maybe one or two of 'em, but that's why jocks and athletes aren't like really the same thing. It's more an attitude thing. (Jimmy—1-8:2)

> Yeah, like jocks rule, girls drool (laughs). Like they drool after us jocks, like because we're so hot (laughs again). (Brent—1-7:2)

Girls could be athletes, but they were not jocks. More often than not, they "drool" while the jocks (the boys) "rule."

As noted in several of the interviews, jocks were "good-looking" and "hot," which made the girls "drool" over them. The ability to attract girls was important for hegemonic boys, and good looks, along with jock status, enhanced their ability to control the desire of girls. And their ability to attract and control girls enhanced their status as jocks.

> Well girls, like, like jocks, we're, OK, we're, I don't know, what they want, and so, that's good for us (laughter) and plus it like makes us, I don't know, cooler, to have them like us; it makes us like even more of a jock. (Brent—1-7:2)

The ability to attract and control young women becomes "part of the performance of hegemonic masculinity that can cement gendered cultural bonds between those boys and men who take up this form of masculinity as their own, creating a sense of identity" (Robinson, 2005, p. 20). The relationship between jock status and the ability to attract girls was predicated upon an assumption of heterosexuality, as well as an assumption that girls would want to "drool" over them. Through their good looks and their ability to attract girls, jocks were able to demonstrate their own heterosexuality to the world. In part, this was also reliant upon their ability to keep girls in a position of desiring, which is perhaps why girls were not within the definition of a jock. If jock status is about the demonstration of hegemonic masculinity, then to define girls as such would require a shift in that definition, and a shift in the power and control of the group.

The attitude that girls could not be jocks permeated student responses, except for those of Josie, who many of the boys identified as possibly the only girl who was a jock. She self-identified as a jock, but recognized that most boys thought girls could not be jocks.

Yeah, like I'm a jock; girls can be jocks. Like I think the guys don't think so, but they're full of it, full of themselves, but yeah. I'd take any of 'em on, and beat most of 'em, a jock, heck yeah. (1-21:2)

However, just like the boys, defining who could be a jock was not simple and clear-cut, and while girls could be jocks, not all athletes could be.

It's athletes, pure and simple. You play; you're a jock. OK, you play good; you're a jock. You play bad; you're a fag. (1-21:2)

Here, Josie relied upon homophobia to define who could and could not be a jock. Josie was one of the few students to use the word "fag" in an interview, and when I asked her about it she spoke honestly about jock culture and the homophobia upon which it relied.

Fags, no, aren't like athletes, like they're different; they do different stuff I guess. They couldn't really hack it in sports, or they wanna be part, but they're just like not very good at it. Usually like, they're weaker, more like girls, ya know. And in sports you can't be that way, can't be weak or a fag or like because, especially like if you wanna be accepted, be like, make a team and be a part and stuff. Jocks just don't want no part of that. (1-21:2)

Within the framework articulated by Josie, jocks were constructed as hetero-sexual, strong, and competitive, the opposite of fags who were weak, like girls, and who would not be able to succeed in sports. Foley (1990) argues that jocks have a need to create a "culturally defined boundary between effeminate and masculine behavior" (p. 32), which solidifies their own identity and position. This boundary creates an opposition between hegemonic masculinity and its di-rect opposite, femininity. Thus, the link made here between fags and girls is not surprising. Everything that was considered not masculine enough was relegated to and constructed as feminine. "Jock" was constructed in opposition to all that which was not masculine enough—whether that was girls or fags. The relational aspect of identity is important here; it was important not only what jocks were, but also what they were not (Eckert, 1989; Weis, 1990). The connection between homosexuality, femininity, and weakness is apparent, perhaps contributing to why students did not define girls as jocks.

The homophobia Josie articulated was also present in other interviews, al-though never stated quite as explicitly. Her need to engage in this form of op-pression may represent internalized oppression and a way for her to deflect the homophobia that victimized her, as a girl who participated in jock culture. In order to be successful as a jock, Josie needed to repudiate those who did not dis-play or attain the standards of hegemonic masculinity. Although not the focus of this chapter, the homophobia women in sport face is a powerful force that is explored in other chapters in this text.

Homophobia is a central organizing principle of hegemonic masculinity, and schools are clearly important places where it is learned. Recall the opening story of the two boys I observed in the middle school hallway. A cocky, self-assured "jock" hits a smaller boy, and calls him a "faggot." The other boy cowers with his books at his locker and yet deigns to call the other boy "stupid." Here it matters not at all what the sexual preference of the smaller boy actually is. What matters is that the one boy emasculates the other in order to assert himself as the stronger, the "real man." Indeed, it isn't hard to understand that homophobia is more than likely strong for the other boy as well. For as Kimmel (1994) points out, more than just the fear of gay men, homophobia represents "the fear that other men will unmask us, emasculate us, reveal to us and the world that we do not measure up, that we are not real men" (p. 131).

I Don't Tell Many People This, but I Play the Piano: Hiding the "Feminine" Self

Kent was a very tall, quiet young man with braces and dark, wavy hair. He played several sports, but was one of the basketball stars, and hoped to make the high school basketball team the following year. In our first interview, Kent made it clear that basketball was one reason that he thought kids accepted him.

> Like they think because I play basketball I must be OK. OK, some girls like it too (he smiles broadly), but I play because I like to play, not because it's going to get me anything. (1-2:1)

However, as we began our third interview (1-2:3), Kent smiled, looking down shyly, saying:

Kent: I don't tell many people this, but I play the piano.

SSP: So why don't you share that fact with many people?

Kent: Because guys might, you know, think things about me; it's just not something I want people to know.

SSP: What kind of things do you think they'll assume about you?

Kent: You know, that I'm a sissy or that like I'm gay or something, which I'm not, and not that I have anything against anybody who is or anything. They're just different than me. It's just that I'm not and I don't want people to think things just because they know something about me. But I took piano lessons since I was like 5 or so, so for a long time, and I like it. It makes me happy, and plus my parents want me to do it, so I do. I just, I guess, keep it hidden.

SSP: Are you afraid for people to find out?

Kent: No, not afraid, well maybe afraid, because of what they'd say and stuff, but not too much, not too, because as a basketball player, I think people would know, wouldn't maybe still think I was like gay or anything. And plus, and even though I'm shy, I've like had girlfriends, and that kind of, kind of ya know, shows I'm OK, I'm not, I'm normal, OK.

I thought immediately of my own eighth-grade son who was afraid to let his peers know that he plays violin, for fear of being labeled a sissy, or gay. The imperative to present a heterosexual self to the world, and to expel any inkling of homosexuality, is one of the most important components of the developing masculine identity. Arnot (1982) argues that in a male-dominated society, femininity is ascribed, but masculinity must be attained through a process that involves constant negotiation and confirmation. And those who confer it are other boys and men (Kimmel, 2000; Mac an Ghaill, 1994; Messner, 1990). Kent was afraid to let other boys know he played piano, because of assumptions they, the "guys," might make about him, which might call his heterosexual status, and thus his masculinity, into question. In addition, Kent also made his interest in and association with girls very clear, reinforcing his heterosexual status despite an action that might put it into question.

This fear circumscribed the behavior of many boys at PMS, causing them to engage in particular activities and not in others—often forcing them to deny parts of themselves.

Well, I used to dance, but like I wouldn't tell no one that, but I liked it, but I still dance, just not ballet or nuthin, but hip hop like that's cool and it's OK for guys, but you gotta be careful. Ya know? So now, I like play basketball and all that stuff, cuz that's what people expect, want ya to do, or at least for me like. But dance, yeah, it's not what you like or like wanna do, but what you need ta do. Damn, that makes me sad. I guess I didn't never say that before to no one for a long time, maybe never. Does that make you sad? (Jimmy—i-8:1)

I read a lot. It's like something that makes life good, and I know a lot of kids think it's weird, like girl-like or something, but I don't care. I read all the time and a lot of my guy friends don't get it and think it's queer or stuff, but tough shit, oh sorry. Like I'm reading this 750-page book now and every minute I get, in school, out of school, around school, I read. And if they think it's gay, then they lose. But I don't worry too much. Like I do too many other things like football and sports and stuff that nobody's gonna take me for gay or anything. (Brian—1-4:1)

Cooking, I like to cook, but don't be telling nobody that. . . . Football is what's like important, for you know, like friends, and girls, and, you know, like, everything. So you can tell everybody I play football; that's cool. (Mario—1-9:1)

Jimmy was afraid to dance, Brian worried about the message reading sends to others, and Mario did not want anyone to know he liked to cook. Heteronormativity insists that young boys not engage in behaviors traditionally associated with girls and women, like dancing, reading, and cooking, because when boys engage in them they move outside the boundaries of gender-appropriate behavior. When boys participate in activities typically linked to girls and femininity, their masculinity gets called into question, along with their heterosexual status. In addition, heteronormativity insists that boys participate in those activities, like sports, that confer appropriate gender status. It is interesting to note that all of these boys, self-identified jocks, made it a point to mention that they played sports. This activity was what defined them as men and solidified their heterosexual status. This policing of activities curtailed their lives, and their emotions, in many ways, and boys at PMS clearly had to watch what they did in order to portray a masculine, and thus heterosexual, image to the world.

Kimmel (2000) argues, "Homophobia is more than the fear or hatred of homosexuals; it is also, for men, the fear of being perceived as unmanly, effeminate, or worst of all, gay" (pp. 238–239). He goes on to argue that boys engage in particular kinds of behaviors to ensure that no one gets the "wrong idea" about them, from the way they dress, to the way they act, to the activities they engage in, to the interactions they have with their friends. Boys at PMS referred to this demarcation repeatedly in interviews, and it was the source of Kent's fear about playing the piano—someone, especially the "guys," might misperceive him to be gay because of it. Boys at PMS enjoyed activities often associated with girls and femininity. However, some of them had either learned to give them up or to hide them so that others would not question their masculinity. In so doing, they lost part of themselves, and as Jimmy said, "that makes me sad" (Jimmy—1-8:1). They no longer danced or cooked; instead, they were becoming "real men" and learning to curtail their actions and emotions.

Sports, School, and the Spectre of the Sissy

As discussed above, masculinity at PMS was based on heteronormative standards, and circumscribed by homophobia and heterosexism. Boys who will grow into "real men" are expected to be heterosexual, athletic, competitive, tough, and physically developed and attractive, even in middle school. These characteristics conferred the highest status for boys at PMS and represented the hegemonic norm against which other forms of masculinity were judged and evaluated. For example, jocks at PMS were the male peer group with the highest status in the school, based on the ranking activity described previously. As demonstrated earlier, to become a jock did not necessarily mean to participate in a sport, although that was sometimes one way to gain entrance into the group. It had more to do with appearance and attitude than with athletic prowess. One reason that participation in sports was important was that it developed other characteristics associated with hegemonic masculinity, such as competition, aggression, and toughness.

Kent, who played the piano and played basketball, recognized that one thing he had going for him was his physical prowess on the basketball court. Messner (1992) argues, "Boys learn early that to be gay, to be suspected of being gay, or even to be unable to prove one's heterosexual status is not acceptable" (p. 34). One way to reinforce heterosexual status is through participation in competitive, physical activity—in sport (Messner, 1992). Thus, Kent made it clear that while he played piano, he also played basketball. He was physical, active, and competitive, all hallmarks of masculinity as described by many boys in this study. While he feared others finding out about the fact that he played the piano, and what they might infer from that, he knew that playing basketball would protect him to some extent from those inferences.

When I asked Kent whether he thought boys like Ken suffered from the same fear, since he played football and also violin, he replied:

> No, not really. Ken, he, he plays a school instrument, I don't know, maybe it's more accepted. But I think really that it's just that Ken is, you know, like really good. He brings lots of attention to the school; people love him. He's a guy. Everyone knows it, so he doesn't have to worry. (Kent—1-2:2)

Ken's virtuosity, on the football field, with his violin, or through his academics, highlighted the school's achievements and therefore conferred status upon him. His masculinity was not called into question, and he did not need to fear repercussions. Ken recognized this as well.

> Like I don't worry too much about what other people say. I just do (long pause) things I like. It's not even like I try to be the best, but I think because I'm good, at football or violin or whatever, that people think I'm OK. No one like thinks it's strange that I play violin, or get all A's, or do whatever. They just, I don't know, accept it. No one calls me a fag or thinks I'm weird or anything. Maybe, I don't know, maybe because of football. (Ken—1-3:3)

Within this context, Ken's prowess on the football field proved his masculinity and as a result he did not need to fear his masculinity being called into question. Kent also believed that because Ken engaged in activities that brought accolades to the institution, he was more likely to be accepted and less likely to face questions about his sexuality or his masculinity. This was not as true for boys who also brought accolades to the school that were not sports-related.

Jonathon was a quiet and soft-spoken boy, with dark hair and glasses. He was the only boy, other than Ken, chosen to represent the school as an all-conference scholar. He was one of the top students in the school and all of his teachers reported how much they liked him and enjoyed having him in class. He also played in the band, excelling on his instrument, played soccer for a travel team, and ran track at school. However, on more than one occasion, Jonathon's masculinity was called into question by his peers, who concluded that his behavior was effeminate, and thus homosexual. This was demonstrated in the interview below that took place with Brent, one of the boys who exhibited strong hegemonic masculinity.

> *Brent:* Well, yeah, I think playing sports makes you tougher, makes you, I guess, like, more male, more of a guy, but that's because we just act more like guys.
>
> *SSP:* So what do guys act like who don't play sports?
>
> *Brent:* You know, like they're just more, I don't know, they're not as tough, like physically or anything. Like Jonathon for example. He's a nice guy and stuff, but he acts more like the girls, more like, not a guy. He's smart and all and stuff, but just different. I mean, I know he's a guy, but he just acts different is all. And sports, well, uh, it, uh, makes like men out of you, like you get hard. It's competitive, and we work to like win, like always. (1-7:3)

Brent spoke about how boys who do not play sports are somehow different than their male peers; they are more "like the girls" and thus perceived differently. He believed that because Jonathon did not play sports, did not engage in physical competition, and did not get "tough" and "hard," he was perceived as "not a guy." It is interesting to note here that Jonathon does play sports, playing soccer with a travel team and running on the school track team. This participation obviously did not count in Brent's construction of masculinity, perhaps because he did not associate Jonathon with jocks, an assessment with which Jonathon agreed.

Other students also associated a lack of athletic participation, or a lack of ability in athletics, as an indicator of homosexual status and less-than-masculine behavior. Josie, in a previous quote, talked about how "you play good; you're a jock. You play bad; you're a fag" (1-21:2). Other students expressed similar ideas about boys who did not play sports.

> Well, I think like guys are just like expected to play sports, and be good at 'em, or, well, then like you're not really a guy. Ya know? (Sam—1-5:2)

> I think it's stupid, but sports are stupid, but this school, like it expects us to do sports, and so kids think that you're like, you know, cool, or more of *a man* (lowers his voice here) if you do it, and especially like if you're good at it. (Landon— 1-6:3)

> Like in this school a lot of people play sports, a lot of guys, and a lot of girls too, but like you're not a jock just cuz you play, and you're not like, I don't know, really good, or if you're really good then it's OK, but if you just are OK, or like aren't *really* (emphasized) into it then you're still, I don't know maybe they think you're gay. (Ben—1-14:1)

Athletic prowess was one means by which to prove one's heterosexuality and align with hegemonic norms of masculinity. Thus, homophobic and heterosexist norms of the culture at PMS ensured that all of the students who qualified as jocks, the highest-status peer group there, were hegemonic boys, thereby preserving this privileged status as the sole domain of hegemonic males.

In addition to the homophobia and heterosexism of sports, violence was often a hallmark of participation, another factor that contributed to hegemonic status. Anthropological research has shown that in societies where men are permitted to acknowledge fear, lower levels of violence are seen (Howell & Willis, 1983). However, in societies where the denial of fear is a defining characteristic of masculinity, the likelihood of violence is much higher. Kaufman (1993) argues it is fear that creates and sustains the need for dominant forms of masculinity. However, men must hide and deny their fear, because this would demonstrate their vulnerability. This fear, and the denial of it, leads to the repression of all emotion other than anger, which often erupts into violence. Men are able to express their anger because it does not violate codes of vulnerability and fear. Kimmel (2000) argues that "the spectre of the 'sissy'—encompassing the fears of emasculation, humiliation, and effeminacy that American men carry with them—is responsible for a significant amount of masculine violence" (p. 253). He goes on to argue that masculinity is more often than not associated with the capacity for violence. "From the locker room to the chat room, men of all ages learn violence is a socially sanctioned form of expression" (p. 254). One of the main arenas where violence is socially sanctioned, especially in the school setting, is within the context of sport. Messner (1992) argues that "males often view aggression, within the rule-bound structure of sport, as legitimate and 'natural'" (p. 67). As a result, students like Brent and Kent came to associate playing sports with being violent and competitive, and therefore sufficiently masculine. Other activities or ways of being must be hidden, for fear of being labeled or discovered as not masculine enough, as gay.

For boys at PMS, pain and violence were often part of the landscape of sports, and something that conferred status on those that participated.

> If you're careful you don't, won't, maybe get hurt, but the point isn't to like be careful, and so you do have to like push, and sometimes that might mean you get hurt, but hopefully, no, like not. (Jason—1-1:3)

> Kids do get hurt playing sports. It's like part of the game, but like it's also what people want, ya know, like they like to see that. I think they don't say that, but they like it. And so do athletes, like it's status to be injured, to get hurt; everybody is oohing and aahing, and all like gaga over you. You can take it; you're a man, ya know. (Brian—1-4:3)

> I got hurt last year, playing basketball, and everyone was like "Oh, are you all right?" and stuff and it was like I was cool or something. And it hurt and stuff, but

I guess it hurt less when I figured out it was cool maybe. Sometimes I worry about it, about getting hurt and stuff, but I think you just have to be smart, think about it. (Kent—1-2:3)

These boys articulated the potential for injury and pain involved in playing sports. However, they also talked about the status and privilege such injuries conferred. Being injured while playing sports made them "cool," and also made them into real men.

My field notes portray similar ideas, especially those that include observations of Brent, a high-status athlete. Several weeks into my observations, Brent came to school with his right leg immobilized. When I asked what had happened, he replied that he had just had knee surgery, because <I blew out my knee, but it was cool> (FN19:1). He went on to explain that he played ice hockey, <because it's the coolest sport, [because] there's lots of fights> and that last year he had had other injuries as well. <But this is the best because I get to go around on crutches, and girls get to help me> (FN19:1). When I asked Brent about whether playing hockey was worth getting injured, he was quick to reply. <Heck yeah, like no pain, no gain, ya know. And I really got the guy too> (FN19:1). He explained that someone had taken the puck from him earlier in the game and that he <needed to get him back.> So he went after him later in the game, and even though he was the one who got hurt in the end, <it was all worth it. People see I'm tough. Oh yeah. (shaking his head and laughing)> (FN19:1). As noted above in an interview quote, Brent also articulated the notion that sports make boys into men: "And sports, well, uh, it, uh, makes like men out of you, like you get hard. It's competitive, and we work to like win, like always" (Brent—1-7:3).

Sports make men out of boys because they teach them how to be aggressive, violent, and competitive, and because they teach them how to expect and accept pain. As Brent and others suggest above, the violence they engage in while playing sports is often sanctioned by rules of the games, as well as by their coaches and fans, who reward them for their willingness to engage in it. Messner (1992) argues that this results in violence becoming "normative behavior" in sports, and that "athletes who earn reputations as aggressive 'hitters' are afforded high status in the community and among peers" (p. 66). Athletes like Brent often wear their scars and injuries with pride, "as badges of masculine status" (p. 76), and bask in the glory of their victory, a victory which is over their body as much as over their opponent.

Conclusion

This chapter explores the dynamics of defining, constructing, and enacting the category of jock, both individually and collectively. While it presents data from individual understandings of this culture, it also demonstrates the ways in which these individual understandings lead to a broader social and collective representation and acknowlegment of what it means to be a jock, of who can and cannot be a jock, and of how this inclusion and exclusion occur. In understanding the dynamics of group affiliation, it is clear that as a group, jocks are comprised of heterosexual boys (at least this is the assumption based upon the public identity they portray to the world) who play sports well and who are good-looking, or boys who like sports and are also good-looking. They are boys who have known each other before, and who have been friends for a while, often having played sports together for many years. Perhaps most importantly, they are not girls, and they are not fags. Thus, jock identity is about social class, gender, sexuality, and, while not explored in this chapter, race/ethnicity.

However, while the identity of a jock seems stable and fixed given this definition, it is clearly contested and contradictory territory. Many boys articulated a very different private self than the public persona they put forth to the world. In private they played music, danced, and cooked, while in public they played football, basketball, and hockey, in order to prove themselves sufficiently as masculine and thus qualify for jock and hegemonic status. The importance of proving their masculinity to the world relied upon presenting a heterosexual identity to the world, and demeaning anything that did not adhere to heterosexual and hegemonic norms of masculinity. Jock identity was about the ability to achieve hegemonic norms and how successfully these were performed, and was often measured by the ability to dominate and control others, through inclusion and exclusion practices, as well as by other means. Thus, the construction and enactment of jock relies upon powerful cultural binaries—male/female, heterosexual/non-heterosexual—that operate to regulate heteronormative and gendered power relationships.

In many ways, comprehending how young people understand and inhabit the social categories they create is important for educators today. There is certainly room for more research in this area, but also for a greater understanding on the part of schools and sport programs about the ways in which masculine identity, specifically hegemonic masculinity, operates to limit all students, those who are jocks as well as those who are not. Understanding what it means to be a jock allows us to work with students and athletes to challenge some of the negative ways in which jock identity is constructed and enacted. At the same time, it provides us with opportunities to help students (re)think the identity work that is so important in their lives. Recognizing the gendered, heterosexual, and social class dimensions of jock identity may help us as we engage with students and athletes in the important work of identity construction. It may also help us move toward a space in which anyone can be a jock, in which jocks do not always rule and girls do not always drool, and in which being a jock does not mean having to "hide" parts of yourself from the world.

References

Arnot, M. (1982). Male hegemony, social class and women's education. *Journal of Education, 164* (1), 64–89.

Butler, J. (1990). *Gender trouble: Feminism and the subversion of identity.* New York: Routledge.

Connell, R. (1987). *Gender and power.* Stanford, CA: Stanford University Press.

Connell, R. (1989). Cool guys, swots and wimps: The interplay of masculinity and education. *Oxford Review of Education, 15,* 291–303.

Eckert, P. (1989). *Jocks and burnouts: Social categories and identity in the high school.* New York: Teachers College Press.

Eckert, P. (1993). *Status and subordination.* Paper presented at the Annual Meeting of the American Anthropological Association, November 1993.

Foley, D. (1990). *Learning capitalist culture: Deep in the heart of Tejas.* Philadelphia: University of Pennsylvania Press.

Howell, S. & Willis, R. (1983). *Societies at peace.* New York: Routledge.

Kaufman, M. (1993). *Cracking the armour: Power, pain, and the lives of men.* Toronto: Viking Books.

Kimmel, M. (1994). Masculinity as homophobia: Fear, shame, and silence in the construction of gender identity. In H. Brod & M. Kaufman (Eds.), *Theorizing masculinities.* Thousand Oaks, CA: Sage.

Kimmel, M. (2000). *The gendered society.* New York: Oxford University Press.

Mac an Ghaill, M. (1994). *The making of men: Masculinities, sexualities and schooling.* Buckingham, England: Open University Press.

Messner, M. (1990). Boyhood, organizational sports, and the construction of masculinities. *Journal of Contemporary Ethnography, 18* (4), 4–16.

Messner, M. (1992). *Power at play: Sports and the problem of masculinity.* Boston: Beacon Press.

Robinson, K. H. (2005). Reinforcing hegemonic masculinities through sexual harassment: Issues of identity, power, and popularity in secondary schools. *Gender and Education, 17,* 19–37.

Weis, L. (1990). *Working class without work.* New York: Routledge.

Willis, P. (1977). *Learning to labour.* Hampshire, England: Bower Press.

5

The Frontrunner Failed to Land a Knockout Punch

Sports Metaphors, Masculinities, and Presidential Politics

Jackson Katz

A COUPLE OF YEARS AGO, I TURNED on my car radio in the middle of a newscast and heard the end of a report in which the correspondent was quoting a politician about the painful process of pushing through a major bill that had recently been passed into law. All I caught was the end of a sentence: ". . . it felt like giving birth." I didn't know the identity of the politician, but I was intrigued by the unusual birth reference. I remember musing about what kind of political leader would use that sort of language. It didn't make any sense. Politicians didn't talk like that. A few seconds later I felt chagrined when I realized my potential mistake. Was the sexism in my psyche so deeply ingrained that I had overlooked the possibility that the reporter was quoting a *female* politician for whom such a metaphor might come naturally?

If the same politician—of either sex—had said something like "We stumbled across the finish line," I am sure I wouldn't have raised an eyebrow. Sports metaphor is such an integral part of U.S. political discourse that even commenting on its ubiquity runs the risk of exposing oneself to the charge of stating the obvious. But in spite of the fact that everyone from political scientists to op-ed columnists has written about our culture's obsession with seeing the political world through the lens of sports experience and language, relatively few academics or journalists have analyzed the particularly gendered aspects of sports metaphor. There is widespread agreement that men are more likely than women to appreciate statements like "So far, we've been waging this campaign between the forty-yard lines; we've got to begin to move downfield." In fact, much of the journalistic treatment of the topic of sports metaphors and politics highlights gender differences, with commentators frequently poking fun at men's sports obsessions and the way they creep into other areas of life. The

Republican pollster Frank Luntz says that men's use of sports analogies "drives women insane" (Luntz, 2007).

But it is a mistake to dismiss this subject as light fare or merely fodder for pop psychological speculation. Particularly in an era when for the first time in U.S. history a woman (Hillary Clinton) emerged as a major candidate for the presidency, much more attention needs to be paid to the process by which cultural constructs of masculinity—including those shaped by the dominant male sports culture—impact voters' perceptions of the people, parties, and interests that seek to attain and exercise power at the highest levels of American government.

This essay is about the relationship between sports metaphors and the construction of presidential masculinity in U.S. politics and media at the beginning of the twenty-first century. What effect does it have on our political system when mainstream commentary about politics is infused with the kind of language one hears every day on ESPN, in sports bars, and in locker rooms? To what extent is bitter partisanship in the two-party system merely a political manifestation of the sort of quasi-tribalism that is routinely on display in sports rivalries? What are the particularly gendered features of sports/political discourse, and how do those influence which qualities in potential leaders are regarded as important? For example, presidential debates are routinely covered by the mainstream media as if they were boxing matches. Does this subtly—or not so subtly—influence voters' perceptions of various candidates? Can a male political figure who does not embody certain traditionally masculine qualities—such as being a "team player" or being able to converse comfortably in "sportspeak"—succeed in such an environment? Can a woman? Will we get any closer to finding solutions to complex twenty-first-century problems when political commentary focuses not on what candidates say or stand for, but on the fact that the "frontrunner" failed to deliver a "knockout punch"?

I intend to sketch out a number of questions about the ideological influence of (male) sports culture with which serious students of presidential politics, gender, media, and sport need to grapple. These questions are especially relevant in the context of a 24/7 media environment in which information and propaganda come fast and furious, and where notions of discrete electoral cycles have given way to the realities of the perpetual campaign. This does not pretend to be a comprehensive examination of this subject. It is, rather, a preliminary discussion of one aspect of a much larger cultural studies project that examines the centrality of constructed notions of masculinity to American (and world) politics in an age of ubiquitous media. At the very least, this brief essay should be seen as a statement about the need to take "sportspeak" seriously, especially at a time when the phenomenon that communications scholar Sut Jhally (1984) terms the "sports/media complex" continues to grow exponentially, and when the very integrity of democracy is threatened by the steady rise of sound-bite philosophy and entertainment values.

Sports Studies, Cultural Studies, and the Electoral Gender Gap

In an article that summarized recent developments in the study of sport sociology, Michael Messner (2005) wrote that scholars of sport increasingly frame their object of study not as the "sports-world," but instead as "sports in the world." He located the study of sport within broader cultural studies approaches, and identified the analysis of media imagery as one of the most fruitful dimensions of an interdisciplinary "cultural turn" in studies of gender and sport. As Jhally (1984) had argued in an earlier essay, most people do "the vast majority of their sports spectating via the media (largely through television), so that the cultural experience of sports is hugely mediated." It follows that sports culture and its many constituent parts—such as sports metaphors—are thus important sites for cultural studies critique—and critical media literacy efforts.

In his book *Media Culture* (1995), the philosopher and cultural theorist Douglas Kellner provides a powerful rationale for the importance of studying media:

> A media culture has emerged in which images, sounds and spectacles help produce the fabric of everyday life, dominating leisure time, shaping political views and social behavior, and providing the materials out of which people shape their very identities. . . . Media culture also provides the materials out of which many people construct their sense of class, of ethnicity and race, of nationality, of sexuality, of 'us' and 'them.' . . . For those immersed from cradle to grave in a media and consumer society, it is therefore important to learn how to understand, interpret, and criticize its meanings and messages. (pp. 1–2)

Among the media meanings and messages that are important to understand, interpret, and criticize are those—such as elements of sports culture—that are involved in shaping gendered perceptions of presidential candidates. Why? Sports metaphors and other references help to define political reality for millions of men—and women. Listen to *National Review* editor Rich Lowry's (2005) analysis of George Allen, the former senator from Virginia who was once a leading Republican hopeful for president. "Football gives Allen a conversational entree with nearly any American male," Lowry writes. "And it is one he never leaves unexploited. What Shakespeare is to the sonnet, Allen is to the football analogy. Over a period of a couple of months, I heard him compare every significant event in Washington to a football play or situation" (p. 33). But sports metaphors in politics—whether they're used by politicians, media pundits, or co-workers at the watercooler—do more than provide a shared language for members of the good ole boys' club. They also help to define key characteristics of manhood, and to identify who measures up—and who does not.

It has been well-documented and often discussed that gender differences in voting patterns have been pronounced over the past few presidential elections (Center for American Women and Politics, 2004). Consider: In 2004, George

W. Bush won 55 percent of the total male vote, to John F. Kerry's 44 percent. Kerry actually beat Bush among all female voters 51 percent to 48 percent (although he lost 55 percent to 44 percent among white women). In 2008 Barack Obama won a landslide victory among all women, but while he failed to capture the white male vote, he did much better with white men than John Kerry did in 2004. Kerry lost among white males by twenty-five points; Obama lost by only sixteen. As a result, he won the overall men's vote, however slightly. These (racialized) gender disparities offer clues to some of the differences between women's and men's political priorities. They highlight differences in women's and men's perceptions of the world. But these perceptions are not formed in a vacuum. Ideology is transmitted through various institutional, cultural, and individual practices that not only can be studied, but can also be altered. And precisely because media is the great pedagogical force of our time, it should go without saying that any serious discussion about gendered patterns in political beliefs and electoral choices needs to account for the breadth and depth of its enormous influence.

Most analyses of the gender gap have focused on women—how their gendered identities impact their political choices, and how their voting habits are changing the face of U.S. politics. Only recently have political scientists and journalists begun to look at the male side of the gender gap, in order to understand how men's gendered identities and sense of themselves *as men* impact their political choices. One way to frame this debate is to ask not why do women tend to support Democrats, but why do (white) men in such great numbers support Republicans?

There are, of course, many possible explanations for this electoral gender gap. For example, the linguist George Lakoff (2004) has theorized that Republican ideology embodies an authoritarian "strict father" perspective, while the Democrats are better characterized by the values of "nurturant parents." In political shorthand, this means the Republicans are perceived as the "daddy party," and the Democrats the "mommy party." In addition, since at least 1972, when the Democratic presidential nominee was the liberal Senator George McGovern, a former World War II fighter pilot who opposed the Vietnam War, polls have consistently shown that a majority of voters believe the Republican party to be more trustworthy on "national security" (Griffith, 2005). One way to interpret this belief is that—for whatever reasons of substance or style—the GOP is perceived to be the party that is "tougher" on communism/terrorism, which translates to mean it's more willing to increase military spending and resort to military force to project strength and defend U.S. interests around the world. Because violence is seen as a masculine prerogative (Katz, 2003), the Republican party attracts a greater percentage of votes from men, who are more likely than women to prioritize "foreign policy" as an issue that determines their vote for president.

Other factors contributing to the electoral gender gap include the decline in recent decades of organized labor's political influence, white male opposition to gender- and race-based affirmative action policies championed by Democrats, and single-issue voting on issues like gun control. (Note: There are significant racial and ethnic dimensions to political identities and voters' preferences, although the complexities of these dimensions are beyond the scope of this paper. It is worth noting that men of color, especially African Americans and Latinos, are much more liberal and Democratic than white men. It is quite possible that for them, the masculine discourse of politics—or the masculinity of specific candidates—is less important than racial/ethnic issues, identities, and politics. This discussion is primarily about white voters.)

A further reason to do a cultural studies analysis of how media conventions influence the political views not only of white male voters but of *working-class* white male voters is that their voting patterns over the past quarter-century confound the traditional assumption among liberal and progressive economists and political strategists that people are likely to vote their "pocketbooks," i.e. their economic/class interests. Millions of (mostly) non-union blue-collar white men have for the past couple of decades voted for the presidential nominees of the Republican party, which favors tax cuts for the wealthy and reduced federal spending on education and health care programs that serve middle- and working-class families. Consider: In 2000, George W. Bush won the support of 63 percent of white men without a college degree, a stunning 29-point margin over Al Gore. Pundits and writers inside and outside of academia have for years sought to understand this phenomenon. Why do so many non-wealthy white voters—men and women—consistently vote against their own (economic) interests? One of the most popular political books of the past decade, *What's the Matter with Kansas? How Conservatives Won the Heart of America* by Thomas Frank (2004), addresses this very question. Frank argues that the conservative movement has convinced millions of working-class whites that their true enemies are liberal "elites" who have contempt for good old-fashioned American values, and that the solution to cultural decline is to elect conservative Republicans. The tragedy for these working people, though, is that the economic policies pursued by these same Republicans are designed to ease the tax burden on big business and to steadily erode both the rights of workers and the social safety net that protects them from the harsh realities of economic and social inequality.

Interestingly, Frank and many others neglect to explore in any depth the role of media culture in this critical process—much less the role of sports/media culture. But it is impossible to deny the central role of media *and* sports in contemporary presidential politics. For a long time, television advertising has been the single biggest campaign expenditure. The 2004 presidential race was at the time the most expensive in history. *USA Today* reported that the Bush and Kerry campaigns, along with "independent" groups, spent approximately $1.6 billion on TV ads in the 2004 race, more than double the $771 million spent in 2000 (Memmott & Drinkard, 2004). It is estimated that in the "battleground" states alone, there were 675,000 television commercials broadcast (Anderson, 2004). Estimates of the money spent on the presidential race in 2008 put the total at over $2.4 billion, with advertising and other expenditures shattering all previous records (Schouten, 2008; Schneider, 2007). And that doesn't even begin to measure all of the *unpaid* media—the many thousands of hours of political news and talk shows on cable TV, radio, newspapers, magazines, and the Internet.

Even so, relatively little attention has been paid—in scholarship or journalism—to the relationship between white men's voting habits and media-driven constructions of masculinities (and femininities)—including the political impact of sports. One notable exception is a brilliant book-length study by Stephen J. Ducat, entitled *The Wimp Factor: Gender Gaps, Holy Wars, and the Politics of Anxious Masculinity* (2004), which features brief discussions of sports metaphors, talk radio, and other media phenomena. The lack of this type of analysis elsewhere is unfortunate but perhaps not surprising. It could be that the politicized use of sports metaphors is nearly invisible, even to cultural critics, precisely because they are such a part of our daily speech that they "fly under the radar" of critical consciousness. And how realistic is it to expect serious examination of this subject in media, especially when some key opinion leaders in that realm— such as MSNBC's Chris Matthews, host of the aptly named *Hardball*—are men who themselves are frequently caught up in the masculine mythmaking that often passes for insightful political analysis?

Sports Metaphors and Class Politics

What follows are some reflections about the relationship between sports metaphors and the construction of hegemonic masculinity in contemporary U.S. presidential discourse. Hegemonic masculinity is a conceptual tool, identified by the sociologist R. W. Connell (1987), that refers to the idealized and dominant form of masculinity in a given cultural context. In our culture, it is white, middle- and upper-class, and heterosexual, and is further characterized as aggressive and competitive. Not surprisingly, the qualities considered "presidential"—to date—track closely with those associated with hegemonic masculinity. My purpose is to sketch out some of the ways that sports metaphors help to shape voters' perceptions about the masculinity of various candidates for president, which in turn affects male voters' propensity to positively identify with them, and both male and female voters' willingness to think they have the "right stuff" to be president.

More specifically, I am going to explore, in brief, some of the intersections of gender and class in sports and political discourse. The language of sports in mainstream journalism and presidential campaign rhetoric not only helps to shape masculine norms and present special challenges for female candidates, but it also plays a crucial role in either highlighting or obfuscating class differences. It is thus an important area of study, not only for academics and practitioners in the field of political communication, but also for anyone interested in gender and class politics. It should be noted that this discussion is a preliminary examination of a topic that will require a much greater degree of theory, research, and political activism in coming years.

The Populist Appeal of Sports Metaphors

With some variation, certain sports are identified not only with men, but with men from specific social classes. For example, racquetball in the U.S. is largely viewed as a sport primarily for middle- and upper-class men in health and fitness clubs, whereas boxing and football are considered more blue-collar (although their fan base draws heavily from the middle and upper classes, as well). The "masculinity" of a given sport thus has a class dimension. As Nicholas Howe (1988) points out, American politicians "especially those of patrician background, have long appreciated that the use of sports metaphors allows them to affect a common touch or forge a bond with average voters" (p. 89). By making references to sports that are popular with working-class men, sports metaphors and other references are surefire ways to demonstrate populist appeal. A famous example from the pre-television era is the aristocrat Teddy Roosevelt's use of boxing metaphors. More recent examples include Richard Nixon's frequent references to baseball and football, or Ronald Reagan's close identification with football.

Reagan's football credentials were enhanced by his having been a college football player, and from his role as George Gipp in the 1940 film about a famous football coach, *Knute Rockne: All-American*. (The movie was the source of the famous line, "Win one for the Gipper," which became part of Reagan lore.) Reagan also effortlessly employed gridiron metaphors, such as when he stated in 1981 that European opponents of the neutron bomb were "carrying the propaganda ball for the Soviet Union" (ibid., p. 92), or when he asked in 1984, "Isn't it good to see the American team, instead of punting on third down, scoring touchdowns again?" (ibid., p. 90). Reagan's ability to talk the populist language of football while cutting programs that served working-class families and pursuing an economic policy that redistributed income upward is one of the reasons he earned the nickname the "Great Communicator."

On the other hand, politicians who get the class politics wrong—or who are characterized by their opponents as getting them wrong—run the risk of revealing themselves as elitist, out of touch, or aristocratic in a way that is not read as manly by millions of working- and middle-class male voters. For example, during Michael Dukakis' run for the White House in 1988, the former Massachusetts governor repeatedly referred to his campaign as a "marathon," invoking his Greek heritage. The effectiveness of this was questionable, because while many Americans admire and in some ways are in awe of marathon runners, marathon running is not seen in the dominant U.S. culture as a "masculine" endeavor. Additionally, Dukakis' penchant for "power-walking" with the TV cameras rolling did not help bolster his masculine image, as this form of exercise is more often the object of ridicule than emulation in traditional male culture.

In the 2004 presidential campaign, news commentators and conservative media personalities had a field day with footage of John Kerry skiing and snowboarding in Sun Valley, Idaho, and windsurfing off Nantucket Island. While these visuals showed him to be athletic and adventurous, and symbolically reinforced Kerry's similarities to and identification with fellow Massachusetts senator and former president John F. Kennedy, they also accentuated the idea that his sports passions were upper-class in nature. (The class and cultural imagery surrounding the Democratic and Republican parties in the early twenty-first century have changed dramatically since the Kennedy era. Hence, widely circulated images of Kennedy engaged in upper-class pastimes in the early 1960s played out very differently—and much less negatively—for him and his political persona.) This placed Kerry's constructed masculine image in sharp contrast with his opponent and fellow aristocrat George W. Bush's carefully stage-managed image as an average guy who rides in pickup trucks and loves baseball, as someone with whom plain folks could identify. The windsurfing photos also served as another kind of sports metaphor: They were the perfect visual illustration of the Republican theme of John Kerry as a "flip-flopper" who did not stand for anything and would just blow with the prevailing winds.

Cultural Specificity

There are no universal sports metaphors that work equally well to define manhood across national or cultural boundaries, in part because different cultures have varying definitions of what is considered "masculine." For example, in most parts of the world, soccer is considered a manly sport (even if women also play it), and male soccer stars are often national icons. This is not true in the U.S. Although soccer is our most popular youth sport in terms of athletic participation, it is not even close to American football in its cultural influence, masculine identification, or metaphorical power. It is rare to find a national-level politician in the U.S. who uses soccer metaphors, precisely because to do so would call into question the strength of their American identity, as well as their masculine credibility. Thus it is important for people who use sports metaphors in their speech or writing to know which sports are identified with the hegemonic masculinity of a given society, and to use references to those sports while avoiding others. For politicians or political commentators in media, failure to do one's "homework" in this area would expose oneself as either oblivious to local norms and customs, or in the case of a man, as not masculine enough because he discusses, plays, or enjoys feminized—or otherwise "wrong"—sports. Political professionals are well aware of this trap, which accounts for the fact that in 2004, John Kerry's presidential campaign downplayed his collegiate soccer record and emphasized his hockey credentials.

It is possible to interpret this de-emphasis on Kerry's soccer past as an attempt by his handlers to steer clear of biographical information that reinforced his European—especially French—sensibilities, as this was a line of attack that right-wing activists and media pundits used to paint him as elitist and out of touch with average (read: working-class) American voters. Right-wing critics of Kerry are undoubtedly well aware of the gender and class politics that surround soccer in mainstream U.S. culture. As Franklin Foer points out in his book *How Soccer Explains the World* (2004), in most of the world, soccer is the province of the working class. But in the U.S., with the exception of Latinos, and recent immigrants from Asia and Africa, "the professional classes follow the game most avidly and the working class couldn't give a toss about it . . . [and] half the nation's soccer participants come from households earning over $50,000 . . . the solid middle-class and above" (p. 239). Moreover, Foer argues that when a "generation of elites" adopted soccer in the 1960s and 1970s, it gave the impression that they had "turned their backs on the stultifying conformity of what it perceived as traditional America" (p. 239). This naturally caused resentment toward Democratic "elites" in "red state" America and other bastions of traditional values. Thus another sports metaphor functioned to reinforce a major tenet of right-wing propaganda, one that Republicans have used to their advantage for decades.

Violence in Sports Metaphors

U.S. political discourse is infused with metaphors from a range of sports. From former Central Intelligence Agency director George Tenet's infamous assertion that the presence of weapons of mass destruction in Iraq was a "slam dunk," to the criticism that some journalists are known to ask "softball" questions during presidential press conferences, to United States Supreme Court Chief Justice John Roberts' assertion during his confirmation hearings that "judges are like umpires. . . . They make sure everybody plays by the rules" (Roberts, 2005), to then-presidential candidate Barack Obama's statement that "a nuclear Iran would be a game-changing situation not just in the Middle East but around the world" (Zeleny, 2008), everyday speech by and about politics and politicians routinely contains sports terminology whose meaning resonates with a large number of voters.

But while metaphors from sports such as basketball and baseball regularly surface in political speech, arguably the two most metaphorically influential sports in presidential politics are boxing and football. Not coincidentally, they are both violent sports, and they attract a disproportionate percentage of male participants and fans. It is not within the scope of this study to estimate how much of the white male vote is determined by impressions about the relative "manliness" or "toughness" of candidates or political parties. But the frequent use of boxing and football metaphors in political discourse surely contributes to the fact that presidential campaigns in the mass media era (to date) are less about issues and complex political agendas than they are about the selling of a certain kind of executive masculinity, embodied (prior to Obama) in a particular white man whom the public comes to know largely through television and other media and information technologies. What follows is a brief discussion of the role of boxing and football metaphors in this process.

Boxing Metaphors

Boxing metaphors help to construct presidential campaigns as the ultimate arena for masculine competition. Boxing is a prototypical working-class or poor man's (or more recently, woman's) sport that strips the notion of physical combat to its barest essence: Competitors go "mano a mano" in a fight to the finish. Through the campaign of 2004, the (almost exclusively) white male candidates who have vied at the highest level for the presidency have in effect been competing to be their party's *champion,* who if victorious becomes the champion of the entire country, the man who stands in for the home team in international political competition against the champions of other countries (e.g., Saddam Hussein, Hugo Chavez, etc.).

For many decades, newspapers have covered presidential debates with language taken directly from coverage of title bouts, complete with "Tale of the Tape" features that quantify a candidate's strengths and weaknesses. To this day, the political fortunes of various candidates are in part determined by whether or not political and media elites describe them as "heavyweights." Anyone who follows contemporary U.S. politics even superficially knows that politicians and journalists constantly use boxing metaphors to describe political machinations. There are countless examples of this: Before his first debate with Ronald Reagan in 1984, Walter Mondale was urged by Tip O'Neill to "come out slugging and come out fighting" (Howe, 1988, pp. 93–94). The *Los Angeles Times,* during the presidential primary season in 2000, ran an article about a dramatic speech by Arizona senator John McCain under the headline "McCain Delivers Hard Left to

Christian Right" (Miller & Brownstein, 2000). And in a lead-in to a jocular and substantive exchange on National Public Radio with commentator Michael Eric Dyson about the first debate between George W. Bush and John Kerry in 2004, host Tavis Smiley stated: "Once the lights and cameras are off, media pundits and voters are still left to decide which punches actually landed, which political jabs will be felt throughout the rest of the campaign" (Smiley, 2004). Later in the discussion, Dyson, commenting on a previous debate performance by Kerry, said, "I ain't saying he was dancing like Ali, but at least he wasn't plodding like some ham-fisted contender for the crown" (Dyson, 2004).

Boxing has historically been a male bastion, and it remains so in the twenty-first century. But women's boxing now occupies a small—but highly visible—cultural space. It is probably too early to tell how the increased popularity of women's boxing has affected the power of masculine symbolism associated with the sport. In any case, the 2008 political season broke new linguistic ground, at first because the presence of Hillary Clinton in the ranks of political "heavy-weights" complicated the boxing metaphors. Politicians and political commentators had to choose whether or not to use language that had men metaphorically hitting a woman (and vice versa). Republican Sarah Palin's entry into the race as her party's vice presidential nominee and the second woman on a major party ticket provided another watershed cultural moment. In her first nationally televised speech, at the Republican National Convention in early September, Palin sharply attacked Barack Obama's character and record. A typical headline in the media coverage read "Defiant Sarah Palin Comes Out Swinging" (Barabak, 2008), and the *New York Times* editorialized that Palin's rallies had become "spectacles of anger and insult" ("Politics of Attack," 2008). One of Palin's most-quoted lines on the campaign trail in the fall of 2008 was "The heels are on, the gloves are off," which she typically delivered to wild cheers of approval. In coming years, when this historic campaign and those yet to come are analyzed, it will be particularly interesting to see how female and male voters respond to language where a woman throws the "knockout punch." Does this masculinize and thus help to make them more credible as potential commanders-in-chief? Or do women who are seen as "too aggressive"—even if only in a metaphorical sense—turn voters off? What are the differences between how the sexes view a woman "throwing punches" if she's a conservative (like Palin) or a liberal feminist (like Hillary Clinton?).

Football Metaphors

Football is a hugely popular sport across the United States, and it provides a wealth of metaphors in contemporary American politics. Journalists wonder whether a politician will do an "end run" around his/her opposition in the legislature. TV pundits preface their remarks about a candidate's debate performance by apologizing for doing a little "Monday-morning quarterbacking." Newly energized campaign volunteers claim to have been inspired to "get off the sidelines" and join the political battle. An op-ed in *USA Today* runs under the headline "Don't Punt on Iran: U.S. Shouldn't Throw Bombs or Play a Soft Defense" (Schweizer, 2007). And interestingly, the general election campaign season—when political ads increase exponentially and political talk fills the airwaves—corresponds to the main part of the football season. In fact, Election Day is the first Tuesday in November, right in the heart of the football schedule.

Because football is a violent sport, football metaphors bring violent language and imagery to political discourse. They also subtly and overtly link politics to warfare. As Howe (1988) puts it, "The element of physical conflict in football . . . makes football metaphors effective . . . because it establishes that politics is a violent exercise of power with clear winners and losers" (p. 92). Football metaphors with military analogues that are used commonly by sportscasters and sportswriters, such as "throwing the bomb," "penetrating the zone," and "air game vs. ground game," insure that the language of football and the language of war cross-reference each other. Establishment politicians—men and women—who use this sort of language can thus prove their mastery, or at least familiarity, with two important masculine domains: football and the military. As Reagan and many others have proved, this can be an effective way for wealthy candidates to show blue-collar males that they're "one of the guys" (especially if they're a man)—whether or not their economic program addresses working people's concerns or represents their interests.

It is certainly not difficult to find examples of football metaphors in the speech of contemporary politicians. During the 2004 Republican National Convention in New York City, Rudy Giuliani praised George W. Bush as a "great president" because "he turned around the ship of state from being solely on defense against terrorism to being on offense as well" (Giuliani, 2004). Speaking to reporters about the Iraq war several years later, Secretary of Defense Robert Gates made a similar point, with even more explicit football terminology: "It's important to defend this country on the extremists' 10-yard line, and not on our 10-yard line," he said (Richter, 2007). Republican senator Richard Lugar compared the Bush plan for a "surge" in Iraq to ". . . a draw play on third down with 20 yards to go in the first quarter. The play does have a chance of working if everything goes perfectly, but it is more likely to gain a few yards and set up a punt on the next down" (Lugar, 2007).

No discussion of football metaphors in politics would be complete without mention of George Allen, the former senator from Virginia. Allen, a former college quarterback and the son of the late Washington Redskins coach, has taken the political use of football metaphors to a new level. As reported by Dana

Milbank (2005) in the *Washington Post*, Allen filters nearly everything political through a football lens. He once said that critics of Condoleezza Rice, who went on to become secretary of state, "have used some bump-and-run defenses and tactics against her." A couple of years ago, when the Republicans won a Senate seat in Louisiana, he said it "was like a double-reverse flea-flicker and a lateral." As head of Senate Republicans' campaign efforts in 2004, he called his candidates in the Southern states the "NFC South" (ibid.).

According to Milbank, "In Allen's world, primaries are 'intrasquad scrimmages,' his Senate staff is the 'A-team,' Senate recess is 'halftime' and opponents are flagged for 'pass interference.'" Allen accused the Democrats of "Constant delay of game, constant holding, constant pass interference and, once in a while, even piling on." Years without elections are the "offseason." Primaries are the "preseason." Senate Republicans are President Bush's "teammates." Big political donors join a "Quarterback Club" or a "Special Teams" committee (ibid.).

It is important to note that Allen's near-obsessive use of football metaphors did not hurt him politically. In fact, while his football language was the object of ridicule in some quarters of mainstream journalism and also the blogosphere, until late in 2006 he was a major star in conservative Republican circles, when his use of an alleged ethnic slur tarnished his reputation and contributed to the loss of his Senate seat. George Allen's precipitous fall was a reminder that race and ethnicity remain central issues in presidential politics, and will likely remain so for years to come. As increasing numbers of men and women of color enter U.S. politics, including presidential politics, it is interesting to speculate about what effect race—and racism—will have on the way sports metaphors are used, and discussed. For example, if an African American male politician used football metaphors as promiscuously as does former senator George Allen, would people find it humorous, perhaps a little "goofy," but still an indication that he's a "man's man"? Or is it possible that his stature would be questioned, as African Americans constantly have to fight the stereotype that they're "natural" athletes who lack intellectual heft? Barack Obama is a good basketball player, and often played pickup games on the campaign trail for exercise. Basketball is a highly popular sport in this country, yet players at the elite level in college and the pros are overwhelmingly African American. Do Obama's hoop skills reinforce his "otherness" to the white majority, his *black* masculinity? Is it overdrawn to suggest that in its own minor way, this might have been one of the reasons—along with his poor bowling performance on the campaign trail in Pennsylvania—why he was slow to win the votes of working-class whites in the 2008 Democratic primaries? Furthermore, playing pickup basketball has not traditionally been seen as "presidential" behavior. Could this have contributed to the perception among some white voters that he was young and inexperienced, and therefore not ready for the highest office in the land?

Female Candidates: Do They Play the Game?

In coming years, as (presumably) more women enter presidential politics, a number of questions will arise about the role of sports in politics, including the role of sports metaphors. Will women candidates need to perfect the language and style of male "sportspeak" in order to succeed in a political world that is still dominated by men, much as female sportscasters and sportswriters have had to adjust to the male-dominated sports/media complex? It might be too early to tell. As one journalist stated in an article about Hillary Rodham Clinton's athletic credentials, "There is no playbook for a woman running for president" (Healy, 2007). Clearly, this is treacherous terrain for women candidates, in part because they are expected to be comfortable with what has been a predominantly (but not exclusively) masculine sports discourse. But they can't be too comfortable, lest they commit the unforgivable sin in politics of appearing "inauthentic."

One conundrum for women seeking the presidency is whether or not it is possible to talk—and be talked about—in the violent language of boxing and football metaphors, thus bolstering their image as "tough enough" to be commander-in-chief, without appearing to be wannabes in the "jockocratic" world of male politics. One woman with some relevant experience in this regard is Condoleezza Rice, secretary of state in the George W. Bush administration. Rice has stated publicly numerous times that she would like to be commissioner of the National Football League. In a *New York Times* article, she asserted that she is a "student of the game," but that despite her knowledge of football and her passion for it, men often underestimate what she knows because she is a woman (Freeman, 2002). Would male voters be comfortable with a woman running for president who knows more about football than many of them? Would women? It remains to be seen. Rice has never faced the electorate as a candidate for office.

There is growing evidence that voters have become more comfortable with women in positions of political power. But it is still too early to tell how this new acceptance of female leadership will play out in presidential politics over the next generation, and how the language of politics might change to reflect this. Will the presence of women candidates prompt interest in a new set of metaphors that resonate with voters, such as the birth metaphor that I referenced at the beginning of this essay? Or will a new sort of politics emerge, where female—or male—candidates will be able to forge and embody new kinds of gendered identities that do not fall along predictable or traditional lines?

It is also difficult to do anything but speculate about the process by which new styles of manhood emerge and evolve into acceptable presidential qualities to a significant number of white male voters. The election in 2008 of President Barack Obama surely marked a turning point in terms of ethnic and racial diversification at the highest level of political power. But as anyone who watches cable TV or listens to talk radio can attest, Obama's masculinity—not just his policies—has been under attack from the moment he took office. (Even before

Obama took office, right-wing talk radio host Rush Limbaugh derided him by saying, "He can't take a punch, he's weak, and he whines"[Brownstein, 2008].) It remains to be seen whether Obama's personal brand of cerebral cool, his talk about the importance of "empathy" in Supreme Court justices, and his attempts to articulate a less-aggressive U.S. foreign policy represent a potentially lasting shift in the gender order, or whether more traditionalist conceptions of presidential masculinity will ultimately regain power.

Conclusion

This paper attempts to provide readers with some key aspects of a cultural studies analysis of a subject that is often discussed but infrequently taken seriously as a topic for systematic theory and research. Sports metaphors are a ubiquitous part of political speech and journalism in the United States in the twenty-first century. They help to produce and reproduce dominant constructions of masculinity (and femininity), and establish and reinforce norms for both candidates and voters. Yet without further study, it is premature to make broad or specific claims about exactly what effect they have on presidential politics.

This study poses a number of questions about the relationship between conventions of dominant male sports culture and the political beliefs and choices of white men, especially working-class white men. There are many more questions raised by this line of inquiry: What affect, if any, does political discourse filled with sports metaphors popular in *male* sports culture have on *women's* political beliefs and choices? Are there significant class dimensions to these, as well? This study focuses on white men. What, if any, impact does the political use of sports metaphors have on men of color? On women of color? As increasing numbers of men and women of color enter U.S. politics, including presidential politics, what affect will race—and racism—have on the way sports metaphors are used and discussed? For example, as Latinos increase as a percentage of the U.S. population and electorate, will Latino politicians—and Anglo politicians seeking Latino votes—choose to use soccer metaphors in their speeches or press conference banter? How will that play out in Anglo culture, especially among sports talk radio hosts and other media personalities who are used to ridiculing soccer as "wimpy" in relation to American football? These are just a few of the countless lines of inquiry for further exploration in this fruitful and important area of cultural studies.

References

Anderson, N. (2004). Silence of the wolves, and their ilk, in swing states. *Los Angeles Times Online*, November 2.

Barabak, M. (2008). Defiant Sarah Palin comes out swinging. *Los Angeles Times*, September 4.

Brownstein, R. (2008, September). Reconcilable differences. *The Atlantic*, p. 58.

Center for American Women and Politics. (2004). Rutgers, NJ. November 5, 2004. Retrieved from http://www.rci.rutgers.edu/~cawp/Facts/Elections/GG2004Facts.pdf.

Connell, R.W. (1987). *Gender and Power*. Stanford, CA: Stanford University Press.

Ducat, S. (2004). *The Wimp Factor: Gender Gaps, Holy Wars, and the Politics of Anxious Masculinity*. Boston: Beacon Press.

Dyson, M.E. (2004). The Tavis Smiley Show, *National Public Radio*, www.npr.org, September 30. http://www.npr.org/templates/story/story.php?storyId=4054526.

Foer, F. (2004). *How Soccer Explains the World*. New York: HarperPerennial.

Frank, T. (2004). *What's the Matter with Kansas? How Conservatives Won the Heart of America*. New York: Metropolitan Books.

Freeman, M. (2002). On pro football: Dream job for Rice: N.F.L. commissioner. *New York Times*, April 17.

Giuliani, R. (2004). www.CNN.com, August 31. Retrieved from http://www.cnn.com/2004/ALL POLITICS/08/30/giuliani.transcript/index.html.

Griffith, L. (2005). Where we went wrong: How the public lost faith in Democrats' ability to protect our national security, and how to stage a comeback. The Truman National Security Project, May. http://www.trumanproject.org/trumanpaper3.html.

Healy, P. (2007). Hillary Clinton searches for her inner jock. *New York Times*, June 10.

Howe, N. (1988). Metaphors in contemporary American political discourse. *Metaphor and Symbolic Activity*, 3(2), 87–104.

Jhally, S. (1984). The spectacle of accumulation: Material and cultural factors in the evolution of the sports/media complex. *Insurgent Sociogist, 12*(3).

Katz, J. (2003). Advertising and the construction of violent white masculinity: From Eminem to Clinique for Men. In G. Dines & J. Humez (Eds.), *Gender, Race and Class in Media: A Text Reader*, 2nd ed. Thousand Oaks, CA: Sage Publications.

Kellner, D. (1995). *Media Culture: Cultural Studies, Identity and Politics between the Modern and the Postmodern*. New York: Routledge.

Lakoff, G. (2004). *Don't Think of an Elephant: Know Your Values and Frame the Debate*. White River Junction, VT: Chelsea Green Publishing Company.

Lowry, R. (2005). Buckling his chin strap: Sen. George Allen—likable, conservative, and tough—prepares to run for president. *National Review*, November 7.

Lugar, R. (2007). Beyond Baghdad. *The Washington Post*, January 30, p. A17.

Luntz, F. (2007). *Words That Work: It's Not What You Say, It's What People Hear*. New York: Hyperion.

Memmott, M. & Drinkard, J. (2004). Election ad battle smashes record in 2004. *USA Today*, November 25.

Messner, M. (2005). Still a man's world: Studying masculinities and sport. In *Handbook of Studies on Men and Masculinities*. M. Kimmel, J. Hearn, & R.W. Connell (Eds.), (pp. 313–325). Thousand Oaks, CA: Sage Publications.

Milbank, D. (2005). Mixing politics, pigskins: When Allen talks, football jargon flows. *Washington Post*, February 6, p. C01.

Miller, T.C. & Brownstein, R. (2000). McCain delivers hard left to Christian right. *Los Angeles Times*, Feburary 9, p. 1.

Politics of attack. (2008). *New York Times*, October 8, p. 24.

Richter, P. (2007). Bush sees long-term role for troops. *Los Angeles Times*, May 31.

Roberts, J. (2005). Text of John Roberts' opening statement. www.*USAToday.com*, September 12. Retrieved from http://www.usatoday.com/news/washington/2005-09-12-roberts-fulltext_x.htm.

Schneider, W. (2007). Presidential fundraising hits record pace. CNN.com, July 6. Retrieved from http://politicalticker.blogs.cnn.com/2007/07/06/schneider-why-are-dems-winning-the-money race/#more-729.

Schouten, F. (2008). Political spending races toward record $5.3 billion. *USA Today*, October 23, p. 1.

Schweizer, P. (2007). Don't punt on Iran. *USA Today*, June 26, p. 13A.

Smiley, T. (2004). The Tavis Smiley Show, *National Public Radio*, www.npr.org, September 30. Retrieved from http://www.npr.org/templates/story/story.php?storyId=4054526.

Zeleny, J. (2008). Obama meets with Israeli and Palestinian leaders. *New York Times*, July 24, p. A16.

6

The Rutgers Women's Basketball Team Talks Back

Intersectionality, Resistance, and Media Power

Mary G. McDonald and Cheria Thomas

O N APRIL 3, 2007, TWO BASKETBALL teams competed for the women's National Collegiate Athletic Association (NCAA) championship: the University of Tennessee and Rutgers University. One of the most compelling storylines heading into that title game was the performance of Coach C. Vivian Stringer's Rutgers team, who had started the season slowly with a 2-4 record. Through determination and teamwork, the freshman- and sophomore-laden squad completed a fine regular season with a 23-8 record and played exceptionally well throughout the NCAA Tournament to earn their way to the championship game. However, not all stories have happy endings, or in this case, produce an NCAA championship: The Scarlet Knights fell to the University of Tennessee, 59-46. Still, their run through the tournament was widely regarded in basketball circles as a remarkable journey for the young squad.

Despite these achievements, the Rutgers women soon found themselves at the center of a firestorm that erupted on April 4, 2007, because of the controversial comments made by Don Imus, host of *Imus in the Morning*. The talk radio show aired on WFAN radio in New York, and also was syndicated on CBS Radio and simulcast on MSNBC cable television. Imus, along with executive producer Bernard McGuirk, co-host Charles McCord, and substitute sports announcer Sid Rosenberg, made disparaging remarks about the predominately African American Rutgers team in their discussion of the NCAA basketball championship. Imus, specifically, reported that he had watched part of the title game and noted that the Rutgers team was composed of "some rough girls." McGuirk chimed in by offering that the Rutgers players were "some hard-core hos." Imus immediately responded, "That's some nappy-headed hos." This dialogue between Imus, McGuirk, and McCord continued for over a minute and a half and included out-of-context references by McCord to a Spike Lee movie, *School Daze*. Rosenberg further stated that the Rutgers team physically resembled the National Basketball Association's Toronto Raptors, while McGuirk suggested that perhaps the Memphis Grizzlies would be a more appropriate comparison for the Rutgers team ("Imus Called," 2007).

This discussion was flagged and critiqued as offensive by the watchdog group Media Matters for America, and it subsequently sparked protests and demands from several organizations including the National Association of Black Journalists (NABJ). (These responses are archived on the Media Matters website and the NABJ website.) Several visible spokespeople and activists including the Reverends Al Sharpton and Jesse Jackson, as well as many writers/bloggers on the Internet, called for the cancellation of *Imus in the Morning* and the immediate dismissal of Imus and his colleagues from WFAN/CBS Radio and the MSNBC network. As the controversy grew over the course of several days, a number of sponsors including Procter & Gamble dropped their support from the show and/ or networks.

Most of the escalating public outrage focused on the broadcasting of Imus' "nappy-headed hos" comment, even as Imus suggested that the conversation was all meant in good fun. Claiming that he was only making a joke, Imus offered repeated public apologies and later apologized in a private meeting with the team. Despite these expressions of regret, the Imus/CBS/MSNBC incident triggered a broader public debate about media power. Given the power of the media to frame stories, critics suggested the aired remarks denigrated women, especially African American women and women athletes, by turning their accomplishments and bodies into targets of racist and sexist humor. Numerous groups and individuals pointed out that the term "nappy-headed hos" conjures both sexist and racist meanings. While the slang term "nappy" has multiple definitions, it has been frequently used to disparage the form, texture, and style of black women's hair. The term "ho" is shorthand for "whore" and most frequently serves as a pejorative for a prostitute; all three terms have historically been deployed to denigrate and control female sexuality. In short, the words broadcast on CBS and MSNBC do not reflect isolated, individual thoughts but are illustrative of lingering inequalities that need redress, both within and outside the world of sport.

Several days after the controversy began, Coach Stringer and the Rutgers team held their own nationally telecast press conference to publicly voice their outrage and emotional hurt over the demeaning characterizations aired to the nation and the world by CBS Radio and MSNBC. (For transcriptions, see Press Conference Transcribe, 2007.) The women spoke about the way in which broadcast and public debate had profoundly impacted them and inspired them to action. Team captain Essence Carson noted that the team had not "done anything to deserve this controversy" and that it had "taken a toll on us mentally and physically."

She argued that the case "had stolen a moment of pure grace from us" and asked the public to "not recognize us in a light as dimly lit as this, but in a light that encompasses the great hurdles we've overcome and goals achieved this season" (Press Conference Transcribe, 2007). Later, during an appearance on *The Oprah Winfrey Show*, Carson observed that "no one's even paying attention to who won the game. So he didn't only steal from us our moment, but he also stole the moment away from Tennessee's great team" (Potempa, 2007).

Still, during the press conference Carson was proactive and optimistic in observing that

> . . . there are a lot of positives that can come from this. One thing is that we finally speak up for women, not only African American women, but all women. That's just going to be a major step forward in society, just to finally understand that there isn't that equality that we all wish was there. It's something we all hope for, but until we make those great strides to achieve that, we're going to continue to fall short. I'm glad we're speaking up. I feel like we can achieve that [equality]. (Press Conference Transcribe, 2007)

With resolve and respect, Carson also stated that the team would like to meet with "Mr. Don Imus" in order to "come to some type of understanding of what the remarks really entailed, his reasons why they were said. And we'd just like to express our great hurt." After meeting in person with Imus, the team issued a press release stating that they accepted his apology. Stringer noted that Imus' "comments are indicative of greater ills in our culture. It is not just Mr. Imus, and we hope that this will be and serve as a catalyst for change. Let us continue to work hard together to make this world a better place" ("Rutgers Coach," 2007). And while the team never publicly demanded Imus' resignation or the cancellation of his show, apparently preferring to use the case as a teachable moment, the *Imus in the Morning* show was subsequently cancelled by both MSNBC and CBS Radio.

In this chapter we build upon the team's call for social change by first demonstrating the ways in which Imus' words are part of "greater ills"—that is, the broader intersecting forces of racism and sexism in U.S. culture. And much like the Rutgers women, who decided to "talk back" at their telecast news conference, we also believe that resistance to the intersections of racism and sexism in sport and the wider culture, while already well under way, must be enhanced and more widely embraced if the interests of social justice are to be served. In this spirit, we point out several of the successful strategies employed by the Rutgers team and their allies, and suggest that other athletes, sport fans, and their allies might consider these ideas when advocating for justice, within both sport and the wider culture. We conclude this chapter by arguing that the considerable power of media monopoly practices frequently reinforce and legitimize conditions of inequality, and thus must be continuously challenged in the interests of democracy and fairness.

The Importance of Intersectionality

The public responses to the Imus/CBS/MSNBC incident reveal the importance of understanding the concept of intersectionality: the acknowledgment that racism and sexism are not independent systems of domination, but are instead powerful, interacting forces both within and outside of sport. The last decade has seen an increased appreciation for intersectional analysis, partially thanks to the acknowledgment that identities are always multiple, shifting, and shaped by power via additional cultural categories such as social class, sexuality, and nationality (McDonald & Birrell, 1999).

First coined by legal scholar Kimberley Williams Crenshaw (1989), the theory of intersectionality grew from her desire to expose the ways that the law frequently ignores the interlocking systems of racial and gender bias. Discounting the profound impact of these intersections means that the law typically only permits narrow notion of redress based upon either race or gender discrimination. For example, employment law is largely configured to address gender independently of race; thus, it fails to understand that while they are the targets of inequality, white women also experience structural advantages due to whiteness, while men of color are also privileged by gendered constructions in the workplace. In the United States, one result of this segmented focus is that the unique experiences of and issues faced by women of color are frequently left unaddressed in legal theory, popular practices, and activisms.

Intersectionality additionally posits that groups, such as women, are not homogenous—everyone faces opportunity and discrimination depending on the amalgamation of identity within particular contexts and circumstances. From this perspective, it is evident that "everyone is positioned at the intersections of a cluster of identity categories that together interact and produce an effect that is different from the sum of its parts" (Duncan, 2007, p. 69). Given these insights, efforts to ensure social justice for all must take into account the ways in which complex matrices of domination and subordination work simultaneously within particular contexts (Collins, 1990).

The Imus/CBS/MSNBC incident is illustrative of this point. As several critics have noted, the broadcast comments reflect a general cultural misogyny toward women and disrespect toward female athletes. As previously noted, the term "whore" has long been used as an insult to suggest that particular women are sexually promiscuous or corrupt. This sexualized assault on female bodies additionally diverts critical attention away from the sexist structures that seek to control and curtail female autonomy and self-authorizing expressions of sexuality. In short, the term derives from a broader set of social relations that position women, especially strong and assertive women, as second-class citizens.

In a similar way—and despite considerable progress—female athletes continue to be positioned as second-class citizens within the masculine domain of sport.

Sport is still structured to offer greater rewards and status for men in relationship to women (Messner, 2002). Some female athletes, for example, have been additionally subject to homophobic taunts and labeled by the culturally stigmatized term, "lesbian." Once again, such characterizations shift critical attention away from dominant normalizing systems within and beyond the world of sport—in this case, those seeking to naturalize heterosexuality as the only appropriate form of sexual expression. Such "lesbian-baiting" practices additionally represent attempts to reinforce traditional gender expressions and conventional standards of physical appearance while disciplining those who challenge these body norms (Griffin, 1998).

Similar attempts at demonization are additionally linked to race in complex and contradictory ways. Indeed, racist mythology dating back to slavery has especially targeted black women as extraordinarily sensual, promiscuous, and deviant, particularly in relationship to their allegedly more restrained and sexually repressed white middle-class counterparts (Collins, 1990). Given this history and contemporary racial politics, we can understand Imus' broadcast remarks as illustrative of what Carson characterized as a "race-specific" attack on women (Kelly, Starr & Conant, 2007, p. 32).

Appearing on CNN with Lou Dobbs, cultural critic Michael Eric Dyson additionally articulated the ways in which the Imus/CBS/MSNBC "nappy-headed hos" characterization reveals the unique issues regarding beauty that don't just target the Rutgers basketball team and women more generally, but have significant influence on women of color living in the U.S. According to Dyson:

> . . . [what Imus] said about those particular black women is symbolic and representative. Those black women represent women who work at MSNBC, who work at CNN. Black women in corporate America who have, quote, "nappy hair," who wear their hair in a way that is alternative to the mainstream, straightened hair.
>
> So the reality is that nappy hair is as equally lethal as the so-called "hos" statement. Because it's signifying upon the choices that black women make aesthetically and what they look like. That's the deepness of the harm. And all of us have to confront that in every circle in America. (Lou Dobbs Tonight, 2007)

Dyson's quote invites us to further delve into a central element of intersectional analysis: the symbolic and lived effects of intersecting inequality mediated through body norms. Specifically, Dyson's words suggest the need to examine the broader impact of white-dominated notions of beauty and physical attractiveness among diverse groups of women.

These ideas about beauty not only set unrealistic standards in an attempt to police the bodily expressions of women, but also are grounded in centuries-old ideological beliefs about racial difference and skin color. As black feminist Patricia Hill Collins (1990) argues:

Race, gender, and sexuality converge on this issue of evaluating beauty. Judging White women by their physical appearance and attractiveness to men objectifies them. But their white skin and straight hair privilege them in a system in which part of the basic definition of whiteness is its superiority to blackness. Black men's blackness penalizes them. But because they are men, their self-definitions are not as heavily dependent on their physical attractiveness as those of all women. (p. 79)

Read from this perspective, the Imus/CBS/MSNBC incident evokes a much longer history relative to expressions of sexuality and norms of physical appearance and attractiveness. Indeed, both within and beyond the world of sport, a disproportionate amount of disempowering scrutiny is aimed at women's physical features and physicality, while a phrase such as "nappy-headed hos" also evokes a set of shifting social relations whose demeaning impact is additionally contoured by the intersections of race and gender.

Talking Back: Learning through the Rutgers Team

Just as the broadcasting of Imus' words is suggestive of complex intersecting forces of racism and sexism, this incident also reveals strategies of resistance and challenges to these inequities. One notable element is the manner in which the Rutgers women repeatedly and passionately called for others to join them in "talking back." The Rutgers team refused to see this issue as merely related to one individual's opinion. Stringer urged:

> We all need to make changes, all of us beyond Imus. We need to serve as examples of how to be winners on the basketball court and we also need to serve as examples of how to be winners in life. (Press Conference Transcribe, 2007)

Carson echoed this sentiment in arguing that we have to attack "an issue that we know isn't right" (ibid.). These and other varied responses reveal that sport culture and popular culture are contested territories—that is, sites where meanings and values are struggled over. This conceptualization further suggests that attempts to ensure equity must by necessity include public engagement in dialogue and struggle.

While time, place, and circumstance may ultimately demand different tactics, the multiple responses by the Rutgers team and their supporters are potentially instructive for those wishing to challenge inequalities in their own local settings. Space does not permit us to detail the myriad of resistant responses in this case, but we do wish to highlight four responses that are potentially useful for others challenging the status quo, both within and beyond the world of sport. These tactics are consistent with the Rutgers team's actions in talking back. These include utilizing cyberspace to communicate counter-narratives and activist practices, bringing economic pressure on key institutions, forming alliances across difference, and anticipating and challenging backlash.

Utilizing Cyberspace to Communicate Counter-Narratives and Activist Practices

The watchdog group Media Matters for America first alerted the broader public to the Imus/CBS/MSNBC incident on its website, and the National Association of Black Journalists followed suit. Bloggers also played a crucial role in disseminating the story. Several bloggers offered advice on where to send e-mails, letters, and phone calls of protest to WFAN radio, CBS, MSNBC, the *Imus in the Morning* show, and related corporate sponsors. The conversation between Imus and McGuirk as well as Imus' visit to the Al Sharpton radio show, were re-broadcast on numerous websites and accessible on YouTube. Some blogs, like the Unapologetic Mexican, offered social commentary connecting Imus' disparaging "nappy-headed" remarks to gendered beauty standards embedded in white supremacist beliefs. Blogs for college basketball fans discussed how the flippant remarks garnered more attention than the NCAA tournament and urged fans to pressure the media to offer greater coverage of women's sports.

The web also served as a repository for the statements of self-representation from the Rutgers team, illustrating how it can serve as a readily accessible archive of information produced by those challenging inequality. For example, at the press conference, sophomore center Kia Vaughn offered an alternative characterization, or counter-narrative, symbolizing her refusal to accept the broadcast depiction of the team. This form of self-representation was disseminated throughout the web as organizations and individuals linked to the transcripts of the press conference. In discussing her desire to meet Imus, Vaughn noted:

> I would like to speak to him personally and . . . ask him, after you've met me personally, do you still feel this category that I'm still a "ho" as a woman and as a black, African American woman at that? I achieved a lot and unless they have given this name, a "ho," a new definition, that is not what I am. (Press Conference Transcribe, 2007)

Vaughn's words, and those of the Rutgers allies, clearly reveal how the Internet and new media technologies can offer fresh formations of political and civic engagement, offering a space for analysis, information dissemination, mobilization, counter-narratives, and alternative expressions of social life.

Bringing Economic Pressure on Key Institutions

Many activists spoke out against the racist and sexist characterizations of the Rutgers team by calling for a boycott of *Imus in the Morning*, CBS, MSNBC, and their corporate advertising sponsors. That advocates would use this strategy is not surprising, given the pervasiveness of exerting economic pressure on key institutions within civil and human rights movements across the globe. For example, during the 1980s, sport teams from several nations participated in broader economic boycotts against apartheid in South Africa, refusing to compete against South African national teams until legal segregation was ended. This broad coalition ultimately helped to end the oppressive regime (Birrell & Theberge, 1994). In the Imus/CBS/MSNBC case, rallies were held on the Rutgers campus, and students were at the forefront in calling for others to exert their economic power to bring about change in the media. Alpha Kappa Alpha, a 200,000-member African American women's sorority, not only called for Imus' resignation but also encouraged fellow members to divest themselves of CBS, NBC, and their affiliates' (i.e., Microsoft) stock ("Alpha Kappa Alpha Assails," 2007). Proctor & Gamble, American Express, General Motors, GlaxoSmithKline, Geico, and Staples all eventually pulled their financial support, and this lack of corporate support ultimately led to the firing of Imus.

Forming Alliances across Difference

Given their understanding of identity and inequality as multiple and shifting, feminists have been at the forefront in advocating for the need to work across culturally constructed social and political gulfs. As with other progressives, one aim has been to connect fair-minded individuals in either long-term or short-term alliances in order to bring about social change. The commitment to building alliances assumes that we all embody multiple statuses and identities, and thus can work for change even if an issue does not in that moment directly impact our lives (McDonald & Birrell, 1999). Such a foci moves activists away from an exclusive focus on the authenticity of identity of those protesting (e.g., only women can fight for women's issues) and toward building networks of diverse people of all backgrounds committed to ensuring political and social justice for all. Indeed, one notable element in the response to Imus' broadcast words has been the diversity of groups and individuals across the social and political spectrum who have helped counter the claims made by Imus on CBS Radio and MSNBC.

Among the most visible groups responding were Media Matters for America, the National Association of Black Journalists (NABJ), the National Organization for Women (NOW), the National Association for the Advancement of Colored People (NAACP), the Rutgers University administration, and the basketball team itself. The Reverends Al Sharpton and Jesse Jackson, who both have a long history of civil rights activism, were both vocal and visible in linking the event to broader forces of racism and misogyny. Retired baseball superstar Cal Ripken Jr. refused to appear on the *Imus in the Morning* show. The highest-ranking black woman ever in U.S. government, Secretary of State Condoleezza Rice, argued that Imus' characterization of the team was "disgusting. . . . I just thought that it was an attack on women's sports, first of all, and secondly an attack on very accomplished young black women in a way that was really offensive" (Associated Press, 2007).

The Rutgers women were able to draw upon the status and resources of Rutgers University in responding to Imus' statements in a nationally telecast news conference that was later streamed on the university's web page. Most people are not so fortunate as to have immediate access to such a global stage, but many still have the potential to connect with other individuals, groups, and organizations locally to build strength in numbers. Whether or not the players and Coach Stringer actively sought the support of progressive organizations and sympathetic individuals, this event reveals that there are resources and organizations that can help form powerful coalitions to challenge the status quo.

Such coalition building has already occurred in other sport-related cases. For example, in the spring of 2005 former Penn State University basketball player Jennifer Harris teamed with the National Center for Lesbian Rights (NCLR) to ask Penn State administrators to stop then-coach Rene Portland from contributing to the formation of a homophobic and racially hostile climate on her team. NCLR offered legal support that helped shed light on the case, and an internal investigation by Penn State University subsequently vowed to make changes to what they found to be a "hostile, intimidating, and offensive environment" ("University Concludes," 2006).

Anticipating and Challenging Backlash

Engaging in activist work for social justice frequently is accompanied by public backlash against progressive voices. Indicative of competing ideologies, such backlash also potentially serves to divert attention away from the initial critique and calls for change. In the Rutgers scenario, the diversionary tactics most often focused on activist Al Sharpton's activist past as well as the use of the word "ho" by black male rappers in hip-hop music. One such comment posted on the Internet is reflective of both foci:

> Funny, I don't recall hearing Sharpton and Co. excoriating the rap singers who reap millions spreading Imus-type messages to a whole generation of young people.

Many of today's kids are falling over themselves to emulate the rappers, thug life, which regards all women as 'ho's. Sharpton might actually do some good if he took on rap's toxic messages. But then he would have to point fingers at some in the black community. So it won't happen. ("Al Sharpton Takes On," 2007)

History has shown that backlash techniques often focus on the messenger rather than the message, and this was certainly the case in criticism of Al Sharpton. Any interpretation of Sharpton's past and/or motivations does not change the sentiment promoted by Imus/CBS/MSNBC. And while it would be difficult to defend the misogyny and homophobia of music culture, closer inspection reveals that long before the Imus/CBS/MSNBC controversy many people, including Sharpton himself, had already protested against some violent and degrading elements of music culture, both within hip-hop and other genres ("Al Sharpton Proposes Ban," 2005).

In this case, those who attacked the messengers of change missed opportunities to explore commonalities of interest that might be formed in exposing the corporate media structure, which glorifies particular forms of racism, homophobia, and sexism in both music culture and the *Imus in the Morning* show. Indeed, some media conglomerates may have an even bigger economic stake in the promotion of particular forms of rap music. While both the audiences for Imus and hip-hop are mostly white, hip-hop is targeted to the currently more desirable, allegedly edgy youth market.[1]

In sum, countering backlash involves understanding that marginalized communities and those critiquing the status quo frequently serve as scapegoats in attempts to divert attention from the social, political, and economic stakes involved. In this case, diversionary tactics focused on the actions of black bodies—rappers and Al Sharpton most prominently—while the white-dominated corporate media culture escaped broader scrutiny. This case thus reveals that concerted efforts must also be placed on discussing and exposing the people and groups that benefit the most from relations of inequality and backlash strategies.

Concluding Thoughts: The Need to Challenge Media Monopolies

Throughout this chapter, we have labeled this story as the Imus/CBS/MSNBC incident to illustrate the incredible power of our current network and cable media structures to promote a narrow vision of social life, one that too frequently marginalizes people through the interacting forces of race, gender, sexuality, class, ability, and nation. In this way, this incident reflects a series of important issues related to intersectionality and the monopoly power of the media. At present, the public has yet to fully understand the need to reform the monopoly power of the media (McChesney, 2005). Perhaps this is partially due to the fact that the media consist of many apparently divergent elements, including various network, cable, television stations, radio stations, and satellite radio. The Internet offers an additional amalgamation and consolidation of these elements, as well as previously mentioned opportunities for alternative production possibilities. This proliferation of apparently diverse network, cable, and satellite outlets belies a larger problem: "a handful of corporations" continue to exert "awesome power over our news, information and entertainment" (Copps, 2005, p. 117).

The Imus/CBS/MSNBC case reveals that concentrated media ownership remains an important issue, because the consolidation of ownership has translated into less local control, as well as less ideological and content diversity (McChesney, 2005). And while the commercial and corporate status of U.S. media means that there are opportunities to pressure advertisers to evoke short-term change, as happened with the cancellation of *Imus in the Morning*, broader structural changes in corporate media are needed to enhance democracy.

Of course, we don't mean to suggest that the current media system is completely devoid of editorial freedom—indeed, most mainstream journalists analyzed and critiqued Imus' broadcast words, and several explored the intersecting forces of racism and sexism operating in the case. Yet these responses mostly existed in reaction to the voices of watchdog news media groups who actively publicized the case until it received coverage by the mainstream press. The initial broadcast comments from Imus and company support the contention from media scholars that a few multinational corporations still exert incredible "gate keeping control over the civil dialogue of our country; and veto power over the majority of what we and our families watch, hear and read" (Copps, 2005, p. 118). The gatekeeping power seems to be to be especially evident in this case, because Imus had previously made disparaging remarks that marginalized groups of people and individuals (for examples, see "Racism to Be Expected," 2007). That he was able to continue on the airwaves for thirty years speaks to a corporate media system that too frequently values demographics and profits at the expense of equality and fairness.

A handful of corporations still maintain awesome power to shape and frame narratives that in turn influence how we come to view, for example, female athletes and their accomplishments, as well as our own bodies and those of citizens around the globe. Several scholars argue media monopolization and consolidation greatly impact our ability to consistently encounter alternative and diverse images and ideals (McChesney, 2005). They suggest that new broadcast policies are necessary to open up more diverse public and private ownership arrangements to better promote multiple perspectives and varied images. Despite making some inroads, progressive change will be difficult to achieve given the economic incentives that bolster and link seemingly disparate media organizations, which promote stories and issues of social justice more as products and entertainment to be consumed and enjoyed. But such a struggle is especially necessary as large corporations continue to attempt to consolidate their power within new media technologies such as the Internet (ibid.).

Tracing the partnerships of the *Imus in the Morning* show reveals the awesome power of media consolidation. Space does not permit us to fully detail the web of connections, but notable connections begin with the show syndicated on CBS Radio. CBS Radio is a division of CBS Broadcasting Corporation (once Viacom), which in turn has several divisions including Paramount Pictures, Showtime, CW, CBS Outdoor, CBS Interactive, CBS Consumer Products, Simon & Schuster books, and CBS Management Television. The show was simulcast on MSNBC, a cable network and news organization originally launched in a joint venture with Microsoft and now a holding of NBC Universal, which in turn is a division of General Electric (80 percent) and Vivendi (20 percent). General Electric also owns GE industrial, which includes GE aviation, GE health care, and of course GE appliances, all of which can be advertised throughout this vast network.[2]

Vivendi is based in Europe, and among its holdings is Universal Music Group, one of the largest holders of record labels in the industry. Universal Music Group is an umbrella of record labels in partnership with Interscope/Shady'G-Unit Records, which has primary artists such as Dr. Dre, Emimen, Fifty Cent, and G-Unit. It owns Geffen Group, which also has various rap and alternative artists such as Fred Durst, Snoop Dogg, and Timbaland. A third record label that this group partners with is Universal Motown Group, which has such artists as Ja Rule, Nelly, Lil' Wayne, and Neil Bogart. Universal Music Group also includes Def Jam Records and Show Dog Nashville, who employ such artists as Jay-Z, Ludacris, Kanye West, and Toby Keith.

This brief tracing of ownerships and partnerships reveals interesting connections between the Imus/CBS/MSNBC story and the problems of media monopoly: Imus continually made disparaging comments on multinational networks designed to secure profits and, in particular, on a network owned by a corporate group that also distributes music, some aspects of which also promote racist and sexist ideas. Legislative and policy changes to diversify ownership and reverse consolidation are needed to lessen this awesome representational power. The quest for a media system that serves the public interest must recognize the necessities of what the Rutgers women's basketball team and their allies have also called for: fair representation and a commitment to justice and democracy for all.

Notes

1. Several commentators have noted that the increasing commodification of hip-hop music has denuded its historical role in offering social criticism. The Imus/CBS/MSNBC discussion about the imagery of rap music largely ignored the critical contributions of rap in delineating and critiquing

the racial and class politics that have produced oppressive living conditions for the poor of urban America and across the globe. See Dyson (2004) for an analysis of the critical vision of hip-hop.

2. In an era of consolidation and divestment, media subsidiaries and partnerships are frequently in flux. We retrieved the information regarding ownership and partnerships May 29, 2007, from the following websites: CBS Corporation, http://www.cbscorporation.com/; General Electric, http://www.ge.com/index.htm; NBC Universal, http://www.nbcuni.com/; Vivendi, http://www.vivendi .com/corp/en/home/index.php; Columbia Journalism Review, http://www.cjr.org/resources/; Take Back the Media, http://www.takebackthemedia.com/owners.html; Universal Music Group, http:// en.wikipedia.org/wiki/Universal_Music_Group.

References

Al Sharpton proposes ban on rappers—wants those connected with violent acts to be denied airplay. (March 8, 2005). Retrieved June 7, 2007, from http://www.fradical.com/Al_Sharpton_violent _rap.htm.

Al Sharpton takes on the latest loose tongue. (April 11, 2007). Retrieved June 7, 2007, from http:// www.startribune.com/blogs/kersten/?cat=57.

Alpha Kappa Alpha assails remarks of Don Imus and Bernard McGuirk: President urges members to flex economic muscle. (April 10, 2007). Retrieved May 7, 2007, from http://www.aka1908 .com/pdf/imus_press_release_4_07.pdf.

Associated Press. (April 13, 2007). Secretary of State Condoleezza Rice calls remarks about Rutgers players disgusting. Retrieved May 20, 2007, from http://www.foxnews.com/story/ 0,2933,266049,00.html.

Birrell, S. & Theberge, N. (1994). Feminist resistance and transformation in sport. In D. M. Costa & S. R. Guthrie, (Eds.), *Women and sport: Interdisciplinary perspectives* (pp. 361–376). Champaign, IL: Human Kinetics.

CBS Corporation. (n.d.). Retrieved from http://www.cbscorporation.com/.

Collins, P. H. (1990). *Black feminist thought: Knowledge, consciousness and the politics of empowerment.* Boston: Unwin Hyman.

Columbia Journalism Review. (n.d.). Retrieved from http://www.cjr.org/resources/.

Copps, M. (2005). Where is the public interest in media consolidation. In R. McChesney, R. Newman, & B. Scott, (Eds.). *The future of media: Resistance and reform in the 21st century* (pp. 117–126). New York: Seven Stories.

Crenshaw, K. W. (1989). Demarginalizing the intersections of race and sex: A black feminist critique of antidiscrimination doctrine, feminist theory and antiracial politics. *University of Chicago Legal Forum,* 139–167.

Duncan, M. C. (2007). Response to Carrington's "Merely identity: Cultural identity and the politics of sport." *Sociology of Sport Journal,* 24(1), 67–75.

Dyson, M. C. (2004). *The Michael Eric Dyson reader.* New York: Basic Civitas.

General Electric. (n.d.). Retrieved from http://www.ge.com/index.htm.

Griffin, P. (1998). *Strong women, deep closets: Lesbians and homophobia in sport.* Champaign, IL: Human Kinetics.

Imus called women's basketball team "nappy-headed hos." (April 4, 2007). Retrieved May 7, 2007, from http://mediamatters.org/items/200704040011.

Kelly, R., Starr, M. & Conant, E. (April 23, 2007). A team stands tall, *Newsweek*, p. 32.

Lou Dobbs Tonight. (April 9, 2007). Retrieved May 7, 2007, from http://transcripts.cnn.com/ TRANSCRIPTS/0704/09/ldt.01.html.

McChesney, R. W. (2005). The emerging struggle for a free press. In R. McChesney, R. Newman, & B. Scott (Eds.). *The future of media: Resistance and reform in the 21st century* (pp. 9–20). New York: Seven Stories.

McDonald, M. G. & Birrell, S. (1999). Reading sport critically: A methodology for interrogating power. *Sociology of Sport Journal*, 16(4), 283–300.

Messner, M. (2002). *Taking the field: Women, men and sports.* Minneapolis: University of Minnesota.

NBC Universal. (n.d.). Retrieved from http://www.nbcuni.com/.

Potempa, P. (April 14, 2007). Oprah proud of Rutgers basketball team's "grace" while handling Don Imus' insults/firing. Retrieved June 4, 2007, from http://nwitimes.com/articles/2007/04/14/columnists/offbeat/doc0cd5f048f16a1c52862572bc0073fd7d.txt.

Press conference transcribe. (April 10, 2007). Retrieved May 7, 2007, from http://www.scarlet knights.com/print.asp?prID=5226.

Racism to be expected from Don Imus. (April 9, 2007). Retrieved June 4, 2007, from http://www .fair.org/index.php?page=3082.

Rutgers coach, players accept Imus' apology. Retrieved May 7, 2007, from http://www.msnbc.msn .com/id/18089620/.

Take Back the Media. (n.d.). Retrieved from http://www.takebackthemedia.com/owners.html.

University concludes investigation of claims against women's basketball coach. (April 18, 2006). Retrieved June 4, 2007, from http://live.psu.edu/story/17387.

Vivendi. (n.d.). Retrieved from http://www.vivendi.com/corp/en/home/index.php.

7

Come Out and Play

Confronting Homophobia in Sports

Brandon Sternod

Homosexuality is an obsession among ballplayers, trailing only wealth and women. The guys I played with just didn't like "fags"—or so they insisted over and over again. . . . Over time, I realized their antigay prejudice was more a convention of a particular brand of masculinity. Homophobia is a ballplayer posture, akin to donning a "game face," wearing flashy jewelry or driving the perfect black Escalade. (Former NBA player and openly gay athlete John Amaechi, 2007b)

IN THE SPRING OF 2007, *Man in the Middle*, a memoir written by former National Basketball Association (NBA) power forward John Amaechi, was released and reignited a fiery public discourse regarding homosexuality and sports. In the book, Amaechi openly discusses his life as a gay black man and vividly recounts stories about the homophobic attitudes and actions he observed from fellow players as well as coaches. While the public reaction from the NBA community regarding Amaechi was mostly positive (Dallas Mavericks owner Mark Cuban went so far as to declare Amaechi a hero), not everyone was willing to accept the man or his lifestyle. Most notable were the comments made by another former NBA player, African American Tim Hardaway, when asked about Amaechi and the prospect of having a gay man as a teammate. In a radio interview with Miami journalist Dan Le Batard, Hardaway boldly stated: "You know, I hate gay people, so I let it be known. . . . I don't like gay people and I don't like to be around gay people. I am homophobic. I don't like it. It shouldn't be in the world or in the United States" (ESPN.com News Services, 2007c).

Attitudes such as this regarding lesbian and gay athletes, while rarely stated out in the open, are nothing new in the world of sport and have most certainly not disappeared completely. In 2002, a parallel situation occurred when a former

National Football League (NFL) player, Hawaii-born Samoan Esera Tuaolo, came out on HBO's *Real Sports* television program (Dolin, 2002). Like the reaction to Amaechi, several NFL players publicly expressed their support for Tuaolo. But others were not as supportive or accepting. Then-San Francisco 49ers running back Garrison Hearst, an African American, was quoted in the *Fresno Bee* (2002) in response to the Tuaolo piece, saying that he was against having "faggots" in the locker room and that anyone who happens to be gay is a "punk" (Kaufman, 2003). And New York Giants tight end Jeremy Shockey, a popular white player, said in an interview on the *Howard Stern Show* (done shortly before the television program aired) that he hoped he didn't have any gay teammates and wouldn't "stand for it" if he found out that he did (Kaufman, 2003; Zeigler, 2002).

Similar intolerant beliefs regarding homosexuality could also be found in collegiate sports and, in one case, were part of a long-standing anti-gay policy. In December 2005, former Penn State women's basketball player Jennifer Harris sued the university, claiming that white head coach Rene Portland discriminated against her because she suspected that Harris, an African American, was gay. In an interview with the *Chicago Sun-Times* (Figel, 1986), Portland clearly states her anti-lesbian policy and apparently supported this policy with her actions (Belge, n.d.; Griffin, 2007). According to Harris, Portland erroneously believed that the player was violating this policy, openly questioned her about her sexuality, ridiculed her in front of her teammates, and eventually kicked Harris off the team due to her suspicions. The lawsuit was recently settled out of court, and Portland resigned from her position after twenty-seven years on the job.

If these recent cases are any indication, it is apparent that homophobia is still prevalent in the sports world and in American society, even at their highest and most public levels. It is also clear that homophobia and homophobic beliefs cut across many social categories such as race, class, culture, and gender. Amaechi, Tuaolo, and Harris, despite their differences, have all experienced homophobia firsthand and have joined the exclusive ranks of athletes such as tennis legends Billie Jean King and Martina Navratilova, Women's National Basketball Association (WNBA) superstar Sheryl Swoopes, and former Major League Baseball (MLB) player Billy Bean who have been brave enough to come forward and fight back against the oftentimes unquestioned heteronormative standards of sexuality. But what about other, lower-profile lesbian, gay, bisexual, and transgendered (LGBT) athletes who also struggle against these standards? What are their experiences? And what can parents, coaches, teammates, and allies do to help create a cultural atmosphere where gay and lesbian athletes feel safe to openly be themselves? In this chapter, I take a closer look at these highly visible cases of homophobia in sport and critically examine the normative roots of such attitudes towards homosexuality and homosexual athletes. I will also discuss the experiences of other LGBT athletes, both positive and negative, and ponder the possibility that the homophobic landscape of sport can change for the better.

And finally, I will discuss ways that anti-gay attitudes in sport can be combated and how safe environments for LGBT athletes and their allies can be fostered.

The Performance of Gender and Sexuality in the Locker Room and on the Playing Field

According to Judith Butler (1990), gender is not something someone *is* but rather something someone *does*. Being a man or a woman is not the same as being biologically male or biologically female; masculinity and femininity are social norms of behavior that are discursively produced and reproduced in a given society. Individuals feel compelled to perform the gender assigned to their sex in the ways they dress, the ways they interact, and the ways they desire. It is this category of desire that is the most intricately linked to gender, and the area of performance as a man or a woman that is perhaps the most rigidly enforced. Just as biological sex is seen as the "natural" root of gender, gender is seen as the cause of "natural" desire toward its opposite. Heterosexuality, then, is understood by many as an essential element in how one correctly "does" being a man or a woman, and any deviation from it is viewed as abnormal, immoral, and distinctly un-"natural." Nowhere is this more evident or more strictly enforced than in sports.

For men and boys, the locker room and playing field are prime locations for learning and/or performing heterosexual masculinity (Curry, 1991; Dworkin & Wachs, 2000; Messner & Stevens, 2002; Sabo & Messner, 1994). Even at an early age, boys and young men are performing heterosexual masculinity by competitively bantering with teammates about sex and their sexual exploits with females. In these very public discussions, these male athletes are expected to express not only their sexual desire for females but, more importantly, their dominance over them (and hence the dominance of all things "masculine" over all things "feminine"). Failure to do so or failure to do it in a correct way often results in ridicule, which causes a high amount of pressure, even for heterosexual males. So where does this type of banter leave gay athletes, who not only fail to desire females sexually but who actually have desires (for other males) that are understood as "feminine?" As Messner (1994) explains:

> The need to prove one's manhood through sexual conquests of women is experienced as a burden by many young heterosexual men, but it is especially oppressive for gay athletes. The pressure to be seen by one's peers as "a man"—indeed, the pressure to see one's self as "a man"—makes most young males play along with the homophobic and sexist locker room banter. But gay men are far more likely to perceive this behavior as a strategy for constructing an identity. (p. 48)

In his interview with *Real Sports* (Dolin, 2002), Esera Tuaolo discussed this heterosexist banter and his own construction of an acceptable heterosexual identity.

He made a point of engaging in such conversations, and of being seen by his teammates with various women. He even managed to gain a reputation as a "player," someone with a high number of sexual conquests over females. However, this identity work was not without consequence. Tuaolo saw himself not as a real person but as an actor, and sat idly by while teammates repeatedly told one another gay jokes. He felt a high degree of shame because of his desires, slipped into depression, and even contemplated suicide. Tuaolo feared that if his teammates found out his secret, they would turn on him based upon the homophobic remarks that some had made. Former Green Bay Packers wide receiver Sterling Sharpe, interviewed for the same *Real Sports* segment, agreed with Tuaolo and stated that he believed that Tuaolo's fears were not unfounded: "He would have been eaten alive and he would have been hated for it. Had he come out on a Monday, with Wednesday, Thursday, Friday practices, he'd have never gotten to the other team." LeRoy Butler (2002), former teammate to both Tuaolo and Sharpe, agreed with this assessment in a special column written for ESPN.com:

> It's terrible, yes, but the reality is that a lot of players would treat him badly. I would guess that he'd find graffiti on his locker and maybe even on his car. Perhaps more devastating would be the isolation he would endure. An openly gay player would be treated like the kicker who missed the winning field goal in the last seconds of the game. There would be a noticeable absence of high-fives if he scored a touchdown and he'd be celebrating by himself after a win.

John Amaechi (2007b) was also witness to sexist and homophobic locker room talk but, as he explains, he was often considered exempt from certain standards of masculinity because he is from Great Britain and hence expected to be a little peculiar. "It's an old phenomenon, dating back to the film stars of the 1920s, when audiences would ask, 'Is he gay or is he British?' Every time I did something eccentric . . . people would quip, 'Oh, he's just English. Leave him alone.'" (p. 74). However, being a gay man in such an environment, he couldn't help but notice the irony in the ways his straight teammates bonded with one another. "The NBA locker room was one the most flamboyant places I've ever been. Guys flaunted their perfect bodies. They bragged about sexual exploits. They primped in front of the mirror, applying cologne and hair gel by the bucketful," Amaechi explains. "They tried on each other's $10,000 suits, admired each other's rings and necklaces. It was an intense camaraderie that felt completely natural to them. Surveying the room, I couldn't help chuckling to myself: And *I'm* the gay one" (p. 72).

These comments mirror the work of Brian Pronger (1990, 1999), who contends that the gender-segregated yet homophobic locker room and playing field spaces allow men who boldly uphold heterosexist norms of masculinity to simultaneously surround themselves with the naked bodies of other men, to engage physically with them, and to participate in homoerotic play without the stigma of being labeled as homosexuals. In an environment where heterosexuality is assumed to be an absolute and behaviors that might otherwise be considered "gay" in another environment are the norm, it is not hard to imagine how a gay man like Amaechi could pass as straight. For straight men, however, the locker room and playing field serve as arenas where they can be free of some of the constraints of hegemonic masculinity without losing their places in our heterosexist, patriarchal society. So, as Pronger (1999) writes, "they can have their (beef)cake and eat it too."

For women and girls, normative heterosexist femininity is also upheld though sport in similar yet different ways. Just as gay men are feared and stigmatized in sports, lesbian women are also seen as threats, but not just to hegemonic gender norms; they are also viewed as threats to the livelihood of the sports themselves. In an era where sports are a major industry, women's athletics struggle to find its niche in the American sporting conscience. Competitive women's sports have historically been viewed as non-feminine and have carried the stigma of rampant lesbianism (Lenskyj, 1986, 2003). To combat this "problem," numerous executives, athletic directors, athletic merchandise manufacturers, and coaches made concerted efforts to emphasize the femininity (and hence heterosexuality) of female athletes and to promote attractive, heterosexual women (for example, Anna Kournikova) over more successful lesbian or suspected lesbian athletes (Martina Navratilova). Thus, for the modern female athlete, success on the field often takes a backseat to success at being sexually attractive to men, or, as Dworkin and Messner (2002) and Griffin (2002) call it, being "heterosexy."

Griffin (2002) contends that homophobia in women's sport manifests itself in several ways. The first and most enduring manifestation is silence. Because many female athletes and those who coach, support, and promote them are fearful of the lesbian stigma, female athletes who desire other females are encouraged to remain silent about their sexuality. "Lesbians in sport are treated like nasty little secrets that must be kept locked tightly in the closet. Lesbians, of course, are expected to maintain deep cover at all times. Not surprisingly, most lesbians in sport choose to remain hidden rather than face potential public condemnation" (p. 195). The second manifestation of homophobia is denial, or the refusal by athletes, coaches, and other interested parties to admit that any lesbians participate on their teams or in their sports.

The third manifestation is apology: "In an attempt to compensate for an unsavory reputation, women in sport try to promote a feminine image and focus attention on those who meet white heterosexual standards of beauty" (Griffin, 2002, p. 196). Female athletes are often encouraged to maintain a feminine (and hence heterosexual) appearance by being seen off the field or court having a "feminine" appearance and being in the company of boyfriends or husbands. As Lenskyj (2003) writes:

Many coaches, administrators, and sponsors, female as well as male, continue to express concern over the "image problem" of women's sports and to put considerable energy into making superficial changes aimed at convincing the public that female athletes are "normal" heterosexual women. Coaches and sponsors of women's teams often impose dress codes that impose revealing uniforms, long hair, shaved legs and makeup. (p. 36).

Other more recent manifestations of homophobia in women's sports include the related promotion of a "heterosexy" image, a preference for male coaches, and attacks on lesbian athletes and coaches. In the case of Jennifer Harris and her dismissal from the Penn State women's basketball team, this last manifestation is particularly relevant.

It was a well-known fact among the collegiate women's basketball community that Penn State head coach Rene Portland had a strict policy prohibiting lesbians from competing on her teams. "Everyone I know who is familiar with women's college basketball has heard the rumors or has talked privately to former PSU basketball players or recruits who confirmed the stories: Rene Portland has enforced a 'no lesbian' policy for over 20 years," Griffin (2007) explains. "I myself talked to a mother and daughter years ago who told me that Portland had announced, unasked, during a home visit that she did not allow lesbians on her team." Despite this fact, Portland was never reprimanded by the university and was allowed to stay in a position of power over young female athletes. It took the legal action of Harris, with the help of the National Center for Lesbian Rights (NCLR), to bring sufficient attention to this blatant discrimination and force Portland's resignation in the spring of 2007. "Because Coach Portland thought that I was gay, I was treated in a very demeaning manner," Harris explains. "Coach Portland created an offensive, hostile and intimidating learning environment for players she believed were gay. She created divisiveness on the team by instructing players not to associate with other players she believed to be gay, or they would be kicked off the team also" (Belge, n.d.). Sadly, Harris is not alone in receiving this type of treatment. Other lesbian or suspected lesbian athletes have also endured taunting from spectators, teammates, competitors, and like Harris, their own coaches. Female coaches suspected to be lesbians also face similar treatment, and a number of coaches have been dismissed due to their suspected sexuality (Griffin, 2002, p. 198).

For gay athletes, male and female alike, homophobia in sport can have devastating social, psychological, and even physical effects. In numerous accounts (Anderson, 2002; Griffin, 2002; Lenskyj, 2003; McKay, Messner & Sabo, 2000; Messner & Sabo, 1994; Pronger, 1990, 1999), research and scholarship show that gay athletes are often under a tremendous amount of pressure to hide their sexuality from teammates and coaches, live in fear of being outed and/or physically assaulted, and can even internalize homophobic attitudes that erode their sense of self-worth.

For example, consider again Esera Tuaolo. A large man, standing six foot three and weighing three hundred pounds, Tuaolo is an imposing figure. Yet he led his life in fear that someone would discover he was gay and that his life as an athlete would be over. On the exterior, he was a man who participated in a physically brutal sport, drank alcohol to excess, and womanized—all very stereotypically masculine behaviors. But on the inside, he was lonely, depressed, and at times suicidal (Buzinski, 2002a; Dolin, 2002). Although his career was long by NFL standards (eight seasons), his accomplishments in the league were unremarkable. According to Tuaolo, he was wary of doing too well on the field and attracting undue attention to himself, fearful that the attention would lead to his secret being exposed and the end of his career.

In "Openly Gay Athletes: Contesting Hegemonic Masculinity in a Homophobic Environment," Eric Anderson (2002) presents the case of Greg Congdon, a former Pennsylvania high school football player who was coerced into coming out after attempting to take his own life. When his teammates discovered his secret, he was warned not to rejoin the team, threatened with physical violence, repeatedly taunted with homophobic slurs, and ostracized by friends, coaches, and his community. For Congdon, this icy response to his sexuality served to make him hate himself even more (p. 869). Although the treatment Congdon received was extreme in comparison to the other athletes in his study, Anderson insists that even those who were supposedly accepted by their peers were still not allowed to fully be themselves. The main element in these athletes' experiences coming out was not the outright resistance to their sexuality but the denial (oftentimes self-imposed) of it. These athletes were tacitly accepted under "don't ask, don't tell," like arrangements where their sexuality was known, just not talked about. As Anderson explains, "the gay athletes failed to recognize that their identities were being denied, and they often took part in their own oppression by self-silencing and partaking in heterosexual dialogue" (p. 870). These young men were not accepted wholly by their peers or coaches but were accepted as athletes. In many cases, the athletes believe that to be enough.

In another notable case, WNBA superstar and Olympic gold-medal-winning basketball star Sheryl Swoopes recently made the decision to come out as a lesbian and to reveal that she was engaged in a long-term relationship with another woman. In an interview with *ESPN the Magazine* done after she came out in October 2005, Swoopes, an African American, discussed what it had been like for her to be a closeted lesbian:

> Not being free to be who I am, not being OK with other people knowing who I am—it has been miserable. And it hurts. I'm a very affectionate person. Going out to the movies or dinner, seeing so-called normal couples show affection in public

and knowing that I can't, that hurts. It's frustrating to keep everything inside and not be who I want to be. I'm sure life is not going to be easier for me just because I'm coming out. But at least I'll be free. (Swoopes, 2006)

Like Tuaolo, hiding her feelings for a person of the same sex was a major element in Swoopes' unhappiness as an athlete and public figure. But unlike Tuaolo or Amaechi, who both came out after they retired, Swoopes has come out as an active player, which implies that she does not live in fear of reprimand or rejection from her teammates or organization. As a major star and former league MVP, Swoopes has not been run out of her sport or off her team in the two seasons since her public announcement. But because she has publicly admitted to being a lesbian in a homophobic society, Swoopes has stated that she is fearful that people will no longer see her as a feminine role model for young girls. This fear again emphasizes the association of femininity with heterosexuality and reiterates the stigma of lesbianism with women's athletics.

Whether it is heterosexist locker room banter by boys and men, homophobia as a means to justify homoeroticism in the locker room and the playing field, or individual and/or institutional compliance with dominant notions of femininity, gender and sexuality are intricately linked in and through sports. Many male athletes learn from an early age by way of locker room discourse that to "be a man," one must reject and dominate femininity, and that to be openly gay is, for the most part, not acceptable. Gay or straight, boys and men routinely "do" gender by performing a certain brand of heterosexual masculinity in order to be accepted by their peers. For female athletes, the performance of gender is also closely tied to sexuality. Because of the historical stigma of female athleticism being associated with homosexuality and the desire to make women's sports more appealing to the public, compliance with heterosexual norms of femininity has become, in many instances, compulsory. Openly lesbian athletes, who by these standards are deemed to be distinctly unfeminine, are often viewed as liabilities to a sport's success and are frequently asked to hide, keep quiet, get out of the way, or risk being removed. But is this the whole story?

The Possibility of Change

The recent experiences of high-profile athletes like Amaechi, Tuaolo, and Harris could reasonably lead one to believe that homophobia in sports is as prevalent as ever. But while the rejection of homosexuality is still rampant both in sports and in American society in general, there is evidence that sporting culture is taking steps towards more inclusive and accepting attitudes towards both gender and sexuality.

In the case of John Amaechi, the response to his memoir and the possibility of there being a gay man in an NBA locker room ranged from Hardaway's hateful comments quoted earlier to "don't ask, don't tell" indifference (former teammate Troy Hudson stated, "If you keep it to yourself, I don't care what you are"), to acceptance based on performance (according to former coach Doc Rivers, "You look at it and say, 'So what? Can he rebound? Can he shoot? Can he defend?'"), to unconditional positive feelings based on who Amaechi is as an individual (from former teammate Michael Doleac: "John was a smart guy, a great guy, a fun guy to be around on the team, a good teammate" (ESPN.com News Services, 2007a). Yet despite these mixed reactions by his former NBA peers, Amaechi has stated that so far 95 percent of the correspondence he has received from the American public has been positive. In a speech given to the nation's largest gay Republican organization, the Log Cabin Republicans, Amaechi acknowledged that, while there is still work to be done, he "underestimated" the American public's attitude regarding homosexuality (Associated Press, 2007).

Responses to Esera Tuaolo's admission from around the NFL were also somewhat mixed. Many former teammates, including Todd Steussie, Byron Chamberlain, and LeRoy Butler, were supportive of the former lineman (Buzinski, 2002b). Stuessie, a former teammate with the Minnesota Vikings, stated, "I really don't see it as being that big a deal. It might make some people uncomfortable, but to me it's a non-issue." Chamberlain was quoted as saying, "It really doesn't concern me, because I'm definitely not homophobic. I know that there are homosexuals in every occupation, and with the number of homosexuals out there, I wouldn't doubt there are some in athletics. The odds are, with the number of guys I've played with, I've probably been in the locker room with some." And Butler wrote in his *ESPN.com* column: "I'm proud of Esera Tuaolo. By coming out to the world, he did something a lot of guys would never have the guts to do" (2002). Butler continued, "We were teammates in Green Bay, and I know him pretty well. And now, knowing that he's gay, it doesn't change anything. I don't have any bad feelings about it. To me, it's not that big of a deal. But the reality is, I may be in the minority." Clearly, these players have a certain level of sensitivity concerning Tuaolo and the struggles that he and other LGBT athletes endure. While some former teammates and current NFL players have made remarks about not wanting to shower with a gay man or have expressed fears that a gay teammate might check them out or make a sexually aggressive move on them, the players quoted above serve as examples that not all male athletes share such stereotypical, homophobic perspectives.

In the case of collegiate women's basketball player Jennifer Harris, she has transferred to James Madison University, where she'll have the opportunity to continue her athletic and academic career. And, as noted earlier, Rene Portland is no longer the coach at Penn State University, thanks to Harris' lawsuit and the work of the National Center for Lesbian Rights. It is cases such as this that should give LGBT athletes and coaches (as well as their friends, family members, and allies) reason to feel optimistic. Athletes who stand up against institutionalized discriminatory practices based on sexual orientation now have an example of how to fight back. As Griffin (2007) writes:

> I believe that one of the positive outcomes of the Harris case is that university and athletic leaders are increasingly clear about the necessity of developing policy and instituting education programs that protect student-athletes from the discriminatory practices apparently tolerated at Penn State for over twenty years. Jen Harris represents a new generation of student-athletes and their families who are willing to challenge discrimination rather than suffer in silence as so many have in the past. I also believe that Penn State and Rene Portland represent the last generation of institutions and coaches that tolerate or practice discrimination against athletes on the basis of their presumed or actual sexual orientation.

So while homophobic attitudes, heterosexist beliefs, and hegemonic norms of masculinity and femininity may still be prevalent in locker rooms and on the playing field (as they are in most of American society), a precedent has been set that they will no longer be allowed to become policy in the world of sport, whether official or de facto.

But these cases aren't the only reason to feel positive about the future for LGBT athletes and coaches. In his study on openly gay high school and collegiate male athletes, Anderson (2002) found that most of the gay athletes he interviewed were surprised about the open-minded and accepting treatment they received from many of their coaches and teammates. The author argues that the athletes themselves, by being openly gay in the hegemonically masculine world of athletics, represent sites of contestation and serve as evidence that the heterosexist, masculine hegemony is far from seamless. Griffin (2002) points to the example of Martina Navratilova and the "accepting, if not warm" response given to her by tennis fans around the world; she argues that the sporting world needs more courageous individuals like Navratilova to take a chance, come out, and inspire other LGBT athletes.

After the John Amaechi story was released, *Outsports.com* writer Cyd Zeigler Jr. (2007) agreed with Griffin's position and went so far as to pronounce that "pro sports are now ready for gay athletes." Zeigler cites a recent *Sports Illustrated* survey that showed that most Americans, athletes and non-athletes alike, would either welcome a gay teammate or would not feel differently about their favorite athlete if he or she came out. He also quotes Dallas Mavericks owner, savvy businessperson, and multimillionaire Mark Cuban, who hinted at a positive future for gay and lesbian athletes, particularly those at the upper levels of their sports (ESPN.com News Services, 2007b; Zeigler, 2007). In response to Amaechi's admission of his sexuality, Cuban applauded the former player and declared that if an active gay player came out, the American public would accept him as a hero. "When you do something that the whole world thinks is difficult and you stand up and just be who you are and take on that difficulty factor, you're an American hero no matter what," Cuban explains. "That's what the American spirit's all about, going against the grain and standing up for who you are, even if it's not a popular position" (ESPN.com News Services, 2007b). In addition to the admiration of the public, Cuban also claims that a high-profile, active gay athlete would also stand to benefit financially:

> From a marketing perspective, if you're a player who happens to be gay and you want to be incredibly rich, then you should come out, because it would be the best thing that ever happened to you from a marketing and an endorsement perspective. You would be an absolute hero to more Americans than you can ever possibly be as an athlete, and that'll put money in your pocket. On the flip side, if you're the idiot who condemns somebody because they're gay, then you're going to be ostracized, you're going to be picketed and you're going to ruin whatever marketing endorsements you have. (Zeigler, 2007)

In his article, Zeigler (2007) agrees with Cuban and points to WNBA superstar Sheryl Swoopes as an example of this very idea. After she came out, her team stood by her, her sponsor Nike stood by her, and she even picked up an endorsement deal from Olivia Cruises. Although he admits that homophobia and homophobic beliefs still exist in professional sports, Zeigler argues that very few teams or sponsors would risk the public backlash (or the possible lawsuit) they would face if they dropped a player shortly after he or she came out.

The Construction of Safe Environments for LGBT Athletes at All Levels of Competition

While the above cases certainly provide cause for confidence in a bright future for gay and lesbian athletes and hint at the potential eradication of homophobia in sports, almost all of them deal exclusively with high-profile collegiate and professional athletics with the exception of the Anderson study (2002). And even Anderson concedes that of all the athletes he surveyed, it was only the elite athletes (i.e., the best players on their respective teams) who felt comfortable enough to come out. The gay athletes he talked to who were of average ability tended to feel unsafe revealing their sexual preference and remained closeted. For the gay or lesbian professional or top-tier college athlete, coming out may be an increasingly safe, emotionally beneficial, and financially lucrative decision. But what about other, lower-profile gay and lesbian athletes, especially children and young adults? And what about other athletes, those who may not be gay but are nonetheless discriminated against because of the heteronormative suspicions of coaches and teammates, or who live in fear that they might be? What can be done to create safer, more accepting environments for them?

In "It Takes a Team! Making Sports Safe for Lesbian, Gay, Bisexual, and Transgender Athletes and Coaches," Griffin, Perrotti, Priest, and Muska (2002) describe an educational program designed to raise awareness of LGBT issues and eliminate homophobia in sports. The authors list several ways in which athletes, coaches, athletic directors, and parents can address and combat negative attitudes towards LGBT athletes and coaches and create a more positive environment for all. As they argue, homophobia impacts the lives of all athletes, not just LGBT athletes. It is fear and the lack of understanding that leads to unjust treatment of LGBT athletes and straight athletes who are suspected of being gay or lesbian, as well the unwillingness of straight athletes and coaches to stand up to such attitudes for fear that they themselves might be labeled gay or lesbian. Therefore, it is imperative to not only confront homophobia in all levels of sport, but also to educate individuals about homosexuality and the harmful effects of homophobia.

Responsibilities for those who choose to educate others on this topic include creating a safe learning environment, having a respect for difference, recognizing the legal liability of protecting the rights of LGBT athletes, fulfilling the role of community leadership, and finally, removing fear and ignorance (Griffin, Perrotti, Priest & Muska, 2002). Creating a safe learning environment means that one must acknowledge that all sports organizations include LGBT athletes, staff members, and parents, whether they are public about their sexual preference or not. Therefore, schools, athletic organizations, and other sports institutions are obligated to ensure that discriminatory practices are never to be allowed. Having a respect for difference means that coaches and other individuals in leadership roles have the responsibility to model accepting behavior towards diverse populations. These individuals should not just teach athletic skills; they should also teach athletes how to appropriately interact with people of all backgrounds.

Being aware of the legal liability in protecting the rights of LGBT athletes or those harassed under suspicion of being gay or lesbian is also important. Like with the Jennifer Harris case, institutions that allow discrimination to occur can find themselves liable for the actions of homophobic athletes and coaches. Athletes, coaches, parents, and athletic directors alike need to be aware of such rights and take action when appropriate. Next, athletes and coaches must realize that they are "highly visible community members who can influence how safe and welcoming schools and sports organizations are to students and student-athletes who feel marginalized" (Griffin, Perrotti, Priest & Muska, 2002, p. 1). What this means is that through sport, athletes and coaches are in a position of leadership in a community and should see that position as an opportunity to make all students feel safe to participate and be involved. And finally, the last responsibility of educators is to help remove fear and ignorance in the community about LGBT individuals. Whether that person is out or not, everyone has an LGBT individual in his or her life. Therefore, "young people need an opportunity to develop attitudes and beliefs based on respect for differences rather than fear or ignorance" (p. 1).

I agree with these authors that for an anti-homophobic educational program to be effective, homophobic attitudes and beliefs not only need to be confronted as Amaechi, Tuaolo, and Harris have done, but also need to be questioned and disrupted to ensure that such erroneous views no longer persist. High-profile cases of elite athletes can serve as models and inspire other LGBT athletes to come out despite the dangers that exist. It is fear and ignorance that have allowed discriminatory treatment of LGBT athletes and coaches to persist for so long, and without education, that dual-headed serpent will continue to plague both sports and American society in general. But I also argue, echoing Butler (1990), that homophobia is not just a matter of sexuality or desire but also of gender. Heterosexuality is understood by many as the correct and "natural" way to "do" gender. If the popular assumption that being a "man" or a "woman" is a "natural" product of biological sex and that heterosexual desire is a "natural" product of those gendered identities is not addressed and confronted, then programs that seek to end homophobia can never truly be successful. While communities can learn to become more tolerant of LGBT athletes and coaches, the athletes will never be fully accepted because the undercurrent of hegemonic femininity and masculinity will still exist.

Athletic communities must also be educated about gender and the impossibility for most to live up to dominant notions of masculinity and femininity. Gender must be understood as a limiting social construction, with heterosexism functioning as one of the most powerful elements in maintaining that construction. In the locker room and on the playing field (as in other social institutions), homophobia and normative gender ideals are continually being produced and reproduced, reminding gay and straight athletes alike that they need to properly perform their gender, keep quiet about any same-sex desires, and live in fear that their failure to live up to hegemonic norms may be discovered. By working to unravel and demystify both hegemonic gender norms *and* heterosexist beliefs, educators, coaches, parents, and other community leaders stand a better chance of creating safe environments for all athletes.

References

Amaechi, J. (2007a). *Man in the middle.* New York: ESPN Books.
Amaechi, J. (2007b, February 26). John Amaechi busts out. *ESPN the Magazine,* 70–74.
Anderson, E. (2002). Openly gay athletes: Contesting hegemonic masculinity in a homophobic environment. *Gender and Society,* 16(6): 860–877.
Associated Press (2007, May 5). *Amaechi says '95 percent' of feedback positive.* Retrieved May 18, 2007, from http://sports.espn.go.com/nba/news/story?id=2861621.

Belge, K. (n.d.). *Lesbians and sports*. Retrieved May 18, 2007, from http://lesbianlife.about.com/od/sports/a/RenePortland.htm.

Butler, J. (1990). *Gender trouble*. New York: Routledge.

Butler, L. (2002, October 25). *Tuaolo would have been ostracized*. Retrieved May 18, 2007, from http://sports.espn.go.com/espn/print?id=1450926&type=story.

Buzinski, J. (2002a, October 27). *No more hiding: Former NFL player Esera Tuaolo comes out: "I feel wonderful."* Retrieved May 18, 2007, from http://www.outsports.com/nfl/20021027eseramain.htm.

Buzinski, J. (2002b, November 20). *Players react to Tuaolo*. Retrieved May 18, 2007, from http://www.outsports.com/nfl/20021027eserasplayerreax.htm.

Curry, T. (1991). Fraternal bonding in the locker room: Pro-feminist analysis of talk about competition and women. *Sociology of Sport Journal, 8*, 119–135.

Dolin, N. (Producer). (2002, October 29). *Real Sports* [Television broadcast]. New York: Home Box Office.

Dworkin, S.L. & Messner, M. (2002). Just do . . . what? Sports, bodies, gender. In Scraton, S. & Flintoff, A. (Eds.) *Gender and sport: A reader* (pp. 17–29). New York: Routledge.

Dworkin, S.L. & Wachs, F.L. (2000). The morality/manhood paradox: Masculinity, sport, and the media. In McKay, J., Messner, M. & Sabo, D. (Eds.). *Masculinities, gender relations, and sport* (pp. 47–66). Thousand Oaks, CA: Sage Publications.

ESPN.com news services (2007a, February 8). *NBA local special: February 8*. Retrieved May 18, 2007, from http://sports.espn.go.com/nba/news/story?page=nbalocal/amaechi.

ESPN.com news services (2007b, February 12). *Cuban says openly gay player would clean up*. Retrieved May 18, 2007, from http://sports.espn.go.com/nba/news/story?id=2762656.

ESPN.com news services (2007c, February 14). *Retired NBA star Hardaway says he hates 'gay people.'* Retrieved May 18, 2007, from http://sports.espn.go.com/nba/news/story?id=2766213.

Figel, B. (1986, June 16). Lesbians in world of athletics. *The Chicago Sun-Times*, p. 119.

Gatz, M., Messner, M. & Ball-Rokeach, S. (2002). *Paradoxes of youth and sport*. Albany, NY: SUNY Press.

Griffin, P. (2002). Changing the game: Homophobia, sexism, and lesbians in sport. In Scraton, S. & Flintoff, A. (Eds.). *Gender and sport: A reader*. New York: Routledge.

Griffin, P. (2007). *Settling can mean victory*. Retrieved May 18, 2007, from http://outsports.com/campus/2007/0206harris.htm.

Griffin, P., Perrotti, J., Priest, L. & Muska, M. (2002). It takes a team! Making sports safe for lesbian, gay, bisexual, and transgender athletes and coaches. *Women's Sports Foundation*.

Kaufman, K. (2003, January 8). *Football: America's favorite homoerotic sport*. Retrieved May 18, 2007, from http://www.salon.com/news/sports/col/kaufman/2003/01/08/homoerotic/print.html.

Lenskyj, H. (1986). *Out of bounds: Women, sport and sexuality*. Toronto: Women's Press.

Lenskyj, H. (2003). *Out on the field: Gender, sport, and sexualities*. Toronto: Canadian Scholars' Press.

McKay, J., Messner, M. & Sabo, D. (Eds.). (2000). *Masculinities, gender relations, and sport*. Thousand Oaks, CA: Sage Publications.

Messner, M. (1992). *Power at play: Sports and the problem of masculinity*. Boston: Beacon Press.

Messner, M. (1994). Women in the men's locker room? In Messner, M. & Sabo, D. (Eds.). *Sex, violence, and power in sports: rethinking masculinity* (pp. 42–52). Freedom, CA: The Crossing Press.

Messner, M. & Sabo, D. (1994). *Sex, violence, and power in sports: Rethinking masculinity*. Freedom, CA: The Crossing Press.

Messner, M. & Stevens, M. (2002). Scoring without consent: Confronting male athletes' violence against women. In Gatz, M., Messner, M. & Ball-Rokeach, S. (Eds.). *Paradoxes of youth and sport* (pp. 225–239). Albany, NY; SUNY Press.

Pronger, B. (1990). *The arena of masculinity: Sport, homosexuality, and the meaning of sex*. New York: St. Martin's.

Pronger, B. (1999). Outta my endzone: Sport and the territorial anus. *Journal of Sport and Social Issues,* 23(4): 373–389.

Swoopes, S. (2006, April 12). *Outside the arc.* Retrieved June 1, 2007, from http://sports.espn .go.com/wnba/news/story?id=2204322.

Zeigler, C. (2002). *A New York Giants' gay problem.* Retrieved June 1, 2007, from http://outsports .com/nfl/2002/0922shockeystern.htm.

Zeigler, C. (2007). *Pro sports now ready for gay athletes.* Retrieved May 18, 2007, from http://www .outsports.com/nba/20062007/0214sportsready.htm.

8

Title IX Literacy

What Every Citizen Should Know about Title IX, Gender Equity, and College Sport

Ellen J. Staurowsky

O N A FALL FRIDAY AFTERNOON IN LATE September of 2006, James Madison University (JMU) officials assembled athletes in their convocation center to share the news that seven men's teams (swimming, cross country, indoor and outdoor track, gymnastics, wrestling, and archery) and three women's teams (gymnastics, fencing, and archery) would be eliminated by the next academic year ("JMU Enacts," 2006). Simultaneously, members of the JMU Board of Visitors along with Dr. Linwood Rose, president of JMU, held a press conference to announce the news to media outlets. Due to the fact that the cross country teams were competing away from campus that day, David Rinker received word of the elimination of two of the sports he coached (men's cross country and track) via cell phone during the middle of the meet. Imagine the scene as runners finished an exciting race, only to encounter their coach in tears, blindsided by the realization that the fate of the men's team and his own future had been determined in their absence (Pennington, 2006, 2007).

The arresting thought that athletes and coaches could leave their home institution on a given day, focusing on nothing other than the hope of a promising meet ahead, only to return in turmoil despite a successful performance is haunting. In explaining the decision to eliminate nearly a third of their entire athletic program, the JMU Board of Visitors explained that the plan was a response to an "insurmountable challenge" to comply with Title IX of the Education Amendments of 1972, due to the athletics program being "unusually large for a public university" of its size ("JMU Enacts," 2006). Offering assurances that every avenue had been explored prior to reaching the decision, associate vice president of communications Andy Perrine elaborated, "We would not have done it [cut teams] if not for Title IX. There was just about no way we could add more women's programs and afford it and be in compliance" (Redden, 2006).

In the aftermath of the announcement, students from the affected sports and their allies rallied on campus to voice their opposition to the decision and their frustration with the federal law that they were led to believe had dictated that the cuts occur (Staurowsky, 2006). Finding support from the College Sports Council (CSC), an organization whose stated mission is the "reform of Title IX," a protest that drew a crowd of between 100 and 150 athletes and coaches was staged in front of the U.S. Department of Education (USDOE) in November of 2006, calling for government officials to intervene (Goldenbach, 2006; McCarthy Communications, 2006).

Taking a position that Title IX is no longer necessary because "more females are interested in sports and female enrollment outpaces male enrollment," the rally concluded with protesters running several laps around the building and meeting with USDOE officials to air their grievances (Lemke, 2006). With the assistance of the CSC and the Pacific Legal Fund, affected JMU athletes filed suit against the United States Department of Education and James Madison University, seeking to stop the elimination of the teams and alleging that the enforcement scheme of Title IX has a disparate impact on male athletes (*Equity in Athletics, Inc. v. U.S. Department of Education and James Madison University*, June 2007). The 2007–2008 academic year opened with JMU executing its intended plan to downsize its athletic program. The preliminary injunction sought by Equity in Athletics, Inc., to prevent the cutting of the teams at James Madison, was denied by U.S. District Court Judge Glen E. Conrad in August of 2007.

As often happens in cases where cuts in athletic programs garner media attention and the ingredients for a Title IX controversy exist, the JMU case has become a focal point around which various groups have registered concerns. While Eric Pearson of the CSC called for a more "athlete-centered" approach to providing sport opportunities on college campuses, Marcia Greenberger of the National Women's Law Center observed that JMU erred on two fronts: first by cutting men's and women's sports, and second by falsely attributing those cuts to the requirements of Title IX (Goldenbach, 2006). Whether Title IX reformer or advocate, it is notable that the JMU case generated agreement on both sides that reductions in teams and athletic opportunities was not a desirable course of action or in the best interests of either female or male athletes (Lemke, 2006; Lopiano, 2006a). In point of fact, USDOE spokesman Chad Colby reiterated that the Office for Civil Rights (OCR), the office charged with Title IX enforcement, is "always concerned when schools choose to eliminate or reduce opportunities for [their] students and has strongly discouraged such actions as a means of complying with Title IX" (Lemke, 2006).

In an unprecedented step, the chief executive officer of the United States Olympic Committee (USOC), James Scherr, publicly challenged JMU's position, writing, "We have seen universities across the nation inappropriately use Title IX as an excuse to eliminate sport programs" (Dixit, 2006). Alison Truglio, one of the JMU gymnasts whose team was cut, did not join her colleagues in protesting Title IX. In an interview with the *Washington Post*, she commented, "I do think that Title IX has nothing to do with this decision. It is possible my peers are directing their energy in the wrong direction. It's sad that JMU felt obligated to take these opportunities away from us" (Goldenbach, 2006). In a speech before the National Press Club in October of 2006, Myles Brand, president of the National Collegiate Athletic Association (NCAA), similarly commented that institutions have unfairly used Title IX as an excuse to cut men's teams. As he put it, this kind of restructuring is the result of "institutional priorities and financial circumstances . . . not the unintended consequences of Title IX" (p. 13).

The notion that cutting athletic teams could remedy concerns about gender equity on the JMU campus emerged during the 2000–2001 academic year in a report issued by a group called the Centennial Sports Committee (University Council Minutes, 2000–2001). In minutes from a University Council meeting, students expressed concerns that they had not been adequately represented and that the committee had failed to publicly address alternative proposals to eliminated sport programs. Significant to what would eventually happen in September of 2006, students identified among their concerns about the process unfolding at JMU that "Title IX, the federal gender equity statute that is cited as the prompt for the Committee's proposal, was not intended to eliminate opportunities but to enhance them" (University Council Minutes, November 2, 2000–2001). A news release issued by JMU echoed a similar understanding in February of 2001. In explaining the decision at that time to keep twenty-eight sports: "A university spokesman said the university administration's recommendation was made with the belief that the framers of Title IX did not intend for compliance efforts to result in the elimination of men's sports opportunities" ("Keep All 28," 2001).

As consumers of Title IX controversies playing out on the airwaves and on the web, in the blogosphere and in the news, and sometimes on our own campuses, how are we to make sense of the disparate readings of what happened at JMU? The dramatic cuts and traumatic effect of JMU's decision on their athletes and student body warrant sympathy. At the same time, the lingering question of whether Title IX was the culprit is one that deserves careful scrutiny, especially in light of the fact that James Madison University was, at one time, an all-women's institution. With a rich history of offering "opportunities for women in sports when many other colleges and universities did not," one wonders why JMU had such difficulty complying with the equity considerations under Title IX ("Dr. Lee Morrison," n.d.).

The JMU case is an instructive one for exploring a list of persistent questions that circulate about Title IX, program cuts, and college sport decision making. When confronted with headlines and news stories about Title IX being a "perversion of the law" that unfairly penalizes male athletes (Lopez, 2006; Swift, 2006), are most Americans literate enough about Title IX's requirements to make an informed decision on these issues? Does Title IX require the cutting of men's sports in order to achieve compliance? Were the cuts at JMU really prompted by Title IX, or did other issues factor into the decision-making process? Do men have fewer opportunities to compete in college programs as a result of Title IX? The remainder of this chapter will address each of these questions and finish with a few thoughts about the significance of the James Madison example.

Does Title IX Require Cutting Men's Sports?

Featured prominently in discussions about the JMU case is a measure of Title IX compliance in the athletic participation area referred to as "the three-part test." Under this test, institutions can comply with Title IX by (1) offering athletic opportunities that are substantially proportionate to the representation of men and women in the student body, (2) expanding athletic opportunities for the underrepresented sex, or (3) fully accommodating the interests and abilities of the underrepresented sex (National Women's Law Center, 2007; United States Department of Education, 1996). (See textboxes 8.1–8.3 for more details on the specifics of the three-part test.)

The construction of the test provides insight about the choices available and the latitude higher education administrators have in developing gender equity compliance plans that not only satisfy Title IX requirements but also most favorably serve students. Importantly, the test requires schools to work towards equality, but recognizes that compliance may entail a long-term process (Tracy & Fromson, 2002, p. 3).

When analyzing the facts in the James Madison case, alternatives to cutting sports are evident. In 2004–2005, during the time institutional decision makers were considering options, females comprised 61 percent of the overall student population compared to 47 percent of the athlete population ("JMUE Enacts," 2006). Given James Madison's failure to meet the first part of the three-part test, the university could have added women's teams in response to existing levels of interest and the abilities of female athletes on their campus.

What this analysis demonstrates is that James Madison was not in compliance with Title IX at the time the announcement regarding program cuts was made. However, what remains to be determined is whether the cuts in the athletic department were motivated by a desire to address the needs of female students on their campus or other considerations.

TEXTBOX 8.1
Title IX—The Three-Part Test: Part 1

Substantial Proportionality—The percentage of female-to-male students in the general student population is about the same as the percentage of female-to-male students in the athlete population. Although there is no specific percentage that the Office for Civil Rights uses to determine when a school meets the substantial proportionality standard, generally that figure is 1 percent to 3 percent (Acosta & Carpenter, 2004).

How did James Madison fare on the substantial proportionality standard at the time the cuts were announced (data drawn from 2005–2006 EADA report)?

Percent of females in the general student population: 61 percent
Percent of females in the athlete population: 47 percent
The gap: 14 percent

Note: The percentages above reflect unduplicated numbers!

TEXTBOX 8.2
Title IX—The Three-Part Test: Part 2

History and Continuing Practice of Program Expansion—This part of the test looks at the record of program expansion for the underrepresented sex, which most often is female (United States Department of Education, 1996).

How did James Madison fare on the program expansion standard? At the time the program cuts were announced, JMU had not added a women's sport in seven years (in 2001, softball was added as a varsity sport) ("James Madison University," 2005–2006).

Could James Madison argue that it had a "continuing practice" of program expansion? The elimination of women's archery, fencing, and gymnastics precludes a determination that JMU had a continuing practice of expanding opportunities for female athletes within its athletic program.

> **TEXTBOX 8.3**
> **Title IX—The Three-Part Test: Part 3**
>
> Fully Accommodating Interests and Abilities—There are numerous ways that an institution can determine if the interests and abilities of female athletes are being met. Some of those include requests for sports to be converted to varsity status, number of teams participating in intramurals, participation in physical education, responses to surveys, and teams that exist within regions and at the conference level (Cantu, 1996; Manning, 2005). Another way is by assessing participation of females in club sport activities.
>
> On the JMU campus, female athletes are active in an array of club sports from equestrian to rugby to water polo (James Madison University, 2010).

Did Other Considerations Impact the Decision to Cut Programs at JMU?

At the time of the announcement, the university stated that there was simply not enough money available to continue to fund existing programs and address the requirements of Title IX. In effect, the institution decided that certain athletic programs could not be run as "loss leaders" any longer. From a financial accounting perspective, this makes perfect sense. However, the elimination of ten sports resulted in the recovery of approximately a half a million dollars ($550,000), which would be redistributed within the athletic program to fully fund the remaining women's programs, partially fund men's golf and tennis teams, and increase scholarships for selected women's and men's teams ("Title IX Statement," 2007). Whereas the institution did not wish to encumber further debt by adding women's programs, it is nevertheless notable that the football team, according to data in the institution's Equity in Athletics Disclosure report for 2005–2006, reported an $800,000 deficit that year in operating budget. Additionally, when comparing deficits for the 2004–2005 fiscal year based on NCAA reports, football ran a deficit in excess of $250,000 while all of the other non-revenue-producing sports combined (men's and women's) amounted to a deficit close to $33,500 (Alesia, 2006).

The financial hardships identified with the minor sports are also problematic when considered in light of the opening of a new $10 million athletic facility designed to primarily meet the needs of the football program. Whereas the campaign for the Plecker Athletic Performance Center generated "the largest amount of donations ever made for a JMU project," it is significant that $2.8 million for the completion of that project was drawn from "JMU reserves and other non-tax sources" (Staff, 2003).

From a public perspective, as well as from the perspective of what is passed on to future generations of college students seeking to understand the motivations behind a plan of this kind, the representation of Title IX as the promoter of unreasonable and irrational decision making serves to obscure the institutional values and priorities reflected in the JMU decision. Beyond the obvious impediment to the belief that women's interests were at the core of this decision, as seen in the incongruous cutting of women's sports within this plan and the anticipated scholarship benefits that would eventually accrue for both female and male athletes, there is also the matter of football's strategic absence from the rationale at the time the cuts were announced (Staurowsky, 2006).

The plan to cut sports at JMU coincided with the timing of the Colonial Athletic Association's (CAA) sponsorship of football starting in the fall of 2007. The CAA released this statement, regarding the caliber of football to be played in the conference: "The conference is already considered one of the finest in Division I-AA football, having produced the past two national champions in Delaware (2003) and James Madison (2004) and three of the last seven with Massachusetts claiming the title in 1998. Ten of the twelve teams have reached the Division I-AA playoffs at least once in the past five years" (CAA, 2007).[1]

By examining this part of the overall JMU athletic program story, we begin to see that the issues facing the athletic department were not merely about gender equity, but were attributable to the institutional decision to participate in a conference where the level of competition requires that financial resources be distributed to a select group of sports. A comparison of the allocation of resources within the JMU athletic department reveals that competing in the CAA creates considerable strain. As is shown in Figures 8.1 and 8.2, James Madison devoted 6 percent more to football and 5 percent less to their other men's non-revenue sports compared to other NCAA Division I-AA programs in 2005–2006.

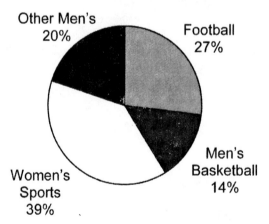

FIGURE 8.1
NCAA Division I-AA Budget Breakdown (2005–2006 EADA Report)
Adapted from: James Madison University Equity in Athletics Disclosure Act Report, 2005–2006. Retrieved December 4, 2006, from http://ope.ed.gov/athletics/InstDetail.asp.

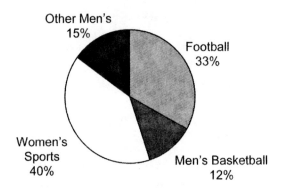

FIGURE 8.2
James Madison Budget Breakdown (2005–2006) EADA Report
Adapted from: James Madison University Equity in Athletics Disclosure Act Report, 2005–2006. Retrieved December 4, 2006, from http://ope.ed.gov/athletics/InstDetail.asp.

A consideration of the budget streams that contribute to the overall profitability of each program within the JMU athletic department deserves attention, as well. For example, according to a revenue statement submitted to the NCAA for the year 2004–2005, JMU football reported revenue just under $3 million (Alesia, 2006). However, over half of that revenue came from student fees. Out of a $21 million budget for the entire athletic department, close to $18 million, or 85 percent, came from student fees (ibid.). Whereas the vast majority of NCAA institutions rely on subsidies to support their sport programs (Fitzpatrick, 2007), JMU's heavy reliance on a student fee structure to fund the athletic program reveals the appropriateness of asking whether the athletic department is in compliance with Title IX. Given the fact that 61 percent of the student body is female, the majority of female students on the JMU campus are paying for both men and women to compete. The institution's strategic refusal to increase opportunities for female athletes while cutting men's sports not only hurt the male athletes involved but ensured that female students on the JMU campus would be taxed disproportionately to support men's athletics, even with the cuts that were made.

Do Men Have Fewer Opportunities as a Result of Title IX?

As the above analysis shows, the cause-and-effect relationship often attributed to Title IX and program cuts obscures the underlying priorities taken into account when a college or university athletic program is restructured in the manner done by James Madison. Thus, the restructuring was a reflection of the need to reorder priorities and to use scarce resources in a way that would allow the university to successfully compete in an increasingly competitive conference in football and other sports. As athletic director Jeff Bourne acknowledged in the weeks following the announcement, "the broad elimination of teams was necessary for the future management of the athletics program" (Lipka, 2006).

Regardless of motive, the cuts in the athletic program at James Madison tapped into the fears of many that Title IX has been responsible for reducing opportunities for male athletes on college campuses. But is this fear grounded in facts or misperceptions?

Contrary to claims that men's athletic participation has seriously declined over time, research findings indicate that declines have occurred in selected men's sports, but not in the overall pattern of participation. As Cheslock (2007) reports, "participation in men's wrestling and tennis declined substantially over time, but other men's sports (football, baseball, lacrosse and soccer) experienced much larger gains" (p. 3). More specifically, while opportunities were lost for male athletes in the sports of tennis (−678 athletes) and wrestling (−488) in 738 NCAA institutions during the decade between 1995–1996 and 2004–2005, the number of athletes in four other men's sports grew by much larger amounts. During the same period of time, increased male participation occurred in football (+4,056), baseball (+1,561), lacrosse (+1,091), and soccer (+758).

Examining the trends more closely, Cheslock (2007) also found that in 1,895 institutions aligned with the major intercollegiate athletic organizations, including the National Collegiate Athletic Association (NCAA), National Association of Intercollegiate Athletics (NAIA), National Christian Collegiate Athletic Association (NCCAA), and National Junior College Athletic Association (NJCAA), overall increases in men's participation levels were realized (2007).

It is the case that increases in women's programs have outpaced those for men's; however, these differences are to be expected, especially as college and university athletic programs change to meet increased female enrollments and the demands of gender equity. It is notable, however, that the pace of change has slowed as we have entered the 2000s. As shown below, between 1981–1982 and 1998–1999, there was an 81 percent increase in the number of female participants in college sports (+72,683) compared to a 5 percent increase among male participants (+11,688) (see table 8.1). During the time period between 2001–2002 and 2004–2005, female athlete participation increased by 11,043,

TABLE 8.1
Changes in Intercollegiate Athletic Participation by Gender from 1981–1999

Gender	1981–1982	1998–1999	Change in Number of Participants	Percentage Change
Female	90,100	162,783	72,683	81%
Male	220,178	231,866	11,688	5%

Source: National Coalition for Women and Girls in Education (NCWGE). (2007, May 10). Title IX athletics policies: Issues and data for educational decision makers. Retrieved April 23, 2008, from http://www.ncwge .org/.

TABLE 8.2
Changes in Intercollegiate Athletic Participation by Gender, 2001–2004

Gender	2001–2002	2004–2005	Change	Percentage Change
Female	198,623	209,666	11,043	5.6%
Male	285,215	295,180	9,965	3.5%

Source: National Coalition for Women and Girls in Education (NCWGE). (2007, May 10). Title IX athletics policies: Issues and data for educational decision makers. Retrieved April 23, 2008, from http://www.ncwge.org/.

representing only a 5.6 percent change, while male participation increased by 9,965, representing a 3.5 percent change (see table 8.2). This slowing in the growth of athletic opportunities suggests that "progress towards more equitable participation numbers for men and women has been stalled" (Cheslock, 2007, p. 4).

The only level within college sport where men's participation has declined is in NCAA Division I-A. At the same time, men's participation in NCAA Divisions II and III has increased, while men's participation in Divisions I-AA and I-AAA (non-football-playing schools) has remained stable. This phenomenon lends credence to the argument that cutbacks in men's sports in Division I institutions occur most frequently at the pressure points between college sport and escalating commercial interests. This is seen in the increasing amounts of money being spent on the sports where most of the corporate attention is directed: football and men's basketball. Within the context of what has been described as the college sports "arms race," in which 70 to 80 percent of budgets are being devoted to those two sports at the Division I-A level, maintaining market position becomes the central organizing principle for athletic department decisions (Lopiano, 2006a). For institutions that have limited financial means to draw upon, program cuts signal programmatic and economic shifts—schools no longer able to compete at higher levels within their existing business models must make difficult decisions in order to remain financially and competitively viable. As economist Roger Noll (1999) wrote about college sport and the high cost of winning, ". . . for major sports outside the top group of colleges, intercollegiate athletics is a financial drain" (p. 25).[2] An alternative, which was certainly available to James Madison, would have been to play in a lower division.

Final Thoughts

Whereas the JMU case has been presented at times in the press and elsewhere as a cautionary tale about the unreasonable demands of Title IX, the lessons to be learned from this case are best found in the business model in place, which established program priorities well in advance of the final decision to cut sports.

In 1998, the JMU athletic department underwent a significant organizational change, committing to maintaining twenty-eight varsity sports but electing to fund scholarships for only thirteen of those programs. With that decision, the athletic department adopted a tier system among the sponsored teams ("Institution Self-Study Instrument Report," 2005–2006).

Programs within the department were placed into four tiers, with sports in the top two tiers receiving both operating and scholarship support up to the NCAA limits, while the remaining fifteen sports were designed to receive operational support only. There was a further expectation for the teams in the top two tiers that they would "consistently perform among the top teams in their conference and frequently appear in national rankings" (p. 50). Athletic teams at JMU were classified into tiers according to the following configuration in 2005–2006:

- Tier One
  - Men's Sports—Football, Basketball
  - Women's Sports—Basketball
- Tier Two
  - Men's Sports—Baseball, Soccer
  - Women's Sports—Cross Country, Field Hockey, Indoor Track, Lacrosse, Outdoor Track, Soccer, Softball, Volleyball
- Tier Three
  - Men's Sports—Cross Country, Golf, Gymnastics, Indoor Track, Outdoor Track, Swimming/Diving, Tennis, Wrestling
  - Women's Sports – Golf, Gymnastics, Swimming/Diving, Tennis
- Tier Four
  - Men's Sports – Archery
  - Women's Sports – Archery, Fencing

Within the context of this configuration, JMU elected to effectively eliminate the bottom two tiers of their overall program, investing resources in the programs designed to perform well in the conference and rank in the national polls on a frequent basis. When examined in this light, JMU had attempted to maintain a balance between the competing models of commercial college sport and participatory college sport within its athletic program. When a move to the more competitive Colonial Athletic Association no longer allowed for that balance to be sustained, the lower tiers were most vulnerable to elimination.

James Madison's decision to situate their athletic program as they have within Division I-AA is a matter of institutional autonomy, an assertion of what some call academic freedom. The idea that 144 athletes' lives are forever changed—their trust in their alma mater violated, and their opportunities to participate in college sport cut short—is deeply troubling. At the same time, James Madison University officials exercised institutional prerogatives in a fashion similar to what other higher education administrators do when academic departments are retrenched or eliminated in favor of redistributing resources to support flagship programs. As Donna Lopiano, former CEO of the Women's Sports Foundation, pointed out, "The question that should be asked by alumni and students in either case is whether it has the resources or appetite to pursue such an objective and whether the outcome, even if achieved, justifies the means" (2006a).

To identify Title IX as the cause of the events that occurred at James Madison is to misinterpret the requirements of Title IX. There is nothing in the legislation or regulatory scheme that requires colleges and universities to participate at a given divisional level or to emphasize certain sports over others. These decisions are left to administrators on individual campuses. Title IX comes into play after those priorities are established and equity is then defined in accordance with the philosophical position of the institution. Though invoking Title IX incited anger and calls for reform, the mechanisms for reinstating those eliminated teams were unlikely to come out of a claim of reverse discrimination. A case for reinstatement would need to be directed toward the fundamental decision made by JMU to compete in Division I-AA, given their resources and reliance on student fees.

To characterize female enrollment as problematic—as James Madison did in its rationale for eliminating athletic teams—should be viewed as the affront to fairness that it is. As can be seen in table 8.3, the institution expanded their enrollment by one-third during the decade between 1996–1997 and 2005–2006, relying more and more heavily on female enrollment to sustain that growth model. Thus, if 85 percent of the athletic budget is based on student fees and 61 percent of those student fees are being provided by female students, why should the institution be so reluctant to offer athletic opportunities at a rate consistent with that level of contribution?

In closing, if there is hope to be found in the James Madison case, it is in the loyalty female athletes showed toward the affected male athletes. Some of the most vocal champions calling for JMU to reconsider its position were female athletes, most notably Jennifer Chapman, a cross country and track athlete at JMU who was also chair of the athlete advisory board. It was Chapman who served as the liaison between the affected men's teams and lawyers for the group that attempted to contest JMU's decision in court, moved to action because she witnessed what she believed to be unfair treatment of her male colleagues (Brady, 2007; Goldenbach, 2007; Pennington, 2006).

Contrary to claims about the "unintended consequences" of Title IX, it was the intention of Title IX that female and male athletes have access to an athletic education that would foster and promote mutual respect and appreciation. The fact that female athletes were willing, in partnership with and on behalf of male athletes, to speak up and engage in activism to resist the cuts made at JMU may never have surfaced if not for Title IX.

TABLE 8.3
James Madison University Student Enrollment and Athlete Participation Rates

Year	Undergraduate Enrollment				Athletes				Substantial Proportionality
	Male	% Male	Female	% Female	Male	% Male	Female	%Female	
2005–06	6,422	38.81	10,124	61.19	361	49.72	365	50.28	–10.91
2004–05	5,805	39.55	8,872	60.45	371	53.23	326	46.77	–13.68
2003–04	5,697	39.69	8,657	60.31	379	50.40	373	49.60	–10.71
2002–03	6,484	40.61	9,481	59.39	414	53.21	364	46.79	–12.6
2001–02	5,930	41.17	8,472	58.83	387	50.85	374	49.15	–9.28
2000–01	5,391	39.00	8,433	61.00	457	54.86	376	45.14	–15.86
1999–00	5,565	42.21	7,620	57.79	457	59.27	314	40.73	–17.07
1998–99	5,522	43.22	7,254	56.78	358	58.02	259	41.98	–14.8
1997–98	5,363	44.14	6,786	55.86	348	58.39	248	41.61	–14.25
1996–97	5,001	44.62	6,208	55.38	350	60.34	230	39.66	–15.73

Source: For the years 2003–2004 through 2005–2006, data was taken directly from the Equity in Athletics Data Analysis Cutting Tool, from http://www.ope.edu.gov/athletics/SelectDownloadOptions.aspx.
For reporting years prior to 2003–2004, data was found at the Chronicle of Higher Education Gender Equity Project database: Chronicle of Higher Education. (2006). Gender equity in college sport. Retrieved November 1, 2006, from http://www.chronicle.com/stats/genderequity.

However, for all of the goodwill this kind of support represents, so long as institutions are not fully forthcoming about their reasons for embracing the value system at the core of a commercial model of college sport that emphasizes participation for the few in a highly competitive atmosphere, and opt instead to mislead athletes and the general public about the causes of program cuts, there is a terrible danger that college and university officials will pit the interests of female athletes against the interests of male athletes in a way that does justice to neither the higher ideals of the academy nor the professional standards of truth telling that form the ethical core of higher education. To set up Title IX smokescreens further undermines the ability of the citizenry to hold institutions accountable for continuing sex discrimination.

Until institutions are more forthcoming about their motivations, those confronted with controversies about cutbacks in college sport programs will need to develop the Title IX literacy necessary to distinguish motives and the political forces at work in triggering fears about the mistreatment of men in situations, like the James Madison case, where women's interests were actually undermined as well. The stakes are high for our democracy and our culture if we fail to comprehend that the playing fields of our country can be sites for the enactment of important lessons about treating each other as equals. The stakes are equally high if institutions of higher education intentionally set up scenarios that lead to the populace harboring hostility towards legal mechanisms designed to remedy sex discrimination.

The way to achieve Title IX compliance is elegantly mapped out in the three-part test. When seen for what it is, the three-part test serves as a road map for how to progressively and temperately make equitable provision for female athletes, if only the athletic community would take heed and commit. But Title IX requires something that is difficult to acquire in the present athletic structure. It requires a creative and bold rethinking of the commonly held assumptions and practices at the core of the athletic enterprise—a gender-integrated mind-set, as it were, to address the challenges of a gender-segregated structure. As Welch Suggs (2007) argues persuasively, "Parents, coaches, and athletics administrators need to take a fresh look at what gender equity really means." Real change will come when current and future decision makers no longer view Title IX compliance as a chore or a mandate or a problem, but as an invitation to invest in the next generation. Those who are Title IX literate, who can see through the smokescreens, will be better able to formulate solutions that are in the best interests of female and male students.

Notes

1. NCAA Division I-AA has since been renamed the Football Championship Series (FCS). Data for the years cited were organized under the label NCAA Division I-AA, thus the use of the term here. As an informational item, JMU football reported a record of 8-4 in its first year in the Colonial

Athletic Association and played Appalachian State in the playoffs. Appalachian State made head-lines during the fall of 2007 when it beat Michigan early in the season.

2. Economically, the NCAA continues to expand the business enterprise of sport in a way that blurs the distinctions between professional and amateur sport. In February of 2008, International Management Group (IMG) continued to expand its accumulation of collegiate marketing rights, joining CBS in selling NCAA packages (Gallagher & Byrne, 2008). The NCAA also announced in January of 2008 an agreement with TicketReserve, which will increase revenue from Final Four ticket sales through the secondary ticket market (Hopkins, 2008). As all of these ventures move forward, wealth accumulation will pool among the established powers, creating a greater likelihood that the gap that already exists between Division I-A and I-AA will create even greater strain on those schools trying to maintain market position.

References

Acosta, V. & Carpenter, L. (2004). *Title IX.* Champaign, IL: Human Kinetics Publishers.

Alesia, M. (2006). "NCAA financial reports database 2004–2005." Retrieved from http://www2 .indystar.com/NCAA_financial_reports/.

Brady, E. (2007, April 19). "James Madison's hard cuts spur Title IX." *USA Today.* Retrieved February 25, 2007, from http://www.usatoday.com/sports/college/other/2007-04-19-title-ix -jmu-cover_N.htm.

Brand, M. (2006, October 30). "Speech to the National Press Club." Retrieved December 4, 2006, from http://www.ncaa.org.

Cantu, N. (1996). "Clarification of intercollegiate athletics policy guidance. The three-part test." Retrieved May 14, 2010, from http://www2.ed.gov/about/offices/list/ocr/docs/clarific.html.

Cheslock, J. (2007). "Who is playing college sports?" Retrieved February 15, 2007, from http://www .womenssportsfoundation.org.

Chronicle of Higher Education. (2008). "Gender equity in college sports database. James Madison University 1995–96 to 2005–06." Retrieved March 1, 2008, from http://www.chronicle.com/.

Colonial Athletic Association. (2007). "CAA football announces 2007 schedule." Retrieved April 23, 2008, from http://www.caasports.org.

Conrad, G. (2007). "Opinion in Equity in Athletics, Inc. v. Department of Education et al." Retrieved May 14, 2010, from http://docs.justia.com/cases/federal/district-courts/virginia/ vawdce/5:2007cv00028/63921/79/0.pdf.

Dixit, R. (2006, October 19). "USOC protest cuts: U.S. Olympics Committee interferes for first time in Title IX compliance." *The Breeze.* Retrieved October 30, 2006, from http://www.thebreeze .org/2006/10-19/top2.html.

"Dr. Lee Morrison." (n.d.) The Morrison-Bruce Center for the Promotion of Physical Activity for Girls and Women, James Madison University. Retrieved December 4, 2006, from http://www.jmu .edu/kinesiology/cppagw/leemorrison.htm.

Equity in Athletics, Inc. v. U.S. Department of Education and James Madison University. (2007, June 1). Civil Action No. 5-07-0028-GEC.

"Fall 2005 on-campus enrollment summary." (2005, December). James Madison University Office of Institutional Research. Retrieved December 4, 2006, from http://www.jmu.edu/instresrch/ notes/Vol19no5.pdf.

Fitzpatrick, F. (2007, June 15). Most Division I colleges have to subsidize sports, NCAA finds. *Philadel-phia Inquirer.* Retrieved May 14, 2010, from http://coia.comm.psu.edu/News%20of%20interest/ Most%20Division%20I%20colleges%20have%20to%20subsidize%20sports%20-%20Philly%20 Inquirer%2015%20May%2007.pdf.

Gallagher, J. & Byrne, K. (2008, February 26). "CBS Sports partners with IMG College as sales representatives for NCAA Corporate Champion and Partner Program." Retrieved May 14, 2010, from http://www.imgworld.com/press_room/fullstory.sps?iCategoryID=&iNewsid=535794&iType=13708.

Goldenbach, A. (2006, November 3). "Title IX protest at Education Department Highlights JMU's cuts." *Washington Post.* Retrieved February 25, 2007, from http://www.washingtonpost.com/wpdyn/content/article/2006/11/02/AR2006110201530.html.

"History of James Madison University." James Madison University. (n.d.). Retrieved December 4, 2006, from http://web.jmu.edu/history/.

Hopkins, M. (2008). "Ticket reserve makes 2008 face-value NCAA Men's Final Four tickets available." Press release available at http://www.ncaa.org.

"Institution Self-Study Instrument Report: Equity and student-athlete welfare." James Madison University. (2005–2006). Retrieved March 1, 2008, from http://www.jmu.edu.

"James Madison University Equity in Athletics Disclosure Act Report, 2005–2006." Retrieved December 4, 2006, from http://ope.ed.gov/athletics/InstDetail.asp.

"James Madison University Recreation: Sport Club Teams." James Madison University. (2010). Retrieved April 3, 2010, from http://www.jmu.edu/recreation/Programs/SportClubs/teams.html.

"JMU enacts proportionality plan to comply with Title IX." James Madison University Staff. (2006, September 29). Retrieved September 30, 2006, from http://www.jmu.edu/jmuweb/general/news/general7490.shtml.

"Keep all 28 sports teams, JMU administration recommends." James Madison University press release. (2001, Feb. 22). Retrieved April 26, 2007, from http://www.jmu.edu/mediarel/PR-this release.asp?AutoID=465.

King, C. (2006, November). *James Madison University administrative & finance newsletter.* Retrieved December 4, 2006, from http://www.jmu.edu/adminfinance/news/nov2006.shtml.

Lefton, T. (2008, Feb. 25). "IMG will join CBS in selling NCAA packages." *Street & Smith's Sports-Business Journal.* Retrieved March 1, 2008, from http://www.sportsbusinessjournal.com.

Lemke, T. (2006, November 3). "Group protests Title IX." *The Washington Times,* pp. C01.

Lipka, S. (2006, November 17). "James Madison U. athletes protest at Education Department cuts in the name of Title IX." *The Chronicle of Higher Education.* Retrieved May 14, 2010, from http://chronicle.com/article/James-Madison-U-Athletes/22089/.

Lopez, K. J. (2006, November 15). "*Ms.*ing the point." *National Review.* Retrieved May 14, 2010, from http://article.nationalreview.com/298594/imsiing-the-point/kathryn-jean-lopez.

Lopiano, D. (2006a, October 6). "Public comment: James Madison University's decision to cut women's sports." Retrieved April 29, 2007, from http://www.womenssportsfoundation.org.

Lopiano, D. (2006b, November). "James Madison University and Title IX: Myths and facts." Retrieved December 4, 2006, from http://www.womenssportsfoundation.org/cgi-bin/iowa/issues/disc/article.html?record=1158.

Manning, J. (2005, March 17). "Additional clarification of intercollegiate athletics policy: Three-part test—Part three." Retrieved May 14, 2010, from http://www.totalncaa.net/wps/wcm/connect/9e784b804e0d9725b0d5f01ad6fc8b25/title9guidanceadditional.pdf?MOD=AJPERES&CACHEID=9e784b804e0d9725b0d5f01ad6fc8b25.

McCarthy Communications. (2006). "JMU's reform Title IX rally in front of the U.S. Department of Education." Retrieved April 23, 2008, from http://www.mccarthycommunications.net/photos/.

National Coalition for Women and Girls in Education (NCWGE). (2007, May 10). "Title IX athletics policies: Issues and data for educational decision makers." Retrieved April 23, 2008, from http://www.ncwge.org/.

Noll, R. (1999). "The business of college sports and the high cost of winning." *The Milken Institute Review*. Retrieved March 1, 2008, from http://www.milkeninstitute.org/publications/publications .taf?function=detail&ID=185&cat=MIR.

Pennington, B. (2006, October 7). "At James Madison, Title IX is satisfied but students are not." *New York Times*. Retrieved February 25, 2007, from http://www.nytimes.com/2006/10/07/ sports/othersports/07madison.html?n=Top/Reference/Times%20Topics/People/P/ Pennington,%20Bill.

Pennington, B. (2007). "Fair play? James Madison University's decision to eliminate 10 sports teams—mostly men's—to comply with federal 'gender equity' law is the latest chapter in the debate over the fairness of Title IX." *New York Times Upfront*. Retrieved February 24, 2007, from http://findarticles.com/p/articles/mi_m0BUE/is_8_139/ai_n17216097/pg_3.

Redden, E. (2006, October 3). "Gender equity or finances?" *Inside Higher Education*. Retrieved October 4, 2006, from http://www.insidehighered.com/layout/set/print/news/2006/10/03/jmu.

Staff. (2003, June 3). "JMU to break ground for Athletic Performance Center." Retrieved May 14, 2010, from http://web.jmu.edu/mediarel/PR-thisRelease.asp?AutoID=271.

Staurowsky, E. J. (2006, December). "James Madison University's decision to cut athletic teams: A farce or a tragedy?" *Sport Litigation Alert, 3* (21).

Suggs, W. (2007). "Counting ponytails." *Inside Higher Education*. Retrieved July 17, 2007, from http://www.insidehighered.com.

Swift, E. M. (2006, October 10). "Gender inequality: Title IX was necessary then, but now it's just unfair." *Sports Illustrated*. Retrieved May 14, 2010, from http://sportsillustrated.cnn.com/2006/ writers/em_swift/10/10/title.ix/.

"Title IX statement." (2007, February 7). James Madison University. Retrieved May 14, 2010, from http://www.jmu.edu/jmuweb/general/news/general8145.shtml.

Tracy, C. & Fromson, T. (2002, November 29). "Testimony before the Commission on Opportunities in Athletics of the United States Secretary of Education." Retrieved May 14, 2010, from http://www.womenslawproject.org/testimony/Title%20IX%20Testimony2002.pdf.

United States Department of Education, Office for Civil Rights. (1996, January 16). *Clarification of intercollegiate athletics policy guidance: The three-part test*. Retrieved February 29, 2007, from http://www.ed.gov/about/offices/list/ocr/docs/clarific.html#two.

University Council Minutes. (2000–2001). James Madison University University Council. Retrieved May 14, 2010, from http://www.jmu.edu/commisscommitt/ucouncil/Minutes113000.html.

Other Sources Consulted in Preparation

Anderson, D. J. & Cheslock, J. (2004). "Institutional strategies to achieve gender equity in intercollegiate athletics: Does Title IX harm male athletes?" *The American Economic Review 94* (2), 307–312.

Anderson, D. J., Cheslock, J. & Ehrenberg, R. G. (2004). "Gender equity in Intercollegiate athletics: Determinants of Title IX compliance (CHERI Working Paper #45)." Cornell University, ILR School site: http://digitalcommons.ilr.cornell.edu/workingpapers/44/.

Mahony, D. F. & Pastore, D. (1998, May). "Distributive justice: An examination of participation opportunities, revenues, and expenses at NCAA institutions—1973–1993." *Journal of Sport & Social Issues 22* (2), 127–152.

National Women's Law Center. (2007). "Barriers to fair play." Retrieved from http://www.nwlc .org.

9

Sincere Fictions of Whiteness in New Millennium American Sport Films

Kyle Kusz

O VER THE PAST DECADE, A NUMBER of scholars of race have expanded the scope of their work to not only study people of color and structures of racism in American society, but also to critically examine white people and white privilege as part of their anti-racism scholarship. One of the pioneers of this project, Richard Dyer, explains how this critical study of white people and white privilege—what he calls the critical study of whiteness—involves making visible how being white is taken for granted as the normal way of being in Western societies like the United States and the social privileges that go along with this social position:

> In fact for most of the time white people speak about nothing but white people, it's just that we couch it in terms of "people" in general. Research—into books, museums, the press, advertising, films, television, software—repeatedly shows that in Western representation whites are overwhelmingly and disproportionately predominant, have the central and elaborated roles, and above all are placed as the norm, the ordinary, the standard. Whites are everywhere in representation. . . . At the level of racial representation, in other words, whites are not of a certain race, they're just the human race. . . . This then is why it is important to see whiteness. For those in power in the West, as long as whiteness is felt to be the human condition, then it alone both defines normality and fully inhabits it . . . [and] the equation of being white with being human secures a position of power. White people have power and believe that they think, feel, and act like and for all people. . . . White power nonetheless reproduces itself regardless of its intention, power differences and goodwill, and overwhelmingly because it is not seen as whiteness, but as normal. White people need to learn to see themselves as white, to see their particularity. In other words, whiteness needs to be made strange. (Dyer, 2005, pp. 11–12)

In this quote, Dyer highlights two of the key ingredients of the critical study of whiteness—the need to identify whites as a particular racial group as opposed to allowing them to be "just human," and making visible the social power that goes along with being white in a white-dominant society like the United States. But interestingly absent from his critical examination of the images and stories we tell about white people in American popular culture is any mention of the sports media. As with many cultural observers, Dyer overlooks the prominent place of sports in contemporary American society and fails to consider the sports media, particularly sport films, as a key cultural site offering images of white people that reproduce the idea of whiteness as the normative way of being in American society.

Recently, sport scholars have begun to apply the insights from the field of whiteness studies to examine the stories being told about white people—particularly white men—produced in the American sports media (Brayton, 2005; Douglas, 2005; Hartmann, 2007; King, 2005; King, Leonard & Kusz, 2007; King & Springwood, 2001; Kusz, 2001, 2007a, 2007b; Leonard, 2007; McDonald, 2005; Spencer, 2004). On a basic level, this work reveals how images of white people in sports media are often created in relation to stereotypes associated with whites at the same time that they often rely on stereotypical images of blacks and other people of color. Such representations of race in sports media often reinforce an ideology of white superiority by enabling whites to appear as hardworking, virtuous, powerful, civilized, and morally superior relative to people of color. Even further, these recent sport studies on whiteness have exposed more complex and paradoxical ways in which sports media portrayals of white people make it difficult to recognize white privilege and the continued existence of racism and racial inequities in new millennium America (Hartmann, 2007; Kusz, 2006a, 2006b). We can apply these critical insights from recent sport studies research on whiteness to all sorts of contemporary sports media from video games, television programming, and Internet sites to DVDs, popular music, and films involving sport as a central theme.

Take, for example, the films often cited as the best sport films of all time. ESPN.com recently compiled their own list of such films, and as one might expect, films like *Bull Durham, Rocky, Raging Bull, Hoosiers,* and *Slapshot* occupied the top slots of this list. The appearance of these films at the top of the list is hardly surprising for most American sports fans. Yet if we apply Dyer's call to make whiteness strange, then we might contemplate why virtually all of the so-called best sport films of all time feature white men as lead characters. Interestingly, the list also included a couple of black-white buddy films like *White Men Can't Jump, Jerry Maguire,* and *Brian's Song.* Yet the corresponding images ESPN.com set next to each of these sport-oriented buddy films always featured the main white male character instead of his black counterpart. How do we make sense of the patterned ways in which white men are featured in these well-loved sport films? Can we truthfully say that these patterns are simply random? Or, must we admit they are a symptom of living in American society, where whiteness is too often regarded as the unspoken racial norm of public life and "the natural, inevitable, ordinary way of being human" (Dyer, 1988, p. 6)?

In this chapter, I take seriously sport films as a form of racial pedagogy in contemporary American society. This entails moving beyond an understanding of sport films as solely a pleasurable escape from our everyday lives, in order to think about how sport films teach us—often beyond our conscious awareness—the dominant ways of thinking about race, racism, and white privilege in our time. Too often, these dominant ideologies about race, racism, and white privilege taught to us through media culture like sport films provide distorted, partial, and incomplete images and understandings of race, which tend to serve the interest of maintaining whiteness as the unspoken norm of American society and white privilege as a public force in American social life.

More specifically, I will use Vera and Gordon's concept of a "sincere fiction of whiteness" (which I define and explain below) to critically examine some representations of white people produced in five recent sport films: *Invincible, Rocky Balboa, Dodgeball: A True Underdog's Story, Talladega Nights: The Ballad of Ricky Bobby*, and *Murderball*. I have chosen to focus attention on these films because they have either been commercially successful, marketed to American youth, or brought up in conversations I have had with some of my college students both inside and beyond the classroom. In exposing and interrogating some of the sincere fictions of whiteness that these sport films offer, I hope to reveal the subtle ways in which the cultural dominance of whiteness is reproduced in present-day American popular culture through sport films. Finally, it is important to note the sincere fictions of whiteness I illuminate in this chapter not only are being told within American sport films, but are also representative of the ways in which stories of white people and white privilege are being told in various other cultural sites across American popular culture in the new millennium.

Reading Sport Films Critically

Rather than noticing and critically examining the unavoidable racial dimension of these films, too often, most Americans fail to see the sport films mentioned above as being about race at all. Instead, because they are seen as "just" sport films—since most people consider sport as somehow separate from and uninfluenced by politics and society—there is a tendency not to take their messages about race seriously. Yet the sport film has proved to be a profitable and enduring feature of American popular culture, so the racial messages produced in and through sport films are deserving of critical socio-cultural examination (Baker, 2003).

Most sport films tend to reinforce the racial status quo. Films that reinforce the racial status quo often do so in a number of ways. First, they often celebrate the power of an individual(s) to overcome racial barriers and make it appear that racism is not built into the structure of American society. If racism is portrayed at all in most sport films of the post-civil-rights era, it is displayed as a deplorable attitude held only by one or a few isolated racist white individuals, rather than a social force built into American social institutions like the economy, law, media, and sports that influences all people (albeit in different ways) regardless of their racial identity. Second, they also often promote the notion of America as a truly meritocratic and colorblind society, one where anyone, regardless of race, can be successful if only he or she works hard enough. Third, sport films usually reinforce the idea of whiteness as an American norm by offering stories in which white men are the protagonists and driving forces of the action of a film. Or the films locate racism and racial barriers in the historical past (often taking place in a pre-civil-rights America), thereby allowing post-civil-rights America to appear colorblind and devoid of racism and racial disparities. Because they each use one or more of these representational patterns, sport films like *Remember the Titans*, *Glory Road*, *The Mighty Ducks*, *Hardball*, *Hoop Dreams*, and *White Men Can't Jump* can be regarded as offering racially conservative social messages.

These patterned ways of portraying race in and through sport films make it difficult for casual viewers to realize that racism and system-wide racial inequalities still exist in the contemporary United States. In addition, through their predictable and formulaic storylines where heroic white male underdogs use their extraordinary will and heart (we are told) to overcome seemingly insurmountable obstacles to achieve their desired dream, most white Americans like sport films, at least in part, because they provide "us" (whites) with stories about America as "we" would like to see it and ourselves. Thus, sport films are an excellent cultural site for the critical study of whiteness as the unspoken norm of American society and for offering us representations of race, what Vera and Gordon (2003) call "sincere fictions of whiteness," which need to be taken seriously for the way in which they teach Americans particular ways of thinking about racial issues.

Sincere Fictions of Whiteness

In their book, *Screen Saviors: Hollywood Fictions of Whiteness*, Vera and Gordon (2003) explain sincere fictions of whiteness as public stories about race, racism, and white privilege that enable white people to reconcile the cognitive dissonance created by their investments in American ideals of meritocracy, equality of opportunity for all, and individualism, and their deep-seated awareness of the continued existence of racism, white privilege, and racial inequalities in contemporary American society. Sincere fictions of whiteness are "an invention, a fiction that we take for real and rarely question" (p. 2). These public stories are considered *sincere* because most white people honestly believe them to be true, even if their sincere belief involves some "repression, denial, naïveté, or simple ignorance" of the realities of racial violence and disparities in the United States (p. 16). These public stories are said to be *fictions* because even though they are represented as true stories, in actuality, they are only partial, limited, and incomplete stories told in such a way that they ultimately serve the collective interests of white cultural dominance by masking, minimizing, downplaying, and/or disavowing the systemic character of racism and white privilege. Produced mainly by white authors, rarely, if ever, do sincere fictions of whiteness provide a place for the voices and perspectives of people of color that would contest, interrupt, or complicate a specific sincere fiction of whiteness being offered in a particular Hollywood film. Stated a bit differently, Bell has argued that sincere fictions of whiteness "ignore the enduring realities of racism in favor of an optimistic tale of continuous progress and social reform that bolsters images of white decency and goodness" (2002, p. 237).

To be sure, sincere fictions of whiteness offer images and narratives not only about whites, but also about people of color, particularly African Americans. Sincere fictions of whiteness urge white people to imagine themselves as racial innocents who do not participate in racist or anti-black practices. At the same time, they enable the perpetuation of the racial status quo to continue by denying and masking the continued existence of racism and white privilege in American society.

Thus, the concept of a "sincere fiction of whiteness" alerts us to the particular ways that we tell stories about race, racism, and white privilege in American public culture. Sincere fictions of whiteness are racial stories that most white people believe to be true, but really only offer a limited way of thinking about racial issues—framed from a white dominant perspective—that compel white people to believe that contemporary America is a colorblind society, racism is a thing of the past, and white privilege is something that does not really exist.

This concept of a "sincere fiction of whiteness" is particularly useful to the critical study of racial messages in and through a number of recent sport films with similar themes and storylines. Before addressing these films, we also need to be aware of the way in which the social privileges of being white were increasingly made visible in American public life during the past two decades. This public discussion about white privilege—which too often reductively cast all whites as uniformly privileged while failing to consider the ways in which the axes of gender, class, sexuality, age, and ability complicate simple notions of white privilege—upset a number of white people, particularly whites who hardly felt rich or wealthy in a time of stagnating wages and economic insecurity. During this same era, in reaction to this public visibility of whiteness, there has been a counter-trend of whites portrayed in a variety of ways as lacking or being disconnected from social and economic privileges.

Sport films of the past two decades have produced image after image of white men as authentically unprivileged in one way or another. Examples of this imagery in sport films can be found in films from as far back as the *Rocky* series, *Rudy*, *Field of Dreams*, and *Hoosiers* to more recent films like *Dogtown and Z Boys*, *Jackass: The Movie*, *Cinderella Man*, *The Rookie*, and *Semi-Pro*, not to mention in the films I will examine through the rest of this chapter. This pattern of representing white men as somehow economically and/or socially unprivileged constitutes a new sincere fiction of whiteness. This sincere fiction of whiteness enables white audiences to deny or make invisible the existence of white privilege in American social life by repeatedly offering images of white men who, at first glance, hardly appear to be rich, wealthy, or socially privileged and powerful. In the next section, I show how this sincere fiction of whiteness—white men as authentically socially and/or economically unprivileged—takes a number of forms and has proved to be popular in new millennium American sport films.

Some Sincere Fictions of Whiteness in New Millennium Sport Films

In this section, I identify four variations on the sincere fiction of whiteness of white men as lacking or being disconnected from social and/or economic privileges. The four variations of this sincere fiction are (1) typical sporting underdog stories where the white male protagonist's lack of social and/or economic privileges of any sort is foregrounded in the film (*Invincible*), (2) whites reclaiming an ethnic identity in order to disavow their relation to white privilege (*Rocky Balboa*), (3) lampooning stereotypical white guys to urge audiences to identify with unprivileged white guys (*Dodgeball: A True Underdog's Story* and *Talladega Nights: A Ballad for Ricky Bobby*), and finally, (4) representing "wounded" white men with disabilities as disadvantaged whites who simultaneously serve as symbols of a "wounded" post-9/11 America (*Murderball*).

White Males as Unprivileged

The first variation on the sincere fiction of whiteness of white men without social or economic privileges of any sort can be best seen in Disney's film *Invincible*. This variation can also be seen in a number of other sport films of the new millennium like *Cinderella Man*, *Dodgeball: A True Underdog's Story*, *Murderball*, and *Dogtown and Z Boys*, to name a few. *Invincible* tells the story of Vince Papale (played by Mark Wahlberg), a working-class, average Joe who earns a spot on the 1976 Philadelphia Eagles team after losing his job and being left by his wife. To recognize this sincere fiction of white men being portrayed as economically unprivileged and possessing extraordinary will in *Invincible*, one must take note of several aspects of the film.

First, there's the film's opening imagery of industrial wastelands, which superficially grounds Papale's story. These images of old, decrepit factories signify America's shift from a national economy oriented by manufacturing to a service economy. This economic shift particularly affected working-class men, whose skilled factory labor no longer translated to the needs of the new service economy. To highlight the importance of this shift to Papale's story, the film begins after his recent job loss and reveals his inability to find other work with comparable pay, as well as the stress this puts on him and his marriage.

Through these opening scenes, Papale appears as a white person without social or economic privileges. He has no connections to get himself a new job, and the stress of his situation facilitates the deterioration of his marriage. Without job and wife, it is easy to read him as unprivileged. One can also note how throughout the film, Papale is usually shown either in a dark, rough, local working-class pub where all of his white male friends (who also appear to lack social and/or economic privileges of any sort) congregate, or on the shadowy, gritty, deprived urban landscapes of South Philly. Coming from, and living in, this area makes it difficult to read Papale as a privileged white guy.

Additionally, even after Papale makes the Eagles' roster (and even earns a modest NFL paycheck), there are no scenes showing him enjoying the newfound riches that go along with his earned position: no shopping spree scenes where he is shown purchasing a brand new car, wardrobe, or house. Even after making the Eagles, Papale returns to play in a local tackle football game (on a symbolically rainy and muddy field, which connotes the lack of privilege surrounding the game), signifying how he has not forgotten his working-class roots. Through such portrayals and omissions, Papale's unprivileged white masculinity is reinforced time and time again through the film.

As one might expect in a sport film made by Disney, Papale's story draws heavily upon the formulaic narrative of the American underdog story. Papale is portrayed as the embodiment of the American Dream. His extraordinary will, never-say-die attitude, and strong work ethic serve to affirm the apparent truth of the American Dream and its corresponding ideals of individualism, hard work, and meritocracy. Papale is Rudy, who is Rocky Balboa, who is Jim Braddock (*Cinderella Man*), who is Jim Morris (*The Rookie*), who is Peter LaFleur (*Dodgeball: A True American Story*), who is Mark Zupan (*Murderball*), and so on. In each story, an image of white men as possessing an extraordinary will and work ethic emerges from the silver screen. Such stories are incredibly seductive—particularly for white male viewers of these films (Leonard, 2006). Not only do these stories affirm bedrock American ideals most Americans want to believe about their nation, but they also represent white masculinity as white men want to imagine themselves: as self-determining agents whose extraordinary will enables them to make it "on their own" regardless of their current state of affairs.

In addition, this mundane sincere fiction of white men as unprivileged but able to get by through their own hard work and determination has the potential to urge white audiences of the film to support the elimination of affirmative action programs. These programs were historically created to remedy the social disadvantage suffered by people of color (particularly African Americans) because of systemic racism and white privilege. But, to the extent to which white audiences are seduced by Papale's story that opportunity in America is solely something that a person of any race must make for themselves through good choices, hard work, and determination, the systemic character of racism and white privilege can easily get overlooked, and social supports like affirmative action may become vulnerable to elimination.

White Males Reclaiming an Ethnic Identity

The second variation on the sincere fiction of white men as unprivileged being produced in recent sport films is the reclaiming of white ethnicity in order to portray a particular white person as being seemingly distanced from white privilege. We see this strategy subtly at work in the final film of the *Rocky* series, *Rocky Balboa*. In the 2006 version of Rocky, the "Italian Stallion" returns not as a retired millionaire boxer resting comfortably in his mansion (as seen in previous Rocky films), but as a man of the streets who has returned to his old working-class Philadelphia neighborhood (sound familiar?) and who owns a restaurant where he plays the role of mascot to his past athletic glory for patrons.

Although the central theme of the film is Rocky's quest to recover his masculinity and feel alive again after the death of Adrian, his beloved wife, this quest interestingly requires a racialized contest against the undisputed heavyweight champ of the world, who not-so-coincidentally is named Mason "The Line" Dixon (played by Antonio Tarver). Of course, Dixon's name is a play on the Mason-Dixon line that signified the division between Southern states, where slavery was permissible, and Northern states, where it was illegal. Thus, the Mason-Dixon line is a loaded racial symbol that evokes America's history of racial division, terror, and inequalities. It is interesting that for a film lacking any other explicit racial statement, Stallone knowingly uses this racial symbol to hype Rocky's final battle in the ring. Although the original *Rocky* film is most often remembered today as perhaps the quintessential American underdog tale, we must not forget how Stallone has always made race central to Rocky's various storylines. Rocky's initial rival, the also symbolically named Apollo Creed, was portrayed in *Rocky* as a headstrong, cocky, overconfident, wealthy, and overprivileged black man, to Sylvester Stallone's "Italian Stallion," who represented unprivileged white masculinity. Relative to the well-spoken and commercially savvy Creed, the uneducated Rocky, whose impoverished condition limited him to using his physical body to make money for himself, was originally positioned as the unprivileged white male who came not from the comforts of post–World War II white American suburbia, but from the decaying streets of post-industrial Philadelphia.

Although Rocky largely sheds his Italian accent and surrounds himself with the luxurious trappings of being the heavyweight champion of the world in *Rocky III*, in *Rocky Balboa* American audiences are reintroduced to the heavy-accented, white ethnic Rocky of the first film. This is the Rocky adorned with his disheveled fedora and scarred leather jacket—a man of the people who is most comfortable on the streets of Philadelphia. Although seemingly economically comfortable because of the modest success of his restaurant, Rocky hardly looks economically privileged. As with *Invincible*, in *Rocky Balboa* American audiences are offered the sincere fiction of whiteness in which a white male is coded as economically unprivileged. But *Rocky Balboa* adds another layer to this sincere fiction, because it includes the re-marking of Rocky's white identity as an unmistakable white ethnic—Rocky is once again the "Italian Stallion"! In reviving Rocky's accent, the film demonstrates the contemporary strategy of "resurgent ethnic pride" (King, 2005, p. 397) for specific white people who are reclaiming their ethnic identities as another means of attempting to deny and disavow their relation to, and benefits from, white privilege.

Identifying with Unprivileged White Males: The Use of Lampooning

In *Talladega Nights: A Ballad for Ricky Bobby*, we can discern a third sincere fiction of whiteness in the film's lampooning of a "hyper-masculine" Southern white masculinity from economically unprivileged roots. Like the second sincere fiction of whiteness offered in *Rocky Balboa*, in which whites reclaim their ethnic roots as an attempt to distance themselves from being seen as privileged by being white, in this sincere fiction, stereotypes of Southern whiteness are used to construct a "different sort" of white masculinity that at first glance appears to be detached from the privileges of whiteness. But the sincere fiction of whiteness offered in *Talladega Nights* goes even further, as it lampoons a privileged white masculinity (while endorsing an unprivileged and humble white masculinity) as a means of masking the existence of white privilege in American society.

Talladega Nights is centered on Will Ferrell's caricature of Ricky Bobby, which resonates with some of the other ironic parodies of contemporary white masculinity he perfected on *Saturday Night Live* and in films like *Anchorman: The Life of Ron Burgundy*, *Old School*, *Kicking and Screaming*, and *Blades of Glory*. Much of the film's lampooning is directed at the childlike, hyper-masculine games white men play. But the film's ironic stance can be lost on younger viewers. In conversations with my own students, they often miss the film's ironic stance and enjoy the film because it allows them to take delight in the "old-school" patriarchal pleasures offered in the film—the homophobia, the sexual objectification of women, and the alienating bonds of white fraternity, among others.

At first glance, it seems almost impossible to read Ricky Bobby or his best friend, Cal Naughton Jr., as privileged white guys because both appear to be dim-witted motorheads who come from poor economic backgrounds. Throughout the film, both Ricky and Cal get a taste of fame and fortune as they win various races on the NASCAR circuit. But interestingly, the film lampoons the arrogant, wealthy, narcissistic, and overly competitive versions of Ricky and Cal's white male selves while it sentimentalizes them in their more humble, less privileged, and less competitive moments. In other words, the film urges us to like Ricky and Cal when they are humble and relatively unprivileged white guys, while it ridicules them when they act as arrogant, ungrateful, pretentious, overprivileged white guys. As demonstrated in the subsequent discussion of *Dodgeball: A True Underdog's Story*, this move to lampoon the rich, arrogant, and conceited white male while supporting the underprivileged, humble white male who seemingly has no social connections (read: connections to white privilege) is a representational pattern we see repeated in new millennium American films. Through this representational pattern, white privilege is portrayed as something possessed only by greedy, arrogant, and mean white individuals. Understandings of white privilege as something built into the structure of American social life are avoided.

It is also worth noting that race, and particularly whiteness, is never explicitly mentioned in the film, even as many of the film's jokes require awareness on the part of the audience of stereotypes of Southern whiteness and "white trash." In this way, *Talladega Nights* is part of a counter-trend in new millennium American popular culture of returning whiteness to an unmarked status. In a film where NASCAR's overwhelming whiteness surely holds the potential to provide seemingly endless fodder for explicit jokes about normative whiteness and white people, such jokes never get made, and the only obvious trace of marking Ricky Bobby's whiteness throughout the film is the filmmakers' decision to make Wonder Bread—*the* quintessential American white bread—the main sponsor of Ricky's stock car. Indeed, whiteness is everywhere—yet nowhere—in the film.

The sincere fiction of whiteness offered in *Talladega Nights* also includes another layer: the use of stereotypes of Southern whiteness to manage notions of white privilege. The South appears to have risen again in American popular culture over the past decade (Kincheloe, 2006; Newman, 2007) via the national media attention being given to NASCAR and the popularity of television shows like *My Name is Earl* and *The Blue Collar Comedy Show*, as well as through pop culture icons such as Forrest Gump and Larry the Cable Guy. Critics of whiteness have argued that images of Southern white masculinity have appeared with greater frequency during this era as whiteness and white privilege have become more publicly visible. Like contemporary reclamations of ethnicity by white people, this "Southernized" white identity paradoxically provides a white identity that appears to be different and disconnected from white privilege, yet still serves to keep white people at the center of the stories we tell in American popular culture. In such stories, Southern whites are imagined as coming from and existing on the margins of normative American culture, history, and society. Thus, "Southernized" white identities like the ones offered in *Talladega Nights* enable images of "different" white people who are disaffiliated from the advantages of systemic white privilege to appear in mainstream American popular culture at a time when white people have increasingly been cast in broad brush strokes as uniformly socially privileged because of their race.

Another recent sport film that showcases this sincere fiction of whiteness in which white men are lampooned as a means of masking the existence of white privilege is *Dodgeball: A True Underdog Story*. *Dodgeball* features the story of white everyman Peter LaFleur's (Vince Vaughn) struggle to avoid having the gym he owns (aptly named "Average Joe's Gym") taken over by White Goodman (Ben Stiller) and his Globo Gym empire. LaFleur's gym is in dire straits financially, and Goodman hopes to leverage LaFleur's economic hardship to take over the gym. The film culminates in a contest between LaFleur's underdog cast of out-of-shape slackers and Goodman's fitness professionals, in which both teams compete in a national dodgeball tournament whose $50,000 prize could save LaFleur from having to sell his gym to the heartless, greedy Goodman. I imagine you can figure out who wins in the end.

On one hand, *Dodgeball*'s sincere fiction of whiteness clearly rehearses *Invincible*'s and *Rocky Balboa*'s valorization of the white male underdog figure. But through its rather obvious parody of an arrogant, rich, and self-absorbed white guy, aptly and ironically named White Goodman, *Dodgeball*'s sincere fiction of whiteness also echoes the depiction of Ricky Bobby and Cal Naughton Jr. in *Talladega Nights*, in why they're basking in their newfound status as NASCAR champions. Both films project white privilege onto individual white people who are cast as arrogant, selfish, narcissistic, and uncaring. Portraying white privilege as possessed by a single white individual makes it difficult for white audiences to imagine white privilege as a systemic force in America.

Indeed, much of *Dodgeball*'s humor is directed at getting audiences to find pleasure in ridiculing and punishing Stiller's insecure, narcissistic, and arrogant White Goodman. The film's juxtaposition of LaFleur's unprivileged, underdog everyman to Goodman's embodiment of white male arrogance and self-centeredness reveals how the politics of maintaining a central and normative cultural position for whiteness in post–civil rights America can even include explicit and obvious critiques of white men. But before one jumps to the conclusion that we should read the film as a socially progressive critique of systemic white male privilege because it criticizes a rich, snobbish white male figure, I urge you to consider how Goodman functions in the film as a figure of disavowal for white audiences. More specifically, the film's ridicule and critique of White Goodman urges white audiences to feel good about their desire to criticize the arrogant, overprivileged Goodman as both a "bad guy" and as a symbol of white privilege. By locating white privilege in the figure of Goodman, white audiences are able to avoid contemplating whiteness as a social system that affords privileges to all whites (even if to different degrees, based on one's class, age, gender, sexual orientation, ethnicity, and nationality), and their own possessive investments in whiteness.

Finally, as social and economic privilege is projected onto White Goodman and his right-hand man, who is a very large, muscular, and similarly dim-witted black man, the "average Joe," nerdy, alternative white guys who make up La-Fleur's team become the white figures with whom the audience is urged to identify. And make no mistake, the film places these white everymen as the central figures in this American sport film—they represent the epitome of the average white man. Not only do they win the dodgeball tourney, but the common-man hero, Peter LaFleur, also gets his girl in the end.

Wounded White Males

Finally, in the documentary *Murderball*, which tells the remarkable story of a group of quadriplegic men training to make the U.S. Paralympic quad rugby team, we can see how this story of a group of mostly white male, elite athletes with disabilities reveals another sincere fiction of whiteness through which white privilege can be masked, denied, and disavowed in new millennium America. Like *Invincible*, *Murderball* is based on the "true stories" of the elite, white male athletes with disabilities whose apparent lack of social privileges is dramatically shown through their daily struggles to live "normal," able-bodied lives. These white men are represented as suffering from an ultimate disadvantage: being disabled because of their injured bodies. Thus, the notion of systemic white privilege appears to not exist.

For those who may not have even heard of *Murderball*, the backstory of the film is interesting and unique. The film was produced by a group of independent filmmakers on a shoestring budget. Never intended for mass distribution, in 2005 the film first appeared in only a few small, independent movie houses without much fanfare. Remarkably, the film soon enjoyed an incredible ground-swell of grassroots popularity. Grassroots interest became so great that Paramount Pictures eventually picked up the film, and MTV Films and ThinkFilm distributed the documentary to mainstream cinemas all across the United States. *Murderball* was marketed by MTV through a half-hour show in which a few members of the U.S. Men's Paralympic rugby team were given the "seal" of being cool and hip guys as they hung out and performed a bunch of pain-inducing, sophomoric stunts and pranks with Johnny Knoxville, Bam Margera, Steve-O, and the rest of the *Jackass* crew (Kusz, 2006a). This peculiar articulation of the U.S. Men's Paralympic rugby team with the *Jackass* fraternity by MTV as the means of selling *Murderball* to the public hints at the rather unusual, but telling, way in which their story was publicly framed, which in turn sheds light on the film's cultural politics.

At first glance, *Murderball* simply appears to tell the amazing stories of (mainly white) men who have survived paralyzing injuries of various degrees to compete for a spot on the U.S. Men's Paralympics quad rugby team for the 2004 Paralympic Games in Athens, Greece. Like the other films discussed previously, race is never explicitly made meaningful in the film's narrative. Yet all the key figures in the film are white men. And interestingly, the film goes out of its way to let audiences know that these are white men who may have a disability, but they are still driven by supposedly natural male proclivities to be competitive, rough, tough, strong, and athletic. This theme of masculinization is emphasized through scenes in which the players brag about their ability to seduce attractive, able-bodied women and through the intense rivalry between the United States' current best player, Mark Zupan, and the former top American player and recently dismissed coach of the U.S. team, Joe Soares, who now coaches the United States' biggest rival, Canada. The film's conspicuous masculinization of these white men with disabilities can make it difficult to notice the regressive racialization strategies at work in the film. But it is crucial to understand that the film's obvious masculinization of these white male quadriplegic athletes facilitates the racial politics at work in the film.

To comprehend these intertwined racial and gender politics, I want to focus on the film's main character, Mark Zupan. The pierced, goateed, and tattooed Zupan is introduced as arguably the best quad rugby player in the world. Through interviews with old friends and Zupan's own admissions, he is portrayed as a cocky, if not arrogant, college soccer player prior to the tragic accident that caused his paralysis. The post-paralysis Zupan is said to be much more humble, yet still driven by a fiery love of athletics that is the essential core of his being. In short, he is a "man's man." Sitting in his wheelchair, he is a physically imposing figure whose muscular arms and icy stare immediately catch viewers' attention.

We are told that Zupan suffered his paralyzing injury in a car accident. After getting drunk at a party, Zupan passed out in the bed of his friend's truck. Later, his friend (who also got drunk at the party and was unaware Zupan had passed out in the back of his truck) got into a car accident that launched Zupan into a nearby river. There, Zupan hung onto a tree branch for fourteen hours until help arrived. In this first bit of information we have about him, Zupan is cast as an unprivileged/disadvantaged white male through the "wound" caused by his accident and subsequent paralysis (Robinson, 2000). Although audiences could surely read this "wound" as the product of his own poor choices (i.e., getting drunk and passing out in the back of a pickup truck), the film instead frames his experience as an amazing yet tragic story of survival. The film implies that a white man's racial or gender privileges mean little when he is thrown out of the back of a truck and left holding onto a tree branch for fourteen hours in a stream of freezing water in order to survive.

This framing of Zupan's survival story, like *Invincible*'s portrayal of Vince Papale and *Rocky Balboa*'s portrayal of Rocky, also celebrates the indomitable will and spirit of white men. Important to this tale, Zupan is quick to tell us that he does not ask for anyone's sympathy and does not believe in whining and complaining about his paralysis. On one level, it is important to see how the public appeal of Zupan's story (and perhaps of the film) is that it offers a sincere fiction of whiteness that enables his white masculinity to be authentically marked as disadvantaged (and thus seemingly disaffiliated from white male privilege). Yet his story simultaneously reassures audiences that this disadvantaged, "wounded" white man still possesses an extraordinary will and refuses to assume the position of a victim, choosing instead to be a survivor. In this sincere fiction of whiteness, white men are disadvantaged in a way that white privilege cannot protect or "save" them, while their extraordinary will convinces us that all people (regardless of their station in life) can make their life better if only they choose to do so. The racial implication of this story is that if people living with disabilities can make a better life for themselves despite their "wounded" bodies, then people of color who have not suffered bodily injuries should not whine about America's systemic racial inequities, but should simply work harder to do better. Again, America's racial divisions and differences in opportunity based on one's race, both in the past and the present, get overlooked and forgotten as this sincere fiction of whiteness is told.

Interestingly, this sincere fiction of white men with disabilities or white men having suffered a bodily "wound" has become a repeated public tale in new millennium American popular culture. One can see it played out in the media coverage of cancer survivor and seven-time Tour de France winner Lance Armstrong, whose cancer "wounds" and extraordinary will are central to his popular appeal. This sincere fiction is central to the public narratives told of Pat Tillman, the former NFL player who died tragically and controversially after foregoing his lucrative NFL career to serve his country in the "War on Terror." One can see it in specific white male characters who appear in films like *The Ringer, Remember the Titans,* and even the aforementioned, *Dodgeball: A True Underdog Story.* One can even witness it in the media spectacle made of Jason McElwain, the high school basketball player with autism from Greece, New York, whose story amazed the nation when he knocked down six three-point shots and scored a total of twenty points in four minutes at the end of the only varsity basketball game he was allowed to play in in 2006. Within days, Hollywood studios fought over the rights to retell "J-Mac's story" on the silver screen; President George W. Bush even took time out of his busy schedule to have a photo opportunity with McElwain.

Like many of the other white males mentioned previously who suffered bodily "wounds," Zupan's is also implicitly made into a story about new millennium America. Based on their efforts to make the 2004 U.S. Paralympic quad rugby team, this sincere fiction of whiteness urges these white men to be read as symbols of a wounded American nation following the terrorist attacks of September 11, 2001. One day, each of the white men featured in the film is fine—comfortable, whole, and secure; the next day, each is rendered vulnerable, fragile, and wounded. Of course, none of them ever resigns himself to becoming a passive victim. Instead, as symbols of a wounded nation, the Murderballers show "us" how to become a strong-willed, defiant, resilient, and self-reliant survivor determined to overcome any adversity.

The meteoric rise of this small-budget documentary in cinemas around the United States highlights the value of the sincere fiction of whiteness offered in *Murderball.* The film offers new millennium American audiences a dramatic, compelling, and seemingly true story about white men lacking social privileges of any sort because of their unfortunate, disabling injuries. Especially because this documentary is based on a true story—again, like *Invincible, The Rookie, Cinderella Man,* and *Remember the Titans*—it produces an incredibly seductive sincere fiction of whiteness, enabling white audiences to convince themselves that system-wide white privilege does not exist because these particular white men hardly seem socially or economically privileged.

And because the story of "wounded" white men told through *Murderball* is cast as an American story, this particular sincere fiction of whiteness—with its intertwined racial, gender, and nationalistic meanings—becomes central to some of the most crucial issues and politics of the day. Mark Zupan's "wounded" and Americanized white masculinity becomes an allegory of post-9/11 America. He is both a symbol of the national "wound" experienced by the United States, and is offered as a pleasurably masculinized white everyman whose story of triumph over adversity is an imagined solution to that national "wound" (Kusz, 2007a, 2007b). Through his story and that of *Murderball,* the project of maintaining the centrality and normality of whiteness in new millennium America quietly takes place in front of our very eyes, but too often beyond our conscious comprehension.

Conclusion

In the conclusion of their book *Screen Saviors: Hollywood Fictions of Whiteness,* Vera and Gordon (2003) write:

The movies, along with many other products of popular culture, such as television and music, provide us with the elements we use in our everyday life to think with and to function in an increasingly complex world. We live in the bubble of our stock of knowledge, that collection of ways of thinking, feeling, and acting we share with other members of our society. It is impossible to think and speak a language we do not know. In other words, we live using sincere fictions, those mental templates we use to relate to others. (p. 185)

Keeping in mind how movies provide the public with ideas from which we interpret ourselves and society, the goal of this chapter was to show how a critical reading of some of the most seemingly mundane and non-political films that have sports at their center can reveal some of the key sincere fictions of whiteness. In addition, it reveals how contemporary Americans are being taught to think about race—particularly whiteness—in the new millennium. In particular, four variations of the sincere fiction of whites being portrayed as unprivileged socially and/or economically in order to deny the existence of systemic white privilege in American society were discussed. The first highlighted the many sport films that feature rather typical sporting underdog stories in which the white male protagonist's lack of social and/or economic privileges of any sort was highlighted. The second variation on this sincere fiction of whiteness, as seen in *Rocky Balboa* (or more subtly in *Cinderella Man*), offers an image of whites reclaiming an ethnic identity in order to disavow their relation to white privilege. The third version of this sincere fiction of whiteness lampoons stereotypical white guys to urge audiences to identify with unprivileged white guys. This story about whiteness could be seen through the sport films *Dodgeball: A True Underdog's Story* and *Talladega Nights: A Ballad for Ricky Bobby*. Finally, the sport documentary *Murderball* portrays a mainly white group of men with disabilities trying to earn a spot on the U.S. Paralympic quad rugby team as "wounded"' and disadvantaged whites who simultaneously serve as symbols of a "wounded" post-9/11 America. I argued that each of these variations on the sincere fictions of whiteness, in its own way, offers a story featuring white people who are conspicuously coded as socially and/or economically unprivileged that serves to "maintain the status quo of white privilege" by attempting to deny its existence and by returning whiteness to a public state of invisibility in the twenty-first century (Vera & Gordon, 2003, p. 186).

It is my hope that students will not only develop a greater awareness of some of the sincere fictions of whiteness circulating in contemporary American culture after reading this chapter, but also begin to look more closely at their own lives for other times and places where these (and other) sincere fictions of whiteness are being told, whether in other television shows or movies they enjoy, or through interactions they might have with friends, family members, co-workers, teammates, and others in their communities. I hope students will critically reflect on their own thoughts, actions, identities, and relations with members of other racial and ethnic groups, and critically reflect on those times when their hearts and minds were ensnared by these racial fictions and how such ideas affected their own behaviors. I hope students will begin to see how, through repetition and a lack of alternative ideas about race circulating in American culture, these sincere fictions of whiteness get taken up as racial facts of life by many people. And I hope that students will better understand how these sincere fictions of whiteness, told through popular films like sport films, are far from innocent because they enable those in power to create social policies, laws, and opportunities for achievement that enable white privilege and racial inequalities to persist in the United States.

I also want to make clear that critical analyses of media like the one offered in this chapter are not meant to be an end in themselves, but only a means of teaching people the skills needed to be critical and productive citizens who challenge our social leaders and themselves to make America live up to its democratic ideals. Developing critical media literacy—an ability to critically assess, in this case, the racial meanings and politics of a cultural text—is meant to be just a first step for people to become more aware of how race produces every aspect of all Americans' lives, regardless of their racial identities (Kellner, 1995; Lampman, 2006). The ultimate goal of such critical work is to change people's attitudes about race and their actions toward racial others (whether through their personal relations or the institutionalized rules they may work to create and/or maintain). In other words, the vital aim is to compel people to choose to live a life guided by habitual practices of anti-racism. For white people, such a life would not involve feeling guilty about having white skin, trying to abolish one's whiteness, or attempting to disavow the social and economic privileges they unavoidably enjoy due to their skin color. Having white skin is not the problem, but acting white is. As Lipsitz (1998) explains:

> The problem with white people is not our whiteness [i.e., white skin color or identity], but our possessive investment in it. Created by politics, culture, and consciousness, our possessive investment in whiteness can be altered by those very same processes, but only if we face the hard facts openly and honestly and admit that whiteness is a matter of interests as well as attitudes, that it has more to do with property than pigment. Not all believers in white supremacy are white. All whites do not have to be white supremacists. But the possessive investment in whiteness is a matter of behavior as well as belief. (p. 233)

Such a life filled with daily anti-racist acts can be uncomfortable and difficult at first for white people who choose to walk this path. It can mean temporarily giving up one's social, economic, and/or psychic privileges as one challenges agents of whiteness and white privilege, whether they exist in one's family, workplace, or local or state governments. But living such a life also entails unparalleled rewards—being true to one's ideals, building meaningful relationships with people from diverse backgrounds who are also interested in cultivating an anti-racist life, and earning even the smallest victories against the racial "powers that be."

References

Baker, A. (2003). *Contesting identities: Sports in American film.* Champaign: University of Illinois Press.

Bell, L.A. (2002). Sincere fictions: The pedagogical challenges of preparing white teachers for multicultural classrooms. *Equity & Excellence in Education, 35(3),* 236–244.

Brayton, S. (2005). Black-lash: Revisiting the 'white Negro' through skateboarding. *Sociology of Sport Journal, 22(3),* 356–372.

Douglas, D.D. (2005). Venus, Serena, and the Women's Tennis Association (WTA): When and where "race" enters. *Sociology of Sport Journal, 22(3),* 256–282.

Dyer, R. (1988). White. *Screen, 29(4),* 44–65.

Dyer, R. (2005). The matter of whiteness. In P.S. Rothenberg's *White privilege: Essential readings on the other side of racism* (pp. 9–14). New York: Worth Publishers.

Hartmann, D. (2007). Rush Limbaugh, Donovan McNabb, and "A Little Social Concern": Reflections on the problems of whiteness in contemporary American sport. *Journal of Sport and Social Issues, 31(1),* 45–60.

Kellner, D. (1995). *Media culture.* London: Routledge.

Kincheloe, J. (2006). The South place and racial politics: Southernification, romanticization, and the recovery of white supremacy. *Souls, 8(1),* 27–46.

King, C.R. (2005). Cautionary notes on whiteness. *Sociology of Sport Journal, 22(3),* 397–410.

King, C.R., Leonard, D. & Kusz, K.W. (2007). White power and sports. *Journal of Sport and Social Issues, 31(1),* 1–9.

King, C.R. & Springwood, C.F. (2001). *Beyond the cheers: Race as spectacle in college sport.* Albany, NY: SUNY Press.

Kusz, K.W. (2001). 'I want to be the minority': The politics of youthful white masculinities in sport and popular culture in 1990s America. *Journal of Sport and Social Issues, 25(4),* 390–416.

Kusz, K.W. (2006a). Why be a 'Jackass'?: Media images of young white men in and out of sport in new millennium America. In S. Spickard Prettyman & B. Lampman (Eds.), *Learning culture through sport* (pp. 182–196). Lanham, MD: Scarecrow Press.

Kusz, K.W. (2006b). Interrogating the politics of white particularity in *Dogtown and Z-Boys.* In C.R. King & D. Leonard (Eds.), *Visual economies of/in motion: Sport and film* (pp. 135–163). New York: Peter Lang Publishing.

Kusz, K.W. (2007a). *Revolt of the white athlete: Race, media and the emergence of extreme athletes in America.* New York: Peter Lang Publishing.

Kusz, K.W. (2007b). From NASCAR nation to Pat Tillman: Notes on sport and the politics of white cultural nationalism in post-9/11 America. *Journal of Sport and Social Issues, 31(1),* 77–88.

Lampman, B. (2006). Exploring race with secondary students: Developing critical media literacy. In S. Spickard-Prettyman & B. Lampman (Eds.) *Learning culture through sports* (pp. 119–128). Lanham, MD: Rowman & Littlefield Publishing.

Leonard, D. (2006). "Is this heaven?" White sporting masculinities and the Hollywood imagination. In C.R. King & D. Leonard's *Visual economies of/in motion: Sport and film* (pp. 165–194). New York: Peter Lang Publishing.

Leonard, D.J. (2007). Innocent until proven innocent: In defense of Duke lacrosse and white power (and against menacing black student-athletes, a black stripper, activists, and the Jewish media). *Journal of Sport & Social Issues, 31(1),* 25–44.

Lipsitz, G. (1998). *The possessive investment in whiteness: How white people profit from identity politics*. Philadelphia: Temple University Press.

McDonald, M. (2005). Mapping whiteness and sport: An introduction. *Sociology of Sport Journal, 22(2)*, 245–255.

Newman, J. (2007). Old times there are not forgotten: Sport, identity, and the Confederate flag in the Dixie South. *Sociology of Sport Journal, 24*, 261–282.

Robinson, S. (2000). *Marked men: White masculinity in crisis*. New York: Columbia University Press.

Roediger, D. (2005). *Working toward whiteness: How America's immigrants became white*. New York: Basic Books.

Spencer, N. (2004). Sister Act VI: Venus and Serena Williams at Indian Wells: Sincere fictions and white racism. *Journal of Sport and Social Issues, 28(2)*, 115–135.

Vera, H. & Gordon, A. (2003). *Screen saviors: Hollywood fictions of whiteness*. Lanham, MD: Rowman & Littlefield.

10

Reporting in Black and White

Coverage of Coaching Scandals in Minnesota— Two Different Worlds?

C. Keith Harrison and Richard Lapchick

THROUGHOUT HISTORY, THE LEADERS of athletic teams have come from an exclusive, traditional club of white males, thus mirroring society itself (Marable, 2001). Historically, the African American male has not been represented in these ranks, although there have been coaches over the last decade who have broken through in professional sports (e.g., Tony Dungy, first with the Tampa Bay Buccaneers and now with the Indianapolis Colts, and Maurice Cheeks, with the Portland Trailblazers). There are currently six African American managers in Major League Baseball (MLB), three head coaches in the National Football League (NFL), and nine head coaches in the National Basketball Association (NBA) (Lapchick & Matthews, 2001). Approximately 21 percent of Division I men's coaches are African American. Nonetheless, the number of African American males in the coaching profession (both at the college and the professional level) remains relatively small.

The inequality within the coaching profession (Brooks, 2002) was poignantly depicted in the film *Remember the Titans*. In the film, Coach Boone was told prior to the season that he would be the head coach and given a fair chance. Behind the scenes, however, "the powers that be" had already decided that if he lost one game, they would fire him and replace him with a white coach. This true-life account represents the realities for black male coaches in a white-male-dominated world. They must win big to have a chance to survive, and if their behavior on or off the field is questionable, they will not have the same opportunities for job mobility or continued access to the head coaching profession as white male coaches in similar situations (Lapchick & Matthews, 2001). The phenomenon of minorities (i.e., women, people of color) having to perform at a superior level in the sport industry and display superior character is crucial to their survival. This is why the Minnesota News Council contacted the authors of this paper (in 2001) to determine if bias played a role in the coverage of four coaches in the major papers in Minneapolis, Minnesota, and surrounding areas in the same state.

The Minnesota News Council wanted the authors to determine if a biased mentality by journalists could be analyzed and solutions given to prevent this type of coverage in the future. This is the purpose of the current paper: to summarize the study's findings by applying theories that help explain what role race played in the coverage of four Minnesota coaches, and how racial bias may have contributed to racial tensions in the Minneapolis area and possibly beyond Minnesota's borders. The statements/stories analyzed in this chapter support one of the major interpretations of this study: The *framing* of news reporting is inherently biased and traditionally not conducive to non-status quo populations such as African Americans employed at white institutions (Entman & Rojecki, 2000). This type of media bias raises the following questions: Was there a difference in how black and white coaches were portrayed in the media in Minnesota? And if there was a bias, what role did race play in the coverage of the coaches?

Two of the coaches in this analysis are African Americans: Dennis Green, head coach of the Minnesota Vikings, and Clem Haskins, former head basketball coach at the University of Minnesota. Green has remained as head coach in spite of reported scandals involving women, while Haskins was fired in 2000 after an extensive academic cheating scandal unfolded with his team. Haskins received a large cash settlement from the University of Minnesota, which is now trying to get the money back. Two other coaches investigated are white Americans: Jim Dutcher, who preceded Haskins as head basketball coach at the University of Minnesota, and Doug Woog, the University of Michigan's hockey coach. Dutcher was fired in 1986 after three of his players were arrested and charged with raping a woman in Wisconsin. Unlike today, when more than one hundred sexual assaults involving athletes are reported annually (Lapchick, 2000), the University of Minnesota charges represented a very unusual story in 1986 and were the cause of a major scandal. Woog was fired after allegedly paying a student-athlete $500 for tuition. In the next section, we analyze the foundation of how mainstream media stories are framed and typically consumed, and the role whiteness plays in this.

Whiteness and Media Bias: A Structural Way of Seeing and Believing

Today, theorists and scholars often define whiteness as a form of social, political, economic, and ideological power (Kincheloe, Steinberg, Rodriguez, & Chennault, 1998; Lipsitz, 1998; Roediger, 1998). In other words, whiteness is a system of institutionalized advantages and privileges that are systemically built into the power structure. Complicating this phenomenon is that most people with white skin do not often see these advantages (Rothenberg, 2000). McIntosh (1988) calls this "the invisible knapsack," but is also quick to indicate that many whites will notice when this "knapsack" is taken away. For the purpose of this study, whiteness operates at two major levels. First, mainstream whites are socialized to see the "other" in various situations as different and inferior (Allport, 1954). Rothenberg (2000) explains how this operates:

> I began to understand that in some real sense, right and wrong are defined by the behavior of those with social and economic clout, the right gender, the right color skin. When those people do things, they *become* right or are judged differently than when identical acts are committed by people with a lower socioeconomic status. (p. 94)

In situations with negative press, this has the potential to magnify negative labels attached to people of color. Second, the errors and mistakes of whites, such as the white coaches in this study, are not typically linked in the American mind to the behavior of whites based on racial behavior (Lipsitz, 1998).

This concept of media bias becomes a ritual, and according to Hunt (1999) "we use race-as-representation—even when we have doubts about its validity— to make sense of our own locations in social structure and those of other-raced groups" (p. 263). Thus, difference is constructed and highlighted by electronic media based on race, class, and gender (Biagi & Kern-Foxworth, 1997; Burstyn, 1999; Chideya, 1999). The Minnesota coaching scandals are case examples of how race-as-representation operates in print media, and the effects it can have. The method and design for objectively approaching these scandals will be thoroughly explained in the next section of this paper.

Method and Design: The Statements/Stories

A research team of two primary researchers and two student research assistants reviewed 102 articles on the four Minnesota coaches. We conducted a content analysis focused on all of the local print coverage of the four coaches as designated by the Minnesota News Council. Both student research assistants were trained in content analysis and received information about the relevant literature for two weeks prior to the study. Next, all written responses about the coaches that dealt with social and character issues were "de-identified" from their original sources and then transcribed into a hard copy text for data analysis. Hierarchical content analysis, as suggested by Patton (2001), was utilized in the analysis. Following transcription, each investigator read each of the journalists' transcripts in order to get a sense of what the journalists wrote. The research team then independently identified the raw data statements by the journalists covering each head coach. Before any final categorization of the statements was determined, all four researchers came to a consensus about how to categorize statements as positive, negative, and/or neutral. In this way, we were able to maintain a degree of inter-coder reliability that enabled us to code the statements related to each of the four coaches in a systemic and objective manner (Dixon & Linz, 2000a). In addition, this was coupled with the use of ATLAS.ti® (a computer-based software analysis program often used for large bodies of textual data) to verify and assist with the accuracy of determining the number and percentage of participants who responded within each of the major themes. These approaches were conceptualized as the best way to explicitly qualify and quantify statements and narratives written about each coach. Mutual exclusivity is a sign of good categorization and sequential qualitative analysis, which we used to create categories and identify sections of text that fit into them (Patton, 2001).

Some stories were trivial and discussed only statistics or game-day hype, and were not included in the analysis. The researchers defined positive as "any story or statement that lifts up the character of the coach as a leader or citizen," negative as "any story or statement that damages or demonizes the character of the coach," and neutral as doing neither of these two aforementioned frames. Initially, each raw data statement was assigned to one of these three categories. Subsequently, the design focused more on the meaning of these statements/stories and a more naturalistic and qualitative interpretation of the findings (Patton, 2001). The labels for analysis were derived from the actual words and texts used by the newspaper writers and the language content within each story. Following qualitative methods, the focus was on the raw data themes of the narratives, and then triangulating these statements with descriptive numerical quantification and where the statements fell based on the three tier categories (i.e., positive, negative, and neutral).

In total, we reviewed 102 articles: 66 total articles on the two black coaches (19 on Green and 47 on Haskins) and 36 total articles on the two white coaches (29 on Woog and 7 on Dutcher). Forty-four percent of the articles on the black coaches were negative, 47 percent were neutral, and 9 percent were positive. For the white coaches, 28 percent were negative, 45 percent were neutral, and 28 percent were positive. What follows is an analysis of each coach and an interpretation of the news coverage of each. Within each of these sections is a summary of the statements written about each coach. Due to limited space, only select statements are utilized to represent the broader theme being discussed. The discussion section that follows expands on the specific and broader meanings of the present study.

Findings and Results

The following are major themes that emerged from the data: *History Repeats It-self* (Green; Dutcher), *Still on Campus, Second Chance* (Woog), and *Leadership Is Out of Control* (Haskins). Each of these themes is discussed below in relationship to the coach(es) who are associated with it. Representative data from the statements/stories about the four coaches is used to explore each theme.

Dennis Green

One major idea surfaced in the six negative stories written about Dennis Green. One was that there was a coverup in the Jane Doe story. Jane Doe is mentioned eleven times in the six stories, and begins to become a construct (while generic) that has many connotations in a city like Minneapolis, which is predominantly white and is a place where black-male–white-female interaction stands out.

In this case, the media focused on uncovering confidential information about Green and attempted to demonstrate that there was a historical pattern to his behavior as an African American male. There were only a few negative articles on the white coaches, with far more in the neutral category. Regarding Dennis Green, some analysis is necessary, because the other three coaches will also be discussed in the next few pages. In the discussion section, we will synthesize the media coverage of all four coaches in relation to the statements and quotes. What follows are some examples from the data that illustrate our analysis of the Green situation. Collectively, the quotes demonstrate attention being paid to Green's behavior outside of the Minnesota allegations (accusations of sexual harassment).

A January 1993 settlement between Green and the woman included a confidential-ity agreement that the woman later claimed Green broke.

The woman said she sued Green for breaking the confidentiality agreement after another member of the Vikings organization approached her about a sexual rela-tionship, according to the television report.

The report is the latest off-field problem for Green and the Vikings since allega-tions against Green and assistant coach Richard Solomon surfaced in January 1995. Green was accused of two separate cases of sexual harassment, although he has denied those claims.

The last time head coach Dennis Green appeared before the Vikings board of directors, he predicted that the Vikings would win the Central Division title. But he refused to comment on a lawsuit by a woman known as Jane Doe, information that was ordered sealed by Hennepin County Judge Andrew Danielson.

No one was as openly supportive of Green, whose first four seasons as Vikings coach have been punctuated with two disclosures of sexual harassment allegations, which he has denied.

But the machismo of football and the Vikings' repeated mistreatment of women have been prevalent images during Green's tenure. Domestic violence, deadbeat dads and sexual harassment have recently dominated team news.

What of race? This is a difficult-to-measure reality. Green is a Black man who happens to be an executive for a prominent company in predominantly White corporate environment, in a state struggling with diversity. Can Green's treatment by the news media or the Vikings' board of directors be attributed to his race?

But a professor at Macalester College wonders, "Everything isn't racist, but most things are tinged by racism, especially if you talk about Black-White interaction. It's somewhere in the background."

And if Switzer were caught in the same circumstances as Green, would that change fans' attitudes? "I think not," said one writer. "Besides, Jerry Jones would find a way to hush it up. But that's Texas and this is Minnesota."

Jim Dutcher

Jim Dutcher lost his head coaching position after many years of problems. Dutcher was fired in 1986 after three of his players were arrested and charged with raping a woman in Wisconsin. Prior to this incident, a player quit the team after he was charged with billing $970 in phone calls to university phones in 1982. Another player was accused of using someone else's credit card to get cash. One of the student-athletes charged in Wisconsin in 1986 had been charged and then acquitted of raping a student in her university dorm room in 1985. The question then is how were these incidents during Dutcher's leadership represented by the media coverage?

Some of the data from the media coverage about Jim Dutcher represents writing that is basic and neutral. The focus was on him as an individual and was not about him being part of a broader ethnic group (i.e., white American or African American). Overall, the quotes on Dutcher illustrate that while he faced a negative scandal, he was able to still be on campus and part of the university community as a speaker at high school banquets throughout the state of Minnesota.

. . . He resigned as coach seven years ago in the wake of the Madison, Wisconsin incident in which three players were charged with sexual assault and eventually acquitted.

His friends told him to disassociate himself with the three athletes—and not to return to Madison, where they were arraigned and formally charged Monday. "There are times and places to be expedient, but this is not one of them," Dutcher said.

Dutcher made the rounds within the state to start repairing the tarnished reputation. During his first year, he spoke at 28 high school banquets.

Doug Woog

As stated earlier, Doug Woog was fired after allegedly paying a student-athlete $500 for tuition. However, Woog has been a successful entrepreneur in addition to his coaching expertise. Woog was offered a job at the university after the scandals he faced, but instead chose to run his highly successful business in Minnesota. The following quotes are examples of Woog not only surviving the scandals, but also having options of employment at the same institution, highlighting his leadership in connection with the scandals. The quotes below illuminate that Woog actually joked about having employment options, was assured of coaching another season in light of the scandals he faced, and was still on campus coaching with the option of working on campus in another leadership role despite the publicity surrounding his situation.

> Doug Woog, the University of Minnesota men's hockey coach for 14 seasons, has been offered a fund-raising job in the men's athletic department if he chooses to resign as coach in a scheduled meeting. . . .

> Woog's options—a guarantee of one more season as coach or fund-raising job that would offer more security . . .

> . . . University officials learned in 1996 that Woog had given $500 for school tuition in 1994 to Chris McAlpine, a defenseman who had completed his eligibility.

> I do have the assurance, if I want to coach next season, that's there, Woog said.

> Doug Woog did whatever he could to lighten the mood. He kidded about planning to announce the university had just extended his contract as head coach. He mentioned the sun was shining and nobody had died.

> In his final two seasons as the Gophers' men's hockey coach, Doug Woog had to work to shield himself and his family from growing public criticism. These days, he can hardly go anywhere without hearing a compliment.

Clem Haskins

The Clem Haskins ordeal received the most attention from the writers in the newspapers. This may be due to the high visibility of the sport he coached (basketball) and his race and gender as an African American male, coupled with the broad scope of the scandal itself. We cannot identify any overt racial elements to the coverage based on depictions, descriptions, and characteristics. However, some perceptions persist in the coverage of Haskins. One perception is that the Haskins scandal is framed, in most cases, as being unique to his situation. In other words, academic fraud, rule violations, and inappropriate conduct by him as a leader and his players as subordinates seem to tarnish a clean system. Based on reading all the coverage of Haskins, one is inclined to think that the system of intercollegiate athletics in higher education is a highly moral and rational structure. Haskins made serious transgressions of ethical behavior, and should be punished accordingly. However, his behavior was not unique when considering the incidents and coverage of Dutcher and Woog. At the same time, there is a constant focus on Haskins telling "lies" and regular questioning of the buyout salary package he received upon leaving. It is normal procedure when a coach departs from a top program to buy out his contract. However, allegations that emerged after Haskins' departure have raised new questions regarding the buyout. Another perception is how much money and economic strife Haskins has caused. Although Haskins received the most coverage, only some of the quotes are presented due to limited space. The quotes below are only a few of several statements that support the ideas presented above, regarding the perceptions and interpretations cultivated by the media coverage.

> Clem Haskins leaves the University of Minnesota with a mighty big mess and a $1.5 million parting gift. Next time somebody tells you crime doesn't pay, refer them to big-time college basketball.

> In some businesses, the man in charge of an out-of-control operation gets fired for his failures. In college athletics, he simply negotiates a settlement package.

> Haskins is free to coach again at some other school, while Minnesota's remaining players are stuck in steerage on a sinking ship.

The ethical violations attributed to Haskins happen almost annually at higher education institutions with athletic teams (Thelin, 1994); however, the public only hears about a handful of these. In terms of the third quote above, it is unlikely, based on social and racial politics in sport, that Haskins will "coach again," especially for a major program at a traditionally white institution.

Discussion: A Cross-Case Analysis

In sum, what did the raw data themes tell us about the four coaches as individuals and overall in terms of media coverage? First, there were differences in the coverage of Green/Haskins (the African American coaches) and Dutcher/Woog (the white coaches). For Green/Haskins, the coverage attempted to demonstrate a pattern in their behavior that was indicative of their character, which would ultimately ruin their future. For Dutcher/Woog, the coverage analyzed their situations but ultimately revealed that their behavior was not a character issue but rather something that they could overcome as individuals.

When considering how the perceptions of racial and ethnic groups work, it is clear that the political impact on the African American coaches versus the white American coaches is different. Based on the social psychology literature on prejudice and stereotypes (Steele, Spencer & Aronson, 2002), African Americans tend to be viewed as a group rather than as individuals. For white Americans, it is the opposite: Perceptions are essentially tied to their individual actions and behaviors (Stone et al., 2002). In the final analysis, Dutcher/ Woog were able to overcome their scandals because they were not seen as part of a stigmatized group (white males). However—and the history of African American males in the United States buttresses this point (Hunt, 1999; Wiggins, 1988)—Green/Haskins were seen not as individuals but as part of a larger group composed of incompetent, irresponsible, and ineffective leaders of collegiate athletes at the University of Minnesota.

This study also acknowledges the patterns and outcomes for coaches outside of Minnesota. The primary focus when comparing these coaches to the Minnesota coaches was to examine their current job status and how the eventual outcome of their situation affected their mobility as a leader in sport culture. The findings reveal themes similar to the present study. The scandals pertaining to these coaches range from programs dealing with out-of-control drug use by players to academic fraud to disorderly conduct in public. What is most revealing is that more neutral stories are written than positive or negative stories about the white coaches examined. For the one African American coach in this larger sample, this is problematic when put in the context of the coaching fraternity (traditional, status quo). Of all the coaches, he has had the most trouble staying in coaching after losing his job, in spite of a very good record while at his previous coaching position. Although it may influence public perception, newspaper coverage critical of the character of white male coaches has less effect on their job opportunities (Harrison, 2000; Harrison & Min, 2001; Lapchick, 1991). In terms of African American coaches who work outside of the inner circle of opportunity, this phenomenon appears to be exactly the opposite. However, this is a difficult comparison to make, since there have been fewer blacks and members of other underrepresented groups afforded the opportunity to perform as head coaches (Harrison & Lapchick, presentation given at Macalster College, September 2001).

The cases of African American coaches fit the "cultural script" of squandered opportunity by African Americans. The effect of these cases on public perception reflects variables of black masculinity in sport leadership. In a culture that is historically imbued with biases such as sexism, racism, and homophobia, any negative acts by African American coaches such as Haskins will put them in a potential lose-lose situation: They are simply not afforded the same margin of error as white coaches. Newspaper accounts do not create this reality, but rather reinforce structural biases against those seeking the American Dream.

Two primary conclusions have been reached after examining all of these cases:

1. White coaches who lose their jobs continue to successfully navigate in the system.
2. African American coaches who lose their jobs do not successfully navigate in the system and usually do not get as many chances or opportunities.

Who is at fault for the negative fallout for African American coaches in critical articles? It is a multi-level problem. The media can be more proactive about recognizing bias in the culture and how things can be read based on race, class, and gender. If this happens, then the navigational systems may change. For example, the media can more openly, and in greater depth, discuss the history of African American coaches who have lost their jobs so the public and decision makers in positions to hire people can have a broader perspective with which to make future judgments.

Conclusions, Limitations, and Implications: How Should Reporters Tell the "Facts"?

This study is not without key limitations. Broader and more detailed analyses of the extensive materials cited from the press sources were not the focus of this paper, but would be a fruitful project for future research. Also, the greater part of this research paper lists data extracted from newspaper sources with a pre-assigned categorical (positive, neutral, and negative) analysis of the content. The focus of this initial paper was descriptive and narrative, but the researchers of this project plan to systematically analyze the data by doing a more in-depth qualitative analysis. Acknowledging these shortcomings, this paper still contributes an important analysis of race relations, sport, and media perceptions in the state of Minnesota and the broader society.

America has historically had a separate set of standards for blacks and whites (Harrison, 2000; Harrison & Min, 2001; Lapchick, 1991). In terms of the four coaches examined here, their individual fates are the result of media portrayal, public perception, and performance while employed. In many instances, staff writers may not have intentionally assaulted the character of Green and Haskins. At the same time, many in the mainstream media rarely think about how a story will read in a culture that has significant biases regarding sex, race, and sexual preferences (Leyton-Brown, 2000; Wiggins, 1988).

America is a polarized society (Steinhorn & Diggs-Brown, 2000). At a time in American culture when affirmative action and other access and equal opportunity policies are under attack, any negative press for African Americans and people of color can negatively and permanently impact their futures in the relatively small network of college and professional sports. Extensive social science and related research on race in the media over the last century has indicated that bias is inherent in media reporting in relation to people of color, especially African Americans (Entman & Rojecki, 2000). Coverage is often more volatile, stereotypical, and misunderstood when dealing with African American men (Oriard, 1993; Thomas, 1996). Obviously reporters must tell the facts; how they frame the facts is the key. A pertinent question is, Which facts make the stories more sensational, believable, and/or controversial? Which facts make others question the veracity of the story? Why are white male coaches able to remain in the coaching culture following negative press (violations and infractions), while African American coaches are less likely to be afforded the same chances?

The actions of Dutcher and Woog indicate that while they were involved in negative situations, their behaviors were viewed less severely, as demonstrated by the community's reception. In addition to some favorable articles being written during their respective scandals, Woog was offered a job from his then-current institution. Six years after the scandal involving his student-athletes, Dutcher returned as an analyst for University of Minnesota basketball games. White coaches will often be evaluated by the quality of the program's success in terms of won-lost records, even if the success was relatively brief. On the other hand, African American coaches are often either not given enough time to prove themselves, or in cases where they have won, not given second chances at the "big time" if problems occur off the playing field during their tenures, even with problem programs that were inherited, such as when Clem Haskins succeeded Jim Dutcher. Among the problems with these discrepancies, the negative media attention conditions us to believe that the actions of African American coaches are more unacceptable than those of white coaches.

Sport reflects society (Coakley, 2001), and in this case, the discrimination against African Americans in the society also plays out in the worlds of sport and collegiate coaching. Judging from the outcomes for both white coaches in comparison to Green and Haskins, our early conclusions seem to be underscored.

1. White American coaches who lose their jobs continue to successfully navigate in the system.
2. African American coaches who lose their jobs do not successfully navigate in the system and usually do not get other opportunities.

If Woog and Dutcher switched positions with Green and Haskins, would the same amount of coverage have taken place? Race is ingrained in society and, therefore, in sport. A question of how the black community would read things was raised in one story, while it was never framed in terms of how white communities would receive and react to not only Haskins and Green, but also to Woog and Dutcher. Theories of whiteness inform us that the status quo (white) is not "outed" in these situations. Thus, their whiteness may have protected Woog and Dutcher from the beginning, even if their stories had been very negative, which they were not.

In conclusion, the behaviors of Green and Haskins were portrayed as being traits of both African Americans in general and of African American men in executive positions. This is problematic, not only for future opportunities for Green and Haskins, but also, more importantly, for race relations and integration in general. This correlates with the work of some social psychology scholars (Wheeler, Jarvis & Petty, 2001), who consistently find statistically significant differences in their research investigation(s) on how whites react to behaviors by African Americans and vice versa in situations such as those described in this study in Minnesota. The "in group" (whites) attributes specific attitudes and behaviors to the "out group" (African Americans) using a stereotypical schema about African Americans (Wheeler, Jarvis & Petty, 2001). The opposite holds true when the "in group" (whites) is assessing negative attitudes and behaviors of others in their own group (Aronson, Lustina, Good, Keough, Steele & Brown, 1999). In this case, they are more likely to attribute these attitudes and behaviors to the individual and not see them as stereotypical of the group (Petty, Fleming & White, 1999). Often, African Americans fear that when a negative incident occurs involving African Americans, all African Americans will be "painted with the same brush" and stereotyped (Lapchick, 2000).

Lipsitz's seminal study, *The Possessive Investment in Whiteness* (1998), argues that both public policy and private prejudice have created a "possessive investment in whiteness" that is responsible for the racialized hierarchies of our society. He uses the term "possessive investment" both literally and figuratively:

> Whiteness has a cash value: it accounts for advantages that come to individuals through profits made from housing secured in discriminatory markets, through the unequal educations allocated to children of different races, through insider networks that channel employment opportunities to the relatives and friends of those who have profited most from present and past racial discrimination, and especially through intergenerational transfers of inherited wealth that pass on the spoils of discrimination to succeeding generations. (p. 3)

Lipsitz contends that "the artificial construction of whiteness almost always comes to possess white people themselves unless they develop anti-racist identities, unless they disinvest and divest themselves of their investment in white supremacy" (p. viii). If this was applied to the media, an in-depth diversity management training program could be held in which topics of stereotypes, how they are formed, and how the media reinforces them could be explored. Those in the training sessions could then demonstrate ways to break these patterns.

Finally, it would enhance this study to survey the Minnesota community regarding how people feel about race and ethnicity in news stories. However, social desirability and political correctness can conceal honest perceptions, feelings, and attitudes about African Americans in a predominantly white world (Steinhorn & Diggs-Brown, 2000). The true measure of this study will be told in future years, as Green and Haskins attempt to navigate the coaching and corporate culture with such negative black images (i.e., irresponsible, unethical) in the minds of many whites (Gates, 1997; Golden, 1994).

Recommendations

The following are some solutions that reporters and journalists can apply from the theoretical and empirical findings in the present study.

1. Frame stories equally for all ethnic groups and gender distinctions.
2. If there are inaccuracies, come back with the same intensity and media hype to explain what is true versus what is false.
3. Promote the positive attributes to balance out stories, even when things are negative or fall into a pattern of character demonization.
4. Use photos that are less stereotypical or that do not reinforce historical myths and damaging character attributes about people of color, specifically African Americans.
5. Collaborate with scholars and researchers to examine public opinion of the issues they cover.

In terms of future research, there are a few future projects specifically related to these data that can continue to inform our understanding of race, sport, and media. One, analyzing the photos used in the stories of the four coaches would be informative to test the level of bias in the images and photos selected by the writers. Two, coding the reporters' statements and narratives in the 102 articles to identify raw data themes and sub-themes beyond the categories of positive, negative, and neutral may reveal deeper analyses of the level of bias. Third, all the methodologies used in the present study and mentioned for future studies could be applied to other negative stories in sport and society (i.e., coverage of Latrell Sprewell compared to Kevin Greene). In terms of the broader issue of race and sport, more studies should examine how the public perceives incidents that involve people of color being viewed by mainstream audiences and vice versa. The more data and public discourse we create, the better our chances for creating a world where perhaps things may not be viewed in black and white.

Acknowledgments

Both authors thank Jonathan Adams, research assistant in the DeVos Sport Business Management Graduate Program and Robeson Center at the University of Central Florida, for his assistance with this chapter.

References

Allport, G. (1954). *The nature of prejudice.* Redding: CA: Addison-Welsey.

Aronson, J., Lustina, M.J., Good, C., Keough, K., Steele, C.M. & Brown, J. (1999). When white men can't do math: Necessary and sufficient factors in stereotype threat. *Journal of Experimental Social Psychology, 35,* 29–46.

Biagi, S. & Kern-Foxworth, M. (1997). *Facing difference: Race, gender and mass media.* Thousand Oaks, CA: Pine Forge Press.

Brooks, D. (2002). NCAA African American head coaching opportunities: Unequal access and unequal outcome. Paper presented at the Kinesiology Seminar at the University of Michigan, Ann Arbor.

Brown, D., Firestone, C. & Mickiewicz, E. (1994). *Television/radio news minorities.* Queenstown, MD: The Aspen Institute.

Burstyn, V. (1999). *The rites of men: Manhood, politics, and the culture of sport.* Toronto: University of Toronto Press.

Chideya, F. (1999). Holding the media accountable. In W. Mosley, M. Diawara, C. Taylor, & R. Austin (Eds.), *Black genius: African American solutions to African American problems* (pp. 215–244). New York: W.W. Norton & Company.

Coakley, J. J. (2001). *Sport in society.* New York: McGraw Hill.

Dixon, T. & Linz, D. (2000a). Overrepresenation and underrepresentation of African Americans and Latinos as lawbreakers on television news. *Journal of Communication, 50*(2), 131–154.

Dixon, T. & Linz, D. (2000b). Race and the misrepresentation of victimization on local television news. *Communication Research, 27*(5), 547–573.

Entman, R. & Rojecki, A. (2000). *The black image in the white mind: Media and race in America.* Chicago: University of Chicago Press.

Gates, H. (1997). *Thirteen ways of looking at a black man.* New York: Random House.

Golden, T. (1994). *Black male: Representations of masculinity in contemporary American art.* New York: Whitney Museum of American Art.

Harrison, C.K. (2000, May). Examining the history of whiteness in sport: Gender, class, race, and image. Paper presented at the North American Society for Sport History Annual Meeting in Banff, Alberta, Canada.

Harrison, C.K. & Min, S. (2001, May). Stereotypes and ethnic heritage in sport: Guilty until proven innocent and then still guilty. Paper presented at the North American Society for Sport History Annual Meeting in London, Ontario, University of Western Ontario.

Hunt, D. (1999). *O.J. Simpson facts & fictions: News rituals in the construction of reality.* Cambridge: Cambridge University.

Kincheloe, J., Steinberg, S., Rodriguez, N. & Chennault, R. (1998). *White reign: Deploying whiteness in America.* New York: St. Martin's Griffin.

Lapchick, R. (1991). *Five minutes to midnight: Race and sport in the 1990's.* Lanham, MD: Madison Books.

Lapchick, R. (2000). Crime and athletes: New racial stereotypes. *Society, 37*(3), 14–20.

Lapchick, R.E. & Matthews, K.J. (2001). *Racial and gender report card.* Boston: Center for the Study of Sport in Society.

Leyton-Brown, K. (2000, May). A discourse on race: Jack Johnson in Saskatchewan's newspapers. Paper presented at the North American Society for Sport History Annual Meeting in Banff, Alberta.

Lipsitz, G. (1998). *The possessive investment in whiteness.* Philadelphia: Temple University Press.

Marable, M. (2001). *What black America thinks.* Boston: Houghton-Miffin.

McIntosh, P. (1988). *White privilege and male privilege: A personal account of coming to see correspondences through work in women's studies.* Paper 189. Wellesley College.

Oriard, M. (1993*). Reading football: How the popular press created an American spectacle.* Chapel Hill: University of North Carolina Press.

Oriard, M. (2004). *King football: Sport and spectacle in the golden age of radio & newsreels, movies & magazines, the weekly & daily press.* Chapel Hill: University of North Carolina Press.

Patton, M.Q. (2001). *Qualitative evaluation and research methods* (3rd ed.). Thousand Oaks, CA: Sage Publications.

Petty, R.E., Fleming, M.A. & White, P.H. (1999). Stigmatized sources and persuasion: Prejudice as a determinant of argument scrutiny. *Journal of Personality and Social Psychology, 76,* 19–34.

Roediger, D. (1998). *The wages of whiteness: Race and the making of the American working class.* New York: Verso.

Rothenberg, P. (2000). *Invisible privilege: A memoir about race, class, & gender.* Lawrence: University Press of Kansas.

Steele, C.M., Spencer, S.J. & Aronson, J. (2002). Contending with group image: The psychology of stereotype and social identity threat. In M.P. Zanna (Ed.), *Advances in experimental social psychology* (Vol. 34, pp. 379–440). San Diego: Erlbaum Publishers.

Steinhorn, L. & Diggs-Brown, B. (2000). *By the color of our skin: The illusion of integration and the reality of race.* New York: Penguin Group

Stone, J. (2002). Battling doubt by avoiding practice: The effects of stereotype threat on self-handicapping in white athletes. *Personality and Social Psychology Bulletin, 28,* 1667–1678.

Thelin, J. (1994). *Games colleges play.* Baltimore: John Hopkins University Press.

Thomas, R. (1996). Black faces rare in the press box. In R. Lapchick (Ed.), *Sport in society* (pp. 212–233). Thousand Oaks, CA: Sage Publications.

Thornton, M. (2001). Black newspaper coverage of relations with Asian Americans and Latinos during the LA riots. *African American Research Perspectives,* (7)1, 207–213.

Wheeler, S.C., Jarvis, W.B. & Petty, R.E. (2001). Think unto others: The self-destructive impact of negative stereotypes. *Journal of Experimental Social Psychology, 37,* 173–180.

Wiggins, W. (1988). Boxing's sambo twins: Racial stereotypes in Jack Johnson and Joe Louis newspaper cartoons, 1908 to 1938. *Journal of Sport History, 15,* 3.

11

Duke Lacrosse

An Exploration of Race, Class, Power, and Privilege

Angela J. Hattery and Earl Smith

NONE OF US, OUTSIDE OF THE FEW who were in attendance at the party at 610 North Buchanan Boulevard in Durham, North Carolina—aka the "Duke Lacrosse House"—will ever know what happened the night of March 13, 2006. We are not forensic scientists or attorneys or law enforcement agents, and it is not our job to uncover the facts or proclaim the "truth." We are sociologists, and our concern is for the way that social institutions and membership in status groups shapes behavior at the individual level, specifically examining the decision by a group of college male athletes to hold a party and hire strippers from across town. What we will do in this chapter is examine what we know about the events that transpired at the "Duke Lacrosse House" and attempt to understand how they developed in the first place. We will undertake this examination within the context of a theoretical paradigm known as the race, class, and gender (RCG) theory. We will demonstrate that the events that transpired at the "Duke Lacrosse House" were shaped by the race, class, and gender of the participants and that these events can best be described as an expression of power and privilege that led to exploitation and oppression. Furthermore, we argue that the institutions to which the individuals belonged (the men were members of the Duke University community, and the women were members of a low-income, primarily African American community of Durham, North Carolina) also shaped the ways in which the events at the "Duke Lacrosse House" played out. We begin with a discussion of RCG theory.

Race, Class, and Gender Theory

The race, class, and gender framework was largely developed by black and multiracial feminists (Andersen, 2001; Davis, 1983; Hill-Collins 1994, 2004; King 1988; Zinn & Dill, 2006). This theoretical paradigm rests on the assumption that systems of oppression and domination (i.e., patriarchy, capitalism, and racial superiority) exist independently and are woven together in what Baca Zinn and Thorton Dill (2006) refer to as a matrix of domination. They and others argue that many phenomena from child rearing (Hill & Sprague, 1999) to the wage gap (Padavic & Reskin, 2002) to incarceration (Hattery & Smith, 2007a; Western, 2006) and violence against women (Esqueda, 2005; Hattery, forthcoming; Hattery & Smith, 2007a) are best understood when we consider the independent and interdependent effects of these systems of domination. We begin by discussing each system of domination separately. After we discuss each of the systems separately, we will consider the ways in which the systems of oppression form a matrix of domination.

Gender Domination

Around the world, gender relations are structured by the system of patriarchy (Acker, 2006) that dictates ideologies, beliefs, behaviors, roles, and relations between men and women (Epstein, 2007; Lorber, 1995). As a system of power and oppression, it dictates a set of inequalities based on gender. Gender ideologies are predicated primarily on the belief that there are inherent biological differences between men and women, and that men, as a class of people, are superior to women. The differences that are most frequently cited are those related to women's reproduction (pregnancy, childbirth, and lactation), and to men's greater strength and superiority of intellect. This latter belief is so pervasive that as recently as 2005, former Harvard University president Larry Summers argued that the reason there were fewer women earning Ph.D.s in science and engineering fields than men was because women were naturally inferior in terms of the intellectual skills required for success in these fields. In short, he suggested women were naturally inferior in "math" (Bombardieri, 2005).

Patriarchy infuses both institutions and individual men with power and privilege. In the case of rape, men have the power at the individual level to force women to submit to their sexual needs. And, though rape can be and is about sex—namely that men have the individual power to dictate the terms of sex, such as when they want it, how they want it, and with whom they want it—it is also an expression of power: At its most basic level, it is about the ability to control the body of another person (Brownmiller, 1975; MacKinnon, 1991; Sanday, 2007). At the institutional level, men control all of the institutions that respond to a rape and validate it—or not (Martin, 2005). Men make up the majority of law enforcement officers; they make up the majority of prosecuting and defense attorneys, as well as judges. Therefore, men, not women, define what actions constitute a rape, when a rape has occurred, and when a rape should be prosecuted. Rape, then, at both the individual and institutional levels can be seen as an act that men engage in to enforce gender inequalities: It serves to remind women of their place.

One of the important contributions of RCG theory is that it illuminates the ways in which privilege and oppression are institutionalized. Though many people can see the way in which rape is an example of male power, the usual focus on individual crimes by individual men often renders invisible the ways in which gendered power is institutionalized. This invisibility often results in the belief that widespread discrimination and oppression have ceased to exist in contemporary America. The RCG paradigm allows us to see the ways in which institutionalized privilege continues. Finally, we note what many have said but Acker (2006) so eloquently summarizes, a statement we argue holds true for all systems of domination: "One of the privileges of the privileged, it has been observed, is to not see one's own privilege" (p. 118).

Racial Domination

The United States has been ruled by a system of racial domination from its very inception. As soon as Europeans arrived in the New World, they defined the Native Americans as "savages" and less than fully human. Within the first years of settling Jamestown, European settlers, who had already begun the systematic genocide of the Native Americans, began to import slaves from Africa. African slaves and their descendants were also defined as less than fully human. Their status as chattel was codified in the 1858 Supreme Court decision in the case of Dred Scott (Hattery & Smith, 2007b). Though nearly 150 years have passed since the legal end of slavery, the system of Jim Crow that dominated the post-emancipation period until the civil rights movement firmly ensconced an ideology of racial superiority and patterns of racial domination. As is the case with gender oppression, this ideology of racial superiority dictates patterns of race relations that are based on inequalities. At both the individual and institutional level, whites hold the power, and African Americans and other non-whites face discrimination, blocked opportunity, and outright violence. Evidence of a system of race-based inequalities can be seen in attitudes: Only 6 percent of whites believe racism is still a serious problem—but 12 percent believe Elvis is still alive; 62 percent believe that African Americans would prefer to live on welfare than work (Wise, 2001). During the aftermath of Hurricane Katrina, when thousands of Katrina victims had been evacuated to the Astrodome in Houston, former first lady and mother of the sitting president of the U.S., Barbara Bush, noted that ". . . so many of the people in the arena here, you know, were underprivileged anyway, so this is working very well for them" (*New York Times*, September 7, 2005).

As is the case with gender, the system of racial domination is institutionalized. African Americans, who were denied access to most social, political, and economic institutions for the first 350 years of the history of the United States beginning with the first settlements in Jamestown (until the famous *Brown v. the Board* Supreme Court decision in 1954), are underrepresented in virtually every institution in the United States (Zweigenhaft & Domhoff, 2005) except for prisons, where African American men make up half of the total inmate (male and female) population (Hattery & Smith, 2007a; Western, 2006). The only mainstream institutions in which African Americans are overrepresented are in college and professional football and basketball, though even here they are overrepresented as players but grossly underrepresented as coaches, managers, presidents, commissioners, and owners (Smith, 2007). At virtually every position of decision making in virtually every institution of consequence in the U.S. (the economy, politics, law enforcement, entertainment, education, and the criminal justice system), whites (white men, in particular) hold nearly all the power. At both the individual and institutional levels, the system of racial domination shapes race relations so as to reinforce racial inequalities.

Class Domination

Class inequalities are often more difficult to see in the United States because of our strongly held and shared belief that we are in fact living in a true meritocracy. Most Americans believe in the adage that hard work, sacrifice, and deferred gratification will be rewarded. Those at the top are believed to have earned their position, and those at the bottom (the poor) are believed to have failed. Yet, as many scholars have noted, class advantage is accumulated and passed down inter-generationally in such a way that the best predictor of one's social class is the social class of one's parents (Guinier, 2006; Parkin, 1979; Wright, 1997).

The institutionalization of class privilege is perhaps even more difficult to see than that associated with either race or gender. We illustrate with an example from tax policy. Most Americans are not aware that social security is actually designed as a *regressive tax*. All workers are assessed a 7.65 percent tax (FICA) that provides the funding for social security benefits. Yet this tax applies only to the first $94,200 of earned income. Any income earned above $94,200 is not subjected to this 7.65 percent tax. Thus, the affluent have the *privilege* of not paying FICA tax on a portion of their income, and as a result, their total FICA tax liability is actually a lower percentage than that paid by middle- and working-class employees. Members of the U.S. Congress earn approximately $174,000 per year; because of the $94,200 cap, only 53 percent of their earned income is subjected to FICA tax. Thus congresspeople pay FICA at an overall rate of 4.13 percent (whereas you and I pay the full 7.65 percent). This simple example serves to illustrate one of the ways in which social class privilege is institutionalized and results in the oppression and exploitation of middle- and working-class people (Acker, 2006).

Race, Class, and Gender Intertwined

Systems of race, class, and gender domination can also be intertwined in mutually reinforcing ways that make them even more potent. For example, when we consider the example above of the U.S. Congress setting tax policy that privileges the affluent, we also have to consider the fact that *most of the lawmakers and those who benefit from these tax policies are white and male.* In the next section, we examine the ways in which institutionalized privileges related to race, class, and gender play out in individual lives. We illustrate with an example rampant in Southern communities: the sexual abuse of African American women by white men during slavery and the era of Jim Crow (Davis, 1983).

During the 250 years that slavery legally existed in what is now the United States—including during the colonial period—white men routinely had nonconsensual sex with African American women slaves (Johnston, 1970, p. 217). This behavior occurred at all levels of the social class strata, all the way up to the third president of the United States, Thomas Jefferson (Lanier, 2000). After the official end of slavery, many Southern white households employed an African American woman as a housekeeper or domestic. The systematic sexual abuse of these women is well-documented (Halsell, 1969) and again extends all the way up the social class ladder to longtime U.S. Senator Strom Thurmond, who "sowed his wild oats" with the young African American woman working in his parents' house (Staples, 2003). Herein, we can see the way that a system of racial domination—and, to a lesser degree, social class inequality—can create an environment ripe for gender oppression, expressed as the systematic sexual abuse of African American girls by white men (Halsell, 1969; Hattery & Smith, 2007a).

The Night of March 13, 2006: The Duke Lacrosse House

A Duke Lacrosse team spring break "tradition" involves going out to a strip club as part of the initiation of the first-year players (Hull, 2006). Typically the team is traveling to tournaments during spring break, but during the 2006 season they were at home in Durham. That, coupled with the fact that so many of the players were "underage" and would need "fake IDs" in order to get into the strip clubs, prompted the team to decide instead to throw a party and hire strippers to come to them. Many of the upper-class players and parents judged this decision to be prudent, given the fact that obtaining and using fake IDs would have constituted illegal behavior. We note that they were not similarly disturbed by the fact that serving alcohol to underage players at the party was also illegal. All of these decisions led to several of the upper-class players on the team agreeing to host a party at what would become known as the "Duke Lacrosse House."

The party that afternoon started about 2 p.m. and as the day wore on, the players were in and out of the house. What is not in dispute here is that there was drinking and two exotic dancers were hired to perform that night. By the time the dancers arrived after 11 p.m., 35 players from the lacrosse team were at the party. . . . "I'd say at least half of them were tipsy or better. Tipsy or better," says Kim Roberts, the other dancer paid to perform that night and a central witness in the case. (CBS News, 2006a)

Both of the women who were hired to strip at the "Duke Lacrosse House" are African American, and both can be described as low-income or poor. The alleged victim in the case provided insight into her social class by articulating her reasons for stripping: At the time, she was a single mother of two who was working on her college degree at North Carolina Central University in Durham (one of North Carolina's Historically Black Colleges & Universities, or HBCUs) while also working in a nursing home for $10 an hour. This wage put her and her children barely above the poverty line. Thus, she indicated that stripping was a way to earn the extra money she needed to provide for her children and continue to pursue her education.

There is little evidence available to outsiders about the actual events that transpired between approximately 11:00 p.m., when the women arrived at the party, and 12:30 a.m., when the police were called to respond to the alleged victim who had passed out in a car in the parking lot of a nearby convenience store. What has been reported consistently in the media, however, indicates that the environment at the "Duke Lacrosse House" that night involved both sexual and racial exploitation. Two women were hired to take off their clothes in front of thirty-five or so men who were in various states of intoxication. The women were asked if they had sex toys with them, and when they indicated they did not, they were offered a broom handle, a tool that has often been used in violent rapes (Lefkowitz, 1997). Finally, upon leaving the party, there was tension on both sides. The young men indicated that they felt cheated because the strip act they paid $800 for was supposed to last two hours and the women left after an hour or so (CBS, 2006a); the alleged victim indicated that she had been raped. Layered upon all of this, various individuals, including the "second" stripper, Kim Roberts, corroborate the fact that racial epithets were spewed:

"So, he was mad. And it ended with him callin' me the n-word. And it echoed, so you heard n….. once, and then you heard, n….., n….., n….. ." Roberts acknowledges that her taunting provoked that remark but tells Bradley, "But when I think about it again, I say he could've said black girl. You know what I mean? He could've said black girl. He didn't have to go that route." A neighbor also told police he overheard a player yelling in Roberts' direction "Thank your grandfather for my cotton shirt." (CBS, 2006a)

Though none of us outside this incident will ever know the truth about the events that transpired at the "Duke Lacrosse House," the details that have been made public (and laid out above) can be interpreted as an exercise of power and privilege shaped by the race, class, and gender of the individuals as well as the institutions to which they did or did not belong.

The Response

Within weeks of the "Duke Lacrosse House" party, Durham County district attorney Mike Nifong filed charges against three of the Duke lacrosse players, and on April 17, 2006, two of players, Reade Seligmann and Collin Finnerty, were indicted. The third player, team captain David Evans, was indicted on May 16, 2006. Duke University suspended the players, fired the head coach, and canceled the remainder of the lacrosse season. Throughout the summer and early fall, while the players maintained their innocence, Nifong was re-elected to his post as district attorney, but began facing trouble of his own. Finally, in December 2006, after DNA testing could not link any of the three players to the semen tested, the charges were dropped. In January 2007, Nifong was charged with ethics violations by the North Carolina Bar Association, and Duke University responded by reinstating both the student-athletes themselves and the team, which resumed play in the spring of 2007. We are not arguing in this chapter that the criminal justice system failed by letting guilty men go free. What we are arguing is that regardless of whether or not a legally substantiated rape occurred, the party at the "Duke Lacrosse House" is a clear example of the exploitation of poor African American women by affluent white men.

The Duke Lacrosse Party as an Expression of Power and Privilege

As we outlined above, the framework provided by the race, class, and gender paradigm is useful in interpreting the events that transpired on and around the "Duke Lacrosse House." We begin by analyzing each component of RCG theory separately (gender, race, and class), and then move to a discussion of the ways that these components were intertwined that night.

Gender Dynamics

Regardless of the precise details of what happened the evening of March 13, 2006, at the "Duke Lacrosse House," we do know that the party was a sex-segregated event that involved the sexual exploitation of a few women by many men. Some argue that stripping cannot be considered an act of exploitation because (a) it is a "choice" and (b) it involves economic remuneration. We argue that within the context of patriarchy, a system wherein men can and do enforce their power and privilege through the action of rape, stripping must be understood as a risky, humiliating experience that leaves women vulnerable, *literally naked*, to the men who have hired them. This vulnerability is exacerbated by the fact that the gender composition of the party, which is typical of stripping environments, resulted in the women being numerically in the minority. By many estimates, there were thirty-five Duke lacrosse players—all men—at the party and only two women: those hired to strip. This sex-segregated environment results in a kind of vulnerability whose magnitude is difficult to measure but is certainly powerful.

Many accounts of these types of rituals, from bachelor parties to fraternity initiation practices, highlight the ways in which stripping, gang rape, and other forms of sexual degradation are integral to male bonding (Sanday, 2007). In their investigation into the Duke lacrosse party, ABC News reports:

> By every account, having strippers on campus was part of a male bonding ritual, often with a dozen or more young men present. (2006)

We argue that the events at the "Duke Lacrosse House" were an expression of male power and privilege at both the individual level (the young men who hired the strippers and watched them strip) and the institutional level. At the institutional level, the individual Duke lacrosse players have access to greater power and privilege than they could ever have on their own. First, they have access to the power and privilege imbued to them from the team. An article in *Rolling Stone*, based on interviews with Duke students, confirms the level of prestige these players had on campus:

> This is a coup. "'Laxers,' as lacrosse players are universally known, tend to be the 'most desired and most confident guys on campus. They're fun. And they're hot. It's something that frustrates and often baffles other young men, particularly those who've had girlfriends stolen by these guys. But women understand. "'It's a BMOC thing," Sarah says. She's undecided about the rape charges but is much more certain about the boys. "They have it all—you want a part of that," she says. (Reitman, 2006)

Though not every Duke lacrosse player hired these strippers—nor did every player exploit or abuse these women—all had access to power and privilege based on their membership in an institution, Duke University, that like most other colleges and universities is more concerned about protecting men accused of rape than of finding justice for the victims. According to a January 2007 report by the Judicial Affairs Office at Duke University, there were no reported sexual misconduct cases among students off-campus during the previous year. Yet statistics from national probability studies conducted by the Bureau of Justice indicate that

> *For a campus with 10,000 women, the number of rapes could exceed 350 per year. . . .* The vast majority of the sexual assaults occurred in the evening and in residences, with 10 percent taking place in a fraternity residence. . . . *Respondents in this study reported sexual attacks to law enforcement officials less than 5 percent of the time.* (Fischer, Cullen & Turner, 2000)

Thus, though part of the explanation for low rates of reported sexual assault on the Duke campus could be attributable to non-reporting by victims, the fact remains that like most college and universities, Duke rarely pursues allegations of rape. This is especially the case when the accused are high-profile athletes, as was the case involving the University of Colorado football team that was detailed in an amicus brief filed in the Katie Hnida case against the University of Colorado.

Racial Dynamics

As noted previously, the United States is a society in which a system of racial superiority and domination has been ensconced since our very beginnings. Specifically, whites—as individuals, as a class, and as white institutions—have benefited from this system of domination, whereas African Americans and others have—as individuals, as a class, and at the institutional level—been the victims of racial discrimination and exploitation.

With regard to the specific allegations in the Duke lacrosse case, which involved the sexual exploitation and alleged rape of African American women by white men, we noted previously that this configuration has been a long-standing dark secret in U.S. history (see Halsell, 1969; Johnston, 1970; Lanier, 2000). Furthermore, in terms of the criminal justice system, disparities exist with regard to arrests, prosecution, and sentencing based on the race of the victim and the offender. For example, when white men are sentenced for rape, they are sentenced to ten months less than African American men convicted of similar crimes (Durose & Langan, 2001).

At the institutional level, we note the racial differences between the communities that the individuals in the Duke lacrosse case belonged to. Duke University is a predominately white institution (PWI) that, like most other institutions in the South during Jim Crow, practiced racial segregation; Duke admitted its first African American student in 1963. Today, Duke's "Fact Sheet" (Duke Fact Sheet, 2005–2006) reports that the undergraduate student body is 11 percent African American—and 56 percent white. In contrast, Durham, North Carolina—the community that surrounds Duke—is 40 percent African American—or nearly four times more diverse than the campus, according to recent census figures (United States Census).

At the individual level, the party at the "Duke Lacrosse House" involved white men hiring African American women as strippers. At the institutional level, white Duke students hired African American residents of Durham for exploitation, thus replicating a racial pattern that has been predominant during the more than 150-year history of the institution.

Class Dynamics

Class privilege occurs in many different ways. We focus here on two distinct ways in which class privilege contributed to the events at the "Duke Lacrosse House": the class differences among the individual actors, and class differences at the institutional level. We begin at the individual level.

Shortly after the case "broke" in the media, particularly after young men started to be identified, family members and friends of the accused men started to talk publicly. Among the comments were statements about the fact that not all of these young men were "rich." And, certainly, they all weren't. However, these young men—college students who were on scholarship and thus barred by the NCAA from working for wages—were able to pool enough funds to buy enough alcohol to serve dozens of partygoers who partied, according to reports, for at least twelve hours. Although we don't know the exact amount spent on liquor and perhaps some food, we do know that the Duke lacrosse players paid the strippers $800. To provide some context for this figure, we note that an individual working a minimum-wage job brings home, after taxes, approximately *$800 per month*. In other words, although $800 may not seem like an extraordinary amount of money to many of our readers, the fact that college students were able to cobble together an amount equivalent to the *monthly wages of a minimum-wage worker* and spend it on something as "frivolous" as strippers indicates that they had some class privilege. Though by their parents' accounts these young men were not rich, we can conclude here that they were not poor.

In contrast, the women who were hired to strip *were* poor. As noted previously, the woman who made the rape allegation was, at the time of events at the "Duke Lacrosse House," a single mother. By some accounts, she was not receiving child support from the father of her children; she was, however, working a job that kept her and her children hovering just above the poverty line, and she admits that stripping for her half of the $800 was something she needed to do to make ends meet (Edin & Kefalas, 2005; Edin & Lein, 1997; Hattery & Smith, 2007a). To put the pay ($400) this woman received for stripping in context, if public estimates of her wages are correct, the $400 she earned at the "Duke Lacrosse House" on the night of March 13, 2006, is more than a week's take-home pay from her full-time job at the nursing home. Thus, an amount that clearly meant very little to the young men themselves meant a great deal to the young woman. In turn, this class difference between the Duke lacrosse players and the women they hired to strip created an opportunity for exploitation.

At the institutional level, Duke University has long been known as a "rich" school. Again, according to the "Fact Sheet" (Duke Fact Sheet, 2005–2006) posted on the university's website, Duke's endowment was valued at $3.8 billion on June 30, 2005. To provide a context for this, among the 3,000 or so institutions of higher learning, Duke is ranked in the top fifteen for endowment. As was the case in relation to race, Duke is an affluent "island" in the middle of a lower-middle-class community. Durham's median household income is slightly lower than the median household income for the United States, and the poverty rate is slightly higher.

We conclude that despite any individual variations in the social class of the Duke lacrosse players, these young men had access to privileges that accrue to members of elite institutions. First of all, those in the Durham community would simply stereotype the young men as rich "Dukies," regardless of the financial backgrounds of their families. Access to this type of social class status in and of itself grants an individual privileges in a community comprised of lower-income and working-class residents. Second, these young men had, at least in theory, access to the financial, legal, and overall support of one of the wealthiest, most elite institutions of higher learning in the United States.

Though some of the parents of the Duke lacrosse players believed they were abandoned by the university when their season was cancelled in the spring of 2006, we provide two illustrations of the support these young men received from the university and its members. First,

> Many of the women I spoke to say they are deeply concerned for the lacrosse team, whose "lives have been totally ruined." *They are not overly concerned for the victim, who, many girls point out, was a stripper.* The boys, they add, were the kinds of guys who could get any girl they wanted. "They don't need to stoop to that level in order to have sex with somebody," one girl, a junior, tells me. (Reitman, 2006)

Second, we note that once the charges were formally dropped against these young men in early January 2007, Duke University extended privileges to them, offering that they could move back, re-enroll, and begin taking classes whenever they were "ready." As college professors, we know that institutions of higher learning have strict deadlines for moving in, registering, and attending classes. Thus, any flexibility in the deadlines for these processes is a clear extension of privilege.

With regard to the young men's legal defense, we note that many alumni rallied around them; presumably, had they needed additional legal assistance, it would have been available through a wide network of Duke alumni as well as through the lacrosse community. For example, it was widely reported in the media that the more affluent Duke lacrosse parents immediately promised to fund the legal defense of any player who might be accused and could not afford the best lawyers money could buy (Hull, 2006).

In contrast, though we would never underestimate the kinds of support the community of Durham offered the alleged victim in the aftermath of the events of March 13, 2006, which included rallies and other public shows of support, this is clearly not a community that would easily be able to raise the funds necessary to fight the most elite institution in its midst: Duke University.

Race, Class, and Gender Dynamics Intertwined

In this chapter we have argued that what happened at the "Duke Lacrosse House" was in many ways a very predictable tragedy. At both the individual and institutional level, the Duke lacrosse players had access to at least three vestiges of power and privilege: gender, race, and class. And they exploited individuals who were oppressed based on these same three dimensions: They were poor African American women. We are not the only people who have interpreted the events this way—so did many local residents.

> "We understand that the legal system is that you are innocent until proven guilty," said sophomore Kristin High. "But people are nervous and afraid that these people are going to get away with what they did because of a wealthy privilege, or male privilege, or a white privilege." (CBS News, 2006b)

We noted from the outset that we do not know all of the details of the events that transpired at the "Duke Lacrosse House" in March 2006. What we have done in this chapter is analyze the events we can verify, utilizing the framework provided by the race, class, and gender paradigm. In short, we have argued that the party at the "Duke Lacrosse House" provides an excellent illustration of the ways in which race, class, and gender privilege, at both the individual and institutional levels, can combine to produce exploitation. Using this analysis, we suggest that the Duke lacrosse players' decision to host a party and hire African American women from Durham to strip should not be seen as surprising—or random.

Why not? Men, from an early age, are socialized to see women as sex objects who are available for their pleasure and exploitation (MacKinnon, 1991; Sanday, 2007). For white men, the early lessons are also racialized: African American women's bodies are of little or no value and can be exploited without penalty (Halsell, 1969; Hattery & Smith, 2007a; hooks 2000). Because these messages are embedded so early and so deeply, we suspect that the Duke lacrosse players behaved without being cognizant of them. Evidence for this is clear in the examination of the reactions of their parents and fellow classmates to the events.

Furthermore, we posit the following: If the power and privilege associated with the systems of patriarchy, racial domination, and class exploitation were not at work and were not intertwined, why didn't these young men simply hire some female Duke students to strip at their party? For all the reasons explicated in this chapter, this scenario is highly unlikely. Furthermore, a scenario in which African American male students at North Carolina Central University would hire white, female Duke students to strip at one of their parties is not only less likely; it never would happen. Never.

Epilogue

After we completed the first draft of this chapter on April 11, 2007, all charges against the Duke lacrosse players who were indicted in the alleged rape on March 13, 2006, were dropped by the North Carolina Attorney General's Office. Because our intent in this chapter was never to debate the legal events of March 13, 2006, we do not believe this ruling has any bearing on our argument. The events of that night involved exploitation based on race, class, and gender privilege at the individual and institutional levels.

Some have speculated that the real crime committed in the Duke lacrosse case was committed by Mike Nifong, the district attorney at the time. As of this writing, Nifong faces ethics hearings at the North Carolina Bar Association and could be disbarred if his conduct is found to be in violation of the ethical principles of the office of the district attorney. Some have claimed that he "ran roughshod" over the law. Others have focused on the fact that the media and scholars like us assumed the young men involved were guilty before proven innocent. Finally, many suggest that Nifong charged forward with the indictment of these three young men, knowing he did not have the evidence to convict, because he was up for re-election (in North Carolina, district attorneys are elected), and this action would help him garner the vote in the local black community.

We argue that if, in fact, Nifong behaved unethically in charging three young white men with a crime for which he had no evidentiary support in order to garner the vote in the black community as he sought re-election, then his behavior can also be interpreted using the analysis around which we have built this chapter: Nifong, an affluent white man with the power of an entire legal structure behind him, exploited the tragedies of a poor, African American woman for his own benefit.

Only when the events of the "Duke Lacrosse House" party and the actions of Nifong are examined utilizing the lens provided by the race, class, and gender paradigm can we see that regardless of the legality of the events that transpired, what happened that night is an example of exploitation based on race, class, and gender. Perhaps the district attorney's behavior was based on the same forms of exploitation: He had a victim he could "use" for his own gain in much the same way that the Duke lacrosse players used the bodies of the strippers when they hired them to strip.

References

ABC News. (2006). Duke Lacrosse Scandal Sheds New Light on the Stripper Industry: A Campus Trend? Rape Case Gives Look inside the World of Exotic Dancers and Their Clientele. ABC News. April 24, 2006. Retrieved from http://abcnews.go.com/US/print?id=1882072.

Acker, J. (2006). *Class Questions, Feminist Answers*. New York: Routledge.

Andersen, M. L. (2001) Restructuring for Whom? Race, Class, Gender, and the Ideology of Invisibility. *Sociological Forum* 16:181–201.

Bombardieri, M. (2005). Summers' Remarks on Women Draw Fire. Boston *Globe*. January 17, 2005, A1.

Brownmiller, S. (1975). *Against Our Will: Men, Women, and Rape*. New York: Simon and Schuster.

CBS News. (2006a). Duke Rape Suspects Speak Out. October 15, 2006. Retrieved from http://www.cbsnews.com/stories/2006/10/11/60minutes/printable2082140.shtm.

CBS News. (2006b). Rape Allegations Cloud Duke Lacrosse. March 29, 2006. Retrieved from http://www.cbsnews.com/stories/2006/03/29/sportsline/printable1449886.shtml.

Davis, Angela Y. (1983). *Women, Race, and Class*. New York: Vintage Books.

Duke Fact Sheet. (2005–2006). Retrieved from http://www.dukenews.duke.edu/resources/quickfacts.html#students. Fact sheet for the 2005–2006 academic year. Retrieved April 15, 2007.

Durose, M. & Langan, P. (2001). *State Court Sentencing of Convicted Felons, 1998 Statistical Tables*. Washington, DC: US Department of Justice.

Edin, K. & Kefalas, M. (2005). *Promises I Can Keep: Why Poor Women Put Motherhood before Marriage*. Berkeley: University of California Press.

Edin, K. & Lein., L. (1997). *Making Ends Meet: How Single Mothers Survive Welfare and Low-Wage Work*. New York: Russell Sage Foundation.

Epstein, C. F. (2007). Great Divides: The Cultural, Cognitive, and Social Bases of the Global Subordination of Women. Presidential Address to the American Sociological Association. *American Sociological Review* 72:1–22.

Esqueda, C. (2005) The Influence of Gender Role Stereotypes, the Woman's Race, and Level of Provocation and Resistance on Domestic Violence Culpability Attributions. *Sex Roles: A Journal of Research* 53: 821–834.

Fischer, B. S., Cullen, F. T. & Turner, M.G. (2000). The Sexual Victimization of College Women. *Bureau of Justice Statistics*. Washington, DC: National Institute of Justice.

Guinier, L. (2006). The Meritocracy Myth: A Dollars and Sense interview with Lani Guinier. *Dollars and Sense*, 263, January/February. Retrieved from http://www.dollarsandsense.org/archives/2006/0106guinier.html.

Halsell, G. (1969). *Soul Sister*. New York: Fawcett Books.

Hattery, A. (forthcoming). *Intimate Partner Violence*. New York: Rowman & Littlefield.

Hattery, A. & Smith, E. (2007a). *African American Families*. Thousand Oaks, CA.: Sage Publications.

Hattery, A. & Smith, E. (2007b). Dred Scott, White Supremacy and African American Civil Rights. Pp. 445–447 in W. A. Darity (ed.), *International Encyclopedia of the Social Sciences* (2nd edition). Farmington Hill, MI.: Thomson Gale, Inc.

Hill, S. A. & Sprague, J. (1999) Parenting in Black and White Families: The Interaction of Gender with Race and Class. *Gender & Society*, 13 (4):480–502.

Hill-Collins, P. (1994). Shifting the Center: Race, Class, and Feminist Theorizing about Motherhood. Pp. 45–66 in E. Glenn, G. Chang, & L. Forcey (ed.), *Mothering: Ideology, Experience, and Agency*. New York: Routledge.

Hill-Collins, P. (2004). *Black Sexual Politics: African Americans, Gender, and the New Racism*. New York: Routledge Publishers.

hooks, b. (2000). *Feminist Theory: From Margin to Center*. Cambridge, MA: South End Press.

Hull, A. (2006). Lacrosse Players' Case a Trial for Parents: Faith in Their Sons' Innocence Sustains Them amid Ravages of Scandal. *Washington Post*, June 10, A01.

Johnston, J. H. 1970. *Race Relations in Virginia & Miscegenation in the South, 1776–1860*. Amherst: University of Massachusetts Press.

King, D. (1988). Multiple Jeopardy, Multiple Consciousness: The Context of a Black Feminist Ideology. *Signs* 14(1):88–111.

Lanier, S. (2000). *Jefferson's Children: The Story of One American Family*. New York: Random House.

Lefkowitz, B. (1997). The Boys Next Door. *Sports Illustrated*, June 23, 1997, p. 76.

Lorber, J. (1995). *Paradoxes of Gender*. New Haven, CT: Yale University Press.

MacKinnon, C. (1991). *Toward a Feminist Theory of the State*. Cambridge, MA: Harvard University Press.

Martin, P. (2005). *Rape Work: Victims, Gender, and Emotions in Organization and Community Context*. New York: Routledge.

New York Times. (2005). "Barbara Bush Calls Evacuees Better Off." *New York Times*. September 7, 2005. Retrieved from http://www.nytimes.com/2005/09/07/national/nationalspecial/07barbara .html?scp=2&sq=barbara+bush+september+7+2005&st=nyt; accessed May 15, 2010.

Padavic, I. & Reskin, B. F. (2002). *Women and Men at Work* (2nd ed.). Thousand Oaks, CA: Pine Forge Press.

Parkin, F. (1979). *Marxism and Class Theory*. New York: Columbia University Press.

Reitman, J. (2006). Sex & Scandal at Duke: Lacrosse Players, Sorority Girls and the Booze-Fueled Culture of the Never-Ending Hookup on the Nation's Most Embattled College Campus. *Rolling Stone*. June 1, 2006. Retrieved from http://www.rollingstone.com/news/story/10464110/sex__scandal _at_duke.

Sanday, P. R. (2007). *Fraternity Gang Rape*. New York: New York University Press.

Smith, E. (2007). *Race, Sport and the American Dream*: Chapel Hill, NC: Carolina Academic Press.

Staples, B. (2003). Senator Strom Thurmond's Deception Ravaged Two Lives. *New York Times*, December 26.

United States Census Bureau. *American Fact Finder*. Data for Durham County, North Carolina. Estimates for 2006. Retrieved from http://factfinder.census.gov/servlet/ACSSAFFFacts?_event =ChangeGeoContext&geo_id=05000US37063&_geoContext=&_street=&_county=Durham& _cityTown=Durham&_state=04000US37&_zip=&_lang=en&_sse=on&ActiveGeoDiv=& _useEV=&pctxt=fph&pgsl=010&_submenuId=factsheet_1&ds_name=ACS_2008_3YR _SAFF&_ci_nbr=null&qr_name=null&reg=null%3Anull&_keyword=&_industry=. Retrieved April 15, 2007.

Western, B. (2006). *Punishment and Inequality in America*. New York: Russell Sage Foundation.

Wise, T. (2001, July 17). "Why Whites Think Blacks Have No Problems." AlterNet. http://www. alternet.org/story/11192/.

Wright, E. O. (1997). *Class Counts: Comparative Studies in Class Analysis.* New York: Cambridge University Press.

Zinn, M. B. & Dill, B. T. (2006). Theorizing Difference from Multiracial Feminism. Pp. 193–202 in *Social Class and Stratification: Classical Statements and Theoretical Debates,* R. Levine (ed.). New York: Rowman & Littlefield.

Zweigenhaft, R. L & Domhoff, G. W. (2005). *Diversity in the Power Elite.* New Haven, CT: Yale University Press.

12

Asian Americans in Unexpected Places

Sport, Racism, and the Media

C. Richard King

Q: Name two athletes who broke the color barrier in professional sport in 1947.

A: African American baseball legend Jackie Robinson, as almost everyone knows, began a ten-year career with the Brooklyn Dodgers, and little-known Japanese American guard Wat Misaka played in three games for the New York Knicks.

Q: Name the Asian American athlete selected as a Most Valuable Player for his performance in a Super Bowl.

A: Korean American wide receiver Hines Ward was so honored in 2006.

THESE TRIVIA QUESTIONS ARE ANYTHING but trivial. In fact, the elusiveness of the answers for many readers underscores an unspoken aspect of sport in America: Media preoccupations and audience prejudices erase the presence and excellence of Asian American athletes and coaches, fostering accounts that promote misunderstanding and misrecognition. Too often, fans, journalists, and even scholars act as if Asian Americans do not play sports, and when they do, prevailing interpretations accentuate or efface their Asian heritage, resulting in distorted representations that twist, limit, and undermine the humanity of Asian Americans on and off the playing field. Moreover, collective remembrance through sport routinely celebrates the achievements of African American athletes like Robinson, while all but forgetting the accomplishments of Misaka and countless other Asian American athletes (Franks, 2000). These patterns offer valuable lessons about the biases of sport media and the scope and significance of racism in the contemporary United States.

Previous studies have suggested that popular accounts of sports have great difficulty treating Asian Americans fairly or accurately (Creef, 2004; Franks, 2000; Hanson, 2005; King, 2006; Mayeda, 1999). On the one hand, such accounts have hidden Asian Americans from view (Hanson, 2005), recycling a discourse that is either unable or unwilling to discuss their identities, histories, or athleticism. On the other hand, sport media rely on stereotypes in their coverage of Asian American athletes, often preferring clichés and jokes to grounded coverage of individuals and their achievements (King, 2006). In what follows, I explore the cultural ideologies and social arrangements that render Asian Americans visible and invisible in sport media, detailing the key terms through which fans come to (mis)understand them.

Expectations

In his recent historical analysis, *Indians in Unexpected Places*, Philip Deloria (2004) unpacks what he dubs "expectations" about American Indians and Indianness. Although expectations should seemingly be simple, for Deloria they refer to the complex interlockings of preconceptions and practices through which individuals and institutions have figured and refigured what it has meant to be an Indian. Consequently, he endeavors to expose the ideological arrangements and social formations that have shaped the making, unmaking, and remaking of Indianness by Indians and non-Indians alike. Although concerned with Native Americans during the first quarter of the twentieth century, Deloria's history offers an instructive model for thinking through the ways in which interpretive frames render individuals visible, acceptable, and understandable. Following Deloria, we might argue that sport media and their consumers do not expect Asian Americans to play or coach sports. According to Yun-Oh Whang, a professor of Sport Marketing at the University of Central Florida, "It is common that coaches and teachers at schools presume that an Asian American kid belongs in the science lab, not on the football field" (Lapchick, 2002, para. 7). Such preconceptions, and the racial ideologies that anchor them, foster a context in which sport is an unexpected place for Asian Americans. In turn, those Asian Americans who do enter sporting worlds find themselves out of place. In a real sense, fans, coaches, and journalists encounter difficulty interpreting their presence, which strikes them as incongruous, problematic, and even difficult to comprehend.

More often than not, the reiteration of stereotypes and "sincere fictions" seek to resolve these interpretive problems and ideological contradictions. Following Stuart Hall (1997), I understand stereotypes to emerge from a complex set of cultural relations and practices that condense and communicate simplified meaning about marked groups in unequal social systems. Stereotyping works to naturalize, flatten, and essentialize difference, and, in turn, works to explain and extend existing social hierarchies. Notably, the signifying practices central to stereotyping also lend themselves to the telling of sincere fictions, or sanctioned stories that mystify and mythologize social arrangements and actions and thereby seek to resolve lived contradictions. Moreover, as sociologists Hernan Vera, Joe Feagin, and Andrew Gordon (1995) write:

> These socially accepted fictions are sincere because the actors usually are genuine and honest in their adherence to these rationalizations and are either unaware of or have suppressed the alternative interpretations—psychological, sociological, and historical—of the events or people being fictionalized. (p. 297)

In other words, fans, coaches, and journalists rely on stereotypes of others and familiar stories about the social world to make sense of the presence and absence of Asian American athletes, the extent of their athletic ability, the core of their character, and so on.

The case of quarterback Timmy Chang offers a telling summary of the role of expectations, stereotyping, and sincere fictions in the (in)visibility of Asian American athletes. Chang had an outstanding career at the University of Hawaii, marked by a string of records including total offensive yards, career passing yards, career plays from scrimmage, and most passes completed without an interception. Despite his impressive achievements, Chang was not selected in the 2005 National Football League (NFL) draft, but signed as a free agent with the Arizona Cardinals, before moving on to the Detroit Lions, the Rhein Fire of NFL Europe, and the Philadelphia Eagles. In 2007, he joined the Hamilton (Ontario) Tigercats of the Canadian Football League ("TiCats Sign QB Timmy Chang," 2007). According to Richard Lapchick (2006), Chang's collegiate greatness and professional obscurity turn on prevailing expectations:

> . . . a scout said at the NFL combine that Chang is too short to play quarterback in the NFL. Chang is 6-foot-1, which makes him as tall as or taller than several current NFL quarterbacks. When these comparisons were noted, the scout reportedly answered, "But he plays short." (para. 7)

Much as sincere fictions about African Americans lacking the intelligence and character to play quarterback long segregated them from the position, so, too, do accepted understandings of Asian Americans put limits on public perceptions of them and, in turn, on the positions they play on the field and the pursuits they undertake beyond it.

Naturalness

Even before an Asian American athlete takes the field, then, preconceptions shape interpretations. Significantly, physicality plays an important role in delimiting such interpretations, serving as a transit of sorts between sporting worlds and racial ideologies, both of which depend on popular conceptions of the body. Many Americans cling to the belief that Asian Americans possess superior intellectual gifts, especially in areas like math and science, while displaying a pronounced lack of physical prowess. They are not natural athletes, this line of racist thinking posits further, in part because of feminine characteristics others project upon them, including docility, reserve, and softness. Understood to be smart and feminine, popular sentiments have concluded, Asian Americans could never compete in the physical and masculine domain of sports. If it is not natural—in other words, defies expectations—for an Asian American to be naturally gifted at sports, this does not mean there are not born players. In contrast with the image of feminized, intellectual, and unathletic Asian Americans, popular conceptions of African Americans have long defined them as natural athletes who were thought to be intellectually inferior and hyper-masculine. This complex racial calculus, according to David Leonard (2005), has consequences for the opportunities afforded players and coaches, reinforcing the hierarchical logic structuring sport in the United States:

> The absence of Asian American coaches (and players) embodies the long-standing feminization of all things "Asian," which, in turn, reserves desired athletic and leadership qualities for white coaches. . . . This racialized definition of Asian men as weak exists as a guiding obstacle to Asian advancement in the collegiate ranks. Similarly, white supremacist discourses that position black men as purely physical, without the mental capabilities of their white counterparts, contribute to a scarcity of black coaches. The exclusion of [Norman] Chow and so many black coaches is the effect of the same racist system and hegemony of ideologies. The failure to investigate the links between Chow and, for example, Tyrone Willingham (the recently fired black head coach at Notre Dame), limits the discussion to individual prejudice and to a black/white binary. (para. 18)

Importantly, then, the unnaturalness of Asian Americans in sport affirms a system that appears natural, one that excludes them and contributes to a rigid ranking of racial groups. Rendered overly feminine, Asian Americans cannot be viewed as players or considered for coaching jobs. Moreover, because they are removed from the playing field, barriers to their inclusion and advancement cannot be linked with broader efforts for equity and justice in sport. Instead, familiar images of the natural state of affairs, even when subject to criticism about exploitation and exclusion, remain a conversation that is cast in black and white, a discourse that misrecognizes and marginalizes Asian Americans.

Black-White Paradigm

More often than not, sport does not simply confirm the natural abilities of individuals and groups, but it also reproduces the most prominent means for making sense of racial difference in the U.S.: the black-white paradigm, which dictates that racial inequality can best be understood by an examination of past and present relations between Euro Americans and African Americans. C. Richard King and Charles F. Springwood (2001) worked to expose the limitations of such a framework in their exploration of the interplay of whiteness, blackness, and Indianness in collegiate sport. Rather than a binary, they found that racial meanings, identities, and opportunities were triangular and dialogic, dependent on the articulations of expectations about multiple groups. Previously in this chapter, Leonard affirmed this assertion, underscoring the import of including Asian Americans. Significantly, though, the black-white paradigm displays great resilience and works to recast discussions of race in black and white terms, thus erasing and rendering invisible once again Asian Americans and their contributions.

No individual better illustrates this pattern than golfer Tiger Woods, who has sought to fashion a hybrid identity acknowledging his Asian, African, European, and indigenous ancestors. The media, fans, and other golfers have roundly resisted this desire and have most frequently and vocally represented him as a black golfer—much to the chagrin of some in the Asian American community. Among the more telling public applications of the black-white paradigm—and by extension, erasure of his Asian American-ness—were comments made by Fuzzy Zoeller at the 1997 Masters Golf Tournament at Augusta National in Georgia. Zoeller remarked:

> That little boy is driving well and he's putting well. He's doing everything it takes to win. So, you know what you guys do when he gets in here? You pat him on the back and say congratulations and enjoy it and tell him not to serve fried chicken next year . . . or collard greens or whatever they serve. (Thill, 1997, para. 18)

In what was later described as a joke, Zoeller called on the one drop rule to put Woods in his place, through a play on words and associations with decided racist connotations. Zoeller explicitly figures Woods as black, reducing the complexities of his ethnic heritage and racial identity to a singular and devalued category. In the process, Zoeller not only erases Woods' Asian ancestry, but also the presence of Asian Americans in contemporary sport. Scott Thill (1997) has argued that in this joke, we can see the reassertion of a classification scheme that demands clear social categories and manageable racial hierarchies. Thus, even as racial identities and relations become more diverse and complex, Americans fall back on outdated binaries: "They need the One True Logic or the One True Classification so they can keep that which gave them all they ever had: their power." Clearly, so long as the black-white paradigm serves as the key interpretive framework for Americans, Asian Americans—especially those who are mixed-race like Hines Ward and Tiger Woods—will be out of place in sport, difficult to recognize, and harder to "make sense of."

Disturbing Images

Not surprisingly, sport media and their audiences import established stereotypes and sincere fictions to interpret Asian American athletes. For instance, the large number of Asians and Asian Americans on the Women's Professional Billiards Tour has fostered a discourse that plays off antiquated understandings of sexual power, Oriental exoticism, and feminine charms to portray the players and their achievements. The nicknames of the players highlight this pattern, with Jeanette Lee being dubbed "The Black Widow" and Miyuki Sakai as the "Lady Samurai." Similarly, one fan described a match between two Asian American competitors as "The Battle of the Dragon Ladies"—beautiful but deadly, skilled and seductive (see for instance, "Battle of the Dragon Ladies," 2007). Alongside the sexualized dragon ladies, the effeminate Asian (American) man continues to struggle against superior white and black athletes. A recent Vitamin Water advertisement featured Boston Red Sox player David Ortiz and Chicago Bears linebacker Brian Urlacher trouncing two anonymous Asians (named Yang and Lau) in a world championship badminton match. Whereas the Americans are dominating, polished, and physically imposing, the Asians, supposedly the world's greatest badminton players, are pictured as meek, awkward, and weak. At one point, Ortiz, known as "Big Papi" for his prowess as a hitter in baseball, hits the shuttlecock so hard it penetrates the leg of one of the Asian players. Needless to say, the hypermasculine Americans win. At the same time, one commonly finds the trope of the model minority employed to describe the achievements of Asian and Asian American athletes. Instead of their natural ability, popular stereotypes of Asian American athletes stress hard work, dedication, discipline, and intelligence to account for their success. Mayeda (1999) first identified this pattern in media coverage of Japanese players in Major League Baseball (MLB), but it appears to have gained traction in reporting on other sports.

While the recycling of clichéd characters is noteworthy, so is the manner in which the sport media routinely represent Asian American athletes as foreign. This perhaps has been clearest in coverage of Olympic figure skating medalists Michelle Kwan and Kristi Yamaguchi (Creef, 2004). Following the victory of Sarah Hughes at the 2002 Winter Games, several media outlets ran stories with the headline, "American Beats Kwan." Although later retracted, the headline clearly equates the USA with whiteness, excluding those of Asian descent. Indeed, in an odd reiteration of the Chinese Exclusion Act more than a hundred years before, the headline renders all Asian Americans foreigners, questioning their belonging and contributions while making them second-class citizens. Similarly, Bill Handel, a disc jockey at KFI AM, opined,

> I'm tired of the Kristi Yamaguchis and the Michelle Kwans! They're not American . . . when I look at a box of Wheaties, all right? I don't want to see eyes that are like

all slanted and Oriental and almond shaped. I want American eyes looking at me. (Tuan, 1999, p. 105)

Again, Asian Americans are portrayed as un-American, physically incapable of being "All-American." To be sure, many reporters and fans described both Yamaguchi and Kwan as full Americans; however, in contrast with all other racial groups in the U.S., Asian Americans are always alien. Or, as Henry Yu (2001) eloquently summarizes:

> Americans are constantly convincing themselves that the United States has already become a place where race does not matter, and they are simply wrong. . . . Asians are still exotic, still bearers of an authentic otherness they cannot shake. Like other nonwhites, Asian Americans remain both Americans and examples through their existence of non-America. (p. 203)

So long as this pattern of expectations and misrecognitions persists, it is doubtful that most Americans will appreciate the accomplishments of Asian American athletes or strive to include them as equals on and off the playing field.

References

"Battle of the dragon ladies." (2007). Online Discussion at AzBillilard Forum. Retrieved May 19, 2010, from http://forums.azbilliards.com/showthread.php?t=59450.

Creef, E.T. (2004). Another lesson in "How to tell your friends from the Japs": The 1992 Winter Olympics showdown between Kristi Yamaguchi of the United States and Midori Ito of Japan. In *Imagining Japanese America: The visual construction of citizenship, nation, and the body* (pp. 145–171). New York: New York University Press.

Deloria, P. J. (2004). *Indians in unexpected places.* Lawrence: University Press of Kansas.

Franks, J.S. (2000). *Crossing sidelines, crossing cultures: Sport and Asian Pacific cultural citizenship.* Lanham, MD: University Press of America.

Hall, S. (1997). The spectacle of the other. In S. Hall (Ed.), *Representation.* London: Sage.

Hanson, S.L. (2005). Hidden dragons: Asian American women and sport. *Journal of Sport and Social Issues 29,* 279–312.

King, C.R. (2006). Defacements/effacements: Anti-Asian (American) sentiment in sport. *Journal of Sport and Social Issues 30* (4): 340–352.

King, C.R. & Springwood, C.F. (2001). *Beyond the cheers: Race as spectacle in college sports.* Albany: State University of New York Press.

Lapchick, R. (2002). Asian American athletes: Past, present and future. Retrieved August 23, 2005, from http://sports.espn.go.com/espn/news/story?id=1376346.

Lapchick, R. (2006). From promise to prominence for Asian athletes. Retrieved May 15, 2007, from http://sports.espn.go.com/espn/news/story?id=2449595.

Leonard, D.J. (2005). Beyond black and white: Norm Chow and the case for minority hiring. *Popmatters.* Retrieved October 2, 2005, from http://www.popmatters.com/sports/features/050303-normchow.shtml.

Mayeda, D.T. (1999). From model minority to economic threat: Media portrayals of Major League Baseball pitchers Hideo Nomo and Hideki Irabu. *Journal of Sport and Social Issues 23,* 203–217.

Thill, S. (1997). The importance of being Tiger Woods. *Bad Subjects* 35. Available online from http://bad.eserver.org/issues/1997/35/thill.html.

TiCats sign QB Timmy Chang. Retrieved April 15, 2007, from http://www.ticats.ca/index.php ?module=newser&func=display&nid=15579.

Tuan, M. (1999). Neither *real* Americans nor *real* Asians? Multigenerational Asian ethnics navigating the terrain of authenticity. *Qualitative Sociology 22* (2): 105–113.

Vera, H., Feagin, J.R. & Gordon, A. (1995). Superior intellect? Sincere fictions of the white self. *The Journal of Negro Education 64* (3): 295–306.

Wu, F.H. (2002). *Yellow: Race in America beyond black and white.* New York: Basic Books.

Yu, H. (2001). *Thinking Orientals: Migration, contact, and exoticism in modern America.* Oxford: Oxford University Press.

13

Katrina's Tragic Wake and a Saintly Rescue

A Work in Progress

Richard Lapchick

I FLEW TO BATON ROUGE ON September 7, 2005, with anger in my heart over what had not happened in New Orleans. I was angry that my country could not adequately respond to the horror in those streets, where water became the enemy of the people. I was angry that thousands of Americans were stranded in the Superdome and at the Convention Center, and that almost all of these were poor and African American. It is open to debate whether or not we failed to move to rescue those people, possibly at the expense of thousands of lives, because those stranded did not look the same as most of our government and corporate leaders. For my part, I do believe that if there were 10,000 white people stranded, we would have been mobilized in a heartbeat. If I were African American, I would not have any doubt. Once the forces were mobilized, we became an efficient machine, and those who were stranded were evacuated within days. Food, drink, clothes, and all kinds of essentials were brought to Louisiana, Mississippi, and Alabama quickly. Donations poured in for victim relief from across America and from around the world.

I began to wonder how the rebuilding of such devastated areas could proceed. Most of all, I wondered how the anger, sadness, and great sense of loss could be overcome, and how the racial gap in America could be healed. But I have seen several examples of America's ability to rebuild over the course of history. I have been working in the world of sport for more than three decades and have seen sport and athletes work to transform society and help it heal. Most recently, I saw it with the New York Yankees in the 2001 World Series, after September 11. In the case of New Orleans, I immediately thought of the New Orleans Saints and Hornets, and how they might contribute to such a transformation. However, over the course of the next several months, and indeed the next several years, I was amazed by and proud of the outpouring of support and strength from the sport world. This paper is an attempt to recognize how sport can transform society and the lives of those in it, and the power we hold to help heal the wounds after a tragic event.

Making a Difference: Athletes and Sport Organizations Get Involved

Most of us involved in sport know the power it has to unite and inspire. An examination of the response from athletes and sport organizations after the devastation of Hurricane Katrina demonstrates this power and exemplifies how this event brought forth the best from many different athletes, professional and college teams, athletic departments, and other sport associations. In a time when society focuses on the poor decisions and imprudent actions of a handful of athletes, the efforts of these individuals and groups demonstrate the humanity that also exists within the world of sport. The goodwill and heroism of the sport world emerges, reigniting hope for many. It was sport at its best, and the response was widespread, representing teams, athletes, and supporters of every kind.

What follows are just a few of the examples of generous athletes and sport organizations making a difference for the victims of Hurricane Katrina.

College

- The University of Georgia and the UGA Athletic Association conducted a coordinated collection at the Georgia vs. University of South Carolina football game and received more than $54,000 in donations during the Southeastern Conference (SEC) matchup.
- "Coaches Caring across America" was created to help rebuild the Gulf Coast of the United States by working with Habitat for Humanity. All money raised through the auction went directly to Habitat for Humanity.
- The SEC and its twelve member institutions donated $1 million to various Hurricane Katrina relief efforts.
- The University of Connecticut Student-Athlete Advisory Committee (SAAC), in conjunction with the American Red Cross, raised a total of $30,000 for the victims of Hurricane Katrina at the Connecticut vs. Liberty University football game.

Professional

- A fund-raising telethon that featured more than thirty current and former National Football League (NFL) players raised $5 million for the Bush-Clinton Katrina Fund.

- Major League Baseball (MLB) and the MLB Players Association donated $1 million to the American Red Cross to aid relief efforts.
- The National Basketball Association (NBA) donated $2 million while the NBA Players Association pledged to contribute $2.5 million to the relief efforts.
- The National Hockey League (NHL) and NHL Players' Association donated $1 million to the American Red Cross efforts to assist those affected by the Hurricane Katrina disaster.
- Lance Armstrong, seven-time Tour de France champion and cancer survivor, donated $500,000 to help cancer patients displaced by Hurricane Katrina, in order to prevent the interruption of vital, lifesaving treatments.
- Indianapolis Colts quarterback Peyton Manning and his brother Eli, quarterback of the New York Giants—both of whom grew up in New Orleans—went to Baton Rouge to help distribute 31,000 pounds of nonperishable items, including baby formula, diapers, and water.
- Tennessee Titans quarterback Steve McNair teamed up with Green Bay Packers quarterback Brett Favre and arranged to fill a tractor-trailer bound for Mississippi with water, canned foods, generators, and other relief supplies. McNair, who is from Mississippi, sent twenty-five tractor-trailers filled with supplies. Favre has raised $140,000 through his website.
- Houston Texans owner Bob McNair matched up to $1 million in fan donations towards relief efforts.
- NBA All-Stars LeBron James, Kobe Bryant, Kevin Garnett, Amare Stoudemire, and Dwyane Wade played in the NBA Players Hurricane Relief Game. Participating players donated funds and supplies valued at more than $1 million to victims of Hurricane Katrina.

It was an amazing outpouring of support, and this is only a very partial listing. It is through generous and committed involvement like this that sport and athletes have the power to make a difference, on and off the field.

My Personal Engagement: Understanding the Human Nature of Tragedy

I started this chapter by writing how I went to Baton Rouge that week after Hurricane Katrina with anger in my heart. I accompanied members of the Orlando Magic on both Wednesday and Thursday of that week, each day delivering 6,000 pounds of relief supplies. We worked in the distribution centers and in two large shelters. There about 1,400 people in the two shelters. The refugees looked sad and drained of energy as we arrived, but when they realized that there were people from the Orlando Magic in the room, magic started to spread. These were people who had lost everything, even loved ones in some cases. However, with the arrival of the athletes and team executives, smiles came across faces and eyes brightened. Grant Hill moved around the room as a people's champion, but Magic executives with unknown names received almost the same attention and affection. There was a joy and amazement that a sports team was there with the refugees in the midst of the tragedy. The power of sport to heal was alive that day. My anger began to shift to a reverence for the life that was left, and the spirit of those who were ready to rebuild their city.

Ever since Hurricane Katrina, I have known, like many other Americans, that I hoped I could do something to help the people of New Orleans who were in such tremendous need.

A Call to Action for the Hometown Team

Four days after Katrina hit, I received an e-mail from Casey Knoettgen, one of my former graduate students who worked for the New Orleans Saints. Below is an excerpt from that e-mail, which details his grief about the tragedy, but also his commitment to do something about it.

> For the last couple of days I have understandably been extremely anxious, nervous, concerned about what is happening to my home . . . the City of New Orleans, all the people that are suffering, still trying to survive, and what is happening to the human spirit of this city. I cannot describe to you the feeling of what it's like to send a text message to my friends that reads "Are you still alive?" and then be able to do nothing but wait, hoping to hear from someone. As social order deteriorates in New Orleans, the nights become a terrifying time of waiting, hoping your loved ones live through the night, and that when the sun comes up there will be news of relief and forward progress, instead of more disaster.
>
> Speaking of hope and forward progress. . . . You opened my eyes to the power that sports have to influence people and society into positive courses of action for change. In those 2 years I spent with you at UCF I grew an understanding of how people who are in a leadership position have the responsibility to do something for the betterment of society. I believe that the New Orleans Saints can and should be an extremely instrumental part in rebuilding the spirit of this city and [its] people. . . . I believe that the Saints and the Fleur-de-lis symbol can become something that these lost, displaced, desperate people of New Orieans can rally behind to realize that New Orleans does in fact have a future and that we will find a way to recover and rebuild this community. Can you think of a more immediate thing that people from all walks of life can identify with? I feel like there is such a sense of urgency right now and feel the Saints need to take action immediately.

Soon after I received this e-mail, the Saints traveled to play the Carolina Panthers for the opening game of their 2005 season. In the morning they visited a shelter housing evacuees from New Orleans, and afterward took all of them to the game. The Red Cross made efforts to show the Saints' games in shelters throughout the country, and more than 600 shelters were set up to enable evacuees to watch the games. This was just the beginning of the relationship between the Saints and restoration efforts.

Two star running backs from the Saints, Deuce McAllister and Fred McAfee, spent the weekend before the opening game in shelters set up in Mississippi. Afterward, McAllister, well-known for his philanthropy and commitment to the community, joined McAfee, along with Saints wide receiver Michael Lewis and San Diego Chargers punter Mike Scifres, to form a coalition they called Athletes Making a Difference, to encourage athletes and citizens of the United States to join together in assisting the victims of Hurricane Katrina. All four grew up in Mississippi or Louisiana and were personally affected by Katrina. In addition, once shelters were set up across Texas, Saints players were regular visitors there. They had a commitment to support not only the rebuilding effort, but also those whose lives had been affected by the tragedy. Their work exemplified what sport can do when it decides to take action—especially when that action is off the field.

Opening Day and Opening Hearts:
The Power of a Team to Bring a City Together

By about 3:00 p.m. in New Orleans on the opening Sunday of the season, the Saints had upset the Panthers, who were favored to be a Super Bowl contender. In Charlotte! A field goal with three seconds left. A miracle. The city of New Orleans needed some miracles, and this was one. The divide between the racial and ethnic groups needed healing, and here was an opportunity. It did not matter whether the Saints players were African American, White, Latino, Asian, or Native American, or whether they were Catholic, Protestant, Jewish, or Muslim. They were Saints, teammates, teaching us all that anything and everything is possible. The Saints were able to bring joy to their fans, in spite of a bad season played away from their home in New Orleans. Their fans, who spanned generations, races, genders, religions, and social classes, supported them through it all. This was their team, and it represented their home, even if they were displaced and no longer in New Orleans, just like the team.

I teach a course in moral and ethical principles in sport. In the opening session of that course, we talked about how the sport world had rallied around the Gulf area in the wake of the storm, how many athletes and teams, colleges and universities, got involved with supporting the victims and the rebuilding efforts. The Saints were a visual symbol of that hope. Even losses by the Saints during the 2005 season did not dampen the love for the team. Wins and losses were never the draw for the fans—if they were, they would have abandoned the Saints long ago.

In the midst of all of the tragedy, the Saints were one of the ongoing sources of small hope and minor miracles. When they opened their season in Charlotte with the win over the Panthers with three seconds left, hope spread across the 600 shelters in Louisiana, Texas, Georgia, North Carolina, Florida, and other places where the evacuees had gone. Suddenly, the Saints had shown that there was a symbol that New Orleans could rally around, and that the city could rebuild. Shortly thereafter, NFL commissioner Paul Tagliabue determined that the Saints would play four games in Baton Rouge in their home state of Louisiana and three games in San Antonio. The owner of the Saints, Tom Benson, had relocated the team to San Antonio shortly after the storm. Rumors were that Benson, owner of the team, wanted to permanently relocate the Saints to San Antonio, where he had roots.

A voice for the team to return to New Orleans throughout this period was Arnie Fielkow, the team's top administrator. The community rallied around this idea, wanting and needing their team. Several weeks into the season, in a stunning move, Benson called Arnie Fielkow into his office and fired him. The newspapers reported that the decision was made because Fielkow was urging the Saints to remain a New Orleans–based team while Benson may have had other ideas about the future for the team. While Arnie was, of course, deeply saddened by the termination, he told me he could live with it if it helped the team move back to New Orleans. This would represent the hope of the city, and the team, and become part of the city's rebuilding effort. Arnie expressed his gratitude that the people of New Orleans had rallied behind his position. They wanted the Saints back and, at least for now, the intervention of the NFL made that happen.

The opening game in the New Orleans Superdome was electrifying. The Superdome, a symbol of horror for thousands of the victims of Katrina who lived in squalor in the days after the storm, was reopened on national television. The game and its televised broadcast showed how bad things still were, but also showed the Superdome as a symbol of hope. The 2006 season for the New Orleans Saints became a shining example of the rebuilding of that great city and of what a community can do when it rallies to make something happen for the betterment of society.

The Power of Individuals and Institutions to Make a Difference

The DeVos Sport Business Management Graduate Program is in the College of Business Administration at the University of Central Florida. It is grounded with all the traditional MBA courses and sport-specific courses in law, media, marketing, selling, and professional and college sport. Unlike other programs, it also teaches classes in ethics, diversity, social issues, and leadership. Service is part of the fabric of the DeVos program—all students must work forty-five hours per semester on service projects.

Soon after the Katrina tragedy, students in the program launched a fund-raising effort in which members of the current classes in the DeVos program, as well as alumni from the program, raised more than $36,000. That was matched by the Orlando Magic, making the total contribution $72,000. However, I wanted the students to have the opportunity to experience the way service can have a very real and very human impact on the world, so I contacted my friend Arnie to find a way for us to participate in relief and rebuilding efforts in New Orleans. After Arnie was fired from the Saints, he searched for a different way to serve the city and was elected to the New Orleans City Council. He is currently vice president of the council and works tirelessly to support the rebuilding and revitalization of the city. His work and commitment are shining examples of what we can accomplish. Through him, I hoped to find a way for my family, my students, and myself to help the relief efforts. After several conversations with Arnie, we spent the fall planning for a December 2006 trip to the area. In the end, ten students joined me (along with my wife, daughter, and two friends from Boston) in New Orleans on December 17, 2006.

On our first night in New Orleans, we met to talk about our expectations. I told the students I was confident that we would never be the same people after this week. The next morning we went on a four-hour tour of the aftermath of Hurricane Katrina. Halfway through the tour, it was clear to me that we were starting with neighborhoods that had been hit, but not as badly as those that had been hit the hardest. Everyone had seen pictures, read stories, and seen the horror on television. Our tour showed the story of the tragedy in full graphic detail. We went from neighborhood to neighborhood. We began in Lakeview, where we saw where the canal was breached on London Avenue, and then went to Gentilly Woods and Pontchartrain Park. We saw many uninhabited homes with FEMA trailers out in front. It was devastating and I could see the students were, like me, becoming angrier and angrier that the people of New Orleans were still living in these conditions, fifteen months after the tragedy.

Then we arrived in the lower Ninth Ward, where the worst devastation took place. We pulled up to a spot where two barges had crashed through the levees, letting the waters pour into the Ninth Ward. Any area where the levees broke received the full force of the terrible power of the water that had been held back by the levees. Those areas also took the pressure off of other areas. For example, nearby was the French Quarter, which became relatively safe because the levees broke and flooded the Ninth Ward. Slowly, we began to understand what we were seeing. Straight ahead we saw remains of homes that had clearly not been re-inhabited. As we looked more closely at the land around us, we realized that there were slabs of concrete representing all that was left of the homes in the three blocks nearest to the breach. Before FEMA would set up trailers and help people return, there had to be water and power. Water and power were only restored in the Ninth Ward approximately one year after Katrina.

We asked our guide (an aide for one of the city council members) about what the priorities were for the city. We were told that a decision had been made to bring back the areas that were economically strong and had resources before attending to areas like the Ninth Ward. He told us that developers felt this incredibly valuable piece of real estate could be developed in a different way. This meant that generations of families who had lived in the Ninth Ward because of its close proximity to the French Quarter might be displaced. This was an area where a substantial portion of African American families in New Orleans had lived. In one fell swoop, New Orleans had gone from a city with a majority of African American residents to a city with a minority African American population. Many residents felt the decision to not restore water or power in the area for twelve months was done to keep former residents away, thus allowing the city to call for the land to be used for other purposes. While there was plenty of reconstruction going on elsewhere, the Ninth Ward was a quiet wasteland. No saws or hammers were heard anywhere in this once-thriving community.

We were dismayed, sad, confused, and angry as we headed to St. David's at St. Maurice, a Catholic church where we were scheduled to help put together bicycles for children in the Ninth Ward. Although no one said anything, I knew everyone was thinking, "What good will these bicycles do in light of all of this devastation?" At the church, we were greeted by Mary, an activist from the group All Congregations Together. She was grateful that such a large group had come. However, it seemed apparent that when she saw our group of fifteen people, she knew there would not be enough work for everyone to do. There were also three college-age students at the church. They had come from Chicago after collecting bikes to donate to children. Their spirit seemed greater than their organizational skills, but they were working hard on putting bikes together. They trained a group of our students to put the bikes together. Another group began cleaning up the church's courtyard. Mary seemed embarrassed by the lack of organization and soon left. When she returned, she told us that we would be able to spend our time helping a parishioner, Mr. Stewart, tear down the walls of his home so he could rebuild. I went with three others in our group to Mr. Stewart's home.

Stanley Stewart was a 51-year-old man who had lived in what was clearly a beautiful home prior to the storm. He had a courtyard that was made out of brick and wrought iron, and had built his home over the course of many years. We worked with him and listened as he spoke about his home. We felt bad as we ripped out the walls of something that he had lovingly built, but we all agreed that the only way he could rebuild was if we did this. We listened as Mr. Stewart talked about the storm. He spoke about how he, his wife, four daughters, and a niece watched the water come across a field in front of their house after the levees broke. When we were there, they lived in a small FEMA trailer next to what remains of his home. He said the water looked like a tidal wave. He pointed to telephone poles that were thirty feet high and said that the water went completely over the top of the poles. Mr. Stewart said that within ten minutes his home went from being dry to having fourteen feet of water inside of it. He said that he and his wife had never disagreed about anything regarding the house, except that she had not wanted him to build a second story over the main part of the house. As they scurried to the second floor, they realized that without it, they all might have died. Mr. Stewart said that they were stranded in the house for a day and a half and were finally rescued by a friend who came by with a boat to take them to safety. They went to the Superdome, and later dispersed to various parts of the country. The family was separated for the better part of a year before they returned.

After working for several hours with Mr. Stewart, we went back to the hotel to discuss what to do in the coming days. The students talked about how angry they were about what they had witnessed and what little sense of hope they felt after the day. I tried to reinforce for them the sense of hope shown to us by this courageous man, and that seemed to help revive their spirits. Most of the students wanted to work at his home the next day, while some agreed to help with the bike distribution at the church, since the children were scheduled to come to the church. The next day, we arrived at the church and were greeted by Mary, who told us that the schools were open finally and there would be no children coming that day. The distribution had been rescheduled for Saturday. Those in our group who had agreed to work at the church that day were relieved that they could now go to Mr. Stewart's house with the rest of the group. We spent the next two full days ripping down walls, running from rats, stepping on cockroaches, and simply trying to help Mr. Stewart and his family in any way we could.

By the end of the first day, a few members of the team went to purchase garden supplies and began planting a garden in the courtyard we had cleared. The courtyard had been filled with debris, bricks, and an old car. By the end of the second day, there were flowering plants in the ground, and a rusty fence had been painted. With one day left, the students voted not to move to any other project and to stay with Mr. Stewart to finish as much as they could. It was pouring on the last day. Rain was coming through the roof and the ceiling above the areas that we had gutted, but it did not deter the students. Some of us went into the garage and started tearing out the walls so that Mr. Stewart could restore his auto-body shop. The previous day, we had swept it and cleared out the floor so he was able to bring in the first car that he was going to repair. His work was resuming, as was at least a small part of his life. Mr. Stewart had secured a generator, and while we were there he was able to turn on the lights—a symbolic moment for him and his family. That day we worked in the rain, and took pictures of Mr. Stewart and his home so we would have memories to share from this extraordinary experience. By the time we left, I knew we would not need keepsakes to remember Mr. Stewart, who continued to tell us stories about the days after Katrina.

He told us there were people in the Ninth Ward who swear that they heard an explosion before the levees broke. There were others who believe that the levees were deliberately destroyed so that Ninth Ward would get the water and not the French Quarter. He said many people believed that with all of the technology and the advanced weather warnings, they should have been able to prevent the barges from breaking loose outside of the Ninth Ward. Whether or not there was any truth to this terrible thought, the fact that it was believable to some of the people in New Orleans was a sobering reality for us to confront. The bold face of racism was once again unmistakably in our faces. This is not to say in any way that Mr. Stewart was bitter. He was grateful to be alive, full of gratitude for what everyone was trying to do for him, and hopeful for the future of his family. As we began to gather to say our good-byes, Mr. Stewart brought us together in a prayer circle and talked about hope. Afterward, we exchanged addresses and knew that we would be part of each other's lives forever.

Ann and I called Mr. Stewart on the evening of December 23, only a few days after our return. It was as if we were with him again in his home. He talked about all of the hope the students had given him, and gave all of them great praise for the hard work that they had accomplished and the great teamwork they had displayed. He spoke about what all of this meant to his family. He went on to tell us how he had gone to church that Saturday to help distribute bikes. Mr. Stewart did not realize at the time that we had been at the church helping to put the bikes together. He told us how over one hundred children arrived at the church, and they watched Christmas come alive before their eyes. The children were happier than any children he had ever seen. They had not expected to get bikes, and everyone felt the joy in the room. These days, a bike in New Orleans was not only a toy, but also a form of transportation.

It was as if the circle had closed. We thought that our first afternoon in New Orleans had been spent less meaningfully, working on bikes instead of working on devastated homes. Yet unknowingly, we were actually in the process of bringing joy to over one hundred children who otherwise might not have had such a great Christmas. We will never forget everything that we saw and did, and we know we will always be a part of Mr. Stewart's life. I am grateful we had this amazing time together. We left New Orleans inspired to do more for the victims of Hurricane Katrina. As a result, the students of the DeVos Sport Business Management Program, in conjunction with the National Consortium for Academics and Sports and assisted by the New Orleans City Council, announced the Hope for Stanley Foundation. It is an effort to create opportunities for people involved in sport across the United States to help rebuild and revive the city of New Orleans. We recognized the power sport has to provide hope, support, and change.

As I work toward finishing this chapter, I look forward to my ongoing service with the Hope for Stanley Foundation. We are organizing student-athletes from across the nation to join sports management students in this effort. All of these efforts are being supported by and through the National Consortium for Academics and Sport and a generous gift from the Rich and Helen DeVos Foundation. In 2007, we were able to bring in two construction crews from New England. They were organized by Smitty Pignatelli, a member of the Massachusetts legislature who was on our first trip to New Orleans. Smitty said, "In nearly thirty years of public service, I have never had a story move me like the story of Stanley Stewart. While there is so much more work to be done in the Gulf Coast area, our commitment is to ensure that Stanley Stewart can move his family back into their home." The original students, my wife, daughter, and I then returned to paint the inside of Stanley's home. Stanley moved back into his newly renovated home before Thanksgiving of 2007. He is a symbol of all the people of the Lower Ninth Ward who have remained strong and hopeful. Our efforts are aimed at getting many of them back to their beloved New Orleans. We are using the power of sport to bring people together and believe in what they cannot see.

The Power of Sport

This chapter presented examples of the power of sport to create change and have a positive impact in the world. Many people speak and write about how sport teaches positive life lessons, but having witnessed what happened after Hurricane Katrina, I also believe sport has the potential to bring change. While institutions involved with sport, like the DeVos program or the National Basketball Association, can make a tremendous difference, it is also the individuals involved in those programs who contribute to the change in significant ways. We need to hold on to the hope that these individuals and institutions give us, to the hope that sport can create spectacular things, both on and off the field of play.

14

Sports and Economics

An Examination of College
Sports and Big Business

Sanford S. Williams

SPORTS REPRESENT A WINDOW into the soul of the culture of its participants. Show me a popular sporting event, and I will show you fanaticism and a microcosm of the culture of that society. Watch a football game in Texas, a soccer match in the World Cup, a basketball game in New York City, or a NASCAR race in North Carolina. The passion that those events evoke, both in spectators and participants, represents what is important and what is valued in those cultures. Likewise, the impact of economics in sports is illustrative of the impact of economics in our culture. Economics plays a powerful role in our culture, and it similarly plays a powerful role in sports, especially college sports. In this chapter, I will specifically examine the impact of economics in college sports, an impact that has paradoxically propelled college sports to new heights of popularity, while subtracting from the essence of what they are about.

I believe the essence of college sports is building character, educating student-athletes, uniting college communities, and celebrating the joys of competition. Often, college sports are able to attain all of the above goals and more. These goals, however, are often perverted or ignored in colleges' pursuit of economic nirvana. More and more, the focus of college sports is shifting from achieving these goals to attaining riches and winning. The result is a moral conundrum with no easy solution.

College sports and economics are inextricably intertwined. The ubiquity of college sports on television, radio, and the Internet has been fueled by and is directly linked to money—lots of it. The impact of money on college sports may be measured by the enormous contracts between the media and universities to broadcast them in a wide spectrum of venues. The impact is also evident in college coaches' robust salaries and the advertising revenue generated by college sports. It all seems like a win-win proposition. The schools and coaches get money and exposure, the media gets to broadcast events the public longs to follow, and advertisers are able to sell their wares. However, all that glitters is not gold, and while there are many positive consequences from the interplay between college sports and economics, there are also negative ramifications. All of this begs the question: Is the intersection of college sports and economics a good thing? I posit that the answer is yes and no.

The Interplay between Sports and Big Business

The Final Four—March Madness—The Bowl Championship Series—The College World Series—The Rose Bowl—The Orange Bowl—The Sugar Bowl—"One Shining Moment." For some, these events epitomize college sport and serve as the ultimate stage for epic battles between student-athletes. These events produce dramas and stars. Who can forget Larry Bird versus Magic Johnson in the 1979 Final Four? The 2006 Fiesta Bowl cemented the stardom of Matt Leinart and Reggie Bush, while catapulting Vince Young to fame and fortune. Doug Flutie's "Hail Mary" pass for the Boston College football team in a 1984 victory over the University of Miami is one of the most famous plays in college sports history—and it did not even occur in a bowl game. However, it is not just the Rose Bowl; it's the Rose Bowl presented by Citi™, or the AllState Sugar Bowl™, the FedEx Orange Bowl™, the AT&T Cotton Bowl™, the Toyota Gator Bowl™, the Tostitos Fiesta Bowl™, and the Capital One Bowl™. As the names of these games indicate, corporate entities are not disinterested bystanders in college sports—they are part of the action. These corporate entities wield so much economic and political clout that they may be aptly termed "Big Business," an economic group consisting of large profit-making corporations (Merriam-Webster Online Dictionary, 2006–2007). The interplay between Big Business and college sports has helped to create events that are not simply games, but spectacles with compelling storylines. These spectacles are hybrids: part money, part sport, part entertainment, and part capitalism. The result is events that are fun to watch and that economically enrich colleges; however, these events do not necessarily enhance the lives of the participants—college athletes.

College sports currently exist in an environment with a 24/7 sports talk show mentality. The media and fans alike constantly cajole, exhort, excoriate, and praise college athletes on a never-ending basis. Some of the media and many of the fans are the athletes' fellow students, so the athletes can't even count on their campus to be a haven from critiques. Due to the increased interest in college sports, the examination and recruiting of prospective athletes has become more intense and more complex. College recruiting is a big business. Not only has recruiting become a big business; recruiting websites have become big business (BBC News, 2007). Grown men and women spend precious hours of their lives watching, listening to, and discussing college sports and all its accoutrements. The insatiable desire for sports information "has created a cottage industry for coaches' shows" (McCarthy, 2007). Attendance at college football games (Johnson, 2007) and attendance at men's and women's college basketball games (Huliq.com, 2007) significantly increased in 2006–2007. Twenty years ago, college football was basically confined to television on Saturdays, and only a precious few teams earned consistent national exposure. College basketball was also primarily confined nationally to weekend exposure. And college baseball and softball were barely blips on the television landscape. Compare that with 2007–2008, when ABC and ESPN televised more than 400 regular and post-season college football games over their family of networks (ESPN.com, 2007), and with 2006–2007, when the same networks televised more than 1,000 men's college basketball games (ESPN.com, 2006). They also telecast the entire Division I National Collegiate Athletic Association (NCAA) Women's Basketball Tournament, the NCAA Division I Men's and Women's College Soccer Championships, the College Cup, the Division I-AA Football Championship, the NCAA Division I Men's Hockey Championship, the Frozen Four, and the Men's and Women's College World Series.

The yin and yang of a capitalist society are supply and demand. It stands to reason that the great increase in the supply of college sports on television is related to a voracious demand for these telecasts. What's driving the increased exposure of college sports in the media? Is it an increase in population? More discretionary time? A fascination with sports in general? A greater caliber of athlete and competition? All of the above may be factors in the increased popularity and visibility of college sports. The driving factor, however, has been the marriage between them and Big Business. This unlikely, some may say unholy, alliance has indisputably led to the increased exposure of college sports, but it apparently has not led to a commensurate increase in benefits for student-athletes or in the furthering of the goals of college sports.

Media Contracts in College Sports

Networks' substantial investment in college sports affords broadcasters not only access, but also a strong voice in the presentation of the games. Networks are often able to dictate the time, place, and participants for athletic contests they televise. The primary driver for these decisions is not the welfare of student-athletes, but rather the optimal programming choice for the networks. Such a rationale is good for the viewing public, but not always in the best interest of athletes. The primary mission of schools is to educate athletes, and networks love to tout that the participants in college sports are *student* athletes. As the *Daily Utah*

Chronicle noted in discussing a nationally broadcast basketball game between the University of Utah and the University of Nevada–Las Vegas that started at 10:00 p.m. on a Monday night in 2001, it is paradoxical to talk about the importance of education for college athletes and then schedule games at inconvenient times for students ("Red-Eye Games Aren't Good for Anybody," 2001).

The effect of Big Business on college athletics permeates many sports. The impact may be understood best by focusing on the contracts between networks and the NCAA to televise college sports. In 1991, CBS began a seven-year, $1 billion contract to televise the NCAA Men's Basketball Tournament (Jacobson, 2006). It is hard to fathom that sporting events could be worth $1 billion for seven years. However, this stunning figure is surpassed six times over by CBS' current contract, which is $6 billion for eleven years and expires in 2013 (ibid.). If a country had a gross domestic product (GDP) of $6 billion, the country would have ranked 121st worldwide (between Namibia and Macedonia) in GDP in 2005 ("Total GDP 2005," 2007). While this example is not a direct comparison (the CBS contract is over an eleven-year period, while the GDP figure relates to one year), it does provide a sense of the enormity of the money involved. The exclusive deal provides CBS with rights to NCAA Tournament game content on the Internet, and merchandising rights for tournament-related products ("CBS Renews NCAA B'ball," 1999). The NCAA and ESPN have an eleven-year agreement that began in September 2002, granting ESPN the television rights to twenty-one NCAA championships, with the crown jewel being exclusive rights to the Division I Women's Basketball Championship ("NCAA Reaches Agreement with ESPN, INC. for Television Rights to 21 Championships," 2001). The agreement allows ESPN to cover all sixty-three games in the Women's Tournament. The lucrative college sports market is creating niche networks such as College Sports Television (CSTV), which officially began in April 2003 as the first twenty-four-hour network devoted exclusively to college sports ("About Us," 2007). In November 2005, CBS purchased CSTV for $325 million (Consoli & Crupi, 2005). In response to CSTV, ESPN created ESPNU in March 2005, a station that is also fully dedicated to college sports (ESPN.com, 2004). As media increasingly devours the right to broadcast collegiate sports, it is inevitable that their coverage and exposure will increase, while the schools enjoy a financial boost from the increased revenue.

NCAA Division I College Football similarly benefits from the largesse of Big Business. In 1998, the Rose Bowl, Allstate Sugar Bowl, FedEx Orange Bowl, and Tostitos Fiesta Bowl combined with the Atlantic Coast, Big East, Big 12, Big Ten, Pacific-10, and Southeastern Conferences and the University of Notre Dame to form the Bowl Championship Series (BCS). The BCS guarantees the champion of these six conferences a berth in one of five BCS bowl games. BCS participation is limited to schools that participate in what was formerly known as Division I-A, but as of 2006 was changed to the "Football Bowl Subdivision" ("What's the Difference between Divisions I, II and III?," 2007).

In 2004, Fox Television and the BCS announced a four-year deal worth $320 million that gave Fox the broadcast rights to the Fiesta, Orange, and Sugar bowls from 2007–2010 and the national title game from 2007–2009 (Prisbell, 2007). And unlike their basketball brethren who had 336 schools in Division I in the 2006–2007 season, the NCAA Division I Football Bowl Subdivision is composed of only 119 schools, resulting in more money for these schools than if they had to share the money with all Division I institutions. Teams in the Football Bowl Subdivision that were unable to secure a spot in a BCS bowl still had a better-than-average chance to make additional money by participating in a different bowl game. All of these bowl games were sponsored by corporate interests. After the 2006 college football season, there were thirty-two bowl games, ranging from the Poinsettia Bowl on December 19, 2006, which paid $750,000 to each team, to the Tostitos BCS Championship Game on January 8, 2007, which paid $17 million to each participant (O'Toole, 2006). Despite the substantial financial rewards the BCS provides, it does not guarantee that the two best college football teams meet in a national championship game. Thus, the primary driver in crowning a "champion" is not to find the best team, reward the athletes who exhibit the most diligence or work the hardest, or seek to validate any of the other goals that are the essence of college sports. Rather, the goal is to make the most money possible.

The only way to have a true national championship football game is to have a tournament, similar to the NCAA's Division I Men's and Women's Basketball Tournaments. If that model is too difficult to follow, the NCAA could do what is done in every other division of NCAA football: conduct a playoff. A playoff would generate substantial revenues for networks and corporate sponsors, and provide an opportunity for student-athletes to establish a definitive champion on the field. If a playoff were instituted, the importance and visibility of the bowl games would decrease. Moreover, playoff games could be played on college campuses, which would limit the amount of class time missed by athletes and enable more games to take place in a university setting—which, in turn, would enhance the camaraderie on those campuses and allow athletes to play more games in the communities they represent. Networks might pay more money to televise a playoff, but the sponsors of smaller bowl games would either be less viable than they currently are, or be out of business altogether. To avoid having a negative impact on Big Business—in this case, corporate sponsors of and advertisers for bowl games—the status quo prevails. And student-athletes who participate in the NCAA Division I Football Bowl Subdivision are denied an opportunity to do what every other NCAA athlete does: compete for a championship. Ironically, one of the major reasons cited for not having a playoff is that student-athletes would miss too much time from school. This is a highly dubious argument, given the vast amount of class time many athletes already miss. It is interesting that proponents of maximizing revenue, which is vastly inconsistent with the mission of college sports, invoke that same mission to justify their actions. The benefits of the current system over a playoff system to athletes are minimal at best and nonexistent at worst. In this instance, Big Business gets what Big Business wants; and in this case, as in others, what it wants trumps both the opportunity for student-athletes to compete for a championship and the ultimate mission of college sports.

The Specific Example of Notre Dame

The University of Notre Dame football team has also benefited from the interest of Big Business. An examination of the interaction between Notre Dame football and Big Business could take up many volumes. The University of Notre Dame in general, and its football team in particular, has had an intense relationship with sports fans nationally and internationally, in large part due to media coverage and exposure. Notre Dame is synonymous with college football. It has so many fans that have no official affiliation with the school that these supporters have been termed "subway alumni" (Drape, 2006). The scope of the interaction here will be limited to a brief delineation of Notre Dame's national football contracts.

The "Golden Domers" have had a contract with NBC to televise all Notre Dame home football games since 1991 ("NBC Cont[r]act Extended through 2010," 2004). This landmark agreement marked the first, and so far only, time a college sports team has had an exclusive contract with a national network to televise its games. NBC contracted to televise all Notre Dame home games for approximately $9 million a year through 2010 (Martzke & Moran, 2003), and NBC later extended that contract through 2015, which will mark the twenty-fifth year of its partnership with Notre Dame (Miller, 2008). Notre Dame has been able to maintain this contract despite not having won a national championship since 1989. All of the $9 million goes directly to Notre Dame; the university does not have to share the money with any other school. Although Notre Dame is affiliated with the Big East conference in other sports, it is an independent football team; thus, it is able to keep all of the money it receives from NBC. This windfall does not include the money Notre Dame receives from the BCS television deal and other NCAA television money, or revenue that Notre Dame receives from participating in bowl games—which Notre Dame also does not have to share. Furthermore, Notre Dame has a radio contract with the Westwood One Radio Network to broadcast its football games nationally, making Notre Dame the only team, professional or collegiate, to have all of its games broadcast nationally.

In 2004, Notre Dame stated that 111 undergraduates received need-based scholarships averaging $17,600 from an endowment funded by revenue from its contract with NBC ("NBC Cont[r]act Extended through 2010," 2004). It added that since the inception of the fund, 1,263 undergraduate students had received more than $12.6 million ("NBC Cont[r]act Extended through 2010," 2004). This funding of need-based scholarships is a noteworthy aspect of the role of economics in college sports, and an excellent example of how Big Business may have a positive impact on colleges. In fact, the scholarship awards further the mission of both colleges and college sports, by educating students and enhancing the connection between athletics and the college community. However, given the stunning amount of money that Notre Dame has taken in from its contracts, the scholarship money is but a drop in the bucket. Where has the rest of the money gone? Most likely, the majority of money has gone to maintaining and improving the football program, and not to furthering the mission of college sports or that of the university at large. Notre Dame's unabashed pursuit of the top dollar for its football contract seems antithetical to simultaneously striving to accomplish the essence of the goals of college sports. Notre Dame is not the only college in this situation, but its status and financial largesse make it stand out from other colleges. With the money it receives, Notre Dame (and other schools) could take a gigantic leap away from Big Business and towards furthering the mission of college athletics by undertaking initiatives such as drastically increasing scholarship awards, or addressing the physical, mental, and emotional toll college athletics takes on athletes (Pennington, 2008). As long as economics is the primary driver in universities' decision making, the mission of college sports will always take a backseat.

Media Control over College Sports

The clout of networks on college sports is also evident in ESPN's broadcasts of NCAA football games. Once upon a time in the fall, Fridays were for high school football, Saturdays were for college football, and Sundays were for professional football. ESPN has revolutionized this framework by televising a college game on every day of the week during the 2006 and 2007 college seasons, and planned to do so again during the 2008 season. ESPN frequently televises weekday men's college basketball games played on the West Coast at midnight, Eastern Standard Time (EST), which means the games begin at 9:00 p.m., Pacific Standard Time (PST). The late start time allows ESPN to televise *SportsCenter*, its daily show that provides the latest sports news. Women's college basketball games on ESPN and other networks are also played and televised at times that are most convenient for broadcasters. Since the networks are the customers for these services, and high-paying customers at that, it is assumed they are entitled to have a voice in the process of how and when the contests should be staged.

As mentioned above, these late start times are not conducive to an optimal educational environment for student-athletes. With college sport telecasts becoming more pervasive, the question arises whether what is good for the networks is good for college sports. More specifically, are student-athletes educated, enriched, and uplifted by participating in contests at a variety of hours during the day and night, subject to the whims of television, or is such participation detrimental to the mission of schools and to student-athletes? An increase in media exposure has increased the concomitant physical, mental, and emotional demands on student-athletes, resulting in an inevitable decrease in the time and energy these students have to devote to their primary purpose in college, obtaining an education (Pennington, 2008). Many of these college students have to deal with stress similar to or greater than the stress faced by professional athletes. According to the *New York Times*, "The life of a scholarship athlete is so arduous that coaches and athletes said it was not unusual for as many as 15% of those receiving athletic aid to quit sports and turn down the scholarship money after a year or two" (ibid., para. 12). This does not enhance or bolster the mission of college sports. And it is not the type of character building sought for or needed by college athletes. No matter how you slice it, this cannot be a good thing. As the focus of college sports shifts from educating athletes and celebrating the joy of competition to catering to networks and winning, many athletes will likely find themselves in the same predicament as Jessica Richter. Ms. Richter was a NCAA Division I basketball player for the Syracuse University women's team (Wolverton, 2007), who transferred after her freshman season in 2004–2005 to a much smaller school, Vanguard University in Costa Mesa, California. While she enjoyed the many luxuries of playing basketball at Syracuse, including chartered flights and eating filet mignon on road trips, she stated that her coaches at Syracuse routinely criticized players and seemed more interested in winning games than getting to know players (ibid.). This type of disenchantment is inevitable when coaches increasingly focus on winning.

Colleges, specifically their presidents, coaches, and athletic directors, need to become more vigilant and ensure that college athletes are provided with optimal opportunities to succeed in the field and in the classroom. There is some evidence that many colleges have taken this charge to heart. In 2007, the Institute for Diversity and Ethics in Sport at the University of Central Florida released its annual study of NCAA Men's Division I Basketball Tournament teams, and the primary author of the study, Dr. Richard Lapchick, noted that "there is substantial good news for the tournament teams when we examine the Graduation Success Rates" ("Academic Progress/Graduation Success Rate Study of Division I NCAA Men's Basketball Tournament Teams," 2007, para. 2). Despite this good news, Dr. Lapchick also noted in that article that he is "alarmed at the persistent gap between African American and white basketball student athletes" (ibid., para. 6). Moreover, the article stated that approximately 36 percent of tournament teams graduated less than 50 percent of their basketball student-athletes.

Based on these findings, more work needs to be done to ensure that all college athletes achieve their potential in the classroom.

Coaches' Contracts

Colleges and universities are not the only entities that profit financially from Big Business. College coaches are also direct beneficiaries of corporate investment. Financial stability for coaches is wonderful for both coaches and the institutions they represent. However, this profit comes at a price. Coaches have increased pressure to succeed, which shifts the focus of major college sports from building character and educating student-athletes to winning as much as possible. According to a *USA Today* article, head coaches at the NCAA's top-level football schools made an average of $950,000 in 2006, not counting benefits, incentives, subsidized housing, or any additional compensation they frequently receive (Upton & Wieberg, 2006). The article indicates that at least 42 of the 119 Division I-A coaches earn at least $1 million annually, up from a total of five in 1999, and that nine coaches made more than $2 million in 2006, while one coach, Bob Stoops of the University of Oklahoma, made more than $3 million. The article correctly attributes the high salaries to "a tidal wave of money from schools' lucrative television and apparel contracts—and from the latest skyrocketing revenue sources, multimedia and marketing rights deals for entire athletic programs or entire campuses" (para. 17).

While discussing University of Oklahoma (OU) football coach Bob Stoops and his greater than $3 million annual salary, OU's athletics director Joe Castiglione stated that "Bob Stoops is worth every penny he gets" (Wieberg, 2006, para. 2). The University of Oklahoma won only twenty-three games in the five years prior to Stoops' arrival; after his arrival, the article said, the Sooners won fifty-five games and the 2000 national championship (ibid.). Stoops' impact on the success of OU has been substantial. Nevertheless, Stoops has arguably had an even greater financial impact on the university. OU's athletic revenues increased from $26.1 million in 1998–1999, the year before Stoops arrived, to $64.6 million in 2005–2006 (ibid.). In that same time frame, OU increased its ticket sales by $19.5 million and its total revenues by $21.8 million. In 2005–2006, the OU athletic department made a profit of $20 million (ibid.). This dramatic financial impact has to affect the dynamics between the football program, the university, and the university's mission to educate students.

NCAA Division I men's college basketball coaches also are highly compensated. *USA Today* studied the contracts of fifty-eight of the sixty-five coaches of teams that played in the 2006 NCAA Tournament, and reported that the average salaries of the coaches were approximately $800,000 (Upton & Wieberg, 2007). In six major conferences—the Atlantic Coast, Big East, Big Ten, Big 12, Pacific-10, and

Southeastern—the average coach's salary climbs to $1.2 million (ibid.). More telling is that six of the eight coaches of schools who were in the 2006 Elite Eight received raises, illustrating a direct link between competitive success and increased compensation for coaches (ibid.). Big Business has a big impact on these salaries, too. In 2005–2006, the University of Arizona men's head basketball coach, Lute Olson, had a deal with Nike for $500,000 (ibid.). The University of Florida men's head basketball coach, Billy Donovan, was guaranteed at least $525,000 in contracts with shoe and apparel companies in 2006–2007 (ibid.). On May 31, 2007, Coach Donovan parlayed this deal into an even greater contract with the Orlando Magic of the National Basketball Association (NBA) for five years at $5.5 million per year (Gonzalez, 2007). Days later, Donovan had a change of heart and returned to the University of Florida, signing a six-year contract for $3.5 million annually (ibid.). Michigan State University's head men's basketball coach, Tom Izzo, received over $300,000 in compensation from Nike in 2006–2007 (Upton & Wieberg, 2007). George Mason University's men's basketball team had a Cinderella run to the Final Four in 2006. The team's affable coach, Jim Larranaga, cashed in on the team's astounding success, and netted $274,100 in seventy-three speaking appearances between April and December 2006 (ibid.). And in 2004–2005, Texas Tech University's men's head basketball coach, the legendary Bob Knight, sold advertising space on his game-day sweater for $120,000 (ibid.).

Even NCAA Division I women's basketball coaches are starting to reap from colleges' windfalls from corporate coffers. As of May 2007, four coaches of Division I women's teams earn at least $1 million annually: University of Tennessee coach Pat Summitt (whose teams have won seven national championships, including the 2007 championship), Baylor University coach Kim Mulkey (who has led Baylor to one national championship), University of Connecticut coach Geno Auriemma (whose teams have won five national championships), and University of Texas coach Gail Goestenkors (who over fifteen years coached Duke University to a record of 396-99) (Carter, 2007; Davis, 2007). The women's basketball head coaches are not close to approaching parity with their counterparts for the men's teams, but their sizable salaries in a sport that does not generate close to the revenue of men's basketball or men's football indicates an influx of money from Big Business to enable colleges to pay them. As the salaries for women's head coaches increase, it will be interesting to see if their compensation begins to approach the compensation for men's coaches.

The compensation for many coaches of major Division I college football and basketball coaches dwarfs the compensation of other university employees. Upton and Wieberg (2006) cite that the chancellor of the University of Texas system, Mark Yudof, received $693,677 in 2006, but University of Texas head football coach Mack Brown made about four times as much in 2006. In addition, Upton and Wieberg note that the University of Louisville paid its full-time professors an average of $95,024 in 2006, while its head football coach, Bobby Petrino, was guaranteed approximately $1.6 million. The article also quoted Smith College sports economist Andrew Zimbalist stating, "What kind of message does that send? What does that say about the value system? What does that say to students?" (ibid., para. 27). Because the compensation differential between the coaches and other employees of the institutions is so great, what it says to students is that the football coaches are clearly valued more than the president and the professors of these colleges. By extension, what it says is that football is more important than teaching or running a university. This disparity in salaries is so great that there can be no confusion about what is most valued. Coaches can use this fact to their advantage. If there is a debate between a coach and another college employee about the grades of a student-athlete or admitting a recruit, the economic investment the school has made in the coach tilts the resolution of the discussion in the coach's favor. College coaches may also demand personal incentives from their schools, even for activities that are part of their job. Upton and Wieberg (2006) note faculty complaints about "additional compensation for (coaches) doing things they should be doing anyway" (para. 36). In both "real life" and on college campuses, the greater the economic investment, the greater the interest is in maintaining and placating that investment. The significant financial investment in college coaches has given many schools a vested interest in keeping the coaches happy. Thus, coaches derive power from the economic investment.

The marriage of Big Business and college sports has given many coaches lots of money, and by extension, lots of power. As long as many college coaches' earnings continue to greatly outpace the earnings of their university colleagues and bosses, these coaches and their programs will wield increasing and substantial power on campus.

Advertising, Endorsement, and Paraphernalia Revenue

According to TNS Media Intelligence (2007), over $2.73 billion was spent on network television advertising during NCAA Men's Basketball Tournament games from 2000–2006. For 2007, TNS estimated $500 million would be spent on advertising during tournament games (ibid.). In fact, in 2006, more money was spent on advertising during NCAA Men's Basketball Tournament games than on post-season games in professional football ($423 million), professional basketball ($424 million), or professional baseball ($382 million) (ibid.). According to Jon Swallen, senior vice president of research at TNS, among major televised sports championships, only the Super Bowl commands a higher advertising rate than the NCAA Men's Basketball Championship game (ibid.). TNS (2007) states that from 2000–2006, ten advertisers spent at least $48 million in

advertising on NCAA Tournament games (Sprint Nextel - $48 million; Daim-
lerChrysler - $49 million; U.S. Government - $52 million; PepsiCo - $67 million;
Microsoft - $76 million; SABMiller Plc - $84 million; Coca-Cola - $96 million;
AT&T - $111 million; and General Motors - $422 million).

Another source of revenue for college sports comes from sporting goods companies. Of the sixty-four teams in the 2007 NCAA Women's Basketball Tournament, fifty-six teams had endorsement deals with Nike and/or the Jordan logo,
seven teams had deals with Adidas, and one team had a deal with Reebok (Horrow, 2006). In 1999, the University of Georgia (UGA) signed a ten-year deal with
Nike for $13 million; in addition, Nike pays UGA's athletic department $400,000
annually (Strickland, 2006). Strickland notes that in return for Nike's largesse,
Nike expects its apparel to be worn by players and coaches during "practices,
games, exhibitions, clinics, sports camps and other official or university-
sanctioned intercollegiate athletic program activities" (para. 7). In 2001, Nike
signed a seven-year deal with the University of Michigan for $25 million (Strick-
land, 2006). Though Nike is the largest apparel company on campus, its competitor Adidas has a ten-year, $60 million contract with Notre Dame that expires
after the 2013–2014 season ("ND Signs 10-Year, $60M Deal with Adidas," 2005).
Adidas also signed an eight-year, $26 million contract with the University of
Kansas athletic department in 2005 ("KU Announces Contract with Adidas,"
2005). Upstart company Under Armour signed a five-year, $10.6 million con-
tract with Auburn University in December 2005 (Strickland, 2006), and in April
2007, it signed a six-year, $10.8 million contract with the University of South
Carolina to outfit the Gamecocks football team ("University of South Carolina
Partners with Under Armour to Outfit Football Program," 2007).

Corporate collegiate advertising has extended to the construction of on-
campus stadiums. In March 2005, TCF Financial Corporation signed a contract
with the University of Minnesota to be the lead sponsor for a proposed $235 mil-
lion on-campus stadium. TCF Financial received naming rights for the stadium
in exchange for a $35 million sponsorship. In January 2007, the university's
Board of Regents approved a revised budget for the stadium of $288.5 million
to "enhance the fan experience, improve campus aesthetics and incorporate
sustainable or 'green' architecture designs" ("Regents Approve Stadium Design,
New Price Tag," 2007, para. 11).

Universities also have a revenue stream from paraphernalia sales. In the
2005–2006 academic year, the University of Texas (UT) was number one in the
nation in football and in the sale of merchandise ("Longhorns Knock Off Tar
Heels to Lead Nation in Merchandising Revenue," 2006). UT received $6.2 mil-
lion in royalties from merchandise licensing in 2005–2006, and its merchandise
victory ended the University of North Carolina's reign as the premier collegiate
merchandise seller for five consecutive years (ibid.).

Media, advertising, apparel, and to a lesser extent paraphernalia revenue are financial lifelines for the budgets of university athletic directors. As the revenue accruing to universities increases, their budgets concomitantly increase, to improve amenities for athletes and attract new student-athletes. As schools become increasingly dependent on this money, the distributors of the revenues, Big Business, will have an increasingly strong voice in college athletics. If only because of the sheer magnitude of their investments, their voices deserve to be heard. However, their voices should not dictate what is best for colleges and student-athletes.

Conclusion

The link between college sports and economics is a microcosm of the effect money has in society. Money makes the world go round, and economics, specifically Big Business, has a profound impact on college sports. But it shouldn't. Big Business has had a deleterious effect on college sports. The marriage of Big Business and college sports has had a negative impact on the primary mission of college sports: to build character, educate athletes, and celebrate the joys of competition. The ever-increasing physical, mental, and emotional demands on college athletes (Pennington, 2008) may be directly traced ("Red-Eye Games Aren't Good for Anybody," 2001) to the impact of Big Business. In addition to the effects cited in this chapter, there are plenty of other ramifications of Big Business' involvement with college sports, ranging from fans' increasing obsession with student-athletes, to the proliferation of corporate-funded recruiting sites, summer camps, and travel teams. While it is not the intent of this chapter to investigate the full range of involvement between Big Business and college sports, it is worth noting that this involvement extends well beyond the scope cited in this chapter.

In spite of the clear negative impacts Big Business can and does have on college sports, it cannot be denied that the huge sums of money involved also have the ability to bring joy to some. Often, student-athletes are able to attend college because of athletic scholarships, and the revenue generated through Big Business provides for other student scholarships, as discussed earlier in this chapter. However, while many student-athletes receive college scholarships, the trade-off between a college diploma and a lucrative professional contract is not generally financially equitable for athletes in major sports such as football and basketball. It is worth noting that in spite of the staggering revenues reaped by universities, student-athletes are not paid for their efforts. While this issue is important and intriguing, a more in-depth discussion will have to take place another day, since it is not the intent of this chapter to investigate this particular relationship between economics and college sport. However, an example may serve to illustrate its connection. On May 23, 2007, two Georgetown University basketball players, juniors Jeff Green and Roy Hibbert, held a press conference announcing whether they would enter the 2007 NBA Draft, or return to Georgetown for their senior year (Powell, 2007, p. 1). At the press conference, Green announced that he would enter the NBA Draft and forego his final season at Georgetown, while Hibbert announced he would remain at Georgetown. *Washington Post* columnist Thomas Boswell stated that their coach "seemed almost equally happy for both players, perhaps because he has such an unashamed appreciation for two of life's great joys; a large pile of money and a good education" (2007, p. 5). In this case, each of these students was able to determine for himself which of these joys he was more interested in pursuing.

For many people, college sports and the large pile of money Big Business can generate are two of life's great joys, and in many ways they are synonymous and reflective of our culture. At its core, the purpose of college sports is to educate, enlighten, develop, build character in, and inspire college athletes, helping them to bridge the chasm between exuberant and unbridled youth and adulthood, which in turn will help them succeed physically, emotionally, and economically in the future. And to be fair, to varying extents, many college sport programs serve this purpose. The purpose of Big Business is to make money. In order to make money, many businesses attempt to enlighten, develop, and inspire their employees (Fowler, 1991). However, Big Business also worships at the altar of the dollar. The dollar is its master. There is no confusion, no dichotomy. The most visible college sports simultaneously serve two masters—their respective colleges and universities and their concomitant missions, as well as the almighty dollar, which is personified by Big Business. They are committed to one master, their respective missions, and increasingly dependent on the other, Big Business. When serving two masters, inevitably one will suffer. In this case, college sports' devotion to Big Business inevitably detracts from the mission and essence of institutions of higher education.

The poem *Invictus* by William Ernest Henley states: "I am the master of my fate. I am the captain of my soul." College sport neither controls its own fate nor lords over its own soul. It has ceded power and control to Big Business, changing the paradigm of college sports from competitive endeavors engaged in by noble warriors, to contests with high stakes and monetary consequences waged by athletes whose duty it is to produce. While some college sport programs are thriving economically, they are in many ways morally bankrupt, and have deviated from focusing on their mission. Some may see this as progress, but it is progress at what cost? Does it benefit college sports to thrive monetarily while bowing to the whims of Big Business? I believe the spirit of college sports is salvageable. But, for the foreseeable future, the deal has been sealed and the die has been cast. All we can ask is, who will save the soul of college sports?

References

About Us. (2007). Retrieved May 30, 2007, from http://www.cstv.com/online/.

Academic progress/graduation success rate study of Division I NCAA Men's Basketball Tournament teams (2007, March 12). Retrieved July 6, 2007, from http://www.bus.ucf.edu/sport/public/downloads/2007_Womens_Basketball_Tournament.pdf.

BBC News (2007, June 21). New Yahoo boss buys sport website. Retrieved June 26, 2007, from http://news.bbc.co.uk/2/hi/business/6225026.stm.

Boswell, Thomas. (2007, May 24). A big man's clear view. *Washington Post*, pp. E1, E5.

Carter, Rachel. (2007, April 6). Coach G leaves 'comfort zone.' Retrieved May 29, 2007, from http://www.texassports.com/doc_lib/newsstand_wbb/Raleigh_Apr6_CoachG.pdf.

CBS renews NCAA b'ball. (1999, November 18). Retrieved May 25, 2007, from http://money.cnn.com/1999/11/18/news/ncaa/.

Consoli, John & Crupi, Anthony. (2005, November 3). CBS buys CSTV for $325 mil. Retrieved July 7, 2007, from http://www.mediaweek.com/mw/news/recent_display.jsp?vnu_content_id=1001433557

Davis, Brian. (2007, April 8). College coaches raking in cash. Retrieved May 29, 2007, from http://www.dallasnews.com/sharedcontent/dws/spt/misc/weekend/stories/040807dnsponcaasalaries.35c0fe0.html.

Drape, Joe. (2006, November 25) In college football, the pinstripes belong to Notre Dame. Retrieved July 14, 2008, from http://www.nytimes.com/2006/11/25/sports/ncaafootball/25irish.html.

ESPN.com. (2004, December 8). ESPNU to launch on '03-04-05.' Retrieved July 7, 2007, from http://sports.espn.go.com/ncaa/news/story?id=1951755.

ESPN.com. (2006, October 23). More than 1,000 men's college basketball games on ABC, ESPN, ESPN2, ESPNU, ESPN360, ESPN Regional Television and ESPN Full Court. [Press Release] Retrieved July 7, 2007, from http://www.espnmediazone.com/press_releases/Other_Releases/MORETHAN1000MENSCOLLEGEBASKETBALLGAMESONABCESPNESPN2ESPNUESPN360ESPNREGIONALTELEVISIONA.htm.

ESPN.com. (2007, March 12). New assignments and returning commentators highlight ABC, ESPN, ESPN2 and ESPNU college football coverage. [Press Release] Retrieved July 7, 2007, from http://www.espnmediazone.com/press_releases/2007_06_jun/20070628_CollegeFootballCommentators.htm.

Fowler, Elizabeth M. (1991, April 23). CAREERS; Improving employee satisfaction. Retrieved July 15, 2008, from http://query.nytimes.com/gst/fullpage.html?res=9D0CE3D6153BF930A15757C0A967958260.

Gonzalez, Antonio. (2007, June 8). Donovan apologizes to Magic and Florida. Retrieved July 8, 2007, from http://www.wtopnews.com/?nid=177&sid=1107826.

Henley, William Ernest. "Invictus." Retrieved from http://www.bartleby.com/103/7.html.

Horrow, Rick. (2006, March 24). Business of the NCAA Women's Basketball Tournament. Retrieved May 29, 2007, from http://cbs.sportsline.com/general/story/9333466.

Huliq.com. (2007). NCAA basketball attendance enjoys records for both genders. Retrieved July 5, 2007, from http://www.huliq.com/22917/ncaa-basketball-attendancec-enjoys-records-for-both-genders.

Jacobson, Gary. (2006, March 16). March Madness means money. Retrieved July 7, 2007, from http://www.dallasnews.com/sharedcontent/dws/spt/colleges/national/tournament/ncaamen/stories/031606dnsponcaamoney.173e5d7f.html.

Johnson, Gary K. (2007, February 7). NCAA attendance sets new standard. Retrieved July 5, 2007, from http://www.ncaasports.com/story/9981000.

KU announces contract with Adidas. (2005, April 25). Retrieved May 31, 2007 from https://tv.ku .edu/news/2005/04/25/ku-announces-contract-with-adidas/.

Longhorns knock off Tar Heels to lead nation in merchandising revenue. (2006, August 26). Retrieved May 30, 2007, from http://www.usatoday.com/sports/college/2006-08-26-ncaa -merchandise_x.htm?POE=SPOISVA.

Martzke, Rudy & Moran, Malcolm. (2003, December 18). NBC, Notre Dame stretch grid deal through 2010. Retrieved July 7, 2007, from http://www.usatoday.com/sports/college/football/ independents/2003-12-18-nbc-notre-dame_x.htm.

McCarthy, Michael. (2007, November 16). Schools, coaches cash in on lucrative media deals. Retrieved May 30, 2007, from http://usatoday.com/sports/college/football/2006-11-16-cover -coaches-media_x.htm.

Merriam-Webster Online Dictionary. (2006–2007). Retrieved June 29, 2007, from http://www .merriam-webster.com/dictionary/big+business.

Miller, Mark K. (2008, June 19). NBC signs 5-year Notre Dame extension. Retrieved June 19, 2008, from http://www.tvnewsday.com/articles/2008/06/19/daily.8/.

NBC cont[r]act extended through 2010. (2004, Spring). Retrieved July 7, 2007, from http://www .nd.edu/~ndmag/sp2004/nbc.html.

NCAA reaches agreement with ESPN, INC. for television rights to 21 championships. (2001, July 5). [News Release] Retrieved May 29, 2007, from http://ncaa.org/releases/ miscellaneous/2001/2001070501ms.htm.

ND signs 10-year, $60M deal with Adidas. (2005, November 16). Retrieved July 8, 2007, from http://www.msnbc.com/id/9987101/.

O'Toole, Thomas. (2006, December 6). $17M BCS payouts sound great, but . . . . Retrieved May 30, 2007, from http://www.usatoday.com/sports/college/football/2006-12-06-bowl-payouts_x.htm.

Pennington, Bill. (2008, March 12). It's not an adventure, it's a job. Retrieved July 15, 2008, from http://www.nytimes.com/2008/03/12/sports/12lifestyles.html.

Powell, Camille. (2007, May 24). For Georgetown, a split decision. *Washington Post*, pp. E1, E5.

Prisbell, Eric. (2007, January 10). Champion crowned but questions linger. Retrieved July 7, 2007, from http://www.washingtonpost.com/wp-dyn/content/article/2007/01/09/AR2007010901509 .html.

Red-eye games aren't good for anybody. (2001, February 13). [Editorial] Retrieved July 7, 2007, from http://media.www.dailyutahchronicle.com/media/storage/paper244/news/2001/02/13/ Opinion/The-Chronicles.View-29256.shtml.

Regents approve stadium design, new price tag. (2007, January 3). Retrieved May 30, 2007, from http://www1.umn.edu/umnnews/Feature_Stories/Regents_approve_stadium_design.html.

Strickland, Carter. (2006, September 17). Nike the big dog on UGA campus. *The Atlantic Journal-Constitution*. Retrieved from http://www.insidehoops.com/forum/showthread.php?t=11225.

TNS Media Intelligence. (2007, March 6). TNS Media Intelligence releases March Madness advertising trends report. Retrieved July 8, 2007, from http://www.tns-mi.com/news/03062007.htm.

Total GDP 2005. (2007, April 23). Retrieved July 7, 2007, from http://siteresources.worldbank .org/DATASTATISTICS/Resources/GDP.pdf.

University of South Carolina partners with Under Armour to outfit football program. (2007, April 13). Retrieved May 31, 2007, from http://uscsports.cstv.com/sports/m-footbl/spec-rel/ 041307aac.html.

Upton, Jodie & Wieberg, Steve. (2006, November 16). Contracts for college coaches cover more than salaries. Retrieved May 30, 2007, from http://www.usatoday.com/sports/college/football/ 2006-11-16-coaches-salaries-cover_x.htm.

Upton, Jodie & Wieberg, Steve. (2007, March 8). Success on the court translates to big money for coaches. Retrieved May 29, 2007, from http://www.usatoday.com/sports/college/mensbasket ball/2007-03-08-coaches-salary-cover_N.htm.

What's the difference between Divisions I, II and III? (2007, February 1). Retrieved July 7, 2007, from http://www.ncaa.org/about/div_criteria.html.

Wieberg, Steve. (2006, November 16). To Oklahoma, Stoops worth more than his weight in gold. Retrieved May 30, 2007, from http://www.usatoday.com/sports/college/football/big12/2006-11-16-stoops-compensation_x.htm.

Wolverton, Brad. (2007, March 23). What led a top NCAA athlete to transfer to an NAIA program. *The Chronicle of Higher Education.* Retrieved July 7, 2007, from http://chronicle.com/weekly/v53/i29/29a03401.htm.

15

Do Girls Rule?

Understanding Popular Culture Images of "Girl Power!" and Sport

Cheryl Cooky

IN CONTEMPORARY AMERICAN CULTURE, the pinnacle of Girl Power! in sport occurred at the 1999 Women's World Cup soccer final, when the U.S. team defeated the Chinese team in a sudden death face-off. This event was significant, specifically for girl culture and girls who play sport, because it marked a moment where girls were recognized by the mainstream media as key consumers of sport. News media reports noted that more than 90,000 spectators, many of them young girls, had filled the Rose Bowl in Pasadena, California, to watch the game. The media images featured girls in the stands wearing U.S. soccer jerseys, many embroidered with the number nine, the number of women's soccer star Mia Hamm. With sleeves rolled up in the warm Southern California sun, hair pulled back in ponytails tied with ribbons the colors of red, white, and blue, the girl spectators would come to symbolize the impact of the "Third Wave" of female athleticism.

Unlike women in the First and Second Waves (which coincided somewhat with the First and Second Wave feminist movements), women and girls of the Third Wave of female athleticism assume they no longer have to lobby and organize politically for the right to play sport. That right was established during the Second Wave of female athleticism with the passage of Title IX. What has changed since the Second Wave is that today, participation in sport is no longer reserved for an elite group of highly skilled girls and women, but appears as a "normal part of girls' and women's everyday lives" (Heywood & Dworkin, 2003, p. xx). And while other key moments in the history of women's sports occurred during this time frame—for example, the accomplishments of female athletes in team sports during the 1996 Olympics, the emergence of several women's professional sports leagues including the Women's National Basketball Association (WNBA), the challenges to racial ideologies in the world of tennis by the Williams sisters, and so on—the 1999 Women's World Cup was the first time in recent history where *girl* fans (not women) were included in the media frame and in popular understandings of the event. The mainstream media framed the World Cup not just in terms of the accomplishment for the members of the U.S. team; the event was also evidence of a cultural shift in the landscape of girls' and women's sport. The women of the 1999 U.S. soccer team presented to this generation of girls an image of what they could aspire to become; it was an emotionally riveting spectacle of girls' and women's empowerment in sport. This moment became part of the cultural imagery of Girl Power!

While public support for girls' and women's sport, particularly soccer, increased immediately after the 1999 Women's World Cup, the celebratory moment would quickly fade. Shortly after the World Cup, a professional women's soccer league was formed (Women's United Soccer Association, or WUSA). A few years later, the league went under due to a lack of support from commercial sponsors as well as the economic recession in the U.S., which occurred in the aftermath of the attacks on the World Trade Center in New York on September 11, 2001. Unlike the WNBA, which had the support of their established male counterpart, the NBA, the women's soccer league failed to establish a strong fan base quickly enough to satisfy investors and corporate sponsors. The goal here is not to discuss the specific reasons why certain women's professional leagues succeed or fail (although that is a subject worthy of study); I use this example, however, to illustrate how public celebration of girls' and women's sport does not always translate into increased participation, increased opportunities, or broader shifts in the *structural* landscape of sport (see also Cooky, 2009). If we look past the public celebration, the media images, and the representations of female athletes, both in live sport events and in popular cultural discourses, we are presented with a much more complex and contradictory view of girls' and women's sports.

In this chapter, I trace the emergence of Girl Power! as a cultural discourse and discuss how Girl Power! created significant shifts in societal understandings of what it means to be a girl in the contemporary historical moment. Moreover, this chapter will critically interrogate the connections between Girl Power!, sport participation, and girl empowerment to examine, from a cultural perspective, what it means to position sport as a site of empowerment for young girls. Rather than building on the momentum of the 1999 World Cup, Girl Power! eventually faded from the dominant narratives in popular cultural discourses and media representations of girls and girl athletes. Indeed, when examining contemporary popular culture representations of girls today, it is evident that Girl Power! has undergone significant shifts, since the 1990s: moving from the Spice Girls and the women's U.S. soccer team to the Pussycat Dolls and female professional athletes appearing in *Maxim* and *FHM*. Although girls, as consumers and spectators of sport, continue to be a part of the discourse of Girl Power!, the ways in which girls are addressed in popular culture has shifted since the late 1990s. I argue these shifts have defused the potential for Girl Power! to empower "real girls," as well as to lead to broader structural changes in the contemporary landscape of girls' sport.

Girls' Sport and Title IX

Only a few years after the public celebration of Girl Power! at the 1999 World Cup, Title IX was under attack, threatened by the Bush administration. Title IX of the Educational Amendments states that "no person in the United States shall, on the basis of sex, be excluded from participation in, be denied the benefits of, or be subjected to discrimination under any educational program or activity receiving federal assistance" (Education Amendments, 1972). Since its passage in 1972, many groups have attempted to weaken Title IX (Carpenter & Acosta, 2005); this recent battle was no exception. In 2002, the U.S. Department of Education established the Commission on Opportunity in Athletics, whose purpose was to review the current standards for measuring equal opportunity in sport under Title IX. Fortunately, women's sports advocates, feminists, and female athletes successfully defended the importance of and continued need for Title IX and won the battle. Yet the war is not over. Controversy and debate surrounding Title IX continues, even as I write this chapter five years after the commission was formed.

During its tenure, the Bush administration had worked towards significant changes to Title IX; changes, which critics argue, would severely weaken the legislation. There are also women's sports advocates who continue to argue for the importance of Title IX. One advocate who has spoken in support of Title IX is 1999 World Cup champion Julie Foudy. Moreover, in response to the formation of the Commission on Opportunity in Athletics, Myles Brand, then-president of the National Collegiate Athletic Association (NCAA), argued, "Title IX is not broken and it does not need to be fixed. Rather, it needs to be supported, enforced, and allowed to finish the job it was designed to do—provide equal opportunities for athletics participation without gender bias" (2003). Feminists and women's sports advocates feared that the creation of the commission would be a step toward the eventual erosion of Title IX (a similar strategy also used by the Bush administration and right-wing conservatives to attack *Roe v. Wade*). Indeed, feminists have cause for concern. Ironically, because of the gains made by Title IX, many people now believe that girls and women have ample opportunities to participate in sports, and that girls and women who do not do so by choice, not because of any discrimination, lack of access, or lack of opportunity (Cooky, 2009). In a culture where history is quickly forgotten, it is easy for many to believe that Title IX is no longer needed.

Over the past thirty-eight years, Title IX has played an important role in creating more sport opportunities for girls and women, both directly and indirectly (Carpenter & Acosta, 2005). Although many soccer programs were created by grassroots organizing among parents and soccer enthusiasts from middle- and upper-class white communities, not by educational institutions (De Varona, 2004), Title IX had an indirect impact on the growth of girls' soccer in the United States. Title IX helped to create a cultural context wherein girls' participation in sport was "normalized." Thanks to Title IX, the cultural expectations for what girls could aspire to had changed, as well as cultural notions of girlhood and femininity. As part of this cultural shift, the number of elite school soccer programs went from only a few in 1970 to over 1,000 (ibid.). Of course, Title IX had a direct impact on girls' participation, as well. High school girls' participation in sport increased from 294,015 girls in 1971 to 3,114,091 in 2008–2009 (National Federation of State High School Athletics, 2008–2009); and this only includes the number of girls in high school sport programs. Today, girls are participating on private travel teams and in recreational leagues in a variety of individual and team sports.

However, despite these significant gains, not all girls have benefited equally from Title IX (Suggs, 2005). Access to sporting opportunities is necessary for young girls to participate; however, many young girls, specifically girls residing in urban communities, have limited sport opportunities (Sabo and Veliz, 2008). This lack of opportunity is based on a number of factors, including lack of transportation to and from sport activities, lack of funds to pay for equipment and registration fees, lack of organizations that provide sports to girls in urban communities, lack of space and facilities in urban communities, societal gender roles that often confine girls to the home or limit their mobility outside the home (for example, many parents see their sons as athletes and their girls as babysitters and household help), and societal ideologies that conflate athleticism with masculinity.

Although Title IX ushered in an explosion in the number of girls and women who participate in sport and changed the culture such that the female athlete is now considered a "cultural icon" (Heywood & Dworkin, 2003), cultural anxieties about female athleticism, strength, and power persist. Today, girls and women in sport now occupy a liminal cultural space, wherein their participation is simultaneously positioned as empowering and yet often devalued and trivialized (Cooky & McDonald, 2005; Shakib & Dunbar, 2002). Consider, for example, the media coverage of women's sport. Women's collegiate and professional sports are broadcast on television more so than in the past (albeit mostly on ESPN or CSTV, available only to those with a top-tier cable subscription). Women's sport fans can watch televised coverage of women's collegiate softball, soccer, volleyball, and field hockey, women's professional basketball, and a variety of other women's sports. Yet despite the increase in broadcasts of women's sport competition, the coverage of women's sports, in both mainstream televised and print sport news media, is still lacking (for a review, see Smith, 2006). Indeed, longitudinal research has found a continual lack of coverage of women's sports in televised sport news highlight programs over the last fifteen years, despite the tremendous explosion of women participating in collegiate, professional, and Olympic sports during that same time period (Messner, Duncan & Willms, 2005). Moreover, with respect to the coverage of the 1999 Women's World Cup soccer championship match, much of the sport news coverage framed the event as a "strip tease" (Messner, Duncan & Cooky, 2003), a reference to Brandi Chastain's removal of her jersey in a post-win celebration. Interestingly, this is a common form of celebration in soccer; male soccer players frequently remove their jerseys after a win with little to no fanfare from the media. Thus, it can be argued that the news media coverage trivialized the significance of this event for women's sport, fans of women's sport, and girls who play sport (ibid.). Given the media representation of "real" women athletes, girls who play must negotiate the contradictory meanings of empowerment through sport on the one hand (*Newsweek* magazine featured the image of Brandi Chastain's celebration on its cover, with the headline "GIRLS RULE!") and the trivialized representations of female athletes in the media on the other hand (the media frame of Brandi Chastain's celebration as a "strip tease," or references to the U.S. women's soccer team as the "ponytail express").

"Girl Power!": Constructing Empowerment in Popular Culture

Girlhood, as it was understood and experienced in the 1950s and 1960s, dramatically changed for girls growing up in the 1970s and 1980s. Girlhood was no longer a time when girls' aspirations were restricted to the realm of the feminine. Second Wave liberal feminists argued for gender-neutral socialization of children as a strategy to eradicate women's oppression. One consequence of gender-neutral socialization was that girls who grew up in the 1970s and 1980s received cultural messages that they could be and do anything they wanted. In many instances, girls were encouraged to choose traditional masculine pursuits over feminine: playing sports instead of playing house; aspiring to be a doctor instead of a nurse, or an executive instead of a secretary; or pursuing a career instead of motherhood (although structural and ideological constraints still remain in place, which limit girls from achieving these goals or place limits on their success within male-dominated institutions; consider the continuing gender wage gap, for example). In the 1980s and 1990s, even Barbie, the icon of conventional femininity, became an astronaut, the president of the United States, and a professional basketball player.

The 1990s witnessed yet another shift in cultural discourses regarding girlhood. This time, the pendulum swung back toward a cultural embracement of conventional ideals of girlhood. This was due, in part, to the waning influence of the women's movement in society, the emergence of a conservative political climate with the 1980 presidential election of Ronald Reagan, and a subsequent "backlash" against the Second Wave feminist movement (Faludi, 1991). In 1990, *Newsweek* ran a story titled, "The Failure of Feminism," which reported on the inability of the feminist movement to bring about any real improvement in women's lives. In June of 1998, *Time* magazine illustrated the media backlash against feminism in its cover headline, which posed the question to American readers, "Is Feminism Dead?" (for a discussion, see Baumgardner & Richards, 2000). This overall political and social climate in the 1980s and early 1990s was both anti-feminist and post-feminist. (Anti-feminism refers to an overt rejection of feminism and a belief that the Second Wave feminist movement did not benefit women and instead has hurt boys and men. Post-feminism refers to an acceptance that the Second Wave feminist movement did have an impact, and girls and women are now equal to boys and men; therefore the need for political activism for gender equality no longer exists.) This political climate impacted the construction of girlhood. Societal beliefs in individual choice and individual empowerment dominated, and the connection between girlhood and the broader political struggle for women's rights was dissolved.

This shift in the cultural construction of girlhood is best represented by the Spice Girls. The Spice Girls were a British-based pop group, formed from a casting call in 1995 for young women who could sing and dance. The Spice Girls became one of the most successful all-girl pop sensations. In addition to their musical success, the Spice Girls gained notoriety for coining the term "Girl Power!" Although the Spice Girls are most frequently given credit for coining the term "Girl Power!," Third Wave feminists have located Girl Power!'s origins in the underground, young radical feminist movement and post-punk feminism (Harris, 2004).

Each singer in the group had a nickname; one Spice Girl, whose real name is Melanie Chisholm, was named "Sporty Spice" (the other Spice Girls were "Posh," "Ginger," "Baby," and "Scary"). Sporty Spice combined elements of sport and athleticism with girl empowerment. Unlike the other Spice Girls, who wore fashionable dresses, high-heeled boots, platform shoes, or other "feminine" clothing popular during the 1990s, Sporty Spice wore athletic shoes, track pants, sports bras, and other fashionable athletic gear. Sporty Spice performed acrobatic stunts in videos and concerts and became the embodiment of Girl Power! and sport.

As a pop-culture icon of girl empowerment, the Spice Girls' version of Girl Power!, while empowering on an individual level and celebratory of girls' strengths, ultimately contained anti-feminist messages that presented Girl Power! as a "non-political, non-threatening alternative to feminism" (Taft, 2004, p. 70). On the surface, individualist notions of Girl Power! seemed to be empowering, yet they constructed barriers to both girls' activism in general, and girls' engagement with feminist politics in particular. Indeed, in their book *Girl Power!* the Spice Girls completely reject feminism in their claim that Girl Power! "kicks feminism's arse" (ibid).

In the mid-1990s, Girl Power! became part of the mainstream discourse on girlhood and gave rise to a cultural moment wherein all things "Girl" would be celebrated, including girls' participation in sport. Girl Power! discourses were even seen in the U.S. government's public policy, specifically in the aptly named "Girl Power!" campaign (Cooky & McDonald, 2005; Giardina & Metz, 2005). The purpose of this campaign (instituted by Donna Shalala, secretary of the Department of Health and Human Services, in conjunction with then-president Bill Clinton's President's Council on Physical Fitness and Sports) was to "encourage and empower girls to make the most of their lives" (United States Department of Health and Human Services, 2007). Health officials, educators, feminists, and girls' advocates such as the Girl Scouts of America sought to empower girls' lives by promoting sport and physical ability in order to boost girls' self-esteem, launching after-school programs to improve the lives of young girls, and working with girls in collaborative, community-based projects. These forms of empowerment, however, were often muted by the more prominent voices of Girl Power! heard in the commercially driven venues of popular culture. Girl Power! dominated popular culture, embodied in strong female lead characters in television shows such as *Buffy the Vampire Slayer, Xena Warrior Princess, Sabrina: The Teenage Witch,* and the *Powerpuff Girls,* as well as in the films *Lara Croft: Tomb Raider, Terminator 2,* and *Crouching Tiger, Hidden Dragon.* Girls and women who were powerful, who could compete with and defeat male characters, and most importantly, who were unapologetic of their strength and power, literally dominated the popular cultural landscape in the 1990s and early 2000s.

Girl Power! and the Girl Athlete

Alongside the fictional representations, female athletes were also positioned as representatives of Girl Power! During the 1999 Women's World Cup, Brandi Chastain, whose sports-bra-clad body was featured on the cover of *Newsweek* with the announcement that "Girls Rule!" were representatives for and representations of Girl Power! Yet, as was true for the Spice Girls, Girl Power! discourse related to female athletes was employed in ways that dismissed the gains produced by Second Wave feminism. For example, in the article "Changing Face of Sports: World Cup Women Hear the High-Pitched Sound of Girl Power," a *USA Today* journalist informed the reader that it is "Girl Power!" that inspired the women's soccer team, not feminism (Taft, 2004). This further reinforced the idea that Girl Power! was *not* feminism. Surprisingly, with only a passing reference to Billie Jean King and her work for equality in women's sport, there was no mention of the feminist movement, which was responsible for the opportunities the U.S. soccer team experienced (ibid.). Here, the deployment of Girl Power! was post-feminist in its vision: Girls and women are equal to boys and men, and the quest for equality is complete. As such, there was no need for girls and women to challenge boys and men, or any form of male dominance, in any political way (Griffin, 2004). With respect to sport, the alignment of female athletic achievement with Girl Power! sent girls cultural messages that girls and women are empowered, and feminist proscriptions for equality, such as Title IX, are no longer needed or desired (ibid.). Even the Oxford English Dictionary defined Girl Power! as "a self-reliant attitude among girls and young women manifested in ambition, assertiveness and individualism"(Oxford English Dictionary). Here the notion of Girl Power! as a form of feminism or a movement to collectively empower girls and women was erased. Instead, individualism and individual empowerment were valued over collective empowerment.

Girl Power! as a cultural discourse was similar to the contemporary construction of girlhood in that both were inherently contradictory (Banet-Weiser, 2004; Griffin, 2004). On the surface, it would appear that, as representations of Girl Power!, female athletes and female athletic achievements undeniably challenged stereotypical notions of what defined a girl in contemporary culture and the conventional conflation of strength and physicality with masculinity. This challenge created potential empowerment by assisting girls and women in their struggles for equality (Dowling, 2000). Additionally, there was no denying the seductive power in the image of girls and women "just doing it" in a traditionally male-dominated institution constructed to uphold hegemonic masculinity and white, male domination (Messner, 2002; Cahn, 1994). Images of women, succeeding in an area that has been traditionally associated with men's physical (and thereby social, political, and economic) power, disrupted gendered social relations that posit women as weaker and less powerful. These images also challenged our cultural beliefs regarding masculinity and femininity, wherein what it means to be a "real man" is defined in direct opposition to what it means to be a "real woman." In the mid-1990s, Nike successfully capitalized on the challenges posed by Girl Power! in a number of ways, specifically in their appropriation of the insult "you kick like a girl" (featured on a T-shirt showing a girl kicking a goal, for example) and also in their advertising campaign, "If you let me play."

The "If you let me play" campaign drew on feminist struggles for equality in sports (which culminated in the passage of Title IX) to suggest that participation in sport was a basic civil right that should not be denied to anyone, even young girls. Not only is it a basic civil right to let girls play, girls and society in general will benefit. According to this advertising campaign, girls will like themselves, will have more self-confidence, will be less likely to get breast cancer, and will be less likely to be abused or to get pregnant as teens. While the message was quite inspirational, the "If you let me play" campaign presented paradoxical images of empowerment to young girls (Cooky & McDonald, 2005; Lucas, 2000). The girls in the commercial have to ask permission to play; they are featured in black-and-white film, listlessly hanging from tire swings, and not participating in sports. Nike simultaneously empowered girls by encouraging their physicality, yet within the imagery of the commercial, girls were still positioned in passive roles. Despite the academic critique, the "If you let me play" campaign was held as a representation of Girl Power! in sport and received praise from both the public (Giardina & Metz, 2005) and from the advertising community (Cooky & McDonald, 2005). Indeed, the girls in the Nike commercial recited various research findings published in the President's Council on Physical Fitness and Sports report (1997), "Physical Activity and Sport in the Lives of Girls." Nike eventually partnered with the Department of Health and Human Services' Girl Power! initiative (Cooky & McDonald, 2005).

By the end of the 1990s, numerous commercials and advertising campaigns reproduced discourses of Girl Power! In her article on what she calls "Generation G," Geissler (2001) argues that sport and female athleticism were inextricably connected with Girl Power! in sport advertising at the time. In addition to Nike, advertisements for Reebok, Adidas, and Champion, as well as public service announcements, capitalized on this new sense of Girl Power! For example, Reebok's "Women Defy" campaign in 2001 featured images of female athletes defying women's (unspoken) oppression through their athletic achievements. One advertisement in this campaign featured a close-up of Venus Williams' face, her gaze focused on something outside of the frame of the advertisement. She looks strong and determined, yet simultaneously wistful, perhaps longing with hope for the "new future" for girls and women. The copy below reads, "It's A Man's World" with a red line crossed through the text, suggesting that, through sport, women have successfully challenged male dominance and power. The advertisement is also decidedly post-feminist in its assertion that sport itself is no longer a "man's world," equality has been achieved, and the need for feminism has passed. What is not discussed in this post-feminist view of sport is that although elite female tennis players can command the same prize money at the U.S. Open and earn equal pay at Grand Slam events, the needs and issues concerning the majority of women in sport are ignored. In other words, the increased opportunities for elite female athletes rarely "trickle down" to the average female athlete (Spencer, 2000).

The advertising campaigns of the mid-1990s and early 2000s illustrated the paradoxical nature of images of female athleticism. Images of the physicality of female athletes fractured the historical linkage between female physicality and failure. Third Wave feminist and weightlifting enthusiast Leslie Heywood (1998) refers to the "new" image of the female athlete as the "power chick," borrowing the term from professional volleyball player Gabrielle Reese. Heywood writes,

> We don't have to reject our bodies because today "girl" doesn't mean little wuss, woman doesn't mean doormat, giving up all your time and dreams for other people. We can have muscles now and ostensibly those muscles will stand for power, self-determination, presence and place in the world. (p. 205)

Thus, the contemporary image of the female athlete supplanted the "mannish athlete" stereotype that historically plagued women's sport and replaced it with the "power chick": heterosexy, feminine, yet strong and able to "kick some ass" (ibid.). As an embodiment of Girl Power!, the "power chick" served as a representative for girls' and women's empowerment. For Heywood, this is not a contradiction or a step back in feminist principles, but a forward progression of the movement, a re-articulation of feminism in a new historical moment, the Third Wave, where women's struggles for equality have changed. The female athlete could represent feminism to a new generation of girls without girls having to claim the "f-word." For Heywood, the feminism of the 1960s, as a movement and its image, had been replaced with the "power chick"/ Girl Power! of the 1990s.

Thus, Girl Power! encompassed female athleticism and opened cultural spaces for girls and women in sports (Heywood & Dworkin, 2003). This cultural space was, and still continues to be, constructed by the increasing popularity of "real" athletes like Mia Hamm and Brandi Chastain (soccer), Serena and Venus Williams, Maria Sharapova (tennis), Amy Acuff (track and field), Amanda Beard (swimming), Michelle Wie and Lorena Ochoa (golf), Danika Patrick (auto racing), and Lisa Leslie and Candace Parker (basketball)—athletes whose images of physicality, intensity, strength, and competitive spirit seemingly pose a serious threat to sport as the last male preserve (Bryson, 1987). Media representations of female athletes, both in "real" sport events and in "mediated" commercials and advertisements, offered young girls empowering images of the female body. In these real and mediated images, girls could see women's bodies that were strong, athletic, muscular, and active (Heywood & Dworkin, 2003; Dowling, 2000).

At the same time, many female athletes have consciously cultivated media personas that incorporate elements of conventional femininity; all of the aforementioned athletes are viewed as heterosexually attractive and conventionally feminine. Indeed, Serena Williams was a trendsetter in women's fashion on the tennis circuit, Lisa Leslie's media image often focused on her role as a fashion model, and Brandi Chastain, after the World Cup win, posed nude on the cover of *Gear* magazine, with a strategically placed soccer ball. Many female athletes choose these representations either to market their image to attract commercial endorsements, and/or to bring attention to their sport. (Many sport studies scholars, however, argue that while the reproduction of conventional femininity may benefit some individual athletes, it hurts lesbian athletes, who are further closeted by the cultural erasure of "butch" athletes [Kane, Griffin & Messner, 2002]).

More recently, Weiden+Kennedy's 2007 Nike advertising campaign "Pretty" both reproduced and challenged conventional femininity. The commercial depicts Maria Sharapova en route to a tennis tournament. The camera follows Sharapova as she leaves her hotel room at the Waldorf-Astoria. Sharapova walks through the hotel to her car, which drives her to the tournament. The camera follows her journey, cutting to various hotel employees, her car driver, the paparazzi, fans on the street, the announcers, the ball girl at the tournament, the line judge, and fans in the stands as each sings a lyric from the song "I Feel Pretty," which was featured in the film *West Side Story.* Sharapova's facial expression, a concentrated game face with a twinge of disdain, suggests to the viewer that she does not appreciate, nor does she embrace the attention she receives—attention that is based on being "pretty." The commercial ends with Sharapova on the court, waiting to return her opponent's serve. With her classic grunt, Sharapova powerfully returns the serve and wins the point. John McEnroe, shown sitting in the commentators' booth, announces, "Wow, this is *pretty* good stuff already." The camera cuts back to Sharapova with a determined, intimidating expression on her face, wearing a Nike tennis dress. She is focused and concentrating on the next point.

In this commercial, Sharapova, along with Nike, constructed an image that acknowledged Sharapova as a powerful athlete. Moreover, Nike has constructed a marketing campaign that simultaneously challenged and reproduced conventional notions of femininity. Sharapova's glaring expression and distaste for her admirers' sole appreciation of her beauty opens a symbolic space for Sharapova to reject the common practice wherein female athletes receive media attention primarily based on their appearance. The "Pretty" commercial sent the message that Sharapova's athletic accomplishments should be recognized and appreciated. Sharapova, however, is also an attractive woman, according to dominant U.S. cultural standards of beauty. She is tall and thin yet athletic, with straight, long blonde hair, flawless (white) skin, and blue eyes. It would appear that Sharapova, with the help of Nike, produced an image that fractured the dominant cultural expectation that a female athlete must be attractive in order to be validated by the mainstream media, while at the same time utilizing her appearance and athleticism to sell Nike, its image, and its products. Clearly this commercial would not have the same impact if it featured an "unattractive" athlete attempting to challenge the beauty norms in women's sport.

Sharapova's marketing image is much different than that of her predecessor, Anna Kournikova. Although some credit her endorsement deals to her "supermodel bod and Gwyneth Paltrow good looks" (ibid.), Sharapova, unlike Kournikova, has athletic success to back up her commercial appeal, and this fact is conveyed in her commercially mediated image. Kournikova openly embraced and welcomed the attention she received and actively cultivated her image as the "World's Sexiest Athlete," as determined by an EPSN viewer's poll (Kane, Griffin & Messner, 2002). Sharapova, on the other hand, seems to recognize the appeal she has based on her appearance, while simultaneously rejecting the objectification that accompanies that appeal.

When comparing the image of Kournikova in the late 1990s and the image of Sharapova in the mid-2000s, the shift in the representation of female athleticism is evident. Whereas Kournikova was popular with corporations because of her looks, Sharapova is popular with corporations because of her looks *and* her athleticism. Kournikova is a blonde-haired, blue-eyed, conventionally attractive tennis player who, despite never winning a singles tournament in her eight-year career, was the highest-paid female athlete in the late 1990s. In contrast, at one point Sharapova was ranked first in the world, according to WTA rankings, and at the time of this writing, has won twenty-two career tennis titles. Sharapova currently holds the title Kournikova once held: Sharapova is the highest-paid female athlete, with most of the money coming from commercial endorsements with Prince, TAG Heuer, Motorola, Land Rover, and, of course, Nike (Lippert, 2006).

More importantly, the other major shift since the mid-1990s is that of the Girl Power! discourse disappearing from representations of girls' and women's sport. While some may read the Kournikova/Sharapova contrast as a positive shift in the representation of female athletes (now they are recognized for their looks *and* athletic accomplishments), in contemporary popular cultural images, Sharapova and other female athletes are no longer connected with Girl Power! nor with girl athletes. In the "Pretty" campaign, Sharapova has the potential to serve as a new representative of Girl Power! Female athletes, however, are no longer positioned as representatives of Girl Power!, nor is girl empowerment through sport significant in the media or the marketing image of female athletes. The individualism of Girl Power! in the mid-1990s has created a cultural context wherein female athletes are viewed as individuals, rather than as representatives of broader social movements. Moreover, definitions of empowerment for girls and women have undergone re-articulations, wherein girl empowerment and Girl Power! are now based on public and overt expressions of sexuality (Levy, 2005), rather than physicality, strength, and athleticism. Today, in the late 2000s, girl empowerment in popular culture is linked with sexuality and "strip culture" (ibid.) more so than with sport and athleticism. Consider that in the mid-2000s, the Spice Girls have been replaced by the Pussycat Dolls, another manufactured all-girl pop music group whose performances incorporate exotic dancing and burlesque culture and whose songs are overtly sexual in their content.

Empowering Girls through Consuming Sport: Marketing and Girl Power!

While there is no denying that Girl Power! discourse had an impact on young girls and even provided "positive" images of femininity and empowerment, the relationship between girl culture and Girl Power! was more complex. The emergence of Girl Power! in the late 1990s coincided with advertisers' recognition of the untapped girl market, a market that (at the time) spent approximately $50 billion or more each year (Geissler, 2001). Indeed, since the 1990s, marketers have taken notice of the girls of Generation Y and their sport participation, spectatorship, and consumption behaviors. Marketers are aware that girls and women in the U.S. make up almost half the sport market (Bush, Bush, Clark & Bush, 2005). Girl Power! and its athletic representatives were not featured in advertising solely to promote images of girl empowerment; they were also there to sell running shoes and sports bras. Therefore, corporate imperatives must be considered when discussing the cultural representations and meanings of Girl Power!, and their potential to empower the lives of "real" girls (Giardina & Metz, 2005).

Yet this is not an either/or debate, in which corporations are *either* selling products *or* images of empowerment; they do both (Dworkin & Messner, 1999). As Banet-Weiser explains, "Girl Power is profoundly ambiguous; it both appeals to a kind of citizenship that challenges conventional feminine stereotypes, and collapses that citizenship with consumption habits that often celebrate those very same stereotypes" (2001, p. 4). For example, as discussed above, Maria Sharapova's Nike commercials illustrate Banet-Weiser's argument. Nike, Reebok, and the WNBA sold their products through Girl Power! *and* were producing ideas about girlhood, girl empowerment, and girls' sports.

Feminists have raised important critiques about the commodification of feminism and Girl Power! Unlike Second Wave feminism, whose media image was angry and political (Douglas, 1994), Girl Power! was given space in popular culture because it was non-threatening and not angry (Banet-Weiser, 2001). Girl Power! was about a different kind of political agency, one in which girls are primarily "empowered" through consuming popular culture rather than through equal pay for equal work or the right to birth control. Yet, despite this difference between Girl Power!/Third Wave feminism and the feminism of the Second Wave, Banet-Weiser (2004) argues that it is "both misleading and inaccurate" to assume that "girl power as a media-created new commercial avenue has no connection with any kind of real politics" (p. 137). Indeed, one could argue that despite the commercial elements of Girl Power!, the mobilization of girls into sport, along with the shift in increased cultural acceptance of girls in sport, has been sustained by Girl Power! discourse. From this perspective, Girl Power! is interpreted as creating a "real" political impact on the lives of girls. I argue, however, that we must consider both the commercial imperatives of Girl Power! discourse and its discursive fall from popular culture in the mid-2000s *along with* the increase in the cultural acceptance of female athletes. While Girl Power! created a cultural context for the celebration of girls' sport and girl empowerment in the mid- to late 1990s, the lack of popular cultural texts today addressing girls as sport participants, spectators, and consumers in a similar way suggests that Girl Power! served primarily as a marketing discourse, rather than a sustained and ongoing instrument of political change in girls' lives.

The Future of Girl Power! and Girls' Sport

The increase in girls' participation was not simply the result of Title IX (although it has played a significant role in creating shifts in the cultural terrain of girls' sport, as discussed in the beginning of this chapter). As Messner (2002) argues, the growth of girls' participation in sport was also due to shifts in cultural values and understandings that positioned girls' sport participation as beneficial for girls, fostering their health and overall positive well-being, as well as shifts in the marketing of women's sports and female athletes by the sports-media-commercial complex. Understanding Girl Power! and girls' sport requires an examination of these forces, as I have done in this chapter. I have shown that girls' sport is not created in a social vacuum, but is constructed through wider cultural discourses and understandings of girls and Girl Power!

Much of the contemporary popular media discourse on female athletes has centered on this notion of sport as a space of empowerment for young girls, a space where girls can exercise their "girl power." And, as Banet-Weiser (2004) argues, the commercial aspects of Girl Power! were evident and cannot be denied. Yet Girl Power! discourse also created a visibility for girls and women in the media and popular culture—a form of visibility that is highly valued in contemporary U.S. society. While Banet-Weiser was referring to the increased visibility of strong female television characters and programming on Nickelodeon, the same trends existed in the images of female athletes in the mid-1990s to early 2000s. Prior to the 1990s, the mainstream media mostly ignored female athletes and women's sports (with the exception of gymnastics, figure skating, and tennis). However, Girl Power! and Third Wave feminism created a cultural context where girls' and women's empowerment is now, to some extent, embraced by the mainstream media (ibid.). Images of powerful, successful female athletes challenged the historical exclusion of media coverage of women and served to usher in a new Third Wave of female athleticism. While representations of female athletes as both powerful and physically attractive continue to dominate the popular cultural landscape (Heywood & Dworkin, 2003), female athletes as representatives of Girl Power! are no longer a significant cultural discourse through which girls' empowerment or girls' sport are constructed and understood in the mid- to late 2000s. Additionally, in reflecting on Girl Power! in popular culture over the past ten years, the potential for girls' sport to empower "real" girls unfortunately appears to be a marketing fad, quickly forgotten by corporations and advertisers who are under pressure to create new and fresh ways to market their products and images to girl consumers.

The contradictions between the public celebration of female athletes, the challenges to Title IX legislation and its uneven enforcement (Suggs, 2005; Cole, 2000), and the barriers to and complications in increasing opportunities among economically disadvantaged girls (Sabo & Veliz, 2008) raise important questions regarding the potential for sport to empower young girls. It is here at the intersections of race, class, and gender that the complications and tensions in girls' sport become salient. While the public celebration of girls' sport and Girl Power! reflected the experiences of many girls who play sport, it did not reflect the experiences of *all* girls. And yet, this single representation came to dominate the cultural terrain of girls' sport, and often was the only representation of girls' sports made visible in popular culture. Focusing solely on the popular culture celebration of Girl Power! and girls' sports may lead one to make drastically different and somewhat limited conclusions on the state of "real" girls' sports today. Indeed, this conclusion (that Title IX is no longer needed because girls are playing sport), which was given visibility in popular culture, is what the Bush administration and others employed in their arguments against Title IX. Therefore, it is imperative to recognize the power of cultural discourses to shape our societal understandings of sport.

The way in which girls' and women's sport, athletes, and experiences are represented in popular culture serves as a lens through which our society understands the context of girls' and women's sport. These understandings have the potential to impact the way sport is structured and organized, as well as public policy regarding sport and the lives of girls. If the representations are based on a privileged set of girls and women and are linked to commercial imperatives to sell sporting goods to girl consumers, there is a strong potential to enable some girls' (i.e., white, middle-class, educated) sport opportunities while constraining other girls' (i.e., girls of color, working class, under-educated) opportunities. If we, as a society, embrace sport as a site for the empowerment of girls and women, then it is essential to consider cultural constructions of Girl Power! to fully understand both the possibility for and the limitation of cultural discourses to empower *all* girls.

References

Banet-Weiser, S. (2001). A kid's got to do what a kid's got to do: Gender, citizenship, and Nickelodeon. Paper presented at the American Sociology Association, Chicago.

Banet-Weiser, S. (2004). Girls Rule!: Gender, feminism and Nickelodeon. *Critical Studies in Media Communication*, 21 (2), 119–139.

Baumgardner, J. & Richards, A. (2000). *Manifesta: Young women, feminism and the future.* New York: Farrar, Straus, and Giroux.

Brand, M. (2003, April 28). Title IX Seminar Keynote Address. [Electronic Version]. Retrieved May 22, 2007, from http://www.ncaa.org/gender_equity/general_info/20030428speech.html.

Bryson, L. (1987). Sport and the maintenance of masculine hegemony. *Women's Studies International Forum*, 10 (4), 349–360.

Bush, V. D., Bush, A. J., Clark, P. & Bush, R. P. (2005). Girl power and word-of-mouth behavior in the flourishing sports market. *Journal of Consumer Marketing*, 22 (5), 257–264.

Cahn, S. (1994). *Coming on strong: Gender and sexuality in twentieth-century women's sport.* New York: Free Press.

Carpenter, L. J. & Acosta, R. V. (2005). *Title IX.* Champaign, IL: Human Kinetics Publishers.

Cole, C. L. (2000). The year that girls ruled. *Journal of Sport and Social Issues*, 24 (1), 3–7.

Cole, C. L. & Hribar, A. (1995). Celebrity feminism: Nike style post-Fordism, transcendence, and consumer power. *Sociology of Sport Journal*, 12 (4), 347–369.

Cooky, C. (2009). "Girls just aren't interested": The social construction of interest in girls' sport. *Sociological Perspectives*, 52, 259–284.

Cooky, C. & McDonald, M. G. (2005). "'If you let me play': Young girls' insider other narratives of sport." *Sociology of Sport Journal*, 22 (2), 158–177.

De Varona, D. (2004). "M's in football": Myths, management, marketing, media and money. A reprise. In F. Hong & J. A. Mangan (Eds.), *Soccer, women and sexual liberation: Kicking off a new era*, pp. 7–13. London: F. Cass

Douglas, S. J. (1994). *Where the girls are: Growing up female with the mass media.* New York: Times Books.

Dowling, C. (2000). *The frailty myth: Women approaching physical equality.* New York: Random House.

Dworkin, S. L. & Messner, M. A. (1999). Just do . . . what?: Sport, bodies and gender. In M. M. Ferree, J. Lorber & B. B. Hess (Eds.). *Revisioning gender*, pp. 341–364. Thousand Oaks, CA: Sage Publications.

Education Amendments of 1972. Title IX. Department of Labor. Retrieved May 22, 2010, from http://www.dol.gov/oasam/regs/statutes/titleix.htm.

Faludi, S. (1991). *Backlash: The undeclared war against American women.* New York: Crown Publishers.

Geissler, D. (2001). Generation G. *Journal of Sport and Social Issues*, 25 (3), 324–331.

Giardina, M. D. & Metz, J. L. (2005). Women's sports in Nike's America: Body politics and the corporo-empowerment of "everyday athletes." In S. J. Jackson & D. L. Andrews (Eds.). *Sport, culture and advertising: Identities, commodities and the politics of representation*, pp. 59–80. New York: Routledge.

Griffin, C. (2004). Good girls, bad girls: Anglocentrism and diversity in the constitution of contemporary girlhood. In A. Harris (Ed.), *All about the girl: Culture, power and identity*, pp. 29–44. New York: Routledge.

Harris, A. (2004). Introduction. *All about the girl: Culture, power and identity*, pp. xvii–xxiv. New York: Routledge.

Heywood, L. (1998). All-American girls: Jock chic, body image and sports. In O. Edut (Ed.), *Adiós, Barbie: Young women write about body image and identity*, pp. 201–210. Seattle, WA: Seattle Press.

Heywood, L. & Dworkin, S. L. (2003). *Built to win: The female athlete as cultural icon.* Minneapolis: University of Minnesota Press.

Kane, M. J., Griffin, P. & Messner, M. A. (2002). *Playing (un)fair: The media image of the female athlete* [video]. (Available from Media Education Foundation, 60 Masonic Street, Northampton, Massachusetts 01060)

Levy, A. (2005). *Female chauvinist pigs: Women and the rise of raunch culture.* New York: Free Press.

Lippert, B. (2006, August 30). Oh so pretty for Nike. *Adweek* [Electronic version] Retrieved May 21, 2007, from http://www.adweek.com/aw/creative/article_display.jsp?vnu_content_id =1003085464.

Lucas, S. (2000). Nike's commercial solution: Girls, sneakers and salvation. *International Review for the Sociology of Sport, 35* (2), 149–164.

Messner, M. A. (2002). *Taking the field: Women, men and sports.* Minneapolis: University of Minnesota Press.

Messner, M. A., Duncan, M. C. & Cooky, C. (2003). Silence, sports bras, and wrestling porn: The treatment of women in televised sports news and highlights. *Journal of Sport and Social Issues, 27* (1), 38–51.

Messner, M. A., Duncan, M. C. & Willms, N. (2005). *Gender in televised sports: News and highlight shows, 1989–2004.* Amateur Athletic Foundation of Los Angeles.

National Federation of High School Athletics. (2008–2009). *2008–2009 High School Athletics Participation Survey.* Retrieved May 22, 2010, from http://www.nfhs.org/content.aspx?id=3282&linkidentifier =id&itemid=3282.

Oxford English Dictionary. *Girl Power enters the Oxford English Dictionary.* Retrieved May 22, 2010, from http://www.askoxford.com/pressroom/archive/oedjan02/?view=uk.

Sabo, D. & Veliz, P. (2008). *Go out and play: Youth sports in America.* East Meadow, NY: Women's Sports Foundation.

Shakib, S. & Dunbar, M. D. (2002). The social construction of female and male high school basketball participation: Reproducing the gender order through a two-tiered sporting institution. *Sociological Perspectives, 45* (4), 353–378.

Smith, M. (2006). Reconsidering girl power: Examining media images of female athletes. In S. Spickard Prettyman & B. Lampman (Eds.), *Learning culture through sports,* pp. 168–181. Lanham, MD: Rowman and Littlefield Education.

Spencer, N. (2000). Reading between the lines: A discursive analysis of Billie Jean King vs. Bobby Riggs "Battle of the Sexes." *Sociology of Sport Journal, 17* (4), 386–402.

Suggs, W. (2005). "Left behind": Title IX and black women athletes. In D. K. Wiggins & P. B. Miller (Eds.), *The unlevel playing field: A documentary history of the African American experience in sport,* pp. 387–393. Urbana: University of Illinois Press

Taft, J. K. (2004). Girl power politics: Pop-culture barriers and organizational resistance. In A. Harris (Ed.). *All about the girl: Culture, power and identity,* pp. 69–78. New York: Routledge.

United States Department of Health and Human Services. (1997). The President's Council on Physical Fitness and Sports Report: *Physical Activity and Sport in the Lives of Girls.*

United States Department of Health and Human Services. (2007) Girl Power! Retrieved June 1, 2007, from http://www.girlpower.gov/AdultsWhoCare/campinfo/quicknotes.htm.

16

British National Female Coaches on Coaching

Leanne Norman

Historically, men have enjoyed a privileged position over women in sport in terms of opportunities and rewards, grounded in the beliefs concerning the physical differences and abilities between genders. This has then been taken up into commonsense thinking that men are thus naturally superior to women. However, in the twenty-first century in the UK, as is the case in many Western countries, women now participate in a vast variety of sports—more than ever before. Participation rates of men and women in sport and physical activity are almost equal, and no longer are sports viewed as an activity solely for men. Yet there still remains a significant lack of parity, in terms of both participation and status, between men and women in organized, professional sports. Nowhere is that more true than with positions of leadership and power in sport, such as coaching. While there has been a plethora of research examining the sporting experiences of women and girls as athletes, this has not been the case with research into the experiences of the few women who do occupy influential and powerful roles as coaches. It is such positions that still remain masculine "property" and continue to be perceived as the domain of white, heterosexual men. Such gendered division of labor is lingering evidence of the latent, deeply entrenched patriarchal control of sports leadership.

In this chapter, I present an interview with Anna Signeul, head coach of Scotland's national women's football team. This interview, which is grounded in a feminist cultural studies theoretical framework, seeks to understand Anna's experiences as a master woman coach and to gain insight into the complexities and challenges women coaches may face, how women leaders are received in such a male-dominated culture and game as soccer, and how women coaches have contributed to and influenced the sport. The discussion is an account of

Anna's personal journey and career development as a coach, exploring how she has experienced gender relations in sport, as well as what she believes to be some of the most salient causes of and solutions to overcoming women's marginal status in positions of leadership and responsibility. My goal is to increase the production of ideas for empowering and increasing women's political voice and power in sport. Below is the interview with Anna Signeul, followed by an analysis of her ideas and their implications for women in sport.

LN: Tell me about your journey up the coaching career ladder, from when you started to where you are today.

AS: I started to coach in tennis when I was 15 and I enjoyed coaching very much. When I was in school I also helped with PE, because I was a little better than the other girls in the class, so she (the teacher) said, "You take this group; I'll take this group." I enjoyed that—I always enjoyed coaching. Then I thought, I wonder how good I can be at football; then I went from my hometown to another town. So first I had my team, then afterwards I coached, [and] then I played myself. I did that from 1980, when I really started to play football, and I always enjoyed it. And I worked in sport the whole time, so in this club, I worked on a project in the schools over the summer going around the district teaching about the good things about playing football to finally get girls and boys into sports. Then I started to work for a club, the biggest club in the town, and they had different sports. But I was the head administrator for that club and in that job, I set up coaching development, coaching courses for the coaches in that club. I worked on that all day, then I stopped working, I trained the team, [and] then I went to play myself. I did [this] for quite a long time, and then I also played [on] the national team—I didn't do that for long. Then the Swedish Football Association (FA) wanted me to come down and coach at a great camp for one week for the best under-15 players. That's when I started to work for the Swedish FA. I think they opened their eyes to my coaching because of everything I [had] done for the club, and for the youth and girls football I received an award at the Swedish FA annual meeting as "Youth Coach of the Year."

But then I was about 27, and I said I don't want to work for the Swedish FA, you know; we had about two weeks' holiday for the summer. It was getting really tough. We trained more and more and it was really tough to [play for] a team [while] working, so I said I didn't want to get involved anymore. I coached my own club when I stopped playing; then I was offered a job at the Swedish FA as a youth national coach for girls. So in the beginning I trained a club, but that situation was unbearable. I couldn't do it. First of all, [if] you weren't objective enough the other clubs . . . you would try and take talented players to your team. So it was a situation that we didn't want it that way. So I stopped coaching a club team, and I was just national coach. I did all my coaching courses at the same time I played, so I had all my licenses. I thought I was going to get the job [of national coach] but because [of] all of the politics, they wanted a man. They didn't say that, but you could read that between the lines. So that's when I thought, well, I enjoyed my job in Sweden; I thought it was the best job you could have. The circumstances and everything around women's and girls' football has developed so much and become so much better in Sweden in the last few years. So from working with everything when I came to the Swedish FA nine years ago, we had more people in, we had more money, so it was really, really good. I thought, there are not many jobs in the world like this and not many jobs where you can speak English. I thought, well, maybe it was time to move on. So that's why I took this chance to take this job [at the Scottish FA] and I thought also, with the experience of such wide areas that I have, that I could contribute not just in the national team but also in the structure, in the club development and coaching development. On the other hand, when you've been working with women's football for over twenty years, then you have to bang your head against the wall so many times. That was the down side, I thought. If I come here, I know it will be tough because it has been so tough in Sweden. That was the only thing that made me hesitate. "Do I really want to do this again? Do I really want to push myself in a situation where I have to argue and fight for money again and try to convince people who don't believe in women's football, that don't think that women's football is anything to have. Then it's just a burden, and so do I really want to do that again?" I knew it would come with everything else.

LN: Who were the role models or mentors for you during the early stages of your career?

AS: I would say, from when I started, [I think I learnt a lot from] my colleagues. But I never had a role model, no one, because I was the best! But then you become older and you realize you're not the best. I just think it was something I wanted to do when I was young, that I wanted to help and teach and correct. But I think I must have had good coaches when I was young that made it interesting. I can see that as well in my coaching career in football; the experiences I have from individual sport have helped me a lot in coaching football. That is something I've brought into my coaching, a particular-ness in technique and preciseness in technique in individual sports. You had to take responsibility and you always had to learn; it was always up to yourself if you wanted to develop. That is something I have taken with me into football. Teams and environments don't take any responsibility for the players they own, and that's my philosophy as well. You'll never be the best if you don't take responsibility for your future, for your career. That's what I have been working very hard on here for over a year with these players. If someone comes to me and says, "Anna, can I do this?" I say, "Tell me yourself. You work it out yourself. It is not my career. It is not me. What do you think?" Some players can't handle that; they want someone else to make the decisions, and then it is also easier to blame someone else if you're not successful.

LN: Could you describe your daily routine as a national coach: How do you plan for and manage your role each day?

AS: As I have responsibility for the whole elite team and for the youth, you could say the job can change all the time because you have different priorities. So you could say that every day is different because I have to plan everything for the "A" squad— for the matches, the players, the injuries, follow-up individual meetings, help with individual training—so it's very much focused on the "A" squad, but [I] also to try and get a good relationship with all the club coaches. Also [there's] club development and talent identification, we must have a structure for that. Then [there's] also the youth national squads and what they're doing, and we develop that. So it's very busy. It's not just the "A" squad. It's very much other things, also.

LN: We are starting to touch upon barriers and challenges that women coaches have to face. Have you experienced any obstacles or barriers in your development as a coach?

AS: If you're a coach in women's football on the club level and national level, as a coach for women you haven't been able to [just] coach. You're not just a coach. You have to do so many, many other things. The coaching part has been too small. If you are a man and become a coach for a man's club team, you're the coach. You don't have to do all these other things; you don't care about what socks they are going to wear or what the kit should look like or if there's a problem on the board or a problem in the youth teams. You just coach. I think that's the big, big difference, because that's what I thought in the end when I left, that would probably be my best year because the tasks in women's football have progressed so much on a national level so I could actually just coach, [and have] only one thing I was responsible for. But all through these twenty years, it's been too much of other things that we have to do. I think that's a disadvantage for all women. But this is not just a problem for female coaches; it's also a problem for a man who is coaching female football. It's about women's football. There are so many, many other problems, so you can't just concentrate on coaching. We don't have any money; we can't train more because we don't have the players, who work too much. It means development takes a longer time, when you have to spend [your time] on so many other things. That's maybe why the time to develop yourself and the time to go on coaching courses, there is always a lack of it—a lack of time for all development and all coaching development.

LN: Being a woman in what is considered to be a "man's" game, how have you, if at all, experienced any personal conflict between being a woman and a sportswoman?

AS: Since I've been young, I've been a sportswoman and I don't think anyone has seen me as anything else, and I don't know if I've been in other environments where people have noticed that I'm a sportswoman. Do you know what I mean? I've been living in small towns, so everyone knows who you are. So that's maybe why I've not experienced that conflict. You know that I coached all these girls' teams for ten years, and for them, it was very difficult to be a girl and a footballer. When I grew up, I didn't have any problems because I was quite strong and was always listened to when I was in a male environment. My own experience of being bullied or anything, I didn't have that or feel it in any way because I think a large part of my identity as a person when I was young was that I was good at sports. It wasn't to do with [being] a girl or [whether I was] beautiful; it was that my identity was fixed around that I was good at sport.

LN: Going back to what you mentioned earlier, that as a coach of woman's sport you feel there are so many more issues than just coaching to deal with. In what ways do you have or have you had support and guidance from other women coaches?

AS: I must say, during these nine years at the Swedish FA, in the first five years, these two other female coaches and me, we were very close together. Especially one of them and I. We had very inspiring and very good, developing conversations. We did a lot together. As a coach, to work so close to someone, to ask, "What do you think?" it's been very inspiring, it inspired me. You know, it feels like you've found something with someone.

LN: How have you experienced your relations with male coaches?

AS: On average, with most of them, very good. Some of them, men coaches in women's football, they think you have the job because you're female. We have had that situation with the four coaches of the national teams, so we heard that a lot. It's always that you have to win respect; it's the same if you go out and coach the boys' team. You have to show them you can play football; if you did a free kick and put it in the corner, then everyone had respect for you. You have to believe in yourself, you have to think that you are good, that you know things, that you are as good as they are, and don't lower yourself. If you have that feeling, then I think that's the message you send out. But if you are unsure, you lose respect, and then when you lose it, it's hard to get it back. I just went after my heart, what I believed and what I thought. I also had a coach when I wrote my first technical report, he was the national coach for the men and he was like, "oh women are rubbish." When I wrote my first technical analysis, he came in and said, "That was very, very good." He was on the UEFA technical committee, so that made me [realize] how good my knowledge was.

LN: You mentioned a lot of politics occurred in your previous position in the FA and that they wanted to appoint a man. Why do you think that was?

AS: I think this—and this is just what I think and I can't prove anything—but my feeling is that after the success that [the national team] had in 2003 with [a woman] coach and the silver medal, the sponsors became interested in women's football. We had lots more money—the increase in number of spectators and at [the] club level was enormous; the increase in spectators at national games for the women was very good. As the clubs had more money, they could hire full-time coaches, the coaches that came in were better educated, [and] it was much, much more in the newspapers when the women played. The big journalists were writing about the women's national team; they weren't criticizing. I think they thought, now we have to have a man because the pressure from the men in women's football was too big. I think the women were not strong enough to stand up for their philosophy or ideas. How many full-time jobs are there for female coaches in this country? How many full-time jobs are there for male coaches in this country? The jobs you have for full-time coaches, we need to make sure there are females in the posts because they can't get any other jobs. I can coach, but there's no male club [that would have me], and it's just male clubs that have full-time coaches. That was one of my biggest arguments all the time. If female coaches have the criteria and if they are good, then they get the job because [the] men, they can go to men's football and have a full-time job. When it means more and it's tougher, then it's like "let the men take over." That's the feeling I get.

LN: In what ways do you think women possess influence and control in your sport?

AS: They are not on the board, they are not coaches, and they are mainly administrators, treasurers, secretaries. I think the clubs here in Scotland, they are very positive for females in the clubs; however, there is maybe the feeling that it doesn't matter so much. But even the best clubs, they want to have female assistant coaches. Here, coaching is something you can do as a teenager and earn some extra money, so that's why many of the girls in the team are coaching. They go on to these child coaching awards and get their children's license so they can earn a little more money or a little bit more coaching. It's very hard to get women into coaching, and so I think here because of these jobs, like development officer [and] jobs in clubs like youth coaches, there are a lot more opportunities in this country to work as a coach, for girls to work as coaches. That's what makes the difference in England in the development of the clubs, if the clubs in a couple of years can give some money to the coaches.

LN: Having no women on the board, having predominantly men on the board as decision makers, what impact does that have on the women's game?

AS: A huge impact. I think also that I want 50 percent of women on the board in men's clubs and boys' clubs. We always make sure that it is mixed. Where is the mixture on the men's side? But this is because in women's football, there are so many men working, so that's the men wanting the good places in women's football. But there are few girls or no girls working in men's football. I absolutely think it would make a huge impact for boys and girls, because women and men think different. So I think it would benefit girls if there were more females in decision-making positions. Especially [at the] youth [level], when you don't just want competing, you also want social [aspects]; you want so many other things maybe. You want to see the whole picture, and I don't think that men can just see the whole picture.

LN: What would women contribute?

AS: I think women can look at the whole picture and see the wider perspective of things. Maybe women aren't so interested in making money; they are more interested in developing. I think if you have women on the board, they want to sit there because they want to achieve something. I'm not saying that men don't want to achieve anything, but I mean for many men to sit in the club, it is status. That's what I think is a big, big difference between men and women, because a woman wouldn't sit on a board if she didn't think she achieved anything. That's why when you ask a woman. "Do you want to sit on the board?" she says, "What do you want me to do?" If you ask a man, "Do you want to sit on our board?" he wouldn't ask that—it's about status. To have women on the board would make a huge difference in the discussion around the table; I think the meetings are more creative, that you achieve something.

LN: What differences do you see in men and women as coaches?

AS: I think that women are good communicators; they can read body language. Sometimes I think having one man and one woman can be very good, and two women can be very good for women. You have to be a good communicator to coach women's teams. I think there have been men who have been coaching in women's football and stopped because they can't communicate with the women. One thing, if you're a female football player and put up your list of criteria for a coach, one thing that comes very high up is engagement. If a woman sees someone engaged in her, or in her team, she takes that personally. That's one of the criteria you need to have as a coach, or to coach females. If you put a lot of effort or time into these women, they will give everything back to you. I always say if you want to be a successful coach for women, put your heart into it and time, and they will appreciate it so much.

LN: Why do you think there are not more senior women coaches in sport?

AS: I think it's a lack of mentors: I think if we have more mentors to our female coaches, give them advice, talk to them, I think things like that make a difference. Women aren't stupid; if they want to do something, they want to have something back and feel like they're making a good job of it. I think it's tough for women because it's a lonely job. I think the combination of two coaches is much better; if you want to increase the number of senior women coaches, you have mentors; you have a network around them that supports them also. It's a lonely job; many women analyze a lot. If something goes wrong, something isn't good, they take it personally as "what have I done wrong?" and analyze it too much. Men just say, "Let's move on; let's go on to the next step." I think it's important you have support. If you have twenty female players, women can read body language. Men don't always see it: "Don't you see how she looks, what she said?" Men say no. Also, my U-21 coach in Sweden, she had three kids and a husband. They made the decision that he would take care of the kids, even if he was a very successful coach as well. They said that when she got the job as U-21 coach, as long as she had the job that was her priority. How many men do that? It's very tough. You must have a family situation to make it possible. If you have kids, then society says, "What kind of mother are you? Leaving your kids with your husband!" Whatever you do, you do wrong.

LN: In your opinion, how can more women gain senior coaching positions in sport?

AS: I would try and set up a network for female coaches on the highest level, a network that not only supports one another, but also a network that gives special education in communication, self-confidence, etc. But I think that the social situation a woman has, the female coaches just don't have the self-confidence to go on to the next level. They haven't had anyone to give them self-confidence in coaching. We need to help them to make the next step because I think [only a] few of them have the self-confidence to think they are good enough. I think it's a lack of confidence.

LN: What would you suggest to increase their self-confidence?

AS: The only way of doing that is first of all education; you need to give the women coaches much more of that. You have courses just for female coaches, and at these female courses, you have female course leaders and educators. In a female environment, you as a female have self-confidence. When it comes to football and a man, he thinks he knows everything in football and you're just women and you don't know anything about football. "You're just a woman and you're a man, so you know a lot more about football." That's how women see themselves and that's how men see themselves because [this] is their business. This is their sport, this is something they know, so what do you know about this sport. You're a woman! In these courses, I think everyone would learn much more; if you had females sitting together, they would support one another also much better during the course. I also think female course leaders can give self-confidence, can give feedback to let you know you are good, that you can do this. I think all these things you have to do if you want more females as coaches in football, and it must be worth it for the women. You must feel that "if I'm going to go three times a week, I'm going to get something out of it." The important thing for a woman is she learns a lot, she enjoys herself, it feels good, and she meets new friends. That's why all the times you bang your head, the times I feel like quitting, like saying, "I quit," and just getting irritated—at times like that, you think, "I'm right for the young girls to want to play football; I have a responsibility."

LN: Is there anything else you would like to discuss or add in any additional information? Are there any questions you would like to ask me?

AS: I just think it's important to know that there are differences between a male and a female. We are different, and I think when you become good, it's "as good as a man." But I think we are female and continue to want to be female; we don't want to be male. That's not our goal, to be male. We want to be female athletes and continue to do what's best for females. We want to make the game that's good for females.

Conclusion

Much can be learned from eliciting and understanding the lived experiences of those who occupy a marginal, inferior status in sport and as Collins would describe it, the standpoint of the "outsider within" (1991). Using in-depth interviews with master women coaches in this way develops and expands our knowledge and comprehension of what it means to work within the complex and resilient patriarchal power structures that dominate our sporting organizations. This interview with Anna Signeul is particularly insightful because her own coaching education and journey has occurred in a variety of cultures and contexts. Anna demonstrates that for her, coaching goes beyond the mechanistic and scientific; it is a process that is laden with social and ethical responsibilities, and to hold such an esteemed position means to contribute to a team in much more than purely the coaching aspect. Furthermore, the interview with Anna reveals the ideological constraints that operate at the most elite levels of the sports hierarchy, making it difficult for women to act freely and of their own volition (Birrell & Theberge, 1994). For example, it was her ambition to coach her national team, given her progression from national youth coach and substantial involvement in club development and coaching development. However, her progression was restricted by the board, the group that has the power to appoint. The board clearly felt only a man was capable of holding such an important role as national coach, now that the women soccer players had shown their competency as athletes and "threatened" to shake off their secondary and trivialized status. This is a product of the historical and cultural connection between masculinity and authority (Connell, 1987). Authority is a culturally valued skill; other appreciated competencies are those of aggression, force, and strength, all of which are linked to and prescribed to men's sports (Bryson, 1987). The consequence for women's sports and women involved in sport is the undervaluing and misrepresentation of women as being naturally inferior to men (Birrell & Theberge, 1994). Anna's coaching career has been hampered by the negative labels attached to women's sport; she has had to take on many more responsibilities than just coaching the team in an unsupported, underprivileged, and under-resourced environment. The outcome is that many women coaches have not had the opportunity to undergo personal and professional development, perhaps adding fuel to the ideological assumption that women are "naturally" not good enough to occupy positions of power.

This ideology of men's superiority as leaders and athletes also significantly influenced Anna's relations with men coaches. While on the whole she reported positive experiences working with her male colleagues, she did feel that she was continually being "tested," having to prove herself as a competent professional to her colleagues as well as to male athletes. Elite women coaches have to work much harder to earn the respect of colleagues and athletes because the cultural perceptions of women are juxtaposed against perceptions of who is a leader. This then is an outcome of the historical origins of sports, as Sage (1990) describes, and if such perceptions and images of superiority are continually presented, highlighted, and consented to, then male superiority will be unquestionably accepted. Thus, the creation of unequal gender representations and disparate gender ideologies will occur and thrive (Theberge & Birrell, 1994).

Finally, an important motivation for conducting this interview with Anna, a coach who has reached the highest position on the coaching ladder, is to gather her opinions and ideas as to the solutions for how to empower more aspiring women coaches to become powerful leaders of sport. An often-cited answer to the problem of the under-representation of women as coaches is to increase the number of women. This is erroneous in its simplicity and disregard for the covert yet powerful interwoven patriarchal, structural, and ideological forces that have been embedded in our sports structure since the birth of institutionalized sport. Merely having more women in coaching roles also assumes that women "naturally" possess a feminist consciousness, and both an awareness of and will to overcome the oppression that women in sport face. In this interview, Anna clearly demonstrates her appreciation for the problems women coaches struggle with when attempting to operate within such a saturated masculine culture. She believes that women are extremely isolated and have "got the message" that they have no right to be in such roles as leadership and coaching. In response, many women feel that they do not belong in sport. They have incredibly low self-confidence, and this prevents them from wanting to progress through their coaching careers. In this way, women coaches perceive their marginal position to be what Birrell and Theberge (1994) describe as a personal and "private tragedy" (p. 353). But to lead social change and end the oppression of women in sport, the first step is to actively resist; this should be a conscious, intentional act based upon the understanding that our repression on the grounds of gender, race, class, and/or sexuality is systematic (Birrell & Theberge, 1994). Anna argues that if women feel more efficacious, become more educated, and are ascribed much more value, they will have the desire to gain more powerful and senior coaching positions. To facilitate women in becoming strong and confident, sport may then be used as a site to create oppositional meanings that challenge the dominant images of gender (Birrell, 1988; Birrell & Richter, 1994). Of course, it is naïve to presume that this alone will change the structures of power that dominate sports, but it may begin to alter the perception and consciousness of the dominant group in sport—that is, men—of the capabilities of women. Considering that the masculine ideology of sport requires the compliance of men as well as the discrediting of women, perhaps this should be the primary target for the reformation of women's oppression in sport (Connell & Messerschmidt, 2005).

References

Birrell, S. (1988). Discourses on the gender / sport relationship: From women in sport to gender relations. *Exercise and Sport Sciences Reviews, 16*, 459–502.

Birrell, S. & Richter, D.M. (1994). Is a diamond forever? Feminist transformations of sport. *In:* S. Birrell & C. Cole (Eds.). (1994). *Women, Sport and Culture.* Champaign, IL: Human Kinetics, pp. 221–249.

Birrell, S. & Theberge, N. (1994). Ideological control of women in sport. *In:* D.M. Costa & S.R. Guthrie (Eds.). (1994). *Women and Sport: Interdisciplinary Perspectives.* Champaign, IL: Human Kinetics, pp. 341–359.

Bryson, L. (1987). Sport and the maintenance of masculine hegemony. *Women's Studies International Forum, 10,* 349–360.

Collins, P.H. (1991). Learning from the outsider within: The sociological significance of black feminist thought. *In:* J.E. Hartman & E. Messer-Davidow (Eds.). (1991). *(En)gendering Knowledge.* Knoxville: University of Tennessee Press, pp. 4–65.

Connell, R.W. (1987). *Gender and Power.* Stanford: Stanford University Press.

Connell, R.W. & Messerschmidt, J. (2005). Hegemonic masculinity: Rethinking the concept. *Gender & Society, 19* (6), 829–859.

Sage, G.H. (1990). *Power and Ideology in American Sports: A Critical Perspective.* Champaign, IL: Human Kinetics.

Theberge, N. & Birrell, S. (1994). The sociological study of women and sport. *In:* D.M. Costa & S.R. Guthrie (Eds.). (1994). *Women and Sport: Interdisciplinary Perspectives.* Champaign, IL: Human Kinetics, pp. 323–331.

17

Oscar Pistorius, the Paralympics, and Issues of Fair Competition

Carwyn Jones

I N THIS CHAPTER, I EXPLORE SOME of the interesting and important ethical issues that arise in the context of the Paralympic Games and the Paralympic movement. In particular, I examine the tensions inherent in promoting the values of participation and pursuing excellence through sport. A key component in achieving the aims of the Paralympics is establishing competitive categories that are fair, and which encourage healthy competition and excellence. I also examine the principle and practice of classification, highlighting some of the inherent difficulties therein. Finally, I examine some of the ethical implications associated with the Oscar Pistorius case. Oscar Pistorius, the successful Paralympic athlete, was denied the opportunity to participate in the 2008 Olympic Games in Beijing. The decision was made by the International Association of Athletics Federations (IAAF) following extensive tests conducted by leading sport scientists. The results of the tests seem to show that Pistorius' prosthetic blades facilitate a biomechanical efficiency, which means that he can run at a particular speed utilizing far less energy than his non-disabled competitors. Consequently, his prosthetic blades were deemed to contravene IAAF rules which prohibit the use of technical aids. In other words they give him an advantage that is unfair in a non-disabled context. In the Paralympics, however, these prosthetic running blades are sanctioned and arguably constitutive of Pistorius' athletic ability.

The Paralympic Context

The Paralympic Games are held in parallel to both the Winter and Summer Olympics, and from the 2012 bid process onwards, any proposed host must organize both the Olympics and the Paralympics. Etymologically, the term "Paralympics" is thought to have originally been a combination of the terms "paraplegic" and "Olympic," coined during the early days of organized sport for the disabled (largely consisting of individuals with spinal cord injuries). The term later came to refer to a parallel Olympics. The International Paralympic Committee (IPC) is now the umbrella institution for the governance of the Paralympic Games. The IPC is a product of evolution and revolution, but its origins lie in Dr. Ludwig Guttmann's National Spinal Injuries Centre at Stoke Mandeville Hospital, founded in the United Kingdom in 1944. He introduced sport as a form of recreation, using it as treatment and rehabilitation for patients at the hospital (mainly war veterans and civilians using wheelchairs), and in 1948, the first of a series of annual games were held at the hospital. The games became international in 1952, and in 1960 they were held in the same city as the Olympics themselves. The Rome International Stoke Mandeville Games are considered to be the first Paralympic Games, although it was not until 1988 that the games became known officially as the Paralympics. The IPC became the official umbrella organization after the 1992 Paralympics in Barcelona, taking an overall responsibility for the structure and governance of the Paralympic Games. The present situation marks the cooperation of a number of International Organizations of Sport for the Disabled (IOSD), who represent the variety of sport for the disabled; for example the Cerebral Palsy International Sport and Recreation Association (CPISRA) and the International Blind Sports Federation (IBSF) promote, govern, classify, and structure the sports and athletes that fall under their auspices. These individual IOSDs are now represented by the IPC in the organization of the Paralympics and in dialogues with the IOC and other global organizations. Traditionally six disability groups are represented at the Paralympics: amputee, cerebral palsy, visual impairment, spinal cord injuries, intellectual disabilities, and *les autres* (all those who don't fit into other groups), according to the IPC website.

The IPC currently promotes their vision for the games and the movement in the following way: "To enable Paralympic athletes to achieve sporting excellence and inspire and excite the world" (International Paralympic Committee, n.d.). The focus is on athletic achievement rather than disability. The precise meanings of the terms of their vision are listed below.

- To enable: This is the primary role of the IPC as an organization—to create the conditions for athlete empowerment through self-determination.
- Paralympic athletes: The primary focus of IPC's activities, in the context of Paralympic athletes, is the development of all athletes from initiation to elite level.
- To achieve sporting excellence: This is the goal of the IPC as a sport-centered organization.

- To inspire and excite the world: The external result is our contribution to a better world for all people with a disability. To achieve this, relations with external organizations and the promotion of the Paralympic movement as a whole are of prime importance.

The Paralympic motto "spirit in motion," according to the IPC on their website, reflects the athletes' efforts to transcend the limits of possibility and to inspire others through their efforts.

The Nature of Sports Contests?

Although sociologists and historians have been suspicious of attempts to provide a conceptual or ideological account of sport that transcends its different cultural and historical manifestations, there is a rich and informative philosophical body of literature that has been very successful in pointing toward the common uniqueness of sporting practices. Bernard Suits' canonical text, *The Grasshopper: Games, Life and Utopia* (2005), is arguably the single most important contribution to the articulation of the logic of sports contests. Sports, he argues, are institutionalized games of physical skill, and as such are an instantiation of game playing, which he summarized as the voluntary attempt to overcome unnecessary obstacles. In games, individuals strive to complete a contrived test or meet an artificial challenge for no other purpose than a desire to meet that challenge or take a test. The aim of the game and the legitimate means of pursuing this aim are spelled out by the rules, which game players accept in order that they can play the game. By playing games, individuals realize a whole host of intrinsically valuable capacities through their efforts to meet the challenges games provide.

Although modern elite professional sport seems like a far cry from the games that beautifully illustrate Suits' text, they share the same central logic. The aim of a sports contest is to discover which competitor(s) best meet, or successfully complete, the particular challenge or goal of the given contest. The nature of the physical challenge is specified by a formal set of rules (constitutive rules), and also by an ethos conceived as a reasonably shared understanding of how the challenge is to be pursued (D'Agostino, 1991; Loland & McNamee, 2000). It might similarly seem strange to talk about elite sports as voluntary autotelic activities, given the professional status of most athletes; however, like other game players, elite athletes are voluntarily engaging in sport in order to test their physical, mental, and moral qualities. This is a claim about the logical aim of the contest, not an empirical claim about the actual motives of each contestant. This is a crucial distinction, because the motivational value set of any given athlete might be very different from that of his or her fellow competitors, yet the logic of the activity is universal. In light of the foregoing ideas, Fraleigh argues that

The purpose of the sports contest, when conceived as the reason for its existence, is to provide equitable opportunity for mutual contesting of the participants' relative abilities to move mass in space and time within the confines prescribed by an agreed upon set of rules. (1984, p. 45)

For Loland (2002) "the goal of sport competitions is to measure, compare and rank two or more competitors according to athletic performance" (p. 10). Given the logic of games, their normative essence becomes clear. A sports contest, or any good contest, must involve the *fair* comparison of athletes' abilities, be they speed, strength, finesse, agility, or some other quality. To this end, the rules of sports provide the "level playing field" upon which all competitors, at least in principle (if not always in practice) have *ceteris paribus*—an equal chance of victory. The rules stipulate equal opportunities to contest, and if the rules are just and each contestant abides by them, we may have confidence in the fairness of the result. In theory, although not in practice, the rules are to be understood as self-imposed obligations precisely because they provide the conditions (by structuring the contest) that competitors voluntarily seek. From a logical point of view, it makes no sense to enter a contest voluntarily and then set about breaking the rules that provide the very conditions that define the contest you entered.

When competitors take the sporting test and draw on their physical, mental, moral, and technical qualities, victory ought to be dependent on the differential excellence between the competitors. That is the purpose of the test. As Breivik (2000) argues: "The athletes strive to control performance and make the result dependent upon their own intended action" (p. 147). To put it another way, sports contests aim to provide accurate comparisons of the volitional actions of the athletes. We may collectively refer to this as "athletic performance." An ideal sports contest victory ought to be wholly dependent upon athletic performance. Superior athletic performances should *ceteris paribus* be victorious ones. This general account applies to all sports; it is a truth about the logic of sport and its value foundation. How this logic and this value are embodied in actual sports, however, varies significantly from contest to contest.

Fair Play in Sport: From Principle to Practice

In reality, neither the concept of athletic performance itself, nor isolating its superior manifestation in a sports contest, is a straightforward matter. Although we have a certain intuitive grasp of the kinds of performances that we value in certain sports—incisive passing in soccer, graceful vaulting in gymnastics, and efficient stroking in swimming—the lines of demarcation are blurred and sometimes contested. Demarcating between welcome and unwelcome aspects of athletic performance and legislating for their acceptability is a task not without difficulty. Although the aim of the game—comparing athletic performance—is straightforward in principle, the subject of comparison is complex. Athletic performance encompasses causally relevant mental and motor actions that bring about advantages in sport; these actions may include shooting, running, throwing, and jumping. Causally relevant actions might be intentional or unintentional, or we may have intended the action but the result came down to luck. Furthermore, the most causally significant action for victory may be a function of acquired abilities (merit) or of natural characteristics (chance). The status (intentionality and responsibility) of the most causally significant actions is often irrelevant vis-à-vis victory. Being able to block a pass with the back of one's head is not considered one of football's most relevant skills, nor is having a large head that may make such events happen more likely to be considered a key physical attribute; however, both may be causally significant in stopping the game-winning touchdown. Sometimes in sport, the result tells us little about the relative athletic merits of the competitors. This, of course, varies between sports; some, like soccer, are particularly susceptible, while others, like athletics, are less susceptible to the vagaries of luck.

Athletic performance is, and always has been, a delicate mix of natural, moral, technical, aesthetic, psychological, and physical capacities, and the extent and degree to which these are to be considered relevant is not fixed by a formula. There is a significant social and historical dimension to our conceptions of athletic performance, and the acts that are praised and admired are filtered through evolving authoritative lenses. It does not always detract from our admiration of athletes that the performance we admire is tainted by good fortune or predicated upon significant natural endowments rather than acquired traits. In fact, our vocabulary (superior athletes are often described as "naturally gifted") betrays a celebration of naturally gifted competitors. Athletic performance cannot be reduced to a purely meritocratic ideal because some element of it will always lie outside the athlete's control. It is always possible to identify some component of athletic performance for which the athlete cannot claim responsibility. For example, McNamee (1995) argues that "we are due no merit for coming up trumps in the genetic lottery" (p. 77). That the "genetic" lottery plays such a significant role in sporting skills and abilities is beyond doubt, and authors such as Carr (1999) question whether athletes deserve any credit at all for their performances, given the contingency of their talents. Tannsjo (2000) similarly doubts the value of sporting excellence and is particularly dubious of our admiration of these achievements.

In practice, sports fall short of the "scientific" ideal of the ultimate fair test of ability but are not necessarily poorer for this; as Loland (2002) argues, "its (sport's) particular value is to be found in a delicate mix between meritocratic justice, chance and luck" (p. 91). Sports, unlike the analysis of Pistorius' movement, are not scientific experiments that take place in hermetically sealed controllable environments. Poor refereeing decisions, cheating, gamesmanship, weather changes, equipment failure, and so forth may all lead to un-merited victories. Although such things are inevitable, their effects should be minimized, and the administrators and governing bodies should work to reduce their effects. Luck often levels itself out; it might be considered a "variable" error. Its effect is unpredictable—the bounce of the oval ball, the defender slipping on the turf, the gust of wind that changes the direction of the golf ball in flight. Chance, according to Loland (2002), is different from luck and may contribute to a "systematic" error in the comparison between athletes. Chance refers to the effect of factors outside the control of the athlete, such as those discussed above. An athlete's height, stature, muscle type, and physiological predisposition are products of chance, or the "natural lottery" over which we have very little influence. Although luck cannot be eliminated completely, the effect of chance must be reduced where reasonably possible. Sports are not games of chance, after all, but games of physical skill.

Controlling for Natural Differences: The Case of the Paralympics

The foregoing discussion about the complexity of sport provides the background for exploring the aims of the classification process in sports for the disabled. The organization of the Paralympic Games with its classificatory categories represents one of the few attempts—and certainly the most sustained and comprehensive—to control for the excessive influence of chance on the result of sports contests. They manifest Loland (2002) following fairness norm in their organizational strategy where "it is unreasonable to treat persons unequally in essential matters based on inequalities that they cannot influence in any significant way" (p. 54). The premise is that the physical or anatomical condition of Paralympians, whether it is a product of natural endowments, injury, or illness, should not be the overwhelming factor in determining victory. Loland (2002) argues that

> Competitors ought to be differentiated in classes only in cases where inequalities in person-dependent matters that they cannot influence in any significant way and for which they cannot be held responsible have systematic and significant influence on athletic performance. (p. 60)

It is clear that, from their inception, the Paralympic Games have attempted to provide relatively equal conditions to hold athletic contests for individuals who could not find these equal conditions in mainstream sports. The ISODs organize competition so that athletes with similar impairments compete against one another; for example, a blind athlete does not compete against an athlete with cerebral palsy. The focus in this case is on the type of impairment rather than its relative effect on performance. The functional classification system as it's known is based on the ability to undertake certain physical tasks. The tasks are general physical tasks, and the competence relative to the task is taken as the objective or operational measure of function or ability. A team of classifiers consisting of a medical doctor, a physiotherapist, and a sports technical officer assess aspiring competitors' functional capabilities and allocate the athlete to a competitive class with others who have a similar level of functional capacity. The measure is not wholly sport-specific, nor does it evaluate athletic performance in gestalt; rather, it attempts to isolate a baseline physical capacity. Once an athlete has been classified, he or she is observed during competition to ensure that the original classification was reliable.

There is a minimal standard of impairment that must be met to qualify; in other words, qualification depends upon a level of impairment that significantly undermines the potentiality of performance in sport. If the potential athlete meets these minimum standards, then he or she will be allocated to a category to compete against others with similar levels of impairment. The inference is that if athletes are sufficiently similar functionally, the winner of any given contest within a classification category will be the athlete who is superior in matters that he or she can control, such as fitness, technique, and skill.

The functional classification system is by no means foolproof (Howe & Jones, 2006). It operates on the premise that one can "control for" the effects of training. It supposes that functional ability is the foundation upon which athletic ability is constructed—that training and conditioning do not have a significant effect on baseline function. So even if the aim is to pit functionally similar athletes against each other in a contest so as to identify which one has acquired the most skill, in practice that goal is difficult. When assessing an athlete, the effects of "training" cannot be controlled in such a way that an accurate, valid, and reliable baseline measure of function is achieved. As I argued above, the aspects of athletic performance for which one cannot claim responsibility are not readily separated from those aspects for which one can claim responsibility. These difficulties notwithstanding, the Paralympic Games and their precursors proceeded initially with the aim of providing a range of viable competitive categories in which athletes could find challenging and meaningful competition, achieve excellence, and inspire others to take up sport.

Participation versus Fair Competition

It is important to remember that sport for the disabled was initially conceived to offer a particular group of people the opportunity to engage in sport and physical activity for a host of different reasons, which included rehabilitation and integration. The multiple benefits that sports are thought to provide were seen as having particular value for individuals who were recuperating from injuries that had resulted in serious and/or long-term physical impairment. Opportunities for developing physical mobility, social interaction, and self-confidence were provided by a range of adapted physical activities and sports. Much like the development of traditional sports, as more people engaged in the activities, the inevitable regulation and institutionalization of the activities followed. Although physical activity and sports can fulfill a range of important outcomes, the realization of the internal authentic values of sport is predicated upon genuine and meaningful tests (Kretchmar, 1995). In order for the tests offered by sports to be meaningful, they must be fair. Victory in a test must not *simply* be the result of chance or the "natural lottery." On one hand, classification in sports for the disabled attempts to provide sufficiently narrow categories so that the level of disability is not the determining factor in the outcome; at the same time, this classification system tries to maintain enough broadness to its categories, to ensure a sustainable contesting population. The principles of merit and fairness point to increasingly complex classificatory categories for sports for the disabled. In principle, no two people will be identical according to the functional assessments, but absolute fairness must be sacrificed for sustainable classes or categories. Idiosyncratic contests between only a few competitors will not fulfill any of the aims of the sport for the disabled. Nevertheless, a failure to properly delimit competitors based on *significant* differences in functional ability will render certain contests unfair, or in Kretchmar's (1995) words, a "no contest." Getting the categories right is crucial. Elite-level competitors need proper competition to enhance the profile and appeal of the Paralympics but will feel cheated if the categories are too broad. Similarly, people with disabilities will avoid participating in a sport that provides impossible challenges due to the failure to properly categorize athletes. Without any classes, we are left with contests of functional ability rather than sports contests; with too many, we have fair but unsustainable contests.

This tension has been brought to the fore in light of recent moves to streamline the Paralympic Games, primarily for commercial reasons. Because of the range of categories of competition, there can be a significant amount of contests. For example, at the Paralympic Games in Sydney, there were fifteen 100-meter races for men and eleven for women. As a result of the joint TV deal negotiated with the Olympics, there is pressure on the Paralympics to reduce the number of contests featured in its program. One strategy is to combine categories, but this is often seen as a threat both to the principle of fairness and to the aim of providing maximal opportunities for meaningful contests (Howe & Jones, 2006).

The Paralympic Games and the Pursuit of Excellence

The Paralympic Games, like the Olympic Games, are now characterized by the serious pursuit of sporting excellence and victory. The games and the movement, as mentioned in the IPC's mission, seek to encourage sporting excellence. As such, performance enhancement, fair or foul, is a feature of modern Paralympics, much as it is for the Olympics. Paralympians such as Tanni Grey Thompson and Oscar Pistorius have become sporting idols in their own right, pursuing professional sporting careers. Like other elite athletes, they seek the standard physiological, psychological, nutritional, technical, coaching, and tactical advantages that will give them a competitive edge. For many Paralympians, there are other ways of improving performance via the significant technological advantages available from the equipment used. The status of this technological equipment is unclear *vis a vis* athletic performance. Wheelchair users and lower-limb amputees rely on additional equipment for mobility. The technology is constitutive of their daily lives and offers independence and autonomy that would be severely compromised without it. Once individuals decide to participate in athletic contests, however, they explore means of adapting and designing prosthetics and racing wheelchairs that will maximize sporting performance and facilitate safer competition. The development of stable and streamlined racing chairs and flexible and shock-absorbent prosthetics have been closely followed by the deliberate and concerted efforts to maximize the performance potential of the equipment. In the same way that aerodynamic and mechanically efficient bicycles, lightweight and flexible golf clubs, and flexible and durable skis have been developed over the years, aerodynamic and ergogenically efficient racing chairs and flexible and powerful prosthetic running "blades" have been pursued by Paralympic athletes. The use of technology in this way has not been curtailed by the IPC, perhaps because in principle, the technology is available to all (although in practice, there may be financial impediments to equal access).

Pistorius' legitimate pursuit of excellence in the Paralympic sports has led to levels of performance hitherto unexpected; he has, in line with the aims of the Paralympics, "transcended the limits of possibility." He is a paradigmatic and exemplary Paralympian, yet according to IAAF rules, if he were to compete in the Olympics he would be cheating. There is an interesting paradoxical flavor to this decision by the IAAF. It arguably contradicts the dominant logic of elite sport and even the Olympic motto of "faster higher stronger." Hoberman (1995) argues that this dominant logic of elite sport reflects and embodies a broader technological approach to humans. He argues that elite sport is the paradigmatic model of the application of technology to the human mind and body to transcend its natural limits:

It is my view that the comprehensive technologizing of high-performance sport contains, and in some way conceals, an agenda for human development for which high-performance athletes serve as ideal models. (p. 203)

Elite athletes employ the whole gamut of sport-science technologies to transform their bodies into efficient and reliable machines. Those responsible for analyzing Pistorius' technique are leading exponents of the science of improvement and seek themselves to furnish athletes with the advantages that Pistorius purportedly gains through the use of his prosthetics. From Hoberman's perspective, Pistorius might represent the frontier of the technological athlete and in some ways may already transcend the norms of acceptable humanness. Technology, including genetic enhancement, has opened up a debate about the limits of humans and has highlighted concerns about the possibility of "trans-human athletes" in the near future; the logical conclusion of the pursuit of unlimited progress in limited systems is the fully designed and constructed athlete.

These broader, important issues notwithstanding, the IAAF's decision about Pistorius is purportedly just about fairness. It is not as though Pistorius had entered the contest and somehow took a shortcut, or circumvented some of the constitutive rules in another way; even if he abided by the rules of the 400-meter race, according to the IAAF, he could not be said to be wholly responsible for his victory. Based on scientific evidence, it is alleged that a significant amount of credit for his performance is attributable to the technical advantage gained from his prosthetic limbs. He is not wholly responsible for his performance—or at least relative to other competitors, he is not responsible enough. He is privy to an advantage that the other competitors are not, and the advantage takes Pistorius beyond the boundaries of legitimately merited athletic performance.

There is no doubt that Pistorius would be incapable of running without prosthetics. He would presumably be able to run with prosthetics that generate less performance enhancement. In other words, if the Paralympics could decide to standardize the type of prosthetic limb an athlete would be entitled to use and the equipment were standard issue, we could have confidence in the winner's meritocratic status. The issue would then be about line drawing: What "performance" parameters should be used for the standard prosthetic? The IPC might wish to limit the type of sanctioned prosthetics to ones that would cause the user to expend an equivalent amount of energy to a non-amputee when running. If such a move were possible in practice, other numerous problems notwithstanding, Pistorius and other athletes who achieved performances that were comparable to those of non-disabled athletes would not run afoul of the IAAF's rules. In other words, if prosthetics could be designed so their use would not manifest the purported advantages that Pistorius gains with his, then the only condition for competing in the Olympics would be whether the qualifying time is reached. The contest would be open to all.

Using standard compensatory technology in this way might be good for individual athletes (a common practice in lots of sports that require specialist's equipment); however, this solution might create significant problems for the Paralympic games themselves. If it is accepted that athletes using the proscribed prosthetics are essentially being compensated for their disability and nothing more, then there may not be any need for a category in the Paralympics for these athletes. They should compete in the 400-meter race against other athletes, disabled or not. In reality, however, what happens is that individuals with disabilities like Pistorius are given the opportunity to compete and develop within the Paralympic movement. It is unlikely that without the Paralympics and the opportunities it offers in line with its mission and aims, Pistorius would be in a position to try to break into mainstream athletics. Like other athletes, he was assessed and classified, and then competed in the appropriate category. But unlike the others, Pistorius showed incredible talent and ability and quickly came to dominate his event. The Paralympics no longer provide him with a meaningful challenge, and like all good athletes, he wants to test his abilities further. Non-disabled sports he believes, will provide his next challenge, but his ambition has presented sport *itself* with a challenge. The Paralympics might become a kind of second division from which certain top athletes graduate to the main stage. They would *transcend* their disability; however, other athletes whose events are not suited for such progress might become associated with a second-tier event. The IPC has strived to obtain legitimate parallel status for the Paralympic Games, and the progression of its athletes into the mainstream Olympics has a number of implications for its mission and aims. These and other issues provide important material for debate for the governance of the IPC (see Jones & Howe, 2005).

In the meantime, Pistorius is appealing the IAAF's decision. There is no precedent for the testing they are asking for; athletes who have dominated their sports have never been subjected to it. Michael Johnson, for example, was a peerless 400-meter runner and was never tested to see whether his body advantaged him significantly. It might be suggested that this argument misses the point, because Pistorius has been denied his place for using technological aids, not for being uniquely talented. The decision, however, is based on the *amount* of advantage those aids gave him. No tests were needed to draw the conclusion that he was using technological aids. It is clear that technology aids his performance—this is not in doubt. If we are concerned with the principle of technology use, the size of the advantage gained is largely irrelevant. The IAAF judgment, therefore, is not straightforward. Whether Pistorius has an unfair advantage is not a matter of science. It is a value judgment based on the nature of contests, their rules, their aims, and the nature of athletic performance merit and fairness. As I have shown in the foregoing discussion, these are not straightforward matters. The important question, perhaps, is whether Pistorius is actually taking the same test. There would presumably be no discussion if a wheelchair athlete wanted to compete in the 400-meter race. It is clear that propelling a wheelchair 400 meters and covering the same distance on foot are completely different challenges. Although the distance covered is the same and the rules might be similar, the test itself is simply different for the wheelchair athlete and the runner. The evidence from the biomechanical and physiological evaluation of Pistorius seems to support a conceptual point about the nature of the test. Running 400 meters on prosthetic limbs seems to be such a significantly different test that to compare Pistorius with non-disabled athletes is not really a comparison at all. It is not that he gains an unfair advantage; rather, he is doing something different.

Conclusion

In this chapter, I have tried to cover a number of important issues related to the Paralympic Games. My aim is to highlight a number of key ethical issues that arise in the context of the Paralympics in general and the example of Oscar Pistorius in particular. I have argued that the normative principle governing sport contest is fairness. In practice, fair competition is compromised by a whole host of factors, such as chance and luck. The Paralympic Games are structured in a way that minimizes the impact of natural endowments on athletic performance while creating an arena for individuals with disabilities to pursue sporting tests and excellence. Particularly in the case of Oscar Pistorius, however, it is slightly unclear whether the technology he requires to run constitutes an unfair advantage, or is constitutive of a completely different test from the test taken by able-bodied athletes.

References

Breivik, G. (2000). "Against Chance: A Causal Theory of Winning in Sport." In: *Values in Sport.* T. Tannsjo and C. Tamburrini (eds). London: Routledge.

Carr, D. (1999). "Where's the Merit If the Best Man Wins?" *Journal of the Philosophy of Sport*, 26, 1–9.

D'Agostino, F. (1991). "The Ethos of Games." *Journal of the Philosophy of Sport*, 28, 7–18.

Fraleigh, W.P. (1984). *Right Actions in Sport: Ethics for Contestants.* Leeds, UK: Human Kinetics.

Hoberman, J. (1995). "Sport and the Technological Image of Man" In: *Philosophic Inquiry in Sport.* W.J. Morgan & K.V. Meier (eds). Champaign, IL: Human Kinetics.

Howe, P.D. & Jones, C. (2006). "Classification of Disabled Athletes: (Dis)Empowering the Paralympic Practice Community." *Sociology of Sport Journal*, 23, 29–46.

International Paralympic Committee (n.d.). http://www.paralympic.org/IPC/Vision_Mission_Values.html. Accessed October 2009.

International Paralympic Committee. (2008). What Is IPC? Cited 29/02/08. Available from http://www.paralympic.org/.

Jones, C. & Howe, P.D. (2005). "The Conceptual Boundaries of Sport for the Disabled: Classification and Athletic Performance." *Journal of the Philosophy of Sport*, 32 (2), pp. 127–140.

Kretchmar, R.S. (1995). "From Test to Contest: An Analysis of Two Kinds of Counterpoint in Sport." In: *Philosophic Inquiry in Sport*. W.J. Morgan & K.V. Meier (eds). Champaign, IL: Human Kinetics.

Loland, S. (2001). "Record Sports: An Ecological Critique and Reconstruction." *Journal of the Philosophy of Sport*, 28, (2), 127–139.

Loland, S. (2002). *Fair Play: A Moral Norm System*. London: Routledge.

Loland, S. & McNamee, M.J. (2000). "Fair Play and the Ethos of Sports: An Eclectic Philosophical Framework." *Journal of Philosophy of Sport*, 27, 63–80.

McNamee, M.J. (1995). "Sporting Practices, Institutions, and Virtues: A Critique and Restatement." *Journal of the Philosophy of Sport*, 22, 61–82

Suits, B. (1995). "The Elements of Sport." In: *Philosophic Inquiry in Sport*. W.J. Morgan & K.V. Meier (eds). Champaign, IL: Human Kinetics.

Suits, B. (2005). *The Grasshopper: Games, Life and Utopia*. Peterborough, Ontario: Broadview Press.

Tannsjo, T. (2000). "Is it Fascistoid to Admire Sport Heroes." In: *Values in Sport*. T. Tannsjo & C. Tamburrini (eds). London: Routledge.

18

Strong Women, Fragile Closets

The Queering of Women's Sport

Barbara Ravel and Geneviève Rail

WE WILL NOT PRETEND THE RESEMBLANCE of our chapter's title with *Strong Women, Deep Closets: Lesbians and Homophobia in Sport* (1998) is coincidental. Pat Griffin's groundbreaking book is a complete study of the lesbian sporting experience that notably examines homophobia and heterosexism in women's sport. It explores several issues related to the participation of lesbians in sport, including the often hostile climate for lesbians in sport and what Griffin called the "culture of the closet," as she described various identity-management strategies used by lesbian coaches and athletes.

Researchers from different countries have also reported the existence of heterosexism and homophobia in women's sports (e.g. Cahn, 1993, 1994; Hekma, 1998; Mennesson & Clement, 2003). For instance, Cahn (1993, 1994) has explained the emergence of homophobia in U.S. women's sports and physical education in the middle of the twentieth century. In a study on women's soccer in France, Mennesson and Clement (2003) have illustrated the hostile climate within which lesbian soccer players were playing their sport. As the authors have found, homosexuality was seen as "a key problem" (p. 317), and discrimination against lesbian players was sometimes instituted as an unwritten but official policy. For instance, they have reported the case of a homophobic team and its strategies:

> For several years in town X, the struggle against homosexuality occupied a central place in the policies of the club. The managers agreed to no longer recruit anyone but players who were "above reproach" in this area, and to harass attested (avowed) homosexuals, in the team. (ibid.)

Although still frequent, as illustrated in the above example, homophobia tends to be less present in women's sport today than in the past, and a small number of studies offer a more "positive" portrait of the situation for lesbians in sport in certain parts of the world (Broad, 2001; Caudwell, 2003; Shire, Brackenridge & Fuller, 2000). It is worth noting that studies on lesbians in sport now tend to focus less on homophobia and heterosexism, and more on the ways various sexualities are performed in sport. This is without a doubt related to the general evolution of society towards a greater acceptance of non-conventional sexualities, as well as the media's attention to famous out lesbians in the arts and, less frequently, in sport. When the great tennis champion Martina Navratilova came out as a lesbian in 1981, she was one of the first out lesbian athletes, along with Billie Jean King. Martina's coming out was made public only shortly after she became an American because she feared it might harm her application for U.S. citizenship. In the process, she lost many of her sponsors, notably her clothing company, Puma, and it is estimated that she may have lost millions in various endorsements because of her sexuality. More than twenty-five years after her coming out, the situation for non-heterosexual women in sport is less difficult than it once was, particularly in a number of Western urban centers. As for Martina, she eventually received major endorsements, notably in 2005 with the lesbian travel company Olivia. This marked the first time she ever secured a sponsorship for "being gay rather than in spite of it" (Robson, 2005, para. 1). More recently, Amélie Mauresmo, formerly the world's top-ranked women's tennis player, and Sheryl Swoopes, a star in the Women's National Basketball Association (WNBA), have publicly come out, in 1999 and 2005 respectively; both women have continued to have a very large fan base as well as lucrative sponsorship deals!

Away from the highly publicized lives of professional athletes, we conducted a study in Montreal (Quebec, Canada) focusing on women with a non-conventional sexuality who participated in different team sports, from recreational to competitive levels. In this study, we investigated several important issues with regard to sexuality, notably the wide range of non-conventional sexualities performed in sport, the role of sport in the expression of non-conventional sexualities, and the coming-out process in sport. To do so, we relied on data collected through conversations with fourteen young women between 21 and 31 years of age.

Varying Sexualities in Women's Sport

In the 1990s, Griffin (1998) and others (e.g., Cahn, 1993; Fusco, 1998) tended to focus strictly on the experiences of lesbians in sport, thus reinforcing the heterosexual/homosexual binary as well as essentialized notions of sexuality. For instance, in their ten-year study of a field hockey team in Great Britain, Shire, Brackenridge and Fuller (2000) had initially categorized the players as either "lesbian" or "heterosexual." As they explained: "Those who had had sexual relationships with a woman were defined as 'lesbian' and those who had had a relationship with a man were defined as 'heterosexual' for the purposes of the study" (p. 39). As a result, fourteen players were classified as "lesbian," yet only five of them actually defined themselves as "lesbian" or "gay." Concerning the nine other players, several stated that they were attracted to both men and women, even though they were currently in a relationship with a woman. As for the remaining women, they were mostly inclined to refuse labels altogether. In light of these results, the authors' initial classification seemed rather inadequate, and they have concluded that many participants' experiences could be better understood through queer theory, rather than with more conventional conceptualizations of sexuality.

In recent years, researchers on women's sport and issues of sexuality have increasingly acknowledged the fluidity of sexuality and thus the relevance of queer theory (e.g., Broad, 2001; Caudwell, 2003; Sykes, 2006). For instance, the Broad study has brought to light the queer resistance of women's rugby in the U.S., notably "through assertions about the multiplicity and fluidity of sexuality" (2001, p. 195). In the same line, the participants of our study, who were initially recruited with the condition that they be "non-heterosexual," represented a wide range of sexualities. Most of them chose to define themselves as "*gaie*," the feminine and French version of "gay." We decided to keep the term in its original version because the participants were Francophone and the term carried particular connotations. Indeed, it was clearly used by the participants to dissociate from the "old" and negative lesbian image and at the same time to associate with the "light" and "fun" side of being gay (see more on this in Ravel & Rail, 2006). For example, Stéphanie (25 years old, ice hockey) stated that *gaie* "can refer to being happy in life. I like that." Another player reported the following:

> I regularly use this word ["*gaie*"] because it's shorter. [Laughs] No, it's just that I find [that] it sounds less like a disease. It describes what we are but it's less boring [than "lesbian"] if you will. (Marie, 23, soccer)

Despite its acknowledged negative connotation, several participants still preferred the term "lesbian" because of its gender specificity, as one participant explained:

> The word "lesbian" is so ugly! I've talked to many girls and we all find that it's really ugly. But the problem is we don't have an alternative. "*Gaie*," I don't use it often because I find we get lumped in with the guys when we use that term. (Shane, 23, softball)

Apart from *gaie* and lesbian, one participant defined herself as "bisexual" and a few others either claimed an ambiguous sexuality or refused labels altogether. For instance, Gabrielle, a 24-year-old soccer player, stated that "for me, the idea of attaching labels [is irrelevant]." Florence gives another perspective on how sexuality can be conceptualized outside of fixed categories:

> Well, I see myself as a free human being, meaning that, since I was born, I let my heart fall in love with whomever it wanted to, if I can put it that way. At first, it was my best girlfriend from high school; after that, it was a French boyfriend, and then it went back to girls and I think it'll be that way for good. But, as I can't swear to this—because of my past experience [laughs]—I can say that I don't limit myself, nor do I feel that I should fit a particular label for the rest of my life. It's an area in which I want to feel free, so all I can say is that for the moment I'm more *gaie* than straight. (Florence, 31, ice hockey)

In the end, our inclusion criteria (i.e., being a woman with a sexuality other than conventional heterosexuality) proved useful because we were able to witness in the participants' experiences the destabilization of the heterosexual/homosexual binary and, in this respect, our findings were visibly in line with queer theory. As a result, it appears important to not only focus on lesbians' experiences in sport, but rather to acknowledge the possibility of sexualities outside of fixed categories and to examine women with a non-conventional sexuality in sport.

Sport and the Expression of Non-Conventional Sexualities

While many authors have documented the impact of homophobia and discrimination on women's sport, at the same time, sport has long been a refuge for women who do not identify with heterosexuality. Having examined the experiences of lesbians in sport in the U.S. in the middle of the twentieth century, Cahn (1994) described the basic principle at play in that environment:

> Given the danger of open declarations, gay women in sport communicated their presence primarily through action, style, and unspoken understandings. They followed a code of "play it, don't say it," in this way ensuring their own survival in a hostile culture while protecting one of the few social spaces that offered a degree of comfort and freedom. (p. 187)

Cahn's statement suggests that, even decades ago, sport could be a place where non-conventional sexualities could be expressed, at least to some extent, but it also speaks in favor of a certain form of lesbian visibility rather than openness. In this context, lesbian, gay, bisexual, and trans (LGBT) sport appeared to be the solution to homophobia and heteronormativity, providing LGBT athletes with a safe space. Not surprisingly, the three participants of our study who competed in LGBT leagues (in softball and volleyball) clearly emphasized the importance of playing in an environment in which they could be fully out and witness displays of non-conventional sexualities. What is more surprising is that among the other participants (i.e., those playing in mainstream leagues), all but two were out in these leagues, and the two who were closeted were actually involved on two teams and were out in one but not in the other. In general, the young women in our study highlighted the fact that sexual diversity was often embraced by their team, which was sometimes, but not necessarily, related to the fact that there was a significant number of other non-heterosexual players on their team. In other words, even in so-called heterosexual leagues, being heterosexual was not always the "norm." This surprising reversal of the situation must not, of course, be generalized because our study involved a small number of participants, but it nonetheless constitutes a reality for a number of women in various sports.

When our analysis first led us to argue that sport constituted an "open" space with regard to non-conventional sexualities, we attributed this openness to the "Montreal factor." In general, Canada is perceived as an international leader in terms of LGBT rights, notably being one of the very few countries where "gay" marriage is legalized. In addition, within Canada, the province of Quebec as well as its biggest city, Montreal, are renowned for their openness with regard to both cultural and sexual diversity. However, a closer examination of the participants' narratives tended to challenge our first impression and add to the confusion. Indeed, if living and practicing their sport in Montreal was part of the reason why participants were out in sport, we could logically infer that they would be out in other social environments as well. Yet this was not the case. Indeed, many young women reported being less open about their sexuality with their family or at work. This leads us to the conclusion that in a relatively open-minded environment such as Montreal, women's sport appears to be even more tolerant and acceptant towards sexual diversity, thus constituting a space that is quite safe for non-heterosexual women. The story of Amélie, a 24-year-old broomball and ice hockey player, illustrates quite well how women's sport can be a safe space for athletes with a non-conventional sexuality.

Amélie's Story or Sport as a Safe Space

Amélie played broomball with almost the same group of people since she was 16. At the time, she had not yet realized that she was *gaie*, but she could remember that homosexuality was taboo and that many conversations involved heterosexual relationships. But, as she stated, "I was not the type of person who talked about boys because I wasn't interested." She also started to play ice hockey in a recreational league at her school and had many friends who were players on the school's varsity team. According to her, even if there were several out *gaie* players on the varsity team, the climate was not very open towards sexual diversity. As a result, with her recreational team, it was not open, either, "even if you suspected that one or the other was *gaie*." Amélie came out at the age of 19 but was only able to talk about her *gaie*-ness with her best friends who were not related to her team. However, as she explained, the situation considerably changed soon after:

> At the time, everybody was rather closeted but after that, I went to play in another league and it was much more open. Very, very open because, I don't know if I'm right in saying that a majority of the women in this league were *gaie*, but anyway a large part. As a result, that could only open everybody's mind. And, as a young woman who arrived in this league, I think that it really helped me a lot because it's in that league that I realized that I wasn't alone at all and that being *gaie* was normal for many adults—adults who were very stable and all that. I think that it really helped me, to see many women like that, people who looked comfortable in who they were. I found this very positive. It was reassuring, too, for young ones like me, you know; even if I was sure about my sexual orientation, it still wasn't easy to accept at first. I think it's never easy to accept because it's not the "norm" in society. So, I think it was a very positive experience for me. It was very, very open.

For Amélie, ice hockey constituted the first space within which she was able to feel safe and comfortable, even though, as she said, she did not know many people: "It was as if I felt good in that environment as compared to at home."

Coming Out in Sport

There is an old myth in women's sport that suggests sport might "create" or "produce" lesbians. Let us be clear here—we strongly share Griffin's view that "those who encourage the idea that sport participation promotes or causes lesbianism are more interested in controlling women's athleticism by threatening them with the stigma of the lesbian bogeywoman than they are interested in the complexities of sexual attraction and identity" (1998, p. 57). However, it appears, as Griffin put it, that "some women do identify themselves as lesbians for the first time during their participation in sport" (p. 57). This was the case for a few participants in our study, who revealed that sport played an important role in their coming out. Obviously, the presence of other women with a nonconventional sexuality helped them feel comfortable being out to their teammates, but what was mainly emphasized was the *gaie*-friendliness of their sport environment in general, without consideration of the proportion of nonheterosexual players. Marie's case illustrates this quite well because she was the only *gaie* player on her team, yet the information about her sexuality smoothly circulated among her teammates, mostly through ordinary conversations or even jokes, as the following excerpt shows:

> It gradually became known that I was *gaie*. The others were made aware by jokes that are told by some of the players, like when a girl from another team passes by and someone says: "Hey, she might be your type, Marie!" (Marie, 23, soccer)

Along with other participants, Marie's coming out in sport might have been facilitated by the openness of the context, but her teammates were not the first persons to whom she came out. This was not the case for Stéphanie, who realized that she might be *gaie* in sport. Indeed, Stéphanie, a 25 year-old ice hockey player, had long thought that she was heterosexual. Even in her last years of high school, she never questioned her sexuality. She knew that on other teams there were several *gaie* players, but on her team there were none and nobody talked about being *gaie*. It is when she entered university that she joined a team where half of the players, she thought, were *gaie* and half were heterosexual. "It was really, really open," she said. "And we had a deal: One week, we'd go out to a *gaie* bar, and the next week, to a straight bar to please the whole team." As a result, the first time Stéphanie went out in a *gaie* bar was with her hockey team. She explained that she felt quite comfortable, had a lot of fun, and jokingly stated that she even felt proud when an older woman was hitting on her. However, as she said, "I was going out in *gaie* bars but I wasn't considering myself as *gaie*." Eventually she discovered that she, too, might be *gaie* and clearly acknowledged the influence of her *gaie* teammates and of having been in *gaie* bars in the process:

> And at some point, it was gradual but I realized that I was less enthusiastic; I was less energetic. I don't know, there was something that bothered me a little. I say it jokingly but I was like in a depression because really I had less . . . I don't know . . . I was less cheerful. And so I stopped and asked myself what was going on, what was bothering me so much. Finally, I realized that that was it. That, in the end, it was possible that I was attracted to girls and that maybe I knew from the beginning but, you know, that I was repressing my feelings, that I was hiding them and that's what was making me feel unhappy with myself. As soon as I accepted it and it really became a part of my life, you know, I started to smile again and everything was good.

Conclusion

For the tenth anniversary of the publication of *Strong Women, Deep Closets*, we felt that we should acknowledge the influence of Pat Griffin's groundbreaking work (1998) as well as reveal encouraging news for women in sport. First, with regard to homophobia and closets in women's sport, here is how Griffin put it when she explained her book title:

> The title, *Strong Women, Deep Closets*, attempts to capture the apparent contradiction of physically strong and competent women who feel compelled to hide their deepest personal commitments, families, and love relationships in order to be members of the women's sports world. The closets in sport are deep because so many women are hiding there. (pp. ix–x)

Along with Griffin, many researchers focusing on lesbians' sporting participation strongly connected their experiences to homophobia and heterosexism. Second, the encouraging news is that we had no such connection. In our own Montreal study, we revealed how women's sport could be a space of resistance to heteronormativity, thanks to the presence of many out athletes and the existence of a climate of acceptance towards *gaie* sexuality. We also showed how the participants' conceptions of sexuality often challenged the heterosexual/homosexual binary and suggested the possibility of fluid sexualities and sexualities outside of fixed categories. We furthermore highlighted that sport might be a catalyst for questioning with regard to one's own sexuality. Altogether, the findings of our study allowed us to get a better understanding of how sexuality is performed in sport. The *gaie*-friendliness of Montreal's sport milieu was clearly one of the major discoveries. We can only be thrilled to know that the closets in sport are getting more and more fragile and that being out on the sporting field is now a "happy" option for many women with a non-conventional sexuality.

References

Broad, K. L. (2001). The gendered unapologetic: Queer resistance in women's sport. *Sociology of Sport Journal*, 18, 181–204.

Butler, J. (1993). *Bodies that matter: On the discursive limits of sex*. New York: Routledge.

Cahn, S. K. (1993). From the "muscle moll" to the "butch" ballplayer: Mannishness, lesbianism and homophobia in U.S. women's sport. *Feminist Studies*, 19, 343–368.

Cahn, S. K. (1994). *Coming on strong: Gender and sexuality in twentieth-century women's sport*. Toronto: Maxwell Macmillan Canada.

Caudwell, J. (2003). Sporting gender: Women's footballing bodies as sites/sights for the (re)articulation of sex, gender, and desire. *Sociology of Sport Journal*, 20, 371–386.

Fusco, C. (1998). Lesbians and locker rooms: The subjective experience of lesbians in sport. In G. Rail (Ed.), *Sport and postmodern times* (pp. 87–116). New York: State University of New York Press.

Griffin, P. (1998). *Strong women, deep closets: Lesbians and homophobia in sport*. Champaign, IL: Human Kinetics.

Hekma, G. (1998). "As long as they don't make an issue of it . . .": Gay men and lesbians in organized sports in the Netherlands. *Journal of Homosexuality*, 35(1), 1–23.

Iannota, J. G. & Kane, M. J. (2002). Sexual stories as resistance narratives in women's sports: Reconceptualizing identity performance. *Sociology of Sport Journal*, 19, 347–369.

Lauretis, T. de (1993). Sexual indifference and lesbian representation. In H. Abelove, M. A. Barale & D. H. Halperin (Eds.), *The lesbian and gay studies reader* (pp. 141–158). New York: Routledge.

Mennesson, C. & Clement, J. P. (2003). Homosociability and homosexuality: The case of soccer played by women. *International Review for the Sociology of Sport Journal*, 38(3), 311–330.

Ravel, B. & Rail, G. (2006). The lightness of being "*gaie*." Discursive constructions of gender and sexuality in Quebec women's sport. *International Review for the Sociology of Sport*, 41(3–4), 395–412.

Robson, D. (2005). Raising a racket with Martina Navratilova: The legendary lesbian tennis star talks about her new role as Olivia's spokeswoman and dispatches travel wisdom from years on the sports circuit. *The Advocate*, July 5. Retrieved February 28, 2008, from http://findarticles.com/p/articles/mi_m1589/is_2005_July_5/ai_n15399813.

Shire, J., Brackenridge, C. & Fuller, M. (2000). Changing positions: The sexual politics of a women's field hockey team 1986–1996. *Women in Sport and Physical Activity Journal*, 9(1), 35–64.

Sykes, H. (2006). Queering theories of sexuality in sport studies. In J. Caudwell (Ed.), *Sport, sexualities and queer/theory* (pp. 13–32). London & New York: Routledge.

19

Older Athletes

Resisting and Reinforcing Discourses of Sport and Aging

Rylee A. Dionigi

A MAJOR TREND IN CONTEMPORARY Western culture is the aging of the population. Within this demographic shift, more and more people aged in their 50s, 60s, 70s, 80s, and 90s are participating in sport. This trend is occurring within a context of multiple, and at times conflicting, socio-cultural and personal understandings of sport and aging.

To introduce the different ways older individuals understand their sport participation, I present three newspaper articles published during the 8th Australian Masters Games (AMG). From these stories, questions emerge about older athletes' negotiations of diverse cultural understandings of sport and aging. For example, 87-year-old Margaret won "a colossal 24 events" including track and field, long-distance road running, swimming, and indoor rowing (Gadd, 2001, p. 82). She said that the gold medals did not compare "to the fun she is having and the friends she has made at the Games" (ibid.). Why does Margaret choose to compete if she is primarily motivated to have fun and make friends? How do participants (and event organizers) manage the two (apparently contradictory) sides (fun/friendship and competition) to Masters sport? Roy, a 74-year-old field hockey player, "does not know the meaning of 'lay down,'" and said that "he will continue to play until his legs collapse from under him" (Valentine, 2001, p. 31). Why does Roy feel the need to push his body so hard and remain extremely active? Is competing in sport simply an act of resistance to the negative stereotypes of old age as a period dominated by rest, inability, and ill health?

Val, a 76-year-old tennis player who competes in Veteran's competitions, said that she particularly values winning. Her story focused on her "vitality" and recent sporting victories, including her gold medal performance at the

AMG (*Newcastle Herald*, 2001, p. 31). To what extent do older people invest in the understandings and practices of sport performance, competition, youthfulness, and winning? Competition in Masters/senior sport is different from open competitions because it is organized in five- to ten-year age bands. Individual events are typically conducted in five-year increments and team sports in ten-year increments. In Australia, participants in Masters and Veteran's competitions can be as young as 30 or 35 years old, depending on the sport; but the focus in this chapter is on competitors over the age of 55. The Senior Olympic movement in the United States is for competitors who are 55 or older.

The experiences, practices, and interpretations of older people competing in sport can no longer be trivialized, patronized, or ignored. This complex, intriguing, and contradictory cultural phenomenon warrants rigorous sociological enquiry. In this chapter, I discuss how white, middle-class, older athletes simultaneously resist and reproduce conflicting discourses of sport and aging when they talk about and compete in physically demanding sports. Sport can be used (unintentionally or deliberately) by its participants as a vehicle for both resistance and conformity to dominant cultural ideals. In other words, practices and understandings of sport are linked to power relations. From a post-structural perspective, power is available to everyone in their everyday lives, and it is constituted and conveyed through discourse (Foucault, 1978). Discourses are more than words or linguistic phenomena; they are the building blocks that constrain, structure, and produce specific ways of understanding. That is, discourses work to establish and regulate particular practices, "sets of rules," or "perceptions of reality" in different cultures, including understandings of the self and others (Foucault, 1978; Markula & Pringle, 2006). Hence, discourse can be formed, altered, revised, and reproduced at every level of society and in all social settings, including sport (Hayles, 2005). From this perspective, an individual is not passive; rather, individuals actively produce a sense of self via the ongoing construction and negotiation of available discourses (Foucault, 1982). Individuals also have the potential to affect dominant discourses or power relations in society (Foucault, 1978). Therefore, a post-structural approach is used in the chapter because it enables an exploration of the ways in which discourses work in subtle ways (i.e., how they are rebutted, ignored, mobilized, accepted, disrupted, critiqued, and negotiated by individuals). Such an examination also illuminates the different potential consequences or effects of these discourses on individuals and society.

The following section discusses the multiple, conflicting, and intertwining discourses of "mainstream sport performance," "participation or 'sport for older people,'" "aging as decline," and "positive aging" that currently operate in Western societies. The fundamental argument of this discussion is that these discourses carry the same message; that is, in Western capitalist society, competitiveness, activity, and youthfulness are valued, and ill health in old age is undesirable. The next section presents qualitative data on older athletes and interprets their talk and actions within the framework of the outlined discourses. The fact that the majority of athletes in this research are white, English-speaking, middle-class, and considered themselves to be in a state of good health speaks to the racial, class, physical ability, and health bias underpinning this whole phenomenon. My analysis shows that while the workings of these individuals provide alternatives to the dominant understandings of what it means to be an older athlete and an older person in general, they simultaneously reinforce the value Western society places on being competitive, active, healthy, and youthful. Therefore, I conclude by suggesting possible individual and broader social consequences of such an engagement with sport and aging discourses.

Multiple Discourses of Sport and Aging—Same Underlying Message

Coakley (2007) presents two opposing sport models: the dominant power and performance model, and an alternative pleasure and participation model. Similarly, Tinning (1997) differentiates between "performance discourses" and "participation discourses" of physical activity. Two discourses of aging currently operating are the traditional medicalized view of aging as biological decline, and the more contemporary positive aging discourse that aims to promote the health and well-being of older people. These key discourses of sport and aging rely on, inform, intersect with, and at times conflict with each other. They are constructed, permeated, and disseminated through levels of government, the media, the private sector, the education system, medical knowledge and practices, community values, interpersonal relationships, bodily experiences, and personal stories. They function as discursive resources that primarily frame and structure older individuals' talk and practices in the context of sport. In other words, the stories and actions of older athletes depend largely on the sociocultural discourses that are available and how these discourses are drawn upon, used, and/or transformed. While there are many other discourses and personal, local, or global resources available to older athletes, this discussion will focus on the intersection between sport and aging discourses.

The dominant sport form in Western cultures is highly competitive and based on a power and performance model. Participation in mainstream sport is characterized by the use of aggression, strength, speed, and, at times, a "win-at-all-costs" mentality, to push the body to its limit, set records, and beat others (Coakley, 2007; McKay, 1991; McKay, Hughson, Lawrence & Rowe, 2000). This model is based on the belief that competitive success proves superiority and is gained through commitment and training, which commonly involves the use of technology to manage the body (Coakley, 2007). In the same vein, Tinning (1997) argues that through performance discourses, participation in sport and physical activity have become understood as a means for enhancing one's fitness, strength, and skill, and the body is interpreted as a machine. That is, the body is seen as a functioning set of interacting systems that can be trained, compartmentalized, manipulated, and continuously repaired, monitored, and managed (McKay, 1991, p. 141).

Clearly, these discourses and ideals about performance enhancement and winning indicate that competitive sport is most suited to the young, fit, and able. These discourses (and the mainstream sports they frame) exclude the less fit or able. They also support the (problematic) belief that competition is a natural process that "fairly" rewards and recognizes those who are successful (Coakley, 2007, p. 104). Moreover, power and performance sports hold their dominance over alternative sport models because they receive the most media, corporate, economic, political, and spectator support, and they match the interests of people in privileged positions of wealth and influence (Coakley, 2007). Hence, "the ability to compete, to embody competitiveness, is the cornerstone of capitalist ideology" (Hayles, 2005, p. 49).

Generally speaking, sport is a context in which the youthful, robust, performing (male) body is accentuated and celebrated. There is an assumption that older people are not suited to competitive sporting situations because traditional discourses about older people position them as weak, less able, and in a state of biological decline. The dominant, medicalized model of aging as decline links growing older with inevitable deterioration, ill health, loneliness, rest, dependency, and decrepitude (Blaikie, 1999; Featherstone & Hepworth, 1995; Tulle, 2007). Although older age does not always equate to illness, it is hard to deny that the likelihood of chronic disease and frailty does increase with advancing age. Therefore, deep old age is commonly accompanied by illness and disability, often compressed into the last couple of years before death (Blaikie, 1999). Nevertheless, traditional gerontological research has established extensive knowledge about illness (e.g., dementia, cancer, incontinence), frailty, disengagement, and loss in later life. This literature has led to the development of generalizations and negative stereotypes about all older people. One consequence of this dominant way of thinking is that for most of the twentieth century, competitive sports were not readily available, encouraged, or deemed appropriate for older people. In particular, strenuous exercise was considered dangerous for older people because it was believed to place excessive demands on the aging bodies (Coakley, 2007, p. 74; Grant, 2001).

Today, thousands of older people are involved in age-grouped competitions, such as the Masters Games, Veteran's Titles, and the Senior Olympics. They compete in physically demanding team sports (e.g., basketball, soccer, ice hockey, field hockey, badminton) and individual events (e.g., track and field, swimming, cycling, tennis, marathon, triathlon, gymnastics). Some older people participate in more passive competitive activities at these events, such as lawn bowls, golf, bridge, and shuffleboard. The focus here, however, is on physically demanding sports because such activities are not typically associated with older people. Despite these physically intense activities being inherently competitive, when older people are involved, the emphasis shifts from performance and winning to "fun and friendly" participation. In other words, pleasure and participation discourses, which emphasize joy, inclusion, fair play, cooperation, pleasurable movement experiences, personal expression, and growth, are typically used to describe, legitimate, and promote older people's involvement in sport (Coakley, 2007; Tinning, 1997). This way of thinking and experiencing sport appears to challenge the dominant power and performance model. However, in recognizing the need for sponsorship and other types of support, promoters and organizers of senior sport tend to highlight the achievements of high performers *and* emphasize the socializing (and travel/holiday) opportunities (Hayles, 2005). Therefore, organizers attempt to alleviate the potential tension between serious competition and enjoyable participation by creating a convergent or compromising discourse of "friendly competition." How do the athletes experience or negotiate these two sides of senior sport? Before addressing this question, it is important to discuss how participation discourses are parallel to, intertwined with, and formed in relation to contemporary positive aging (and health and fitness promotion) discourses.

Positive aging discourses celebrate later life as a period for enjoyment, leisure, activity, challenge, growth, and exploration (Featherstone & Hepworth, 1995). This "counter" discourse has developed in academic research and as a governmental health promotion strategy to keep people active, independent, and healthy for as long as possible. Businesses have also taken up positive aging discourses to target older adults for products and services associated with active living and anti-aging remedies. According to Hayles (2005), positive aging discourses portray the optimism that many of the advantages of youth can be partly preserved into older age (p. 30). The emphasis here is on self-responsibility for achieving and retaining good health. Regular physical activity is now deemed an appropriate means for maintaining health, resisting the aging body, and postponing deep old age (i.e., preventing or delaying disease and disability) (Gilleard & Higgs, 2000). Other "healthy" practices (e.g., continued mental stimulation, socializing with peers) are also promoted through positive aging discourses. What is strongly communicated to the general public, however, is the link between physical activity and absence of disease. This message reflects the narrow and medicalized view of health that dominates the scientific discourse of fitness (Markula & Pringle, 2006). Therefore, it is well-established that physical activity can contribute to one's health, but this accepted view of health as freedom from disease can overshadow notions of holistic health (i.e., physical, mental, social, emotional, and spiritual well-being). Notably, in regard to sport participation among older people, positive aging and health promotion discourses advocate the pleasure and participation model, not the power and performance model. Encouraging older people to participate in sport and physical activity has also become a key strategy for managing and reducing the potential economic and social burden associated with the aging population.

What these positive aging discourses imply is that regular participation in sport and physical activity is necessary for the good health and well-being of older individuals and for the "good" of society. This message emphasizes that keeping active in later life is primarily a matter of civic duty, individual effort, and personal choice (Katz, 2000). Such imperatives highlight the increasing value of activity, health, youthfulness, and bodily performance in contemporary culture (Gilleard & Higgs, 2000). They also privilege and speak to those older people (usually white and middle-class) who have the means, desire, opportunity, access, and ability to enjoy an active lifestyle. Therefore, these discourses do not consider personal and socio-cultural constraints. Advocating individual responsibility for health is potentially problematic for those who fall ill, are disabled, lack financial resources or education, are from different cultural backgrounds, or do not want to be active. Furthermore, the circulation of traditional and contemporary aging discourses means that ill health in old age can be, paradoxically and simultaneously, seen as expected, pathological, a sign of no willpower, and the result of leading the "wrong" lifestyle. In other words, one's state of health in later life is ironically seen as both naturally determined and a matter of personal choice (Jolanki, 2004).

Despite the similarities, ambiguities, and tensions among these sport and aging discourses, this discussion has demonstrated that they all reinforce the same underlying message—that is, Western society places value on being competitive, active, and youthful, and positions ill health in old age as undesirable and something to be avoided. In other words, these multiple and interacting discourses work to uphold dominant (capitalist) ideals, marginalize other ways of knowing (and doing), and help sustain problematic relations of power (Foucault, 1978). These concerns make it all the more important to examine how the talk and action of older athletes intersect with discourses of sport and aging. More specifically, how do older athletes negotiate such an array of complex, contradictory, and potentially problematic discourses? What are the enabling and limiting (personal and socio-cultural) effects of this engagement?

Older Athletes Negotiating Discourses of Sport and Aging

To illuminate the multiple meanings and practices associated with competing in sport in later life and to interpret these findings within the outlined discursive framework, I draw on observational and interview data of 138 athletes (70 women and 68 men, ages 59 to 94) who competed at the 8th Australian Masters Games

(Dionigi, 2008). The participants in this research are typically white, English-speaking, and middle-class—a cohort largely determined by the demographic of athletes competing in Masters, Veteran, and senior sports. While this cohort may not represent all older athletes (e.g., those from non-English-speaking backgrounds), these research participants reflect the somewhat exclusive culture of older athletes, and their stories reveal the myriad ways in which this culture is experienced, understood, and preserved. Using the words of these older athletes, this section is divided into three interrelated themes: "friendly competition," "competing to win," and "use it or lose it."

"Friendly Competition"

The majority of older athletes indicated that they enjoy both the friendliness and competitiveness of sport participation in later life. A typical statement from Masters Games' participants was

> I just enjoy [competing in sport]. I like the companionship and the friendship, the "mateship" that you make when you go travelling around and meeting all these different people . . . It's great! (63-year-old female field hockey player)

In particular, many older athletes talked about the joy of mixing with younger athletes (i.e., those in their 30s and 40s), because they believed that it "gives them a bit of youth" (64-year-old female swimmer) and keeps them feeling "a little more vital" (70-year-old female swimmer). During my fieldwork at the 8th AMG, I witnessed many hugs between participants who were being reunited with their friends. Also, while off the field, I observed several women's hockey and netball teams dressed up in colorful attire and fancy hats, laughing and generally enjoying themselves. At the venues for men's baseball, men's and women's softball, touch football, and field hockey, many participants wore gaudy wigs while on the field, made jovial comments to opposing players, or smiled and laughed at themselves when they made a mistake.

It is shown in the literature on older athletes that while many say they appreciate the fun and friendship associated with senior sport, very few (if any) say that this is the sole reason for their participation. In particular, Hayles (2005) found that many Masters athletes talked about the pleasure they feel when competing against others, which seems to indicate a convergence between the two (opposing) sides to Masters sport. For example, common descriptors and phrases used by athletes to describe their involvement at the 8th AMG were "friendship," "conviviality," "social interaction," "camaraderie," "fun," "a buzz," "exciting," "keenly contested," "no one gives in," "competitive on the field," and "a good time." The talk of a 66-year-old cricketer typified this contrasting mix of sentiments and discourses:

It's great to play with a great bunch of girls . . . I just love the competitive feeling out there and all the comradeship out there amongst the girls of both teams . . . [it's] wonderful . . . There's nothing else . . . Fitness, friendship, comradeship and just the *oh*, excellent feeling, especially when you *win*! But it's not too bad if you lose, though. I'm only out there just to enjoy myself and just add a bit of whatever I can to the side.

Similarly, many track and field Masters athletes in Hayles' research expressed the desire to win *and* the importance of participation, regardless of the competitive outcome (2005, p. 138). In doing so, many older athletes draw on and reinforce pleasure and participation discourses to describe (and practice) playing sport. For example,

. . . We enjoy the game, we enjoy playing sport, [and] the competition part is secondary. It's just more of the pleasure of being *able* to play sport. (60-year-old male squash player)

I think when you get to our age you have a different outlook on competition. It's just the fact of being *able* to participate. My sister is my age and she has osteoporosis, so being *able* to participate and being *able* to compete is what it's all about and if you win that's just a bonus. (67-year-old female tennis player)

As these older athletes negotiate the discourses that frame Masters sport, they indicate that older people *can* lead active, social, youthful, and engaged lives. Their talk and actions simultaneously resist negative stereotypes associated with the aging-as-decline discourse and reinforce notions of positive aging. Although participants said that they "try hard" to perform well, their strong usage of positive aging and participation discourses (as well as the "less serious" sport practices they promote) was at times in tension with the power and performance model. However, when they talked about competing to win or improving their previous standard, they showed an investment in many aspects of the sport performance model.

"Competing to Win"

Many older athletes said that when they compete they "try to win," and/or aim to achieve a "personal best." However, because sport performance discourses and aging-as-decline discourses position older people as not being suited to competition, several participants expressed feelings of guilt, embarrassment, or avoidance about being competitive. For instance, a 65-year-old male beach volleyball player said that while competition made him "feel good," he was also uncertain about whether he *should* be competitive:

... Maybe I don't want to admit it that I am still competitive and maybe that's pulled apart by playing in these things [competitive beach volleyball and bridge] ... it makes me feel good ... I don't know, maybe because I think I should be retired I shouldn't be like I am.

Some participants said that they are not competitive and then displayed competitiveness on the field. Many considered their age and ability as the main reasons why they cannot (and should not) take competing in sport or winning seriously. They believed that they are "past it," and should acknowledge that they are "too old" to be competitive:

I think it comes, mainly because of age and aspiration. I think when you're young, you want to be the best, that means a lot, or to win ... is what you are really striving for, but, in the latter years, as long as you're enjoying it. I mean you still like to win the game of tennis, but it's not paramount ... but then, I suppose I'm competitive in [tennis], to a degree . . . . (76-year-old female swimmer and tennis player)

Interestingly, the above woman initially appeared to be drawing on participation discourses to make sense of her sport participation. By the end of her statement, however, she acknowledged that she is somewhat competitive. Her final comment points to the notion that many older athletes do invest in some aspects of the sport performance discourse. Notably, many did not invest in the "win-at-all-costs" and aggressive features of this discourse. This finding was common among both men and women of varying ages and sports. For example,

... I am [a competitive person] when I play, but I'm not aggressively competitive, but I like to win, but ... I don't do it at-all-costs ... If I lose that's the end of it ... I don't brood over it and I don't make excuses. (60-year-old female squash player)

... I like competing. I'm a competitor; there's no two ways about that ... You don't go out to lose; you go out to try and win anyhow ... If you don't go out there trying to win, there's no point in going out there, is there? ... I'm not aggressive; I'm competitive, always have been . . . . (60-year-old male badminton player)

These findings about competition are similar to a theme on "serious play" that emerged in Grant's research, which showed older people's focus on fair play and personal bests (2001). Many older athletes seem to purposely play down their competitiveness and mobilize the prevailing attitude that it is not age-appropriate for them to be competitive. While these older athletes in one sense "apologized" for their involvement in sport, they often simultaneously admitted that they are competitive, and they are, after all, out there competing in sport.

In contrast, many older athletes can be quite unapologetic and candid in discussing performance and competition. The majority of participants at the 8th

AMG spoke of the joy in winning and breaking records; appreciating the medals, recognition, and status that accompanied competition; and constantly monitoring their performance levels in comparison to their previous standards, and/or the standards of others of a similar or a significantly younger age. I found that both men and women of varying ages and sporting histories, as well as participants of both individual and team sports, equally engaged with performance discourses to define themselves as competitive. This finding highlights that discourses about competition are pervasive in shaping people's meanings of their participation in sport, regardless of individual differences. For instance, a 76-year-old female tennis player said that she had a "doggedness to win" when she was younger, and that such eagerness remains with her now: "You're out there to outwit your opposition, and if you can do it by powerful play, or clever play, or just good luck [laughs], that's what you do," she explained. Others said, "I like to see how well I measure up to others" or "I love the exercise and the competition against each other." An 82-year-old female track and field athlete, who competed in her first competitive long distance run at age 60, said:

> . . . Competitiveness, I suppose that's . . . one thing that keeps you going, too, because you're always trying to better something . . . If anyone's against me . . . I'll do . . . my best to sort of beat them. It's still there; I've got that little bit of [a] streak still there [laughs] . . . I suppose it's just the competitiveness in me is why I do it anyway . . . I suppose my nature makes me keep pushing.

Case study research by Roper, Molnar, and Wrisberg (2003) on an 88-year-old Masters runner and Tulle's life histories on twenty-one elite Veteran runners (2007) also discuss the importance of competition, performance, and training (among other things) in these athletes' lives. Similarly, an 81-year-old male cyclist from the 8th AMG, who began cycling at age 66, said that he regularly competes in overseas Veteran's cycling tournaments and has bike equipment in his home in order to adhere to a stringent training program. He said:

> Oh, at the Masters Games it's everything. Oh, my word. I mean, I want the lot! I'm greedy . . . When I go into events like in a Masters Games, it is competitive—extremely . . . I want to win . . . I want to be better than the chaps who are with me, right. I know then that, "Ok I have trained right" . . . Oh well [if I lose] I can shake their hand off because they're better than what I am.

A significant number of other participants at the AMG spoke about the need for regular training to be at their physical and mental peak for upcoming competitions and have a better chance of success. I saw many older athletes adopt tactics to enhance their performance, such as using state-of-the-art sporting equipment and wearing sports apparel. Such practices are usually associated with elite or youth sports (Hayles, 2005, p. 115). In particular, cyclists wore

Lycra outfits and clip-in shoes, and track and field athletes wore spiked shoes and used starting blocks for sprints. During a game or event break, many participants warmed up and mentally prepared for their performance. I also saw jubilation when teams or individuals won their game or event. Winning a national medal was considered an immense triumph by most of the participants. Many medal-winners proudly wore their medals throughout the games, even at the nightly social activities. Furthermore, several participants said that they kept accounts of their times, competition rankings, or past performance standards so that they could monitor their physical improvements or decrements.

These findings show that the talk and actions of many older athletes work to reinforce the power and performance sport model, disrupt the aging-as-decline discourse, and partially resist the major tenets underlying participation and positive aging discourses. It appears that these participants are shifting the definition of what it means to be an older athlete, as well as an older person in general. Hayles (2005) argues that Masters athletes adopt the cultural value that those who achieve in sport deserve recognition (p. 162). These athletes show that older people are capable of success in competition and worthy of public recognition in sport. Is this expressed value of competition and winning a "symptom" of the white, middle-class positioning of the participants and the health and fitness imperatives underlying this privileged position?

"Use It or Lose It"

When being asked why they compete in sport, typical responses from older athletes included "it keeps me fit" or "healthy," "it keeps you socially, mentally, and physically alive" and "your mind and body active," "it's good for me," "the longer you keep playing, the fitter and healthier you can stay," and "the more active you are, the better your health is." Therefore, they spoke about their participation in competitive sport as a *means* to improving and maintaining their fitness and health (Tinning, 1997). It is about "making these latter years as enjoyable as you can by keeping fit" (76-year-old female tennis player) or "setting your own quality of life by being fit and active" (60-year-old female squash player).

Many older athletes believed that if they lost their "physical ability," they would also lose their independence, health, a sense of control over their life, and a sense of self. In other words, they were strongly motivated by the concern that if they stopped being active through sport, they would become "old," "rusty," or "dependent on others," or would "age badly" or "end up in a nursing [i.e., aged-care] home." For instance, a 71-year-old female athlete highlighted a common catchphrase among older people who compete in sport:

Well, I'll tell you what [playing badminton] is all about. If you don't use it, you lose it. It's not mine; it's a well-known one . . . You have really got to keep your body going, because if you don't, you just rust up.

Notably, a team of women field hockey players at the 8th AMG wore T-shirts with the slogan "move it or lose it" across the back. While many older athletes recognized that fragility, dependency, and illness are possible outcomes of long life, they also expressed the undesirability of these "risks." They believed that one should attempt to delay their onset for as long as possible—with competitive sport being one such practice to avoid or delay these potential threats:

> I suppose the main thing is to keep it up as long as you can because the alternative of just sitting . . . it wouldn't be a healthy situation . . . I think your body's like a machine in one way; you've got to keep it well oiled and running . . . I have no medical knowledge whatsoever; it's just a sense of well-being, that when . . . you've got it, you want to hang on . . . as long as you can [slight laugh], because some people have strokes and things like that and that must be ghastly . . . just to be dependent, that would be terrible! But still and all, that comes to most of us, doesn't it? But you put it off as long as you can.

Here, the body is viewed as a machine, to be trained, monitored, and maintained (Featherstone & Hepworth, 1995; Tinning, 1997). In particular, it is a machine that needs working on not only to reach peak performance in sport, but primarily to maintain fitness and health, and postpone the onset and duration of deep old age. What is highlighted here is how older athletes negotiate different discourses of aging associated with natural decline *and* the choice to be active. Hayles (2005) and Phoenix and Sparkes (in press) have found similar results in regard to the delicate balance between the inevitable decline of aging and self-responsibility for health. In my research, this "use it or lose it" theme was common across all participants, regardless of age, gender, sporting history, and type of sport played. This commonality in their talk indicates how compelling discourses of positive and negative aging, health and fitness promotion, and sport performance are in shaping how some people make sense of themselves and their experiences.

Evidently, the "use it or lose it" idea is primarily discussed in terms of individual responsibility, and many older people do not situate it in relation to socio-cultural issues or constraints (Hayles, 2005). That is, their talk reinforces the common notion that it is largely up to the individual to "age successfully." In particular, older athletes tend to present a deterministic view of health, which, according to Phoenix and Sparkes (in press), is a dangerous one because it ignores the unpredictability of the (aging) body. Many AMG participants discussed the importance of eating the right foods and doing enough physically intense activities (and different types of them) to maintain and maximize health benefits. For instance, a female tennis player felt:

> It's a way of life when you get to 81 like me . . . People kind of get to 60 and think life's had it, but as long as you keep fit, eat right, exercise [grins]. It's a way of life . . . to wear out, not rust out [laughs] . . . You just have to keep going and keep on keeping on.

A 60-year-old competitive female squash player described how in a typical week, she does a minimum of four aerobics classes, goes for a swim and/or a run, plays two games of squash, and regularly socializes with friends. An 85-year-old male runner, who is also a part-time masseuse, said he regularly competes in fun runs, swims in his backyard pool, works out in his home-based gym, and jogs as part of his fitness program. Both of these athletes said that they plan to keep up this schedule for as long as they can. A 70-year-old swimmer suggested:

> . . . Use your body and your mind, you know; keep your mind active. Do things that involve thinking and concentration [e.g., cryptic crosswords] and also use your body in doing physical things [to maintain] . . . Mobility, flexibility, that's physically and mentally.

By providing detailed descriptions of their weekly physical, mental, and social activities, these individuals presented alternative stories to what were once considered "typical" or "appropriate" levels and types of activity for older people. Furthermore, they constructed themselves as different from "other" (inactive) older people:

> . . . Well, I had a friend . . . and *all she did* was sit in a lounge chair and watch TV, and she'd say, "But I can't, I can't walk" . . . See, she wasn't *active* . . . It is important to *keep* yourself *active* . . . *You've got to do it!* And then, of course, she died at home—no good. (80-year-old female swimmer)

> When I go shopping . . . there's lots of elderly people there . . . but to look at some of those folks. They're grossly overweight, or their legs have gone, their knees have gone, their hips have gone, and I think to myself . . . you know, I could be like *that* if I didn't look after myself . . . You've got to have a certain amount of luck as well, but *most* of it's not luck. It's the work that you put in for it, and that pays dividends. (85-year-old male runner)

> . . . If you've got good health, you've got to *use it* and *keep*, keep fit . . . If I was to sit around . . . I'd get rusty . . . like a lot of old people do . . . They're sitting at home getting around in their pajamas. I know one fellow . . . he retired . . . he'd just given everything away . . . [and] he didn't last very long. (89-year-old male runner and walker)

Furthermore, due to their busy and active lives, many athletes considered themselves an exception to the rule. They expressed pride and a sense of personal empowerment because of this differentiation:

> . . . It's sort of a feeling of POWER [she squints her eyes and really emphasizes this word], all right, when my grandsons can go to school and say, "My grandma runs half marathons," and everybody else says, "Oh no, my grandma's in [an aged-care] home," you know? And so, that's good [she stands erect and puffs her chest out] and I like that kind of feeling. (73-year-old female runner and swimmer)

> I suppose what I'm doing is actually an achievement that thousands of others can't do, you know? It gives me a boost . . . I am so well-known [in his town] . . . I'm somebody. (89-year-old runner and walker)

In this sense, older athletes typically construct and perceive themselves as a worthy person in society who is conscientious about maintaining good health and is keen to "do the right thing." At the individual level, this process appears to be about managing a positive aging identity; however, on a broader scale it may indicate something else. These individuals indeed depict a "busy body" (Katz, 2000), and thus (unintentionally) imply that they have the moral high ground over "inactive" others whose "lifestyle choices" have led to their ultimate demise (i.e., death). Keeping oneself occupied and being a physically active, mentally active, and engaged person were often contrasted in their talk with being idle, watching television, or sitting around all day in one's pajamas. By uncritically taking up the positive aging and health and fitness promotion discourses, these older athletes considered "activity" (including sport) as a means to generate, maintain, and signify health. Also, they candidly spoke of "keeping active" as the preferable and "correct" choice in order to benefit oneself and society. Their talk showed that although they accept the negative stereotype that old people are not usually active or healthy, they also criticize the "inactive" old people who they think uphold this stereotype (Grant, 2001).

It is important to note, however, that in their talk about "other" older people, many participants did indicate that these people may not have the physical or mental ability to keep active or play sport. Despite talk about how much effort, training, hard work, and dedication they exerted to keep fit, they did recognize that luck or fate played a role in determining their health and ability. Therefore, when differentiating themselves from inactive older people, these "active" older athletes acknowledged that it is not entirely about choice, but interestingly they remained silent on structural and cultural constraints that can prevent sport participation, such as financial, access, educational, and racial barriers. The absence of these issues in their talk points to the white, middle-class bias in the sample. It would be interesting to speak to older people from working-class and non-English-speaking backgrounds. What are their beliefs and/or experiences of sport in later life? It would also be fruitful to interview older people from a range of backgrounds who *do not* participate in sport. What do they think of older people who compete in physically demanding sports? Do they perceive older athletes as privileged individuals, as inspirational role models for seniors, or as foolish and excessive?

In regard to extreme behavior, some older athletes I interviewed went so far as to say that they would rather be so active (and competitive) that they die suddenly and avoid ill health in old age altogether. For example, a 60-year-old man said, "Playing badminton keeps me alive! . . . I've always been a competitor and I probably will be when I die . . . If I die on the badminton court, I'd be happy." When talking about his disdain for aged-care homes, a 66-year-old man said, "What we are doing here [competing in gymnastics], we will most probably just go 'plop' one day and that will be a good thing . . . fall from a great height on our head." Evidently, these individuals were more concerned about outliving their independence and vitality than dying. What this finding suggests, however, is the deep societal (and individual) fear or undesirability commonly associated with infirmity in deep old age.

Overall, the talk and practices of participants related to sport, fitness, and health indicate that these athletes accepted the link between physical activity and health-related outcomes that are promoted by governments, fitness industries, medical research, and the media. This acceptance reinforces the positive aging discourse, and simultaneously acknowledges and rejects the aging-as-decline discourse. In addition, many older athletes understood health in later life as involving mental, social, and physical activity. However, their emphasis on maintaining involvement in competitive sport strengthens the argument that they accept and support the somewhat narrow scientific view of health as disease-free *and* invest in the competitive, performance, and youthful ideals framing sport. In particular, the athletes' talk around "use or lose it" and "other" (frail, inactive) older people highlighted their concerns about their aging body, getting old, or ending up in an institution. This talk and its associated practices also showed a relentless attempt to defy the inevitable deterioration of the aging process. These findings indicate that their investment in the fitness aspect of performance discourses and health promotion strategies predominantly works to position ill health in old age as undesirable. These discourses also construct participation in sport and physical activity as unanimously worthwhile, regardless of personal, structural, or cultural barriers. Such constructions support Western ideals, in particular the moral imperative of individualism and maintaining one's health (Jolanki, 2004).

In this sense, these white, middle-class, active individuals could be interpreted as—and perhaps understand themselves to be—"moral citizens" who are "doing their duty" to keep fit in old age, reduce the economic burden on the health care system, and sustain the social and political status quo. Are older athletes merely "cultural dupes" whose workings unwittingly reflect or reproduce society? Or are they empowered individuals actively involved in self-formation, whose collective identity works to (unintentionally or deliberately) resist, disrupt, push aside, and potentially transform social norms? Perhaps they are both, or neither.

Conclusion

On the one hand, this chapter offers alternatives to the dominant understandings of what it means to be an older athlete, as well as an older person in general. On the other hand, it shows how older athletes, through their talk and actions, reinforce the value Western society places on being competitive, active, and youthful. Therefore, the expanding cultural phenomenon of older people competing in sport appears to be a reflection of an ageist society—a society in which many individuals seek to express the ideals of youthfulness and competitiveness and use their bodies in extreme ways to perform well in sport and delay (or avoid) the onset of deep old age. However, it is equally a story of resistance, resilience, enthusiasm, pride, determination, lives well-lived, and lives lived to their potential. This latter finding is encapsulated in the following quote from one of my research participants: ". . . Keep battling on . . . You have just got to face life and make the most of it" (Alison, a 70-year-old runner).

The older athletes' claims about their high levels of energy, strength, and ability to lead active and independent lives (which they saw as direct benefits of their involvement in competitive sport) do not align easily with any of the discourses of sport and aging applied in this analysis. By investing in some aspects of sport performance discourses (i.e., by competing to win, and training, monitoring, and pushing their bodies to maximize their performance) these individuals were challenging the assumption that competition is not suited to older people. Although initially many spoke about sport in terms of participation discourses, their apparent display and talk of competitiveness disrupts pleasure and participation discourses that typically frame senior sport. In line with this, the extreme level of physical activity demonstrated by some resists the aspect of the positive aging discourse that claims the older body should be active, but not overexerted. This process creates possibilities for alternate ways of knowing and participating in sport, such as being competitive in later life without feeling guilty or embarrassed.

Furthermore, these older people resisted traditional understandings of older age as a period of life that is essentially sedentary, diseased, and empty. They defined later life in terms of independence, youthfulness, and vitality by wearing sports apparel, mixing with younger people, and demonstrating that the older body is capable of competition. They engaged in pursuits and practices that were once considered the domain of youth, such as running marathons, overexerting to score a goal in football or ice hockey, outwitting an opponent in racquet sports, breaking records, winning medals, and striving to beat a personal best. Thus, the words and actions of these individuals have the potential to establish new sets of legitimating discourses about sport performance, competition, aging, and later life in Western cultures. At the same time, however, the talk and practices of these individuals work to reproduce many aspects of the dominant discourses of sport and aging, in particular those tied to individual responsibility, sport performance, and the desire to avoid deep old age. This juxtaposition illuminates the potential for discourse to be both the vehicle of power and the means of resisting or exposing it (Foucault, 1978).

The talk of white, middle-class older athletes is very much built around the idea of health, fitness, keeping active, competing in sport, and positive aging as a matter of choice. By promoting the idea of personal choice and the ability to take control of one's health and lifestyle, it appears that aging can potentially be an empowering experience for some. However, this idea of individual responsibility is a fundamental principle of the capitalist economic structure on which much of contemporary Western societies function (Hayles, 2005). In such cultures, inactivity, inability, decline, and ill health remain the signs of old age; however, they become understood as representing immorality, laziness, and/or deviance (Fullagar, 2001; Jolanki, 2004). Consequently, older people who do not have the desire, means, access, opportunity, or ability to participate in regular exercise or remain active are often blamed for causing the social and economic problems associated with an aging population. Evidently, the intersection of notions of positive aging, aging as decline, health, fitness, physical activity, and sport performance heightens the moral contrast between those who age "successfully" and those who do not. "This contrast produces a marginalizing context in which there is almost no excuse for aging poorly. In such a context, guilt and shame are possible effects for those who fall ill, are dependent on others, or require health care in old age" (Dionigi & O'Flynn, 2007, p. 373). Furthermore, in societies where individualism, competitiveness, independence, youthfulness, and physical activity are highly valued, failure of the aging body threatens one's social identity and social worth (Featherstone & Hepworth, 1995).

The older athletes' uncritical embrace of the notion that continued participation in sport and physical activity equates with good health reproduces the narrow definition of health that dominates scientific knowledge of fitness (Markula & Pringle, 2006). It also ignores the potential "negative" individual outcomes of sport. For instance, competing in vigorous team sports and individual events can lead to violence, risk taking, injury, and even death in the pursuit of victory (Coakley, 2007). Interestingly, and perhaps ironically, several older athletes saw the latter as a welcome (and possible) outcome of sports participation and a definite way to avoid deep old age. Their talk indicated that abruptly dropping dead in the field of competitive play or pursuit of athletic success, due to either overexertion or an accident, was preferable to living in a state of dependency, illness, and/or institutionalization. Are older athletes experiencing a heightened fear of the threats associated with deep old age? Indeed, working on the body in such physically extreme ways, not only to win or achieve a personal best in sport, but also to curb or avoid the onset of deep old age, positions the aging or ill body as a problem. This positioning reinforces the popular view that old age is less valuable than youth.

What these outcomes highlight is that the traditional discourse of aging as decline remains pervasive and prevalent. Simultaneously, terms like "aging well," and "successful," "positive," or "active" aging are the catchphrases of much contemporary aging and physical activity research. Furthermore, sport participation continues to be promoted as one way to age successfully. However, it has been argued that there are potential dangers involved in positioning physically active, competitive, youth-like individuals as the ultimate ideal for all older people, given the problematic moral imperative underlying this positioning. Therefore, it is important for researchers, teachers, and students to situate the complex and contradictory phenomenon of older people competing in sport within the socio-cultural context in which it is practiced. Qualitative research that involves thematic, discourse, and/or narrative analysis (as used by the studies discussed in this chapter) presents one way of doing context-sensitive explorations that begin to address these issues. Further questions on this topic that warrant rigorous sociological inquiry still remain. Is it possible to open up spaces for widening (and perhaps transforming) our understandings of, and ways of talking about, sport and aging in Western culture? "We cannot step outside our own culture, but can we develop ways of thinking otherwise within it?" (Jolanki, 2004, p. 502).

References

Blaikie, A. (1999). *Ageing and popular culture.* Cambridge, UK: Cambridge University Press.

Coakley, J. (2007). *Sports in society: Issues and controversies* (9th ed.). New York: McGraw-Hill.

Dionigi, R. A. (2008). *Competing for life: Older people, sport and ageing.* Saarbrüecken, Germany: Verlag Dr. Müller.

Dionigi, R. A. & O'Flynn, G. (2007). Performance discourses and old age: What does it mean to be an older athlete? *Sociology of Sport Journal. 24*(4), 359–377.

Featherstone, M. & Hepworth, M. (1995). Images of positive aging: A case study of *Retirement Choice* magazine. In M. Featherstone and A. Wernick (Eds.), *Images of aging: Cultural representation of later life,* pp. 29–60. London & New York: Routledge.

Foucault, M. (1978). *The history of sexuality: Volume one, An introduction* (R. Hurley, Trans.). New York: Vintage Books.

Foucault, M. (1982). The subject and power. In H. Dreyfuss & P. Rabinow (Eds.), *Michel Foucault: Beyond structuralism and hermeneutics* (pp. 208–226). New York: Harvester Wheatsheaf.

Fullagar, S. (2001). Governing the healthy body: Discourses of leisure and lifestyle within Australian health policy. *Health, 6*(1), 69–84.

Gadd, M. (2001). Margaret's on track. *The Post*, October 10, p. 82.

Gilleard, C. & Higgs, P. (2000). *Cultures of ageing: Self, citizen and the body*. Harlow, UK: Prentice Hall.

Grant, B. C. (2001). "You're never too old": Beliefs about physical activity and playing sport in later life. *Ageing and Society, 21*(6), 777–798.

Hayles, C. (2005). Governmentality and sport in later life. Unpublished doctoral dissertation, University of Queensland, Australia.

Jolanki, O. (2004). Moral argumentation in talk about health and old age. *Health: An Interdisciplinary Journal for the Social Study of Health, Illness and Medicine, 8*(4), 483–503.

Katz, S. (2000). Busy bodies: Activity, aging, and the management of everyday life. *Journal of Aging Studies, 14*(2), 135–152.

Markula, P. & Pringle, R. (2006). *Foucault, sport and exercise: Power, knowledge and transforming the self*. Abingdon, UK: Routledge.

McKay, J. (1991). *No pain, no gain?* Sydney: Prentice Hall.

McKay, J., Hughson, J., Lawrence, G. & Rowe, D. (2000). Sport and Australian society. In J. M. Najman & J. S. Western (Eds.), *A sociology of Australian society* (3rd ed., pp. 275–300). South Yarra, Australia: Macmillan Publishers Australia.

Newcastle Herald. (2001). Veteran aces serve up style. October 8, p. 31.

Phoenix, C. & Sparkes, A. (in press). Being Fred: Big stories, small stories and the accomplishment of a positive ageing identity. *Qualitative Research*.

Roper, E. A., Molnar, D. J., & Wrisberg, C. A. (2003). No "old fool": 88 years old and still running. *Journal of Aging and Physical Activity, 11*(3), 370–387.

Tinning, R. (1997). Performance and participation discourses in human movement: Towards a socially critical physical education. In J. Fernandez-Balboa (Ed.), *Critical postmodernism in human movement, physical education, and sport* (pp. 99–119). New York: State University of New York Press.

Tulle, E. (2007). Running to run: Embodiment, structure and agency amongst Veteran elite runners. *Sociology, 41*(2), 329–346.

Valentine, R. (2001). Roy vows to stick with lifelong obsession. *Newcastle Herald*, October 8, p. 31.

Conclusion

Thinking through the Contradictions in Sport

Brian Lampman and Sandra Spickard Prettyman

R EADING THE SPORTS PAGE OF ANY local, state, or national newspaper can be
disheartening for those who love and believe in sport. Likewise, watching the
local evening news or a cable channel whose programming focuses solely on sport
can prove to be quite depressing for those committed to sport and its positive
effects. And the Internet offers access to non-stop information, whether through
blogs or other venues, that might leave the most positive and passionate fan of
sport with a loss of hope for its future. Clearly, the media provide us with more and
more access to information, and in this case with a myriad of negative images surrounding those involved with sport. For the cynics, each new leading story, newspaper headline, blog, or website that spotlights the latest transgression in the world
of sport is further proof of its corruptive nature. The list is long and frightening:
dogfighting, steroid use, marijuana use, sexual assault, money laundering, gam-
bling, racist hiring practices, sexist hiring practices, child labor violations by major
shoe companies in southeast Asian countries, homophobia in sport, violence in
sports (youth, collegiate, and professional), hazing, and poor graduation rates of
student-athletes. These issues, all from stories occurring in 2009, demonstrate the
ongoing nature of problems within the world of sport, in spite of our best efforts
to create positive changes.

However, the fact that negative incidents continue to occur should come as no
shock to those who love and believe in sport. Sport is a microcosm of society and
will always reflect our most promising achievements, as well as our most horrifying
exploits. Sport has the potential to magnify our imperfections and also reflect our
accomplishments—it has the possibility to encourage the triumphs of the human
spirit and also contribute to its flaws and failures. To discuss the negative elements
of sport is hardly anti-sport, but rather a necessary tool for understanding the role

of sport in society, and potentially for improving its enactment and impact. We must interrogate the contradictions of the sporting landscape if we hope to help sport maintain its promise to those who believe in it, those who participate in it, and those who follow it.

Coaching and Contradictions in Sport: Some Examples of Opportunities Lost and Opportunities Gained

New York Yankees manager Joe Girardi had a tremendous opportunity to create change when his star player, Alex Rodriguez, issued the implausible admission that he did not realize he was taking banned performance enhancing drugs prior to the 2009 baseball season. What an opportunity to publicly denounce Rodriguez's use of steroids and send the message to thousands of kids and young adults about their inherent dangers. Instead, Girardi chose to focus on how the glare of the media spotlight would impact Rodriguez's performance. What an opportunity lost for sport to educate.

University of Connecticut men's basketball coach Jim Calhoun had an important opportunity to recognize the economic difficulties many Americans are facing when he was asked recently about his staggering salary. Instead, he chose to publicly chastise the reporter for daring to ask him about his salary and for insinuating that he was overpaid. Calhoun could have recognized the difficulties many face today while demonstrating empathy for those who have lost their jobs. Instead, he became angry and focused on the revenue he brings to the university and why he deserves such a large salary. Calhoun could have taken this opportunity to demonstrate compassion for others and link sport to larger societal issues. What an opportunity lost for sport to empathize.

Micah Grimes, former coach of the Covenant girls' high school basketball team, had a wonderful opportunity to demonstrate honor and integrity and develop these characteristics in his athletes when his team played Dallas Academy (a school for students with learning deficiencies). Instead, Grimes allowed his team to defeat Dallas Academy 100-0 and gleefully cheered as his team approached 100 points. Grimes had an opportunity to help his athletes and the public learn about sportsmanship, honor, and integrity, and to dislodge negative images and consequences of competition. What an opportunity lost for sport to educate and demonstrate integrity.

University of Colorado head football coach Gary Barnett had an opportunity to dislodge and challenge sexist behaviors and actions following allegations by Katie Hnida (a placekicker for the team) that she had been sexually assaulted by a teammate. Barnett could have supported Hnida and demonstrated compassion for victims of sexual assault. He could also have spoken out against sexual violence, showing his team and the public that sport will not tolerate sexual violence or support the individuals who engage in it. Instead, his initial public comments about Hnida only focused on what an "awful kicker" he thought she was (CNN .com, 2004). What an opportunity lost for sport to support women and create change in the world.

Clearly, coaches are in a position to make a difference—whether positive or negative. If we contrast the above examples of coaches with examples of others who choose to use their platform to heal, teach, nurture, and grow, we have a very different view of sport and its power to have a positive impact.

Rutgers University women's basketball coach Vivian Stringer had an opportunity to demonstrate integrity and dignity in coaching when she responded to radio shock-jock Don Imus' comments about her basketball players without lashing out in anger. Following Rutgers' loss to the University of Tennessee in the 2007 NCAA National Championship game, Imus called Stringer's players "nappy-headed hos" (Stringer & Tucker, 2008). In light of such racist and sexist comments, many people would have pardoned Stringer for responding with anger to Imus' remarks. Instead, Stringer responded with dignity and grace, and chose to focus on the gifted young women she coached and their accomplishments. She reinforced the importance of speaking out against injustice, and of helping our athletes challenge the wrongs of society. What an opportunity gained for sport to confront racism and sexism—in sport and in society.

Grapevine Faith High School's football coach Kris Hogan took the opportunity to create an inclusive athletic environment and to make all players (even the opposing team's) feel valued in times of competition. Grapevine's opponent, Gainesville State School, was no ordinary high school team, but one composed of juvenile offenders from a maximum-security correctional facility. Hogan asked half of his team's parents to cheer for the players of Gainesville State School (by name) for the entire game. For Gainesville players who had not won a game all year, who had only scored two touchdowns all year, who rarely had fans at their games, and who after the final whistle sounded would return to a cold metal cell, the game served as a validation of their importance in the eyes of other human beings. Hogan gave hope to a team that had lost it, and in the process, reminded his players of the power of the human spirit. What an opportunity for sport to develop compassion in those who participate in it, and to show the world the power of sport to lift the human spirit.

Indiana University–Purdue University Indianapolis (IUPUI) men's basketball coach Ron Hunter led a crusade to provide shoes for impoverished children around the world, which has made a profound difference. Hunter learned of an organization based in Charlotte, North Carolina, called Samaritan's Feet, which works to provide shoes for needy children. To raise awareness for this worthy cause, Hunter coached IUPUI's game against Oakland University during the 2008–2009 season in his bare feet. Hunter set a goal to raise 40,000 pairs of shoes; he received $20,000 in donations and 110,000 pairs of shoes (WCNC.com,

2008). He and some of his players delivered the shoes to Africa the summer after the season. Hunter demonstrated the power a coach has to mobilize communities to better the lives of those living in dire need of assistance. His heroic efforts made a difference for thousands of children desperate for proper shoes. What an opportunity for a coach to use sport to actively work to raise money and awareness for a great cause.

This second collection of coaches understands the tremendous potential for positive social change in their positions, and all have worked tirelessly to make a difference well beyond the field of play. All coaches have the power to impart powerful lessons to their athletes and to the public, but they teach much more than just the how-to's of playing the sport. They teach about values, about relationships, about power, and about integrity. However, their responses to this "teaching" epitomize the contradictions in sport. Some continue to promote an institution mired in racist, sexist, and homophobic assumptions and actions, while others believe in challenging them. Some continue to engage in a "win at all costs" mentality, while others work to move sport to even higher levels of conduct and social responsibility. Until all coaches, athletes, and fans take advantage of the opportunities they have to create change in and through sport, the contradictions about the power of sport to create change will remain.

Concluding Thoughts

This book was designed to draw upon the wealth of knowledge and experience of numerous experts in the field of sport and society, all of whom are fans and all of whom express their love for the game through their own unique and critical examination of sport. These authors continue to critique sport and expose some of the ongoing problems in sport. We believe that without such critique, sport is destined to remain as it is—with all of its flaws. More importantly, these authors also champion the possibilities for an institution that is so dear to so many. It is our sincere hope that this book inspires others to examine sport in new ways—to critique sport, but also to find new ways to move it toward its positive potential.

References

CNN.com. (2004). Sixth rape allegation surfaces at CU. Retrieved from www.cnn.com/2004/US/Central/02/19/colorado.football/.

Stringer, V. & Tucker, L. (2008). *Standing tall: A memoir of tragedy and triumph.* New York: Crown Publishers.

WCNC.com. (2008). Barefoot coach sparks thousands of shoes for NC charity. Retrieved from www.wcnc.com/news/local/stories/wcnc-012508-ah-barefootcoach.589151ff.html.

Index

About the Editors

Brian Lampman is a high school social studies teacher in Saline, Michigan, where he also coaches men's varsity soccer. Brian teaches courses in sociology, including a component of sociology of sport, and challenges students to think critically about issues of race, gender, sexuality, and social class as they pertain to sports participation and consumption. Brian is married to Justina Lampman, and they have two children, Kale and Tate. Brian enjoys coaching, running, spending time with his family and aspires to have ESPN cover one of his and his kids' front yard Whiffle Ball games.

Sandra Spickard Prettyman is an associate professor in the Department of Educational Foundations and Leadership at the University of Akron. She teaches courses in multicultural education, sociology of education, and qualitative research methods. She is also the mother of three grown children who are all athletes in their own way and whose experiences prompted her interest in and passion for how sports and athletics are currently experienced and understood by young people.

About the Contributors

Douglas E. Abrams is a law professor at the University of Missouri-Columbia who has coached youth ice hockey at all age levels since 1968. He has written or co-authored five books, including *Children and the Law: Doctrine, Policy and Practice* (3rd ed., 2007), *Children and the Law in a Nutshell* (2nd ed., 2003), and *Contemporary Family Law* (2006).

Jay Coakley is an internationally respected expert on the social aspects of sports. His text, *Sports in Society: Issues and Controversies*, is in its tenth edition with adaptations published in Canada, Australia, and the United Kingdom, and translations in Japanese, Chinese, and Korean. A former intercollegiate athlete, Coakley critically examines social phenomena and promotes changes that will make social worlds more democratic and humane.

Cheryl Cooky, Ph.D., is a joint-appointed assistant professor in the Department of Health & Kinesiology and the Women's Studies program at Purdue University. Dr. Cooky's research interests include the sociological aspects of urban recreation sport programs for low-income minority girls, the role of popular culture and the media in shaping social understandings of gender and sport, the construction of gendered athletic identities among girls who play sport, and qualitative methods in sport. Her research has been published in *Sociological Perspectives*, *Sociology of Sport Journal*, and the *Journal of Sport and Social Issues*, and in several edited collections. In her spare time, Dr. Cooky enjoys running, hiking, and taking her chocolate lab, Wrigley, to the dog park.

Rylee A. Dionigi is associate head of the School of Human Movement Studies, Charles Sturt University, Australia. She is a senior lecturer and has published in the fields of sport sociology, aging and physical activity, exercise psychology, and leisure studies. She is the author of *Competing for Life: Older People, Sport and Ageing* (2008).

C. Keith Harrison is currently an associate professor of the DeVos Sport Business Management Program at the University of Central Florida and the associate director of the Institute of Diversity and Ethics in Sports at the University of Central Florida. He is the founder of the Paul Robeson Research Center for Academic and Athletic Prowess, an author and principal investigator for the Black Coaches Administration Hiring Report Card Study, and a co-founder of Scholar-Baller.

Angela J. Hattery, Ph.D., is professor of sociology and women and gender studies at Wake Forest University (B.A., Carleton College; M.S. and Ph.D., University of Wisconsin-Madison). She is the author of numerous articles, book chapters, and books, including *Intimate Partner Violence* (2008), *African American Families* (2007), *Globalization in America: Race, Human Rights & Inequality* (2008), and *Women, Work, and Family: Balancing and Weaving* (2001). During the 2008–2009 academic year, she was the A. Lindsay O'Connor Distinguished Professor at Colgate University.

Carwyn Jones is a reader in sports ethics at the University of Wales Institute Cardiff (UWIC), UK. He has published a number of articles on Paralympic sports and on other ethical issues in sport. He is a founding member of the British Philosophy of Sport Association and review editor for *Sports, Ethics and Philosophy*.

Jackson Katz is co-founder of the Mentors in Violence Prevention (MVP) program, the leading gender violence prevention initiative in professional and college athletics. He is the creator and co-creator of educational videos including *Tough Guise* (2000), *Wrestling with Manhood* (2002), and *Spin the Bottle* (2004). His book *The Macho Paradox: Why Some Men Hurt Women and How All Men Can Help* was published by Sourcebooks in 2006.

C. Richard King, associate professor of comparative ethnic studies at Washington State University, has written extensively on the changing contours of race in post-civil-rights America and the racial politics of sport. He has recently completed *Native American Athletes in Sport and Society* and *Visual Economies of/in Motion: Sport and Film*.

Kyle Kusz is an associate professor at the University of Rhode Island. His book, *Revolt of the White Athlete*, illuminates how the American sports media at the turn of the twenty-first century produced a set of contradictory images of white masculinity as victimized and unprivileged, yet superior and squarely centered in American culture, that played an overlooked role in a cultural struggle to re-center white masculinity in the U.S.

Richard Lapchick is currently chair of the DeVos Sport Business Management Program at the University of Central Florida, and director of both the National Consortium for Academics and Sports and of the Institute for Diversity and Ethics in Sports. He is a professor at the University of Central Florida, and also a human rights activist, pioneer for racial equality, scholar, and author.

Mary G. McDonald is associate professor in the Department of Kinesiology and Health and in the Western Interdisciplinary Studies program at Miami University in Oxford, Ohio. Her teaching and scholarship focus on the cultural studies of sport and popular culture. She is a past president of the North American Society for the Sociology of Sport.

Leanne Norman is a research fellow in the Carnegie Faculty of Sport and Education, Leeds Metropolitan University. Her research concerns are in utilizing critical feminist sociology to interrogate the culture of coaching. She co-authored *Coaching Knowledges: Understanding the Dynamics of Sport Performance* (2007) and has published widely in academic journals.

Geneviève Rail, Ph.D., is a full professor in the School of Human Kinetics at the University of Ottawa. She is well-known as a feminist critic of body-related institutions (e.g., sport, cultural media, health systems) and favors cultural studies, post-structuralist, and post-colonial approaches.

Barbara Ravel, Ph.D., is professeure adjointe/assistant professor in the École des sciences de l'activité physique/School of Human Kinetics at Université Laurentienne/Laurentian University. She completed her Ph.D. in the Département de Kinésiologie at the Université de Montréal. Her dissertation focused on the discursive constructions of sport, gender, and sexuality in Quebec women's sports.

Earl Smith, Ph.D., is professor of sociology and the Rubin Distinguished Professor of American Ethnic Studies at Wake Forest University. Smith has numerous publications in the area of professions, social stratification, family, and urban sociology, and has published extensively in the area of the sociology of sport. His most recent books include *Race, Sport and the American Dream* (2007) and *African American Families* (2007). During academic year 2008–2009, Smith was the Arnold A. Sio Distinguished Visiting Professor of Diversity and Community at Colgate University.

Ellen J. Staurowsky is professor and graduate chair in the Department of Sport Management and Media at Ithaca College. Considered a leading authority in the U.S. and internationally on topics related to social justice in sport, Staurowsky is an expert in the areas of Title IX, race and sport, athlete rights, and college sport.

Brandon Sternod, Ph.D., is assistant professor in the Department of Teacher Education and Turlock Field Site Director at California State University, Stanislaus. He earned a Ph.D. in cultural studies and social thought in education from Washington State University in 2009. Sternod's research interests include masculinities, gender, and sexuality and the ways in which they impact the lives of teachers and students alike.

Cheria Thomas is from Detroit, Michigan, where she currently works for the Detroit Tigers. She is a 2006 alumnus of Knox College, where she earned her B.A., majoring in political science and history. In 2008, Thomas graduated from Miami University with an M.S. in sport studies.

Sanford S. Williams, Esq., has a bachelor's degree in engineering, an M.B.A. from Cornell University, and a J.D. from the University of Virginia School of Law. Williams is an attorney at the Federal Communications Commission and aspires to teach at a university. He is married to Dr. Anastasia Williams and they have three children, Kiara, Sanford, and Nia.